To

Paul

Best Wishes

Tom

TONY COTTEE
Claret & Blues

TONY COTTEE

Claret & Blues

with Tony McDonald

Independent UK Sports Publications

Acknowledgements

There are many people who have given their time and help to produce this book, and particular thanks must go to the following:

Tony Cottee (for supplying many of the photographs used from his own private collection); Clive Cottee (for jogging the memory and providing useful insights into his son's early life); Lorraine Cottee (for proof-reading and encouragement); Jean McDonald (for transcribing many hours of cassette tape); Steve Blowers (for double-checking facts and the loan of his precious scrapbooks); Danny Francis (for compiling TC's goalscoring record and proof reading); John Keith of the Daily Express (for statistical information and his intimate knowledge of Everton); and to those who kindly provided pictures: Steve Bacon (Newham Recorder), Richard Austin (Hammers News), Roy Beardsworth, Allsport, Colorsport, Empics; the management and staff at Polar Print Group for (again!) meeting our impossible deadlines; the binder who (thankfully, being a Hammers' fan) worked another miracle; Frank McNamara and all at ABS Ltd; and not forgetting the management and staff at Palms, Hornchurch (for use of their facilities and a steady supply of hot coffee and biscuits!).

Published by
Independent UK Sports Publications, a division of Independent Newspapers PLC
7-9 Rathbone Street, London W1P 1AF

First published in Great Britain, October 1995

Filmset & printed by Polar Print Group, Leicester, LE4 7ST
and bound by J W Braithwaite and Son, Wolverhampton, WV2 4HY

Set in 10pt/12pt Sabon

ISBN: 1-899429-02-6

This book is dedicated to
Lorraine and Chloe

Contents

Acknowledgements

Introduction

My Inspiration

Foreword

1   A WAY OF LIFE

2   APPLE PIE AND CUSTARD

3   SWEET FA

4   SMALL TALK

5   SCHOOL'S OUT

6   WEST SIDE STORY

7   THE SPORTING LIFE

8   HAPPY HAMMER

9   MAINE CHANCE

10 GOING DUTCH

11 HERE WE GO

12 ONE STEP FROM HEAVEN

13 JUST LIKE MY DREAMS

14 ON THE ROAD

15 MONEY TALKS

16 CRAZY DAYS

17 DISAPPEARING MAGIC

18 EURO OUTCASTS

19 WHAT'S NEW?

20 HOUSE PROUD

21 SO NEAR, SO FAR

22 WHEN JOHN NEARLY QUIT

23 MISTAKES AND LESSONS

24 FRANK AT WORK AND PLAY

25 STRIKING OUT

26 BREAK POINT ON THE CARDS

27 ON THE MOVE

28 GEORGE GIVES ME THE BLUES

29 TRUE BLUE

30 GUINNESS AND BITTER

31 ROAD TO GLORY

32 SLEEPLESS NIGHTS

33 MERSEYSIDE MOURNING

34 WEMBLEY LET DOWN

35 NATIONAL PRIDE

36 HOPE AND GLORY

37 AUF WIEDERSEHEN

38 CHICKEN RUN

39 ALL CHANGE

40 IN THE COLD

41 ON THE LIST

42 DOWN AND OUT

43 NEW BOSS – SAME OLD STORY

44 HOWARD'S WAY

45 BOND BOMBSHELL

46 SWEET AND SOUR

47 NUMBERS GAME

48 OUT OF THE BLUE

49 GO FOR JOE

50 TALK OF THE TOWN

51 GOING HOME

52 RED MIST ON THE MERSEY

53 FAN-TASTIC FINALE

54 BACK TO EARTH

55 ROVER AND OUT

56 MIND GAMES

57 FAME AND FORTUNE

58 NOW FOR THE BAD NEWS

59 SEASON OF SLEAZE

60 MY TOP 10

61 PREMIERSHIP TEAM TO BEAT

62 DREAM TEAM

63 MANAGING TO SUCCEED

64 TC GOALS TRAIL

65 TC CAREER RECORD

Index

Introduction

WHEN Tony Cottee turned to me on the West Ham team coach travelling to Southampton in March 1995, to ask if I would be interested in helping him write his autobiography, I felt very honoured and immediately keen to accept his invitation.

I had seen, at first hand, his rapid emergence from teenage sensation at West Ham to the first £2 million-plus player in Britain, and then watched him return to haunt the Hammers by scoring several times against them in the blue of Everton.

What I had not quite expected was the total enthusiasm and attention to detail Tony himself would bring to this book. We committed Tony's life and football career to tape. Many, many tapes – TDK should have been approached for sponsorship! Yet the words you read in the following pages are his own – this is no ghosted effort.

If ever his photographic memory almost failed him, and only then to a minor degree, TC would invariably produce one of his many neatly compiled scrapbooks or record books that he has kept updating since his local paper first carried reports of his earliest goalscoring exploits as a precocious seven year-old.

These fascinating volumes of nostalgia are not simply full of newspaper cuttings, but augmented by his own personal account of matches he has played in and assessments of performances. His personal diaries have also proved an invaluable source of reference as well as giving an insight into the mind of a top player.

To Tony, it was not merely a case – as it is with many star players – of following the predictable path through his footballing life. The dynamic little striker, who has shot himself into many newspaper headlines, said from day one that he did not wish to deal in sensationalism for the sake of it, nor commit his thoughts to print in the quest for more money from a game that has already treated him well in his 13 years as a professional.

He simply wanted to tell the truth – about his life, his highs and lows and football in general – from his own well documented experiences.

Read of his constant battle to confound the schoolteachers who warned him against pursuing a career in football and did nothing to encourage the fulfilment of a lifelong dream.

Read of his heartache as football scouts, who knew he had talent in abundance, overlooked him in favour of bigger, stronger (but sometimes inferior) youngsters.

How, driven on by his own sheer determination and the total support of his parents, Carole and Clive, he finally earned his dream chance with the club he and his family had supported passionately all their lives.

His remarkable progress from the Upton Park terraces – where, as a starry-eyed teenager, he stood wearing claret and blue painted 'bovver boots', rugby shirt and a scarf – to the first team dressing room in the space of 12 months, is a Roy of the Rovers journey in its truest form.

Read about his astonishing goalscoring debut as a 17 year-old, against Tottenham Hotspur, on New Year's Day 1983 – the first of more than 130 goals for the Hammers that has earned him a richly deserved place among the club's top five all-time goalscorers.

Tony talks openly about his contractual negotiations with manager John Lyall, a man he has always respected immensely and yet in whose company he never truly felt comfortable. How he became increasingly disillusioned because, in his eyes, the club he loved didn't share his own burning desire and ambition to succeed.

And how, inevitably, he left Upton Park in the summer of '88 with his personal and football future in turmoil.

He badly needed a fresh start and after surprising many, including members of his own family, by rejecting Arsenal's offer, he celebrated his record-breaking transfer to Everton with another incredible debut performance, scoring a hat-trick and going on to play in the FA Cup final at the end of his first season.

Despite enjoying the trappings of success, things soon turned sour on the field for the England international who has won seven caps. Tony talks candidly about the huge burden he carried as Britain's most expensive footballer and the other problems he encountered after moving 250 miles from home. Engulfed in the tragedy of Hillsborough, he explains why he believes the 1989 Cup Final should never have been played.

His long and difficult battle to come to terms with the "£2 million pound man" tag and how, while struggling to make an impression with three successive managers who, at various times, either under-used or under-rated him, he more than once felt like packing his bags and heading back south.

When his third Everton manager in six years also failed to show faith in him, Tony eventually did return to London and his spiritual home, Upton Park.

Married to Lorraine with a three year-old daughter Chloe, he has returned a better, more mature and fulfiled person. On the field, he has added greatly improved qualities as all round team player to the instinctive goalscoring skill that has characterised his turbulent career.

I hope that you enjoy reading Tony Cottee's story as much as I have enjoyed hearing it. At 30, he remains one of the most feared strikers in the Premiership and, I sense, there are a few more exciting chapters in his colourful life yet to unfold . . .

Tony McDonald
Romford
October 1995

My Inspiration

WHEN I was a young boy my favourite reading came in the form of sporting autobiographies as opposed to tedious school books. My enjoyment of these books was increased by the thought of: 'One day, If I achieve something in football, I'd love to write my own book.'

Well, after my return to West Ham, a 30th birthday celebration and the dramatic finale to my 13th season as a professional footballer, I felt it was time to make my dream come true.

I approached Tony McDonald and Independent UK Sports Publications about the possibility of writing a book and they happily agreed. My sincere thanks to them for their help, particularly Tony who has helped me more as a friend than a sports writer, and everybody else who has helped with this book.

I didn't write the book to make a financial killing or to make a poor story sensational. All I have done is told the truth and been honest, as I have done many times in my up and down career. At times I have been critical and strong with my comments but I do believe in 'constructive criticism' and hopefully they will be accepted as just that.

I also hope that the book will serve as an inspiration to young kids, particularly those on the small side, showing that anything is possible if you believe in your own talents.

It's been a wonderful first 30 years of my life and I wouldn't change a thing that's happened. I just hope everyone enjoys reading my book as much as I have enjoyed writing it.

There are a lot of special people who have helped me in my life and I'd just like to take this opportunity to say a big thank you too:

My wife Lorraine and my daughter Chloe, for the love and happiness they bring to my personal life and their support and understanding with my football. My father, Clive, I think I can definitely say that without your influence I wouldn't be the player I am today. My mother Carole, my brother Paul and my sister Joanne, for their loving support on and off the pitch. June and Bill Blackhall, my in-laws, for making me so welcome into their family. Romford Royal FC, my first club. Graham Penn, my school P.E. teacher. Ronnie Gale, the scout who took me to West Ham. Jon & Phil Smith for their help in transfer and contract negotiations. John Lyall, Colin Harvey, Howard Kendall, Mike Walker, Harry Redknapp and Bobby Robson, the managers who have given me lots of good advice (and some bad!) over the years, Trevor Brooking for writing the foreword to my book. All the players I have played with over the seasons – football is a team game and I would be nothing without them. Also, thanks to West Ham United FC and Everton FC, for giving me the chance to play for two magnificent clubs and to both sets of supporters for your constant encouragement.

Finally, a special thank you to my Nans and Grandads who sadly aren't with us today but I know they were all extremely proud of me. I miss you.

Tony Cottee
Hornchurch
October 1995

Foreword

IT is a rather frightening thought that Tony Cottee was born in 1965, which was exactly the same year I joined West Ham as an apprentice professional! I was an East London lad from Barking and as a West Ham supporter, didn't need too much persuading when the club offered me terms as a youngster.

Tony lived even closer to Upton Park in West Ham itself, and so, like myself, had that immediate affinity with the team. I mention this important link with the club because, sadly, these sort of local connections seem to have become a rarity.

The West Ham youth system consistently produced a steady supply of first team players in those days, who had been brought up within close proximity to the ground. The club had established an excellent reputation for encouraging and developing young footballers who were adept at providing an entertaining brand of attacking football.

Tony was a natural goalscorer who immediately found that happy knack of finding the back of the net. He quickly progressed through the junior and reserve teams, finally making his debut and scoring on New Year's Day 1983, at the tender age of 17. Such early recognition says much for his ability, because generally strikers need that bit of extra time to adjust to the physical demands of first team football.

I played regular matches with him during my final season at the club in 1983-84. As a midfield player, I appreciated his constant darting runs, because it always gave me plenty of passing options and alternatives.

But his most crucial asset is his finishing and emphasises that size is not as important as many people make out. He compensates for those lack of inches by being very strong and sharp which gives him good balance and power when shooting for goal. He is very composed and clinical when chances come his way, and like any good finisher, anticipates well where crosses or deflections are likely to land.

Has returned to his roots after his spell at Everton, and once again ended up as leading scorer during a difficult first season back, where attacking support was lacking.

Only Vic Watson, Geoff Hurst, Jimmy Ruffell and John Dick have scored more goals for West Ham, although Tony should comfortably overtake the latter pair by the time his Hammers career ends.

Trevor Brooking
Brentwood
September 1995

CHAPTER 1

Claret & Blues

A WAY OF LIFE

"HE'LL play for West Ham one day, son, you mark my words". They were the prophetic words my Grandad Will Cottee spoke to my dad, Clive, and the two other people with him, Grandad Arthur Griffiths and my Great Uncle Harry Cox.

They were watching me play for Romford Royal one cold winter's morning at Bedfords Park, Romford, back in November 1974, when I was nine years-old.

How true those words proved to be. And how sad I was that, of the four who watched that game, only my dad was still alive to witness my scoring debut for the Hammers against Tottenham in January 1983.

Who knows, I might have made my mark in the French League but for a stroke of fate. It was towards the end of the 19th century when Great Grandad Charles Cottee was brought from his native France to live in England with his parents at the tender age of three. His family settled in the East Ham area of East London, at about the same time a local club called Thames Ironworks was formed. Charles Cottee married and one of his six children, William Richard Albert Cottee, was the man who uttered those immortal words at Bedfords Park.

Born in 1903, just two years after Thames Ironworks changed their name to West Ham United, Will was a builder by trade and very proud of the fact that he helped to construct the main stand at Arsenal's Highbury Stadium in the early 1930s. He married a local girl, Jane Collins, and they lived in a terraced house in Strone Road – just off Green Street, a short walk from the Boleyn Ground. They had five children: Alan, who sadly died in the summer of 1994, Roy, Joan, my father Clive and Janet.

As a young boy, dad always knew when the Hammers had scored because he could hear the roar of the crowd from his terraced house. But soon after war ended, he became a regular supporter himself.

Encouraged by his own father, my dad soon became a big fan of his local football team and, along with his brothers and uncles, was a regular on the North Bank at Upton Park.

The usual route he took to home matches is one that will be familiar to thousands of others. A 10-minute stroll from Strone Road, cutting through the back streets that nestle between Green Street and Katherine Road, winding his way to the little bridge and pathway that run alongside the bus garage behind the old North Bank.

Standing in his usual position down by the front wall of the North Bank, dad's earliest recollections from the age of six or seven include the frightening experience, in season 1947-48, of seeing centre-forward Bill Stephens break his leg, and marvelling at the wing play of West Ham's Terry Woodgate and Tommy Tucker, as well as the legendary Stanley Matthews of Blackpool.

West Ham United has been a way of life throughout generations of the Cottee family. My great-grandfather on mum's side, my dad's father and his uncle were among the estimated 200,000 who attended the famous 'White Horse' Cup final at Wembley against Bolton in 1923. Dad saw Bobby Moore lift the FA Cup in 1964 and then, a little over a year later, returned there to see him lead West Ham to victory over TSV Münich 1860 in the European Cup Winners' Cup final.

Naturally his support of the Hammers rubbed off on his two sons, and my younger brother, Paul, and I both stood on the Wembley terraces to see us beat Arsenal 1-0 in the 1980 FA Cup Final.

Clive Cottee married into another Hammers-crazy family when he wed Carole Griffiths at St. Edmunds Church, Katherine Road, on July 9, 1960. They were childhood sweethearts who grew up together. Dad attended East Grammar School, where one of his best friends was Rob Jenkins, who went on to succeed his father as first team physio at West Ham. Mum went to Plashet Senior school for girls. But my parents didn't start dating seriously until they met up again in their mid-teens while on a school summer holiday in Cornwall.

Mum was a football fan herself, having been surrounded by West Ham supporters in her family. Like the Cottees, the Griffiths also lived only a stone's throw from the ground, in South Esk Road, which runs parallel to Strone Road. Mum, who is an only child, went to home games with her father, Arthur Leonard, and her uncle Harry Cox, who was a founder member of the West Ham United supporters' club. While dad and his family cheered on the team from behind the North Bank goal, they preferred the view and unique atmosphere of the Chicken Run.

Many supporters claim that they devote their whole lives to their favourite club. That can certainly be said of Grandad Griff, as we knew him, who followed Hammers all his life, literally right up to his dying day. He suddenly collapsed beneath the club nameplate on the main forecourt at Upton Park, just prior to our FA Cup tie against West Brom in 1980. We were all deeply upset at the time, of course, but, looking back, I don't think he could have planned a more appropriate place to bow out.

Mum and dad moved into their first home, a two-bedroom terraced house on the Heaton Grange Estate, Harold Hill, near Romford, Essex, in the early part of 1965. Mum didn't make it to Wembley for the ECWC final that year – she was seven months pregnant with me at the time!

I made my entrance into the world just under two months after Hammers were crowned kings of Europe. I arrived two weeks behind schedule and mum was in labour some 14 hours before I finally emerged to face the big, wide world. I suppose that explains my somewhat laid-back, stubborn nature. As a small child, I never said 'no' whenever asked to do certain things. I just simply didn't do them if I didn't want to. No screams, no tantrums, just sheer stubbornness. No one could rush me into doing something.

Although my parents were living in Essex at the time, there were no beds available at any of the local maternity hospitals, so Forest Gate, in East London, was suggested as my alternative birthplace. Not that anyone minded. Like most football-mad fathers do, dad declared that if mum presented him with a son, he would obviously become a footballer and play for the Hammers.

The idea of me being born so close to Upton Park had obvious appeal and, sure enough, I'm very proud of my birth certificate which states that I was born in the West Ham district – the heart of Hammers' territory – at approximately 7pm on Sunday, July 11, 1965, weighing in at 8lbs 2oz. My brother was in fact born at the same hospital in May 1968.

The hospital in Forest Lane – which runs alongside the railway between Forest Gate and Maryland main line stations – has since made way for a new housing estate but Paul and I are both very proud of our East End roots.

My parents christened me Antony Richard Cottee. Richard is dad's middle name, while my christian name was inspired by mum's cousin, Tony Cox, who was a Football League referee.

There was never any doubt that I would follow my parents and their families in supporting the Hammers, but going on to play for the club was something I could only dream about as a little boy. Nobody else in the family had made it to professional level, although the game was a way of life to both my parents' families.

At school, dad was a fairly useful forward, representing East Ham Boys and earning trials with East London and Essex. He once had the distinction of scoring at Norwich City's ground in the final of the English Schools Shield, in front of 15,000 people. He scored the equaliser in a 2-2 draw (and again in the replay which they lost 8-1). Dad gave me stick for years about his scoring feat at Norwich, until I finally managed to find the net at Carrow Road on New Year's Day, 1988. Coincidentally, dad's district team teacher was Bill Elliott, a qualified referee who ran the local district team and, years later, went on to organise the Junior Hammers club at West Ham after I turned pro.

After leaving school, dad had amateur spells with Clapton, Hornchurch and Romford. On completing his national service, he went into insurance, working as a broker for several companies in the City. He learned the business inside out and although he has never lost his love of football, his main priority was working hard to keep a roof over his wife and children.

CHAPTER 2

Claret & Blues

APPLE PIE AND CUSTARD

AS Bobby Moore was preparing to lead England to their greatest-ever triumph in the World Cup finals, one year-old Tony Cottee was already taking his first tentative steps up the football ladder. My dad's 'coaching' sessions began at home when I was barely six months old. He used to throw me a softball to head and I'd allegedly launch myself at it. I began walking by the age of 10 months and was, by all accounts, a bright, lively child.

In that famous summer of '66 we went on holiday with friends to the Isle of Wight and I'm sure I proved to be a lucky charm for 'Mooro' and the rest of the England players. Our holiday camp held its traditional kids' fancy dress competition and I entered it dressed as England's official mascot, World Cup Willie! I was very surprised to be reminded of this last season when a supporter named Garry Haynes, whose mum Iris was on holiday with us at the time and helped to make my outfit, stopped me going into training one morning to recall the occasion! Small world, eh?

After my brother Paul was born, our family moved out 20 miles or so to a slightly bigger, detatched house in Fourth Avenue, Shotgate, Wickford, which became home for the next two years. We lived a little out of town and one of my earliest childhood memories is of sitting by the level crossing, watching the trains speeding between London and Southend. I was always fascinated by the trains – they seemed so big and fast to a three year-old. As it happens, my three year-old daughter, Chloe, gets the same enjoyment as I did whenever I take her to watch the trains pass through Upminster Bridge Station.

But after a while, living in Wickford was beginning to take its toll on dad. As well as working hard to keep his family, he played football for the firm in brokers' matches on Wednesday nights. After a full day at the office, then the football and after having enjoyed a few pints and a game of cards with friends, he would often fall asleep on the train home and wake up stranded at somewhere like Shoeburyness, way past his stop.

Mum was expecting my sister, Joanne, who was born in July 1970, when we returned to the Romford area, moving into a semi-detatched in Highfield Close, Collier Row. I had attended a playgroup while we were at Wickford but my first experience of school was in September 1970, when I joined Clockhouse Infants in nearby Clockhouse Lane, at the age of five.

My first football teacher, when I moved up to the Clockhouse Juniors a few years later, was a Mr. Cook, one of the few who gave me any encouragement towards football during my school days. He ran the school side and seemed pleased for me when I first represented the school in the Havering District side while a fourth year pupil. We were well beaten 4-0 by Newham one day, with a forward called Alan Dickens scoring all four of their goals.

Years later, after I'd turned pro at West Ham, I was asked by the school to write a brief message for the children of Clockhouse Juniors. I recalled one of the funniest memories of my early days in class, when a boy called Paul Galleon made us all laugh at dinner time. Paul, who often commented on his dislike of school dinners, decided one day that he wanted apple pie but not the custard that came with it. Instead of simply eating the pie and leaving the custard on his plate, where it would be seen by one of the teachers and more than likely lead to a good telling off, he chose instead to pour the custard into his pocket. He calmly ate his pie and then emptied the contents of his pocket in the playground a short while later!

My message for the children of Clockhouse was written in a sporting sense and meant to be a source of encouragement. I wrote that 'no matter how good you are, people will always tell you that you won't make it, but if you're dedicated enough and good enough and work on your skills, you can prove that the dream of being a footballer is not as distant as people say it is'. I ended my contribution, entitled 'A Dream Come True', with a poem that had been sent anonymously to Shoot! magazine during my own days at Clockhouse. It's my favourite poem and one that I have referred to many times throughout my career, particularly at times when things have not been going my way.

It reads as follows:

If you think you are beaten, you are.
If you think you dare not, you don't.
If you'd like to win, but think you can't
It's almost a cert you won't.

If you think you'll lose, you've lost,
For out in the world you'll find
Success begins in a fellow's will,
It's all in the state of the mind.

Think big and your deeds will grow.
Think small and you'll fall behind.
Think that you can and you will.
It's all in the state of the mind.

*Sporting battles don't often go to
the stronger or faster man.
But sooner or later the man who wins
is the man who thinks he can.*

It was while I was at Clockhouse Juniors that I met Gary Lewin. He was two years older than me and the best goalkeeper around. He became an apprentice at Arsenal and after giving up the game through injury, has established himself at Highbury as one of the top physiotherapists in the country.

I remember being very upset on my last day at junior school and came home in tears. I didn't want to leave my friends and the teachers there, especially Mr. Cook.. I felt exactly the opposite a couple of years later when senior school became my number one enemy.

With dad continuing to play football with me with in our back garden, my love of the game was becoming intense. On my sixth birthday I was given a portable mini goal. Wearing my replica West Ham kit, I was the proud owner of a pair of Adidas boots and had all the works. Within weeks I had ruined the lawn, which soon became bare, and burst the orange goal net that had to be tied together with string. I'd spend hours hammering the ball into the net, re-enacting the best moves and goals that had glued me to our TV set during Match of the Day and the Big Match every weekend..

It was in our back garden, in the cul-de-sac of Highfield Close, at the age of about six, where I really started to develop ball skills. Our garden was long, sloping slightly downwards, although a little too narrow. But we found the perfect solution to this problem. Fortunately our next-door neighbours were great about having a football-mad kid in their midst and even joined in the fun with dad and me.

We invented a game which saw Alan, who lived on one side of the fence, cross the ball from his garden, over the small wire mesh fence, for me to strike the ball, while Terry, the son-in-law of the people who lived the other side, did the same from his garden.

Two ready-made 'wingers' to supply the crosses! I was lucky to have such accommodating neighbours, because so many kids have their fun with ball sports spoiled by people next door who aren't sports-minded. Some of my shots did not always hit the target, though, and dad had to fit several replacement windows to our garage.

I couldn't get enough of football. On our way to a holiday in Cornwall, we stopped at a fun fair and saw a penalty prize competition advertised. Even though the competition was open to under-15s, I was still keen to take part. I found it quite easy to strike the ball hard to the 'keeper's right. I smashed my first three shots into the same corner but the goalie sussed me out and saved my last two strikes. Three out of five wasn't bad, though, considering the size and age of my rivals, and I was pleased to finish runner-up.

Brother Paul joined me in the garden games and, for his sins, would usually find himself having to keep goal. Little boys and girls can often feel jealous when a new arrival joins the family. There was an age gap of three years between us but I never felt threatened in any way by Paul's presence. On the contrary, I welcomed him on to the scene . . . there was nobody else to go in goal, and he took the blows from my shots. We got on well most of the time, except when I accidentally stuck a nappy pin in his head!

Paul was a useful, little striker himself at school, played for the school team and, later, turned out for my Sunday side now and again. And if I remember rightly, we were short for a senior school game once and Paul helped us out as a 'ringer'.

Paul works with dad at his insurance brokers in Brentwood and is a regular at Upton Park and most of our away matches. Paul has never been jealous of my success in football, although it can't always have been easy for him having an elder brother who is a footballer. He's a great bloke and a special friend.

The local Boys Brigade got word of my passion for football and invited me to play for them, which I was happy to do. I would often find myself up against kids one or even two feet taller than myself. It was a situation I had to get used to in years to come.

I got friendly with a boy at school called Carl Cowley, who went on to sign for Millwall as an apprentice. He also joined us in the garden and we played together in the Boys Brigade team. I can recall an eventful debut. I netted a 'hat-trick' – two in our opponents' goal and the other in my own net! It was the first and, thankfully, only own goal I've ever scored. It still haunts me.

Claret & Blues

SWEET FA

AS I continued to show promise with the ball, mum saw an advert in our local newspaper, the Romford Recorder, in which a club called Romford Royal were seeking new players for their under-8s team.

I was pleased to be accepted into the team and even more delighted to make the first of several scoring debuts. This one didn't quite generate the same euphoria as subsequent goalscoring debuts for West Ham and Everton but it still meant a lot to me at the time.

Unfortunately my goal didn't exactly have a big bearing on the outcome of the game . . . we were hammered 14-1 by West Horndon! Things improved dramatically over the next few years as Royal enjoyed unrivalled success in local junior football.

The side was managed by John Abbott, who turned to my dad when he needed someone to look after the younger under-9s team which had just been formed. A cartilage injury had forced dad to quit playing Sunday morning football so he took up refereeing instead. On the advice of mum's cousin, Tony Cox, he went on a referees' course, qualified and took charge of local senior games.

He realised, though, that at the age of 34, he was too old to progress onto the League list. He also missed seeing me play on Sundays, so reverted to the role of spectator and when the chance came his way to get more involved with Romford Royal, he took it.

He approached the role seriously. Instead of simply letting us kick the ball around as we wished, he took his FA Prelim Coaching Badge, organised proper coaching sessions for the boys and would work hard to improve our ball skills. He certainly wanted us to win but more than anything else, he wanted us to enjoy our football. Dad kept a scrapbook of all the local paper cuttings on the team which appeared each week in the Recorder. This was the start of my own fascination with statistics, which has remained with me throughout my career.

One of the biggest influences on dad was Barrie Williams, an FA area coach and former manager of non-league Sutton United. who caused a sensation when they beat Coventry City 2-0 in the FA Cup a few years ago.Barrie was from the old school who put the emphasis on skill.

Sadly, too many coaches in football today don't share his beliefs, most notably the FA Director of Coaching himself, Charles Hughes. He prefers the 'long-ball, route one' approach to the game. Hughes and his disciples try to tell people, who may have hundreds of League appearances to their credit, how they think the game should be played, and yet they have never kicked a ball themselves at a respectable level. So how are they qualified to coach others?

Look at some of the top managers of the past 20 years – Kenny Dalglish, Big Ron Atkinson, Kevin Keegan and Cloughie. I'll be surprised if they have an FA Coaching Badge between them, but they've won major honours in Britain and Europe, just on instinct, good judgment of players, how to get the best from them and their foot-balling beliefs.

In fact Norwich City's Ian Crook, one of the most talented midfielders in the English game, told me he walked off a coaching course he attended because he couldn't believe what he was hearing.

Although it was right for my dad at the time, I have no intention whatsoever of taking the FA Badge when I pack up playing. To me, and I know many other people in football who share this view, the coaching badge means very little today.

Wearing our blue shirts with red stripes, Romford Royal won everything in sight: The Mid-Essex Sunday League and Cup and became the first local side to win the Metropolitan Essex Cup for under-10s which included the best teams on the fringe of the London area. We went undefeated for 18 months.

At one presentation ceremony, held at Leys Hall, Dagenham, I was thrilled to receive a medal from Trevor Brooking. As West Ham's big star at the time, it was naturally a very big thrill to get his autograph and be photographed with the master midfielder. Little did we know then that Trevor would set up so many of my goals in my early first team days at Upton Park and that he would do me the honour of writing the foreword to this book!

Our under-11s were unstoppable and it says much for our quality that most of the side went on to play a decent level of professional or non-league standard football in later years. In 1975/76 our regular team, in no particular order, included: Carl Cowley (Millwall apprentice), John Cornwell (professional at Orient, Newcastle, Swindon, Southend), Ian Veal (Chelsea app.), David Ridley (Arsenal app.), Steve Castle (pro, Orient, Plymouth and now Birmingham), Malcolm Hawkes (Orient app.), Graham Crandon (trials with Southend, then non-league), Brian Capps, Ronnie Beech, Steve Williams (Barrie's son) and Martin Howard.

Playing to a 4-4-2 system (Graham Crandon was my first regular strike-partner, with Ian Veal supplying the crosses from the right), we were easily the most talented team in Havering and no doubt farther afield than that. Dad was assisted by Barrie Williams and Sid Castle, a useful former player at Ilford who won an Amateur Cup winners' medal at Wembley. They worked us hard in training but were full of good, sound advice and we all enjoyed ourselves.

The fact that it was my dad who was managing the side didn't cause me or him any problems. There was certainly no favouritism shown towards me. He simply wanted to help us all to develop. It was dad who encouraged Dave Ridley to copy the famous Johan Cruyff dummy, performed by the Dutch master in the 1974 World Cup tournament in West Germany, which Dave put to good use in game after game. What's more, we had good parental support and were always cheered on from the sidelines by plenty of mums and dads.

After most home matches at Bedfords Park, we all met up again at the Orange Tree pub on Bedfords Hill. The mums and dads would sup their pints and fruit juices, while the boys stood around drinking orange juice, lemonade and cola and eating crisps. We would usually analyse the game we'd just played for about half an hour and then forget it. Dad had his own opinions and although I didn't always share his views, we never argued. I have a lot of respect for him as a person and as someone who has been closely involved in football for most of his life. He is my biggest supporter, and yet, my sternest critic. We have always agreed on one thing: football should be played with skill and imagination and, above all, it should be enjoyable.

I look a lot like my father and have inherited his organisational abilities. On the night before a game, I'd get all my kit together in a bag, clean my boots and, if the weather looked dodgy, screw in longer studs to give me that extra bit of grip on a slippery pitch.

But I have a more relaxed attitude to things than dad, and in that respect I take after mum for keeping a cool head in a crisis.

In May 1974, we moved a short distance to a new four-bedroom detatched in Ascension Road. It was around this time that dad decided to leave city life and set up a business on his own. He supplemented his earnings by doing part-time coaching. Through Barrie Williams, he contacted Warren Comprehensive School, in Chadwell Heath, and their head of PE Graham Penn, who had played successfully for Ilford at non-league level.

The sports facilities at Warren were impressive. Graham had an obvious enthusiasm for all sports, so when it was time for me to move up to secondary school at the age of 11, I opted for Warren, in the borough of Barking, rather than one of those in my immediate Havering catchment area, Forest Lodge or Chase Cross.

Not that dad, who coached 20 hours a week at Warren, ever came across me in my first year of senior school. In those days, instead of attending the main building in Whalebone Lane South – which is just a few minutes' walk from West Ham's training ground in Saville Road – the first-year pupils were taught at the annex in nearby Rose Lane, across the other side of the Eastern Avenue, at Marks Gate.

It was a three-mile journey from home to school but, to help strengthen my leg muscles, my parents bought me a five-gear racing cycle so I rode to school each morning on that. When I moved to the main school building in year two, by which time dad had left to concentrate on insurance, the journey involved an extra half-mile across the junction of Whalebone Lane and Eastern Avenue at the Moby Dick traffic lights.

It could be hazardous at times and tiring, especially when there was snow on the ground. But I felt it did me more good than harm. Being blessed with the Cottee frame – stocky with big thighs – the ride definitely strengthened my legs and toned the muscles. The only time I came a cropper was while cycling through the park with my brother Paul. I smashed the pedal on the back of my calf and got a haematoma. I've still got the lump as a reminder.

I also used the front wall outside our house as part of my training routine. It was 2ft 6ins high and, with feet together, would jump over it from side to side to further boost the power in my legs. It was especially good for developing my thigh and calf muscles. Carl Cowley and Dave Ridley would often come round for a game of head-tennis over the wall. We'd go on forever and end up with silly scores running into the hundreds.

Claret & Blues

SMALL TALK

BY the time I arrived at Warren, there was already only one thing on my mind: becoming a professional footballer. Revising and doing homework wasn't on the agenda.

The only books and comics I read revolved around football: *Roy of the Rovers, Tiger, Scorcher, Shoot!* and *Match Weekly*. I always enjoyed reading players' autobiographies and maintained my fascination for facts and figures. I would try to memorise facts like who won the FA Cup in 1966 and so on. I used to revise football statistics instead of revising algebra.

My bedroom wall was covered in pictures of West Ham players that I'd cut out from magazines. They were plastered over the walls that were once decorated in football wallpaper. Apart from my wardrobe, the only other main piece of furniture in my room was a cabinet that housed the trophies and medals I won with Romford Royal. Browsing through my dad's coaching manuals was another enjoyable pastime.

In my first year at Warren they sent Alan Richardson, Paul Hammerton, Paul Small and me for trials with Barking District. At the age of 12, I can remember being totally overpowered by a big black kid in Redbridge's defence. He must have been 5ft 10ins compared to me, at 4ft 11ins, and gave me a torrid time. The difference in size between me and George Parris wasn't so great when we played together in West Ham's youth side a few years later.

Football continued to dominate my life. I was playing for Warren and Barking District teams on Saturdays, Essex in midweek and Romford Royal on Sundays. What with all the other sports activities, it was becoming a bit much and dad and Graham Penn feared that I might burn myself out if I didn't ease up. I didn't really want to stop playing for Romford Royal but I took their point. Besides, I could sense an increasing pressure on the boys to win every game we played, which detracted a little from the enjoyment of it all. I continued to play on Sundays, but in a more relaxed atmosphere, for a team called Chase Cross United which was formed by dad and included three or four ex-Royals.

My only regret when I switched to Chase Cross United, whose home ground was in Hainault Road, Fairlop, was that I ended my last season for Romford Royal on . . . 99 goals. I had been stuck on 99 three or four games from the end of the season and my anxiety and frustration increased with each match, until the season was all over and my chance gone.

That's when constant reference to statistical records can be a problem, because the pressure to reach new targets is self-inflicted. If I hadn't diligently logged each result, team line-up and scorer, together with the local newspaper match report, how could I possibly have known that I was stranded on 99? It was a number that would haunt me again at Everton years later.

Trying to break into the Essex team was a tall order – literally. For the first time in my football life, but by no means the last, I encountered the narrow-minded attitude of schoolboy managers and coaches that has hampered the development of so many other little kids like me. I went for Essex under-14s trials but didn't get a look in. A year later, I was rejected again by the under-15s management for the same reason – they said I was too small. My best mate, John Cornwell, and Georgie Parris, who were half a foot taller than me, had no such worries.

My breakthrough didn't come until Essex appointed a new manager, Dave Smith, who couldn't understand why I hadn't been selected earlier. We lost 4-2 on my debut, away to Suffolk at Gorleston, but I scored within 10 minutes of the kick-off and added our second later in the game. Things went much better in my second appearance, against Surrey at Collier Row, where I scored six in our 7-0 victory to break the previous record of five-goals-in-a-game set by former Tottenham stars Jimmy Greaves and Glenn Hoddle. I finished my first season for the county with 13 goals in five matches and I'm proud to say that my six-goal haul still stands as an Essex record today.

My size was continuing to cause concern, though. I'd been overlooked twice by Essex before finally getting my chance and while there were rumours that one or two Football League scouts were watching me play, no one made contact.

My dad and I only felt comfortable after we studied a football sticker book, full of player biographies, and discovered to our delight that the average height of a professional player at the time was 5ft 7½in. As dad was 5ft 8in, the same height as my grandad, we reckoned that it was very likely that I, too, would grow to a similar height.

I'm now five-feet, seven-and-a-half inches tall but I'd be interested to see the results of a footballers' height survey today. It would probably reveal that the average height of today's players is 5ft 10ins!

Claret & Blues

SCHOOL'S OUT

IF I could have left school at the end of the juniors I would have. It wasn't that I was a hopeless pupil. I was very capable and strong on the main subjects like Maths and English. During my junior school days at Clockhouse they carried out an IQ test on all the kids and I registered 142, so I was no idiot.

But apart from the PE teachers, Graham Penn, Clive Avis and Andy Carter, who were very supportive and in fact saw my West Ham first team debut, most of the other teachers at Warren despaired of me. They never had any time for my love of football and in the third year, between the age of 13 and 14, I became a bit rebellious. Nothing serious, like setting fire to the school or anything that drastic, but I started to play truant.

I'd leave home in the morning at the usual time, get my tick at registration and then bunk off for the rest of the morning. I would invariably go round to a mate's house, the park or pass the time in Jif's record shop, on the corner of Whalebone Lane and High Road. I liked to play the Space Invaders machine while listening to the music. Funnily enough, George and Lynn, who ran the record shop then, are still there today, and they reminded me of my misspent youth when I popped into the shop after training one day last season.

My early interest in music centred around the Beatles and Elvis, most pop music and then, in the late 70s and early 80s, dance and soul took over. But by 1979 I was heavily into bands like Madness and The Who and although I claimed I was a 'Mod', I didn't wear the full 'uniform', like a green Parka, and never zapped around on a Vespa, like my mate John.

But I did used to wear button-down shirts, drainpipe trousers and hush puppies – to make sure I looked as silly as everyone else!

I started to experiment in the way most young teenagers do, trying the occasional puff of a cigarette, but couldn't see the attraction in either in smoking or drinking, in the way lots of others kids my age did. My mates would go out every Friday and Saturday night but if I was playing on Sunday, I'd happily stay at home, prepare my kit bag for next morning and watch Match of the Day. In fact, I didn't sample my first alcoholic drink until I was 15, but more of that later.

Dad also made it clear that if I really wanted to make it to the top in football, I should follow a few basic rules: a) Don't smoke; b) Don't drink; c) Keep girls in moderation; and d) Always go to bed reasonably early the night before a game.

It was advice that I was quite happy to follow – nothing was going to get in my way. I would do anything to be a pro footballer.

Back at school, though, I was banging my head against a brick wall. I was basically a well behaved child and a good pupil, at least in my first two years at Warren, but I was beginning to cause my parents a few worries in my early teens with my complete disinterest in school work.

While they did everything to encourage the football career I had set my heart on, mum and dad understandably didn't want me to totally neglect my studies. I was placing them in a difficult position but I never rebelled against them, only the inflexible education system that had no time for budding sportsmen and women. Sadly, it is an attitude that still exists at many schools today.

Teachers would point out to me that for all the many thousands of ambitious, starry-eyed kids who dream every night of one day playing the game professionally, only the very lucky few actually make it. I had so many put-downs: "You're not good enough . . . you won't make it . . . no one ever does . . . it's a mug's game."

To my teachers, football was not something to be taken seriously, and because of their attitude my resentment to school grew. I just switched off from it. My release was to avoid school altogether.

As far as I was concerned, I was one of the few who would make it in football. I was so very determined to prove them all wrong.

Towards the end of the third year the time came to consider options and select specific subjects for the fourth and fifth years. My memorable interview with the careers officer went something like this:

"What are you going to do when you leave school?"

"I'm going to be a professional footballer."

"Fair enough, but what if you don't make it, or you break your leg. What will you fall back on?"

"I'll become a football manager."

She didn't have an answer to that one.

The lack of encouragement from my teachers only fuelled my frustration and I continued to rebel. I was caned in my first year at Warren by Mr Booton, the deputy head, who took great pleasure in punishing me for flicking dried peas at the window blinds during a particularly boring lesson.

The only other time I received the cane was in the fourth year, when Mr Hazdell, the head of Science, accused me of letting air out of one of his car tyres. I didn't, but I still carried the can and received three lashings on my backside, which reduced me to tears.

In the fourth year we had Mr Coe as our commerce teacher – commerce and typing were the two options I liked most. One day I was being particularly loud and boisterous in class and got into a bit of a conflict with Mr Coe.

He picked me up by my ear, dragged me out of my chair and marched me across the corridor into a small storage room. I was acting like Jack the Lad and he gave me the biggest rollocking I'd ever had. He was right to put me in my place. After that I had the utmost respect for Mr Coe and didn't cause him another problem.

Not that I'm against corporal punishment. Indeed, too many schools lack the discipline that applied when I was a kid, and if Mr. Coe did now what he did to me then, he'd probably be sacked. It's a sad reflection of society that teachers aren't allowed to use some much-needed discipline, so that kids of today can grow up with respect for the world.

I didn't get into much trouble at home although whenever I did occasionally step out of line, usually as a result of something I'd got up to at school, dad would remind me that if I wanted him to support me in my football, which he has always done, I, in turn, would have to keep my nose clean at school.

One of the few times I can remember really upsetting him was when a mate called Lee 'Gibo' Gibson and I painted graffiti on the walls of the Hillrise estate near where we lived. Many kids used to scrawl their initials, together with their favourite club's name, on the inside of buses, on the way to school, or on buildings, walls, pavements and lamp-posts. In the classroom, we'd decorate our school books, rulers and desks with the same slogans. My trademark was TC-WHU, with the crossed hammers accompanying the lettering. To me, it was a way of easily identifying my belongings from everybody else's, and I couldn't see any harm in it.

My dad, though, was not so understanding one Friday evening when he and mum were driving home from a do. Dad happened to glance out of the car window and saw my personal graffiti on the side of a wall. He was horrified.

And his mood darkened even more when he drove around the corner to find the same TC-WHU graffiti daubed on the pavement just 100 yards from our front door. He was in no doubt who was responsible and the tin of white paint and brush (still wet), lying inside the garage door, did nothing to help my cause.

Dad came charging up the stairs and said: "I'll see you in the morning – and oh, by the way, don't think you're going anywhere." Next day, dad came to my room to execute his punishment. There was no violence – thankfully, he was never that sort – but this was going to turn out much worse that a whack on the backside or a clip round the ear.

He said: "Right, we can do this two ways: we can go down the nick and tell them what you've done, because you're a hooligan. Or you can give me all your pocket money and we can buy cleaning materials and clean that lot up."

I decided that buying a tin of paint stripper was the better option and duly scrubbed the graffiti from the offending wall and pavement. It was humiliating but I reluctantly did as dad asked. I was quite relieved that the matter was dealt with without upsetting my plans for the rest of the day.

How wrong I was. Dad then delivered his killer blow: "One further thing . . . you aren't going anywhere today."

West Ham were playing Swansea at home. I was absolutely gutted. His 'ban' on me going to Upton Park that afternoon hurt me more than anything else imaginable. What dad didn't know – and I didn't dare tell him – was that 'Gibo' and I had left our mark in several other local places. I didn't want to spend the whole day scrubbing away!

It was a stupid, adolescent thing to do, though. I don't know why I did it – it was just the common thing in those days. It was the most outrageous thing I ever did as a kid.

Well, that and another stunt 'Gibo' and I pulled in the school corridor one day. We got hold of some live maggots and threatened to put them down a girl's back.

Another time in the fifth year, I was sitting at the back of the class, staring out of the window, bored stiff, when my attention turned to this pretty, young girl going past in a P.E. skirt. I thought: "Cor, that's nice," and tried to look up her skirt.

The young third year pupil I am referring to is Lorraine Blackhall, who is now my wife! The episode with the maggots was the start of our relationship. When I was 15 years-old and she was 13, we actually went 'out together' for a month, but it never quite worked out. Then, a couple of years later, when I was 17 and she was 15, we got back together and it went from there.

Claret & Blues

WEST SIDE STORY

MY unfortunate graffiti experience aside, I started to watch the Hammers play regularly during my last two years at school. Initially I went along with dad, then with my brother and John Cornwell, who has remained my best friend since school days.

We used to stand on the old West Stand terrace, near the corner at the South Bank end, roughly between the six-yard and 18-yard box. I used to catch the number 175 bus from Collier Row into Romford, then the 86 to the junction of Romford Road and Green Street. The ground was about a mile away, at the opposite end of Green Street, but I didn't mind walking it. On the way home after the game, it was my routine to stop off at the chippy to grab a saveloy and chips to eat walking along. Most fans have matchday habits that stick with them for years. This was mine.

I really enjoyed the atmosphere on what was then known as the West Side. There were occasional outbreaks of crowd trouble in that part of the ground, usually when London rivals like Chelsea, Spurs and Arsenal were the visitors, but nothing too serious and I always steered clear of it anyway. I was only ever interested in watching the football. I always encouraged the players as much as possible – Pop Robson was my particular favourite, probably because, like me, he was quite small and a natural goalscorer. I never slagged off the players. What's the point?

Our favourite chant went like this:

We're not the North Bank,
We're not the South Bank,
We're the West Side Upton Park

Or, after making progress in either the League or FA Cup, you may have heard the occasional chorus of We Want Tottenham in the Cup.

I don't recall too much about the very first game I saw at Upton Park, except that it was against Nottingham Forest in season 1971/72, when I was six years-old, and they won 4-2.

My clearest early memories as a fan go back to 1975. Dad got tickets for the FA Cup semi-final replay against Ipswich at Stamford Bridge. I got the train to Barking, where I met him, and at that age (nine), bearing in mind my size, the people massed together when we arrived by tube at Fulham Broadway Station seemed overwhelming. They were all pushing and shoving, we were packed together like sardines. I could hardly breath and can remember looking up to the sky in desperate search of fresh air.

There was no hint of trouble. It was just a big mass of people. Very frightening though. Alan Taylor sent the claret and blue fans in the crowd of 45,344 home well happy with both goals in our 2-1 victory. The journey back on the District Line to Barking, where dad had left his car, was much more enjoyable than my pre-match ordeal and made it all worthwhile.

Unfortunately we were unable to get tickets for the Final against Fulham, so we stayed at home to watch it on telly instead. Taylor, enjoying a phenomenal Cup run, scored twice again to bring the trophy back to Upton Park. The club put the trophy on display at Upton Park and invited families along so that children could have their picture taken with the coveted silverware. I waited ages before eventually getting the picture I wanted, and also got it autographed by the whole squad a few weeks later.

Handling the FA Cup was a nice moment – I've still got the photo in my collection. Unfortunately, I'm still waiting to get my hands on that famous trophy again.

From 1975 to 1977/78, when the Hammers were relegated, I used to go to games intermittently because I was usually playing myself on Saturdays. But from 1978/79 onwards, when we kicked off with a 5-2 win over Notts County, my support became fanatical. I went to all the home games and quite a few away – travelling to places like Wrexham, Watford, QPR, Leicester, Luton (where we won 4-1) and Notts County.

Dad started working in a betting shop on Saturdays, to supplement his earnings from the insurance job, but remained just as keen as us and would attend all evening matches at Upton Park.

I was a member of the Irons Travel Club and can look back on numerous eventful trips aboard 'football specials' early in the '78/79 season. My journey would start at Romford, where I got the British Rail overground train to Liverpool Street. We never used to pay for this leg of the journey, though. We'd get off at Liverpool Street Station, jump over the barriers and run through to the Underground. We'd get our money out at this stage and pay the fare to Euston, Kings Cross or St Pancras to catch the 'Special'.

In the main, the West Ham fans were well behaved. We'd pass the time on the longer journeys by reading, playing cards and talking about the game ahead. We always had a laugh on the way to matches. On the way home, the mood was always determined by the result of the match. If we'd won, it was a very happy journey. If we'd lost, the carriages were full of miserable faces.

A bystander who knew nothing about football could tell how West Ham had got on, just by looking at our faces as we got off the train after returning to one of the main line London stations on a Saturday night. If we'd won, there would be singing and plenty of noise. If we'd lost, we simply went our separate ways. Some would vow 'never again'. But they were usually back for more a fortnight later.

Once, a train was wrecked on our way home from a game and I'm sure this contributed to BR's decision to scrap the 'Specials'.

I took a few liberties in my efforts to attend as many West Ham matches as possible. The Hammers were playing an evening game at Cambridge United once and I couldn't see how I could go to school and still make it to Cambridge in time for the game that night. So I hatched a cunning plot that worked superbly. I turned up for school in the afternoon wearing my Hammers rugby top and jeans . . . on the basis that I would almost certainly be sent back home and ordered to change, which they did. Instead of returning to school, I set off for Cambridge!

It was worth the inevitable detention I was given the next day.

My worst experience of travelling away was at Newcastle on March 15, 1980. It's a long haul to the North-East and when we arrived at Newcastle Station I soon discovered that it's also a long way from the ground. We were met by police, who escorted us to St James's Park, where there was an intimidating atmosphere in store for the three thousand Hammers fans.

At that time, there were certain grounds where you were proud to show off your colours. I had a West Ham scarf and regularly wore a claret and blue rugby shirt under my green bomber jacket. St. James's Park is not one of those grounds. My scarf was kept tucked away inside my pocket, while my jacket remained fully zipped to the top. There was no sense in playing the hero!

We were shown into the Leazes End and the Newcastle fans in the terraced enclosure next to us were staring at the London contingent as if we were from another planet. It was awful, just a single bank of terracing and no sign of a roof. From the first whistle, the Geordies were lobbing stones in our direction. I went with John Cornwell (who, ironically went on to play for the Magpies) and we just stood there with our programmes covering our heads for protection. It was unbelievable.

All of a sudden, about midway through the first half, from my position on the middle of the terrace a flash of light caught my eye. A petrol bomb had been thrown and it landed towards the back of the West Ham section. There was chaos all around us. Some fans were set alight, while others rushed to help them put out the flames. I've never seen anything like it at a football match.

After the petrol bomb incident, many West Ham fans retreated to the back of the stand, where they gathered up loose stones to throw back at the Newcastle hooligans. I hardly saw the rest of the game as we were too busy dodging the missiles. I was only 14 at the time and it was a very frightening experience.

At the final whistle, West Ham's fans were kept behind by police – for our own safety. Outside, the Geordies were still baying for blood. When we finally did make our way back to the station, there was the amazing sight of cars overturned in the streets. It was complete madness.

On another occasion, I remember being innocently caught up in trouble between Spurs and West Ham fans prior to the Barry Daines Testimonial game at White Hart Lane. I was in a group of around 20 Hammers' fans, including John Cornwell and Paul, who were chased outside the ground by a mob from Tottenham. We were easy to spot in our claret and blue gear and had to scatter in all directions before re-grouping when the coast was clear.

But the aggro didn't end there. After the match, I was actually punched in the face by a policeman and suffered a cut lip as our train was about to leave White Hart

Lane Station! I gave the copper no reason at all to strike me, but he did so as I wound down the train window to shout to John and Paul (who'd been stranded on the platform as the West Ham fans were herded onto the train) that I'd wait for them at Liverpool Street Station.

Thankfully, unnacceptable behaviour like that by police and scenes of crowd trouble are very rare at football grounds in Britain today.

Season 1979/80 was memorable for our FA Cup run, which ended in glory with a 1-0 victory over Arsenal at Wembley. But, sadly, my family were in no mood to celebrate after the Hammers beat West Brom in the third round replay.

I went to the first game at The Hawthorns, where Stuart Pearson scored our goal and Phil Parkes gave an outstanding performance to keep out everything the Albion strikers threw at him in the 1-1 draw. Paul and I went to the replay at Upton Park, arranging to meet up with dad at the programme hut on the main forecourt after the final whistle.

We were feeling well pleased after goals by Geoff Pike and Paul Goddard ensured a 2-1 win and our passage to a fourth round tie with Orient. We made our way to the programme hut, as agreed, but there was no sign of dad. We waited and waited, for what seemed like ages, but he was still nowhere to be seen.

The ground had completely emptied and the fans were on their way home when he finally arrived. I sensed from the look on his face that something was wrong. He apologised for being so late and then hit us with the tragic news that grandad had died. Paul and I both burst into tears.

Grandad Griff, as we knew him, was 70 years-old and whilst he no longer went regularly to home matches, he liked to see as many of the midweek games as possible. That particular night, dad was queueing for their tickets at the collection point, next to the players' entrance, when he heard a commotion nearby. He heard that an old man had collapsed and had a horrible gut feeling that it was grandad Griff in trouble.

He actually collapsed suffering a heart attack right beneath the West Ham United nameplate on the wall of the main West Stand, near the main turnstiles.

An ambulance rushed grandad and my father to hospital at about seven o'clock, half an hour before kick-off, but of course Paul and I were already inside the ground and oblivious to what was happening outside. It was too late, Grandad being pronounced dead on arrival.

Grandad Griff was West Ham through and through. Every year he placed a bet on them winning the Cup – this was the only year he hadn't. I thought of him four months after that fateful night at Upton Park, when Billy Bonds went up the steps to collect the FA Cup. I'm convinced it was fate but I think if grandad could have chosen a way to go, he would have settled for that.

After beating WBA, the Cup run continued at Orient, before home wins in the fifth and sixth rounds over Swansea and Aston Villa. I saw all three ties but didn't get a ticket for the semi-final clash with Everton at Villa Park as I was playing that afternoon. We beat them in the replay at Elland Road, Leeds, in midweek, but I was disappointed to miss out on that, too, because of another game.

As well as the FA Cup triumph, we also made good progress in the League Cup, reaching the fifth round stage. As I was training with West Ham by this time, Eddie Baily, the club's chief scout, got us tickets for the replay against Nottingham Forest.

We sat and saw the Hammers beaten 3-0 in torrential rain, and got soaked to the skin because Forest hadn't quite managed to fit the roof to their new stand by the time of our visit!

The 1980 Cup Final was very special to all West Ham fans and John, Paul and myself were fortunate enough to get tickets. We arrived at Wembley very early, at about 9.00am, enjoyed a kickaround in the car park, then had some food before entering the stadium at around 1.00pm. I wore my jeans, claret and blue rugby shirt and steel toe-capped Doc Martens painted in West Ham's colours, with the crossed hammers on each boot – with no complaints from dad this time.

It was shortly before the final began that I actually made my TV debut. Mum and dad were watching the telly at home when the cameras panned round the ground and paused on a section of West Ham fans at the tunnel end, where we were standing.

Suddenly, mum shot up out of her armchair when she spotted me and John. It suddenly dawned on her: 'Where was Paul?' It must have gone through her mind that, in a crowd of 100,000, we might have got separated. Her fears were allayed a few seconds later when Paul was lifted onto the barrier by me..

Trevor Brooking scored with his head and the rest is history.

After the game, we decided to go up to Trafalgar Square, along with a few thousand others fans, to celebrate by jumping in the fountains. We got soaked through, just like at Forest, but this time we didn't have a care in the world. We'd won the Cup, that was all that mattered.

The following day, the team paraded the trophy through the streets of East London. We couldn't see much because of all the people there, so we climbed up onto a shop canopy for a better view of the coach carrying the players. An unsympathetic policeman told me to get down – perhaps he supported Arsenal? I enjoyed the day tremendously . . . seeing the streets lined by fans and the presentation at East Ham Town Hall.

I felt part of it because I was a fan, not because I was an associate schoolboy with West Ham and was, therefore, offered the chance to buy two tickets for every game. A lot of the associate schoolboys didn't even support West Ham, so beating Arsenal 1-0 didn't mean as much to them as it did to me and my family.

I recall a funny story when nanny Cottee met John Lyall at an open day the club held at Chadwell Heath, where they put the FA Cup on display soon after the victory over Arsenal. She was admiring the facilities when John said that the new indoor gym cost £75,000 to build. Looking around at the associate schoolboys present, including myself, he told her: "We only need one of this lot to come through and it's all paid for."

It's nice to think that, years later, Everton paid West Ham the equivalent of 26 training facilities like the one at Chadwell Heath when they secured my services!

CHAPTER 7

Claret & Blues

THE SPORTING LIFE

THERE were just two reasons why I got through the latter years of school life – the excellent sports facilities at Warren and Graham Penn who had more time for me than any other teacher.

One day in the gym he challenged me to a competition to see who could keep the ball up most times without letting it touch the floor. We agreed to use all parts of our bodies rather than take the easy option by using our feet. We were standing around waiting to take on Eastbrook at basketball, when Graham threw down the challenge which I gratefully accepted.

He went first and lost control at 240, feeling quite satisfied with his efforts. I managed one thousand and forty touches before retiring bored! It was funny how Graham never challenged me again! Anyway, it was an enjoyable escape from the dreary classroom and that's how I always felt when representing Warren at sport.

I flew the school flag at football, cricket, basketball (yes, despite my size) and athletics. In cricket, I was a good fast bowler, quick in the outfield but no Mike Atherton with the bat. I achieved six metres in the long jump but after football, athletics proved my most successful sport and I excelled on track.

After experimenting at 1500 metre distance, in the fourth year I represented both the school and Barking District at 800 metres, which was more beneficial to football as it involved quick bursts of pace rather than stamina qualities. I didn't lose an 800m race right through my school years, breaking all records at Warren, except once, when I ran against boys a year above my age group and finished sixth in the Essex Schoolboy Championships final.

Against fellow fifth years, a year later, I won the Essex Championship at MacMillan Stadium, Newham, with an impressive time of two minutes and three seconds. I'd signed apprentice forms with West Ham in May 1981, so had to return that July to compete in the race after training through the summer.

I also used to play scrum-half in rugby, revelling in the role of taking drop-kicks and conversions. But as one of the smallest in my year, I dreaded those horrible tackles that came flying in if ever I held the ball too long.

I couldn't get enough of sport. When I left senior school, I wondered how many other talented schoolboys – not just those who love football – have never fulfiled their ability because they were not encouraged. Yet, if the teachers see a pupil who excels at, say, music, you can bet they will do everything possible to develop that talent and help the child to become the next Mozart. Why don't teachers show the same attitude to sport?

When dad found out that I had been bunking off, he decided to put my 'spare' time to good use, by helping me to improve my football skills. He obviously didn't condone me missing lessons, but understood what I was all about and recognised that I had ability.

I can't stress, though, how hard I had to work at my game over the years. People say it's luck, but it isn't. Okay, you may be born with talent, but I've seen many very talented players drift by the wayside because the application and mental desire wasn't in them. And because I was more often than not battling up against kids much taller than me, it was tough going sometimes.

But my appetite for football was insatiable. Many a long hour was spent with dad over at Rise Park, crossing, shooting and heading. It was practice, practice, practice.

Having said my piece about the lack of encouragement I received from the majority of school teachers who couldn't begin to understand my burning desire to make it as a footballer, Warren did make some concessions. As well as the help I received from Graham Penn and his colleagues in the P.E. department, the school took the unprecedented step of allowing me to carry out my Work Experience stint at West Ham's training ground. John Lyall agreed to the unique proposal and Wednesdays became very special to me.

I would go off to Chadwell Heath and spend the mornings training with the apprentices. In the afternoon I'd busy myself performing the duties shared among the other youngsters, who were a year older than me: cleaning kit, tidying the dressing rooms, polishing players' boots and generally keeping the facilities neat and tidy.

On one or two occasions I had the thrill of joining in with the first team. West Ham had a magnificent side at the time – Trevor Brooking, Alan Devonshire, David Cross, Paul Goddard, Ray Stewart . . . they were all there, and I was in awe of them. Every now and again John Lyall would throw me into situations with the senior pros, especially when it was time for shooting practice. As a first team player you usually respond to a kid who shows a bit of talent and can obviously do something with a football, and they were very supportive of me. I do it now if I see a youngster join in and can see that they have promise. I like to encourage them as much as possible.

On the other hand, what senior players don't enjoy is having a kid come along and spoil the session. I don't think I ever spoilt the sessions involving the players who were stars at West Ham in 1980/81 – the side that won the FA Cup and then, within a year, romped to the Second Division championship, reached the League Cup Final and got to the quarter-finals of the European Cup Winners' Cup. I mingled in and did as much as I could for a 15 year-old.

As a fan, that team was great to watch. In 1980/81 we virtually obliterated most teams. Even though it was Second Division football, West Ham were still a real pleasure to see at that time, because they had outstanding players who were playing consistently superb football.

It was a very settled team – as all good teams need to be. Alvin Martin and Billy Bonds were very strong in the centre of defence. Phil Parkes was tremendous in goal, and you had the creative skills of Brooking and Devonshire. And up front, there was Sarge and Crossie scoring all the goals. The perfect blend.

To me, David Cross was a very underrated player, because he used to get some wonderful goals – overhead kicks, volleys and brave diving headers.

A few years earlier, my favourite had been Pop Robson. He was a tremendous all round player, who used to score a lot of his goals from inside the box. Being a small player, I could relate to him a lot. I used to watch him closely – how he found space in the box, how he turned a defender, all the different aspects you would look at in a forward. I'd try to learn from Pop and, later, from Paul Goddard, who took his place.

After Pop Robson, Alan Devonshire became my new favourite. What a great player and one I'd have the pleasure of playing alongside many times once I broke into the first team.

I went to the League Cup Final against Liverpool at Wembley in March 1981, having seen both semi-finals against Coventry and the preceding rounds with Spurs (home), Barnsley (home) and Charlton (away), although I missed the away leg of the second round tie at Burnley. The Liverpool game didn't seem as big as the previous season's FA Cup Final with Arsenal. I don't think many people expected West Ham to beat mighty Liverpool, who were reigning First Division champions. Most of our fans seemed pleased to have reached Wembley again, as we were still only a Second Division side, albeit a brilliant one.

And thanks to referee Clive Thomas, we very nearly lost the first game at Wembley. I stood behind the opposite goal and although it was difficult to see the incident in question, Sammy Lee certainly looked offside when he ducked and allowed Alan Kennedy's shot to fly past Parkesy with just five minutes of extra-time to go. Thomas was never a favourite ref of mine or the West Ham fans after making that bad decision to allow the goal to stand.

We thought we had been cheated (as John Lyall so famously described the incident) and was thinking of a miserable journey home when our ace penalty-taker Ray Stewart ensured justice was done.

There were just seconds left when Alvin Martin rose high for a header which was flying towards the top corner when Terry McDermott stretched out a hand to push it onto the crossbar.

If ever you wanted someone to put your mortgage on in those last-gasp situations, it was Ray. Despite the intense pressure he was under, the hopes of half the 100,000 crowd resting on his right foot, I always thought he would score – and he did, sending Clemence the wrong way with an uncharacteristic side-foot.

We all went crazy at our end of the ground!

I went up to Villa Park for the replay, where we went one up but eventually lost to a very classy Liverpool side who, although beaten by Aston Villa to the First Division title a few weeks later, went on to dominate the championship for most of the 80s.

West Ham's defence of the FA Cup ended at the third round stage thanks to

Wrexham, who won the second replay. That was after the first attempt to play the game was halted by snow. Trouble was, we didn't discover the game had been postponed much earlier in the day until dad had driven John Cornwell, my brother and I all the way to the Racecourse Ground. It snowed all the way but instead of dad tuning in to BBC Radio 5 news and sport as he liked to, we insisted on non-stop playing of our beat music and so arrived in Wales to find the ground deserted. Dad cursed all the way back to Essex.

The one match I really regretted missing that season was the European Cup Winners' Cup tie at home to Castilla of Spain. Due to crowd trouble during the first leg in Madrid, the game had to be played behind closed doors and, as an associate schoolboy on West Ham's books, I was very disappointed not to be chosen as one of the ball boys on the night, like some of the others were.

Claret & Blues

HAPPY HAMMER

THE man who must take most credit for spotting me is Ronnie Gale, a loyal Hammer who has served the club well in a scouting capacity, also discovering Paul Ince, Stuart Slater and Steve Potts amongst others.

I was playing for Chase Cross United in a cup game at Fairlop, Hainault, one Sunday afternoon, when Ronnie saw me play and, unlike all the other scouts who'd been along to have a look, dismissed the size factor.

When Ronnie phoned, inviting me to go for trials at West Ham, I was obviously delighted. Having supported the club since I could walk, and with all my family being die-hard supporters too, it was a dream come true.

My dad didn't go overboard though. He was a little wary of scouts and had a word with Barrie Williams and Graham Penn about West Ham's interest in me. Ronnie, who ran the training ground facilities at Chadwell Heath before his departure in October 1995, immediately came across as a nice bloke and, indeed, our friendship is as strong today as it was when I first joined the club.

Even so, it was agreed that I should go along to West Ham, but not commit myself until I'd been there a while and was totally happy with the set-up and the people in it.

I also trained with Crystal Palace for a short while – not at Selhurst Park, but at their 'satellite' centre at Wapping, East London. Everyone was acclaiming them the 'Team of the 80s' and having just won the FA Youth Cup, they were a club worth considering.

Arsenal also invited me for trials. Dad knew Bob McNab, the old Gunners' left-back, through schools coaching and many youngsters would have been tempted by the lure of Highbury. Arsenal were doing the business under Terry Neill, having reached three consecutive FA Cup Finals between 1978 and 1980 and enjoyed European success.

In fact, I scored a hat-trick playing for Arsenal under-14s and I'm sure Bob fully expected me to put pen to paper and join them as an associate schoolboy. We heard rumours that some kids and their parents were being offered money and other inducements to sign for the bigger clubs, but no one approached us in that respect ... so dad didn't get the chance to tell them to stuff it, as he had every intention of doing.

As far as I was concerned, there was no choice to make. I always wanted to go to West Ham – my team, my first choice. Arsenal didn't interest me then, although within 10 years they would be chasing me again.

Once I signed as an associate schoolboy, in the summer of 1979 at the age of 14, I looked on it as the start of my apprenticeship. We trained on Tuesday and Thursday nights at Upton Park in groups of 10, 15 or 20. I had already come across some of the boys, like Alan Dickens and George Parris, in school and district games, so it wasn't hard to settle in.

We were coached by Ronnie Boyce and Mick McGiven, who took us into the small gym area under the West Stand, which the first team players use today as part of their pre-match warm-up. For the more demanding work, we'd go across to the East Stand, underneath the seats, and run down the steps up the other side, down and up again before running along the corridor which runs the full length of the stand.

Dad was obviously keen to know how I was getting on, so he asked Mick McGiven who happily confirmed that I was doing very well, to the extent that he usually organised training sessions around me and Alan Dickens in particular.

For me, Dicko was head and shoulders above the rest of us. He had everything: great first touch, vision and an ability to make those blind side runs that defenders can't cope with. He scored spectacular goals, as well as his quota of tap-ins, and right from the first session together there was a kind of telepathy between us. I felt then that he had a big future in the game.

I knew, though, that not everyone at Upton Park shared Ronnie Gale's total belief in me when I first arrived. In my first summer as a 'schoolboy', we played friendlies against local youth teams and I invariably found myself stuck out wide on the right, instead of in my natural centre-forward position down the middle. They did so, it seems, for my own protection, as I was significantly smaller than most boys my age.

The size factor continued to become an issue with some people. They were not doubting my ability, but my lack of inches. I had to learn to live with it – from schooldays, through youth, reserve and even first team football at both West Ham and Everton. But at that time, it frustrated me that players would get a game in front of me for no other apparent reason than they were 6ft 1in and I was only 5ft 2ins. It was like David and Goliath at times.

I recalled what the teachers at Warren often reminded me: that no one from Barking Schools had gone on to play professionally at the highest level of football. Steve Hatter, a central defender who played for Fulham, Exeter, Wimbledon and Southend, was their only claim to fame.

Although since I've made the grade in football, Warren can claim Colin McMillan, the former world boxing champion, and England rugby union international Jason Leonard as two ex-pupils.

But I never let the situation get me down for long. I said to myself that West Ham had given me a chance and I was going to get my head down and work hard to make the most of it. I still had two years left at school when I joined the Hammers on schoolboy forms, so we decided to knock Sunday club football on the head.

I had enough going on playing for the school, district and county sides, as well as two nights training with West Ham. I wanted to give myself the best possible chance of earning an apprenticeship contract once my two years as an an associate schoolboy were up.

Claret & Blues

MAINE CHANCE

IMADE my competitive debut for West Ham in the South-East Counties League
Division Two on August 16, 1980. We won 2-0 at Wimbledon with goals from
George Parris and Warren Donald.

As usual, I wrote up my own small report of the match and my own performance,
which read as follows: "Played quite well. Had to do a lot of chasing. One slim
chance that I missed, but other than that the service was very poor." I awarded
myself seven marks out of a possible 10, which was respectable.

Our team that morning: John Vaughan (now in goal for Preston), Mickie Burns,
Ian Cowell (who helps our physio John Green with hamstring injuries), Gerhard
Ampofo (who later suffered an horrific broken leg and was forced to retire), John
Cornwell, Warren Donald (still playing non-league), George Parris, Martin Smith,
myself, Bill Pegram and Alfie Charlton.

Our manager was Dave Woolley, assisted by Jimmy Frith. They both encouraged
the boys to play good football and enjoy ourselves. Sadly, Dave died three or four
years ago, but Jimmy – one of the nicest fellows you will ever meet, with so much
genuine enthusiasm for the game – is still performing the same role at the club today,
alongside youth team manager Tony Carr.

It was a joy to play for Dave and Jimmy. As all youth team matches kicked off at
11 o'clock on Saturday morning, it often meant getting up at six for away games,
then driving to Upton Park to join the mini bus for 8.30am. Even then, we'd pass
time on the journey with a card school at the back of the bus.

My debut for the SECL Division One side soon followed, on September 6, 1980.
I scored my first official goal for the Hammers in a 6-1 slaughter of Gillingham
(away), but Steve Milton took most of the credit with a hat-trick, with Parris and
Wayne Reader scoring the other two.

My report went like this: "Played very well in my first game in the S.E. Counties
Division One. I found the game very fast and hard and very physical. Scored a bril-

liant goal from the edge of the area in the fifth minute . . . screamed into the corner. Hopefully will be in Division One squad next week. Played very well overall, improving with each game." I awarded myself eight out of 10 and the team performance 7 out of 10: "Played quite well against poor opposition."

Our team at Gillingham included Alan Dickens and Glenn Burvill, who enjoyed a good career in the lower divisions of the Football League with Aldershot before going non-league.

It was a pleasure to be part of one of the best youth team squads in Hammers' history and the club seemed reasonably satisfied with my progress when they handed me the following written report in December 1980:

SHOOTING: Good – shows good timing and accuracy.

HEADING: Fair – but does reasonably well for his size.

DRIBBLING: Good – takes people on well and shows good close control.

PASSING: Good – shows good touch and awareness.

TACKLING: Fair – not dominant but shows determination.

RUNNING: Good – shows pace and gets off the mark well.

COURAGE: Good – doesn't shy away from physical confrontation.

STRENGTH: Fair – weights will improve this.

STAMINA: Good – I don't see any fitness problems.

WORK RATE: Fair – could work a little harder when not in possession.

TACTICAL KNOWLEDGE: Good – sees things early and is good to exploit openings.

GROUP MEMBER: Very good – mixes well and shows good understanding.

DISCIPLINE: Very good – no problems here.

REMARKS: Tony has shown steady improvement throughout the first half of the season. I am sure if he is prepared to put in the hard work and dedication needed to be successful in the game his chances of being offered an apprenticeship at the end of the season are good.

The report was signed by John Lyall, coaches Ronnie Boyce, Mick McGiven and Tony Carr as well as by chief scout Eddie Baily. And it's fair to say that the 'Work Rate' comment would have been wholeheartedly endorsed, nine years later, by Howard Kendall!

West Ham's most promising crop of youngsters in many years were on their way to two cup finals that season. For the semi-final of the FA Youth Cup we travelled up to Maine Road, Manchester to face City having already battered them 5-0 in the first leg at Upton Park. Although I travelled up with the squad, I didn't think I had a chance of playing. But manager Tony Carr caught me by surprise when he pulled me aside before the game and told me I would be playing on the right wing.

I wrote in my scrapbook that day: "Came off after 75 minutes, did quite well although I was mainly defending. Didn't get forward as much as I would have liked but it was a good experience though." I rated 7 out of 10.

Maine Road was my first taste of the big time, the first professional ground I'd played on. I remembered it as a big, old ground and I think I was a bit overawed by the occasion. My development continued mainly at Second Division level, making only a handful of First Division appearances in the SECL. Even so, I was still quite pleased to finish my first full season with 26 goals from 49 appearances in all

League, cup and friendlies. My best individual display was four goals in a 9-2 demolition of Bristol Rovers. Happily, there was also a medal to show for it, too, as we won the Second Division championship.

I never got a look in in the FA Youth Cup Final against Tottenham. I felt disappointed not to even make the bench, but in those days only one sub could be named and Dicko got the nod for the first leg at Upton Park. Alan was the outstanding player of our Second Division side, while the First Division team really picked itself. Paul Allen was still eligible at the time, but wasn't used because he was a first team regular by then.

Incredibly, a crowd of 13,000 saw us beat Spurs 2-0. In the meantime we had also reached the Southern Junior Floodlit Cup Final and faced Aston Villa before meeting Tottenham in the return of the more important competition at White Hart Lane. Again, I was confined to the stands for the visit of Villa, who beat us 2-0. We did much better in the return at Villa Park but a 1-0 away win wasn't enough to stop the trophy going to the Midlands.

At least I had 15 minutes' more experience of one of the top grounds in the country. My report reads: "Played very well when I eventually came on but obviously it was too late to do anything. Could have scored if Bobby Barnes had back-heeled it to me."

West Ham's disappointment at losing the SJFC Final was quickly erased by the second leg of the FAYC Final at Tottenham, where another 13,000 turned out to see a memorable match. With a two-goal lead from the first leg, we could afford to go down by the odd goal and still become the first Hammers' side to win the trophy since Bobby Moore led his boys to glory way back in 1958. Again, I watched from the stand and didn't even manage to make it into the celebration pictures of the team on the pitch after the game.

There was no reason to be down though. I was making good progress, my school leaving date was in sight and I couldn't have been happier when I received the news, in a letter from Eddie Baily, that West Ham were going to sign me on as an apprentice. I was doing cartwheels of joy but dad wanted to know more about what was in store for me when I did leave Warren School.

He arranged to meet Eddie, Boycey and Tony Carr after training one night and an interesting conversation between my father and Eddie ensued.

"What's in it for Tone if he signs?"

"There's nothing in it for Tony, let me make that perfectly clear. You don't get any money or anything."

Eddie had, not surprisingly, got hold of the wrong end of the stick, as my dad explained: "I'm not interested in money, I want to know what it's all about for Tone."

"Oh," said a somewhat relieved Eddie, "I thought that you were talking about money, because we don't do things like that here."

Dad told me that Tony Carr had appeared very laid-back about me signing and made it clear that, in their eyes, Alan Dickens was the big star of whom they had the highest hopes.

Undeterred, I was delighted to achieve what I'd aimed for after two years hard work. Along with Dicko and myself, the club took on five more apprentices that summer – George Parris, Warren Donald, Greg Campbell, Alfie Wright and Gerhard

Ampofo. It was one of the most successful years of youth football at West Ham and the fact that five of us went on to play for the first team underlined the quality of the boys coming through the ranks.

Alfie, a coloured winger, never made it, but I think Ger – as we knew him – would also have had a chance on our journey to the first team but for a tragic injury he suffered late in the following season, against Aston Villa in the SJFC.

As always when clubs must decide which boys to offer apprenticeships to and those they don't believe quite have what it takes, there is inevitable heartbreak for the unlucky ones who miss out. My joy was tempered by the news that my best mate, John Cornwell, hadn't been offered a contract at the end of our two years as associate schoolboys.

John and I had grown up together, played for Romford Royal from the age of nine and, although he went to Forest Lodge School while I chose Warren, we were reunited at West Ham training sessions on Tuesdays and Thursdays. On Saturdays we travelled all over the country to support the Hammers, and I was looking forward to us both being apprentices.

I heard that West Ham had doubts about his attitude which, on reflection, I suppose John could understand, but you have got to give him credit for the way he handled rejection. Instead of sulking, he got his head down straight away and wrote to other clubs in search of his big break.

His efforts were rewarded just a few weeks later when he was offered an apprenticeship by West Ham's East London neighbours Leyton Orient, followed by a move to Newcastle United, then spells with Swindon Town and Southend United before retiring due to injury in 1995.

Friday, May 11, 1981 – my last day at school – couldn't come soon enough for me, especially once I knew I'd be going on to an apprenticeship with the Hammers. Three days later, on the Monday, I signed the forms at Upton Park. As I saw it, this was the second stage of my footballing apprenticeship. I had to keep my head down and continue to work very hard if I was to go on and become a pro.

My teachers at Warren must have been glad to see the back of me. I hadn't expected to gain much in the way of GCSE exam qualifications, so there was no disappointment when the results confirmed that I managed only Grade 4 in History and an even poorer Grade 5 in Geography. I did, however, get a Distinction in my RSA Typing exam, just to show that the previous five years had not been a total waste of the education authority's money!

Claret & Blues

GOING DUTCH

THROUGHOUT my career I've been fortunate enough to have enjoyed some memorable debuts – and it is fair to say that my first experience of alcohol was every bit as memorable, though nowhere near as enjoyable, as my goalscoring starts for West Ham and Everton.

I was still 15, having just celebrated becoming an apprentice, when West Ham's successful FA Youth Cup-winning squad embarked upon an end-of-season tour of Holland. From the playing point of view, I did all right in Deventer. I played in a couple of games and was sub in others. Considering I was up against physically stronger 17 and 18 year-olds, I did well enough without getting on the scoresheet.

I made an even bigger impression in our hotel bar one night. The evening began innocuously enough. We'd played a game in the afternoon and had been given permission by the management to go out that evening.

The lads went out and I stayed at the bar, with Mark Smith and Gary Moseley, who were drinking halves of lager and although I initially resisted all offers to join in, I eventually agreed to have one – my first ever beer. I thought: 'Oh this is nice, I think I'll have another'. So I had another. And another. And a few more until I'd drank about eight half-pints of the stuff. I was sitting on my bar stool swaying a little when the next thing I knew, I just blacked out.

I was awakened by a burning sensation around my groin area. Laying on my side, I felt what I thought was water dribbling from my ears, mouth and all down my face.

I was told later by the lads that about four of them had pissed all over me. They put shaving foam in my hair and, just for good measure, applied toothpaste to my genitals. Mark and Gary had carried me back to our dormitory and dumped me onto my bottom bunk, where I crashed out. Then the four other lads, who were well and truly pissed themselves and urged on by everyone, decided to perform their football 'initiation ceremony' on me.

I was fortunate at one stage because, I don't know why, but I had a can of Coke in one hand and, for some reason, threw it across the room. It struck Glenn Burvill on the side of his face and cut his eye. In the morning I asked Glenn how he'd cut his face and he explained what happened. Of course I couldn't remember a thing about it although I was lucky I didn't do him a nasty injury.

The lads taught me an invaluable lesson. I had to wise-up quickly to what the life of a footballer was like. With any group of players on tour, no matter which age group, there will always be a prankster or practical joker waiting to take advantage of some poor unwitting victim. This happened to be my introduction to life at a football club and I had to learn to drink with the rest of the lads without falling over.

My first wage at West Ham was £20 per week plus £25 for lodgings. As I was still living at home with my parents, I handed £100 a month to mum, although I think she only kept £40 and gave me back £60. But at this point dad stopped my pocket money allowance. I spent all my earnings on records and clothes. It was a good wage then but I didn't bother to invest any of it in a building society or savings account.

At West Ham, they were investing plenty of time in their latest group of promising youngsters. It was the year before clubs abandoned the apprenticeship system and adopted the government-backed Youth Training Scheme. We were all very eager to learn and I loved every minute of that beautifully hot summer of '81.

John Lyall clearly knew our potential as players and took a keen interest in all of us. Apart from taking a week's break for a fishing holiday and spending a few days with his family, the manager could be seen every day at Chadwell Heath, planning for the season ahead and getting involved in just about everything that happened. We had our own duties, which John supervised, but there were occasions when both John and Boycey mucked in with the rest of us. They were down to earth people who helped to create a great atmosphere about the place.

The jobs may have been routine but I felt happy to be learning my trade. While the first team stars and the reserves went off on their foreign holidays at the end of the season – very well earned, too, this particular year when you recall that West Ham romped away with the Second Division title and reached the League Cup Final – the young apprentices were slogging away at Chadwell Heath. But whether it was driving the lawnmower around the fields, going round the edges of trees with the strimmer, creosoting the fence, painting walls, cleaning out the toilets or carrying out any number of the other duties, we did it without complaint. It was all part of learning the trade.

I think it is to football's great detriment that clubs no longer get their YTS lads to work on through the summer, before taking a shorter break than the established pro's. Nowadays, when the season ends in the first or second week of May, all the players disperse for their summer break. That's wrong.

When I signed apprentice, after returning from our Dutch tour, we worked at the training ground every day until mid-June, then had just two or three weeks holiday before returning a week ahead of the pro's for pre-season training in mid-July. My daily route to Chadwell Heath began with the 175 bus from Collier Row to Romford, where I would jump aboard either the 86 or 193 along London Road up to the stop before Whalebone Lane, followed by a short walk down Saville Road and into the training ground. On the bus, I'd invariably read a copy of Shoot! or Match

Weekly or the daily copy of The Sun. After a hard day's work, it would be gone 4pm before I was back at the bus stop waiting to start my journey home.

I felt it was right of the club to keep us working. It ensured that we all kept our feet firmly on the ground. I knew that I was starting at the very bottom as a footballer and it was up to me then how far I wanted to work my way up the ladder. There was no room for prima donnas.

If today's youngsters were taught the ropes in the same way we were, I'm sure they would have a much better appreciation of what it means to be a professional footballer, how fortunate they are to be given the chance. In almost every other walk of life the raw newcomer fresh out of school has to work his or her way up. Kids can spend their first year in the office or factory simply making the tea and running errands for their senior colleagues. So why should football be any different?

It is very important that YTS boys at a club have respect for the senior pro's around them, but this is rarely the case nowadays. As an apprentice, I felt in awe of players like Brooking, Bonds and Lampard. We certainly weren't expected to simply go around and involve ourselves in conversations with the senior players. We'd be nervous about entering their dressing room if they were present.

I can't remember whose boots I used to clean at West Ham, but I recall the time Frank Lampard asked me to break in a pair for him. One particular pre-season, Frank threw me a brand new pair with studs and asked me to wear them in, even though the ground was rock hard and totally unsuited to screw-in studs. But I had to wear them as asked.

When I gave them back to Frank, he just laughed, took them off me and they were ready for him to wear for the first game. That's how it was then. You didn't mix with the first team squad and when one of them asked you to do something, you did it willingly. And there was always John Lyall to keep us in line. If he caught you with your hands in your pockets, he'd fine you 50p. It was basic discipline.

But nowadays, many YTS kids don't have the same kind of respect. I saw this for myself in the dressing room at Everton's training ground last year. There was a young kid actually sitting in the first team dressing room listening to our conversation, before he turned round and said: "Oh, Brett Angell's shit – he's no good."

So I looked at this young kid and said: "Excuse me, what team do *you* play for?"

"The youth team," he replied.

"Well, until you get into the first team, keep your mouth shut and don't talk about other players like that. Don't let me hear you saying anything like that around here again and, more importantly, don't let Brett hear you say it because he'll kill you."

You should have seen the kid's face. I'd put him well and truly in his place. He was totally out of order, yet he was sitting there like some big-time Charlie, in the changing room, slagging off a first team player, and he hadn't even played for the reserves.

It's not just at Everton and West Ham where some kids have a big attitude problem. Standards have declined everywhere and I'd like all clubs in this country to act, for the future good of the game and the players in it.

I don't wish to sound like a typical old pro who keeps harping on about the 'good ol' days', because I hate that, but if clubs brought their youngsters down to earth more, worked them harder in the summer instead of sending them off on their holidays for two months, where they tend to indulge themselves in booze, birds and fags (and much worse, I'm afraid), perhaps they might appreciate what they've got a bit more and grow up to become mature people.

A lot of young kids – not just trainee footballers, of course – are getting involved with drugs now. Instead of wandering around in the summer taking Ecstacy pills or whatever, why don't their football clubs get them in to prepare the ground for the following season, like we used to? Let them get down on their hands and knees with a pair of shears to cut the grass. Let them stick their hands down the toilet to clean it out, or paint the goal-posts. Doing those kind of chores would keep the feet of our Jack the Lad's well and truly on the ground.

Working the kids through the summer months might not completely solve the problems of indiscipline among young players we are hearing more and more about, but it would go a long way to improve the situation. It is something I feel very strongly about and I wish our clubs did too.

Claret & Blues

HERE WE GO ...

THE strength, stamina and sheer athleticism of Billy Bonds is legendary at West Ham and has been since the day he signed, right through his 21-year playing career. Even after he hung up his boots in May 1988 at the age of 41 and turned to management, Bill could still embarrass most players much younger than himself when it came to pre-season running.

But in the summer of '81 Bonzo didn't have it all his own way. He had no idea that one of the new intake of apprentices was about to win the 800 metres Essex Schoolboy Championship.

I was probably fitter then than at any other time in my life. As a footballer, I still had to develop more strength in certain muscles, but for pure fitness I was in peak condition as my 16th birthday approached.

I was running as fast as I was ever going to run – about 2 mins, 10 secs on average, although I won the Essex title at Terence MacMillan Stadium, Newham, that July, in a personal best of 2mins 3secs, and ended up disappointed not to break the two minute barrier.

I trained so hard all summer for that athletics final, practicing 200 metres sprints at Westlands Playing Fields (next to our training ground) day after day, so I was in great shape when the first team reported back for pre-season work.

When John Lyall devised this particular cross country run through Hainault Forest, he told us all to follow Bonzo, because he knew the route and, that way, no one would get lost. But John made the point that once we came over Hog Hill, heading down towards where our bus was waiting, it was every man for himself.

So, following John's instructions, I kept Bill in my sights as we ran through the forest, up and down hill. But once we reached the road, I decided to step up the pace and felt confident that I could creep up on Bill's shoulder. I drew level with him as the bus came into view and then, with a sprint finish, I won the race to the line.

I felt really pleased with myself. I'm sure my win didn't bother Bill unduly but, as an apprentice, I was absolutely delighted to have beaten someone as famous as Bill – the senior club captain – who had never been known to lose a cross-country run before. Bill was fine about it. He's a lovely fellow and not the type to hold something like that against you.

He hadn't seen the last of me, though. A couple of weeks later John marked out a track at Chadwell Heath with the sole intention (so I discovered later) of organising an 800 metre race specifically to pit Bill and me against each other. It was a set-up, because before the race John had been winding up Bill by saying: "Oh, I think you'll win this one again, Bill, no trouble," knowing full well that he had the Essex 800 metre champion straining at the leash.

About 15 or 20 players competed but, sure enough, it soon developed into a two-horse race involving Bill and I. Coming off the final bend, I had the acceleration and won quite comfortably in the end. Bill obviously didn't realise that he'd just been beaten by the county champion, but the smug look on John's face said it all. Once Bonzo realised that he'd been set up, he saw the funny side of it.

It was an important time for me at West Ham. My life was changing quickly. The 1981/82 season was on the horizon and I knew that the time had come to concentrate totally on playing and to forget about being a supporter. I had missed seeing a number of first team matches the previous season, anyway, due to the early 11am kick-offs in the SECL, which made it impossible to get back in time for the vast majority of away games in the first team's successful promotion campaign.

To give up supporting from the terraces was a decision I didn't take lightly and it was a big wrench. I missed being a fan and to be honest, I still miss it now at times.

I'm sure that if I could, I'd sit down and watch football all day long, lots of different games. If matches are on the telly, I'll watch them, or I'll check on Ceefax all the time. I watch Sky Sports and listen to the sports news.

To some players football is 'just a job'. They go out there, do their stuff and go home again. With me, it's a lot more than a job. I can't get enough of it, it's my life. As well as watching every televised game possible on TV, I also enjoy the thrill of watching football live – like last season, when West Ham weren't playing and I had the chance to go back north, I went along to Goodison to watch Everton. I really enjoyed myself, being among friends and watching the game from the stand. I never get bored with football. Sometimes, I even watch my brother play on Sunday mornings.

I miss the excitement of sitting in the stand, getting really involved and wanting the team to do well. I was very lucky to have supported the Hammers at a successful time in their history. I saw them play twice in Wembley cup finals, win the Second Division title and then who could forget those European nights. It was a good time to follow West Ham.

But I knew I'd got to the stage where I couldn't combine being an apprentice footballer with being a supporter any longer. I had put school behind me and was now working in an adult environment. I needed to grow up and develop my career. The claret and blue scarves, rugby shirt and Doc Martens had to make way for the suit all young apprentices had to wear to Upton Park on matchdays. I was still in the West Stand, but instead of leaping up and down on the terraces towards the South Bank end, I watched matches with the other apprentices, from the small enclosure behind where the manager and his staff and the substitutes sat.

Midweek away games provided a rare opportunity for me to cheer on the first team and I was very pleased to have been at Tottenham for our first away game to see David Cross score all four in our 4-0 rout, on the night Ray Clemence made his home debut for Spurs following his summer transfer from Liverpool. Away victories like that are few and far between and when they are gained at the expense of old rivals like Tottenham, we savour them all the more.

In fact, West Ham made an impressive start on their return to the top flight and went undefeated for the first nine matches before the run came to an end at Villa Park in mid-October.

At home games, apprentices were allocated specific duties and I was pleased to be assigned to the medical room. Rob Jenkins was physio then and it was my job to make sure the room was tidy before the players arrived. And once everyone had finished throwing everything all over the floor, as players do, I had to clear it all up afterwards.

For me it was great. I'd be standing there in awe as players came in shouting for plasters or bandages or whatever. It was my responsibility to know where everything was kept and produce whatever Rob needed.

I took pride in the job, but that is not always the case with apprentices, as I found out last season, when I ventured into our boot room at Chadwell Heath and asked the YTS lad for my training top. He replied by asking me: "What is your kit number?"

The medical room was a privileged place to be – close to the first-teamers and much better than being asked to clean out the toilets and showers. I remained on duty in the medical room throughout my first year as an apprentice. The second-year apprentices don't have to work quite so hard on matchdays and tend to get the better jobs.

I was very observant and tried to take in everything that was going on around me. It gave me a fascinating insight to the preparations of a First Division team – how different players get ready for the game and the little habits of individuals.

Not that the medical room itself was a busy place at the time. West Ham were winning most home games, the club was enjoying a good run and when things are going well on the park, it usually follows that there are fewer injury problems to deal with. When a team is struggling, it works the other way and the treatment table is in regular use. It's the same everywhere.

On the field, I was determined to maintain progress in the game and the season started very well for the youth team and me in particular. I established myself in the SECL Division One side and on November 17 we battered Derby County 6-0 in the Southern Junior Floodlit Cup replay. I scored my first-ever hat-trick at Upton Park. Yet despite my scoring record over the seasons, I had to wait more than 13 years after that night for my first League hat-trick there– against Manchester City in December 1994. All of my previous hat-tricks were recorded away or in cup ties.

Our defence of the FA Youth Cup began against Orient, which meant I faced John Cornwell. It felt very strange seeing my old team-mate from our Romford Royal days on the opposing side, but we cruised to a 4-0 victory in very wet conditions. We woke up to snow next morning and didn't play again until January 2, 1982.

In the meantime, I'd made my debut for the Reserves against Hereford United at home on September 19. I was substitute, came on in the 78th minute and scored my first goal at Upton Park. The Hammers led 5-0 at half-time and we were seven up by the time I came on and scored from Bobby Barnes' pass. It was the first time I'd made headlines in the local newspapers, *Barking & Dagenham Post* and *Romford Recorder*. *The Recorder* even ran a headline 'COTTEE IN FOR THE KILL', accompanied by a Steve Bacon picture from the match. It was a rarity for the Reserves to receive such coverage, but the fixture obviously gained special merit because our line-up included the likes of Trevor Brooking, who was returning after injury, and Stuart Pearson, who laid on his Cup Final winner in '80.

It was fantastic to be among players of that quality. Our full team that day lined up as follows: Tom McAllister, Everald La Ronde, Mark Smith, Adrian Keith, Keith McPherson, George Cowie, Bobby Barnes, Steve Milton, Ray Houghton, Trevor Brooking and Stuart Pearson.

Unfortunately for me, Hereford struggled to finance the running of their Combination League team and subsequently withdrew from the competition. So, of course, my first-ever goal for the Reserves was erased from the official records!

I had a long wait until my next goal in the Combination, at Leicester on April 24. Our 2-0 win at Filbert Street was memorable for one amusing incident which happened in the first half. Barnesy, commonly described as an 'enigmatic' winger, was playing on the right flank with Mark Schiavi on the left. Ten minutes before the interval Barnesy complained that he'd lost one of his contact lenses. I was sitting on the bench next to Ronnie Boyce when Bobby shouted: "I've lost one of my lenses and can't see out of one eye." To which Boycie responded with a typical classic one-liner: "Well, use your other eye then!"

While the other players were taking a half-time breather, I stayed out on the pitch searching in vain for the missing lens. Bobby completed the game and I was relieved of search duty in the 65th minute, when I came on and scored with my head. It was also pleasing to see that Leicester City completed their fixtures!

Although the Reserves was mainly full of second year apprentices – Paul Brush was the only senior pro in the side regularly – we were still successful and went unbeaten in 12 games at one stage.

In the SECL we remained a force to be reckoned with, too. After the snow disappeared, our defence of the FAYC ended at Birmingham, where we missed quite a few chances, me included, and lost 2-1. It was bitterly disappointing after the way we'd beaten Spurs so well the previous season, but there was still plenty to look forward to.

We absolutely took Fulham apart, thrashing them 10-0. Malcolm Macdonald, the former Newcastle and Arsenal striker, was their manager at the time and showed an interest in me. After I'd scored a couple in that big win, I heard that he approached John Lyall to ask if he could take me on loan to play for Fulham in the Third Division. John turned him down because, after all, I was still only 16 at the time, in my early days as an apprentice and he felt, quite rightly, that I wasn't yet ready for the step up. Years later, 'Super Mac' wrote some complimentary things about me in a couple of his newspaper columns, so I must have made a good impression on him.

It always boosts a player's confidence to know that other clubs are keen on him, but my heart was very much at West Ham.

Under manager Tony Carr, we progressed to the finals of both the SJFC and League Cup. Tony had taught me a valuable lesson at the start of our SJFC campaign when he stunned me by leaving me out of the side for our first round clash with Luton at Upton Park.

As I'd started the season so well, I was naturally full of myself and couldn't believe it when Tony told me I was only sub. for the game – a rare chance to play at the ground. I thought it was a diabolical decision to play Greg Campbell instead of me, especially as I didn't think Greg was as good a player as me and thought he'd only been promised a pro contract because his father, Bobby, was well known in the game.

I was so angry and fired up when, with 20 minutes to go, I came on and scored the only goal of the game.

Apparently, Tony Carr had taken the opportunity to cut me down to size and teach me a lesson for my somewhat stubborn, cocky, arrogant approach.

Tony did me a big favour, because his shrewd handling of that very tricky situation had the desired effect – for him, the team and, as it turned out, myself. He knew I'd been hurt and would be raring to go when I came on determined to prove a point. He never mentioned leaving me out then, or in later years, but he didn't have to.

Although I certainly didn't appreciate what Tony was trying to do on the night, I am older and wiser now and it's true what they say about actions always speaking louder than words. I had to let my goals do all my talking for me.

For the second season in succession we met Aston Villa in the final of the SJFC, only this time we ran out aggregate winners. The players were obviously pleased for themselves but, above all, we were determined to lift the trophy for the sake of Gerhard Ampofo.

'Ger' went in for a 50/50 in the first leg of the final at Upton Park and his leg took the full force of an over-the-top tackle. Not only did he break his leg in two places, but it was a compound fracture and just one glance at him confirmed the extent of his horrific injury. His screams echoed around the empty ground. It was very cruel.

'Ger' endured a terrible time recovering too. He had pins in his leg but the broken bones didn't knit together properly, so doctors had to break his leg again and re-set it. He went through hell in hospital. A couple of days after his operation, some of us visited him. We tried to cheer him up a bit with some girlie mags, but nothing could possibly console him after the injury that ended his career at the age of only 16.

The club granted 'Ger' a Testimonial and 6,000 turned up to see West Ham play Tottenham. With the money raised that night, I think 'Ger' and his brother, Chris, who was a second-year apprentice, set up their own leather business, which I understand has proved a success.

At least 'Ger' can reflect on his role in what was one of the most successful youth team's in West Ham's history. As well as defeating Villa 2-0 on aggregate, our First Division side beat Millwall 4-1 at The Den in the League Cup Final. I got one that night and then two against Millwall again as our Second Division side hammered them 6-2 at Upton Park. We heard that there had been a small bit of crowd trouble outside the ground afterwards. Even at youth level, there is no love lost between West Ham and Millwall.

Another goal in my first full game for the Reserves, at Luton on May 8, rounded off a wonderful season for me. I scored 54 goals in 51 matches, including 30 in SECL Division One and four hat-tricks in total. Taking all cup ties into account, I netted 43 to become divisional top scorer.

It was a great honour to receive the Hawes Trophy, awarded to the South-East Counties League's most outstanding player, at a special presentation evening in London that was also attended by my dad, John Lyall, Tony Carr and West Ham chairman 'Mr Len' Cearns.

A couple of weeks later, after the English season finished, I was among the honours again. In the annual Deventer Tournament in Holland, we won all four of our matches, against FC Schalke 04 (Germany), FC Twente (Holland), RWD Molenbeek (Belgium) and Middlesbrough. I managed six goals to win the player of the tournament award – a much more pleasant experience than my infamous introduction to lager in the same town exactly a year earlier. Some of the second-year apprentices reminded me of my ordeal, but this time I made sure I kept well clear of the hotel bar.

It was the end of a very satisfying season. The only disappointment for me concerned the club's decision to release Ray Houghton. A brilliant member of the Reserve team, Ray made just one first team appearance, in the penultimate away game at Arsenal, before being given the bad news that the club was letting him go on a free transfer. The other players released with Ray were Stuart Pearson, Dale Banton, Steve Milton, Adrian Keith and Wayne Reader.

But there was no doubt in my mind that it was a mistake to show Ray the door. It's true that the club was already very well off for midfielders, with Brooking and Alan Devonshire both outstanding, youngsters like Paul Allen and Alan Dickens fast emerging, and Geoff Pike playing the steady anchor man role. I can still remember coming home from training on the day we heard the news about Houghton and saying to my dad: "I can't believe that they've given him a free."

I could see John Lyall's point of view. He obviously felt that Ray would find it very difficult to break through into the senior side because of the quality of midfielders already established. But he was head and shoulders above the rest in the Combination League that season. Indeed, Ray suffered more than me for Hereford's withdrawal, because he scored four of our 10 goals that were deleted from the record books!

It was a privilege to play in the same side as him and I thought that if ever I get into the first team, he was just the type of player I would like around me. A hard-worker, Ray was a good passer of the ball and gave me the service I appreciated. I was gutted for him when he left.

The rest is history. Ray established himself in the lower divisions with Fulham and Oxford United, before a big £825,000 move to Liverpool, where he enjoyed unlimited success for five seasons, winning all the major domestic honours. Even after leaving Anfield, in an even bigger £900,000 deal, he became an equally vital cog in Aston Villa's midfield before moving on to Crystal Palace.

On the international front, Ray has been an important member of Jack Charlton's Republic of Ireland squad throughout their most successful period and I felt so pleased for him when he scored against Italy in the 1994 World Cup finals in America.

Even now, in his mid-thirties, Ray Houghton continues to play with the same skill and vitality that he showed all those years ago in West Ham's Reserves. All the success he has achieved in his career came as no surprise to me.

Claret & Blues

ONE STEP FROM HEAVEN

AS we returned to our duties at Chadwell Heath in the summer of 1982, I couldn't, in my wildest dreams, have imagined how rapidly my career would progress in the season ahead.

Brazil kept us glued to our TV sets in the World Cup held in Spain. While England were scraping through their qualifying group unconvincingly, the Brazilians – led superbly by Socrates – enchanted the world with their fantasy football.

They were the best team in the tournament but lost 3-2 to Italy in a classic match that decided their group. While I was disappointed that the South Americans didn't lift the trophy, you had to admire the deadly finishing skills of Italy's Paolo Rossi, who scored a brilliant hat-trick to send his country into the semi-final against Poland, which they won before going on to beat West Germany in the final.

The youngsters at West Ham were not only sorry to see England go out of the tournament after managing to only draw 0-0 with Spain, but the fact that a pelvic injury kept Trevor Brooking out of all but the final 20 minutes of that game in Madrid made it an even bigger disappointment for everyone associated with the Hammers.

Ron Greenwood and his players wouldn't have appreciated it, but the English weren't a total loss abroad that summer. Before returning to pre-season training in July, John Cornwell and I took a holiday in Albufeira, Portugal – and beat a team of Portuguese waiters in an impromptu football match at our hotel!

Back at Chadwell Heath, all of us youngsters came back down to earth again. It was time to put our annual summer clean up operation into action although, as a second year apprentice, I managed to get out of doing the less popular jobs, like cleaning the kit and the toilets. Once the 1982/83 season began, I was pleased to keep my matchday role in the medical room, although I probably wasn't as good at it as I had been the previous year. As a second year apprentice, it's funny how you suddenly feel that much more 'senior' than the kids a year younger than yourself, who generally end up with the more menial tasks.

I went into the new season as determined as usual to make my presence felt. I have always had absolute confidence in my own ability to score goals but, at the age of 17, I didn't really know how good I had to be to earn a professional contract.

And I knew I had to earn it. There was a feeling among some of the lads that Greg Campbell, a fellow striker, was 'on a promise'. He was the son of former Fulham and Chelsea manager Bobby Campbell and I got the impression that, right from the start of his apprenticeship, he would be rewarded with a pro contract. I'm not saying that he didn't deserve one anyway, but no one gave me or my dad any idea that I could expect any favours when the day of reckoning came.

Thursday was my favourite day. Every Thursday morning, John Lyall would get all the strikers together for shooting practice. Under the watchful eye of Ernie Gregory, a great club servant who coached the goalkeepers well into his sixties, we used to smash balls at Phil Parkes and the reserve 'keeper Tom McAllister from all angles. But even before training commenced, I'd go out on my own for half-an-hour to work on all aspects of my finishing. Despite all the goals I'd scored the season before, I knew that I had to keep my feet on the ground.

After catching Billy Bonds by surprise a year earlier, Bonzo regained his status as the undisputed king of the cross country runs. I had given up athletics training and hadn't quite reached the level of fitness I had shown in the summer of '81.

What mattered most was how I did on the field and I was delighted to make a flying start to the season, scoring a hat-trick for the youth team against QPR on the opening day. Alan Dickens also hit top form at the same time and we were both honoured to be called up by England Youth for a tour of the former Yugoslavia in early September. It was my first taste of international football, and a tremendous experience, but more of my England career later.

On our return, West Ham offered professional contracts to Dicko and I. Obviously we both signed and our three-year deals were worth £110 a week each, which was a lot to a 17 year-old in those days. It was a great time for me. Before the first team thrashed Birmingham 5-0 on September 11, I was presented with the Young Hammer of the Year award on the pitch by Alan Curbishley, a talented midfielder who had learned his craft at Upton Park before being allowed to leave for Birmingham.

Apart from the occasional appearance in the SECL, I established myself as a regular in the reserves from the start of the season and scored regularly. After playing on a few dodgy grounds at youth level, it was a joy to perform at Upton Park and other top First Division grounds. I felt at this time that I was on course for the first team but if my big breakthrough was to happen, it was more likely to come much later in the season, when the team's position in the table would be more clear-cut.

But in December, things began to happen very quickly. Dicko was called into the first team squad for the visit to Notts County on the 18th of the month. He replaced the injured Alan Devonshire and celebrated his debut by scoring in the opening few minutes and setting Hammers' on their way to a 2-1 win.

Instead of feeling jealous of Alan, his promotion to the big time simply spurred the rest of us on even more. As a youngster, you are always encouraged to see other kids of the same age being given a chance. When Dicko rejoined the rest of us for training the following Monday, he was naturally full of himself. He said how great it was being with the first team players, travelling away to Nottingham and the thrill of scoring. He talked, too, about what it meant to be playing in front of the West Ham fans and seeing them all jumping for joy when his shot hit the net.

Dicko and I had virtually grown up together at West Ham . . . from training as 14 year-olds, on to youth team and then reserves. I knew all along that he would be the first of our crop of youngsters to make the breakthrough and we were all pleased for him that he did so well on his debut as an 18 year-old. Dicko had laid an important foundation, and I said to myself, 'If Dicko can get in, so can I'.

But, in my heart of hearts, I knew that I would have to show patience. Paul Goddard and Sandy Clark were the main strike pairing; Francois van der Elst could play either wide or up front; and even if any of those three weren't available, Nicky Morgan was logically the next option. He was the most senior reserve team forward and had already made several senior appearances as sub. that season.

What I hadn't bargained for was an injury to Paul Goddard, which ruled him out of the home game against arch rivals Tottenham on New Year's Day, 1983. Sometimes you need a lucky break in this game and Sarge's injury effectively turned my world upside down.

Above left: *An early cuddle with dad at home in Harold Hill.*
Above right: *As World Cup Willie – 'Mooro's' good luck charm in '66.*
Left: *Where's the goal?*
Below: *The first of many convertibles.*

Above: Grandad Cottee asleep with
The Sporting Life.
Left: Mum and dad get married, Jul
9, 1960.
Below right: Grandad Griff with Pa
and me at West Ham park.
Below: Me, Jo and Paul prior to
wrecking a camera shop in Romford

Left: *A nice smile, aged three.*
Below left: *Where did I get that shirt and tie!*
Right: *My first day at Warren in 1976 – flares and all!*
Below: *A more serious pose at my first school.*

Left: Carl Cowley and me, aged 10, after winning the Met-Essex Cup.
Below left: A family holiday in Spain, aged 13.
Below right: Me and brother Paul after a Havering district match, 1975.
Below: On my way to runners-up prize in a penalty competition in Cornwall, aged seven.

Left: *Santa meets a future Hammer.*
Centre: *The last time I touched the FA Cup, in 1975 with Ian Veal.*
Below: *Irons Travel Club member, 1981.*

Above: *Romford Royal under-11s, with Jorn Cornwell (back row, right), Steve Castle (front left) and myself (front, third from right).*
Below: *Essex Under-15s in 1980. Future stars include George Parris (back row, second from left), John Cornwell (back, third from left), Alan Dickens (back, fourth from left), Micky Stockwell (back, second from right), myself (front, third from left) and Robert Codner (front row, far right).*

Left: With Trevor Brooking and the police commissioner in 1983.
Centre: Signing associate schoolboy forms for West Ham, watched by Eddie Baily, Eddie Chapman and John Lyall.
Below: With my boyhood hero Frank Lampard – now my assistant manager! – with John Cornwell to my right.

Above: *South-East Counties League Cup winners in 1982.*
Right: *Six handsome apprentices in July 1981 – left to right: myself, George Parris, Greg Campbell, Everald La Ronde, Alan Dickens and Warren Donald!*

Left: *Paul Allen presents me with the Young Hammer of the Year award, aged 16.*

CHAPTER 13

Claret & Blues

JUST LIKE MY DREAMS

ANUARY 1, 1983. A day I will never forget. It was the day 17 year-old Tony Cottee played out his own real life version of fantasy football. In the first team. Against Tottenham Hotspur. In front of 33,000 fans. The TV cameras. G-O-A-L!
My Roy of the Rovers adventure began the previous morning, when I got my first inkling that a first team call up might be on the cards. I reported for training as usual with the youth team. Before we started, Mick McGiven pulled me aside and said: "I think you might be needed for training with the first team. You'd better go home and report back tonight at five-thirty." Dicko, who hadn't played in the previous two Christmas holiday games against Swansea and Watford, was told the same.

Obviously we were both excited about the thought of being in the first team squad, but the possibility of actually playing still seemed very remote to me.

I even remember thinking, 'blimey, it means that now I won't be able to go out celebrating on New Year's eve, just as every other 17 year-old would be!' I always went out and had a good time on Christmas and New Year's eve, as does just about everyone who isn't preparing for a football match the next day.

I was really surprised by my call up. Although I had played well and scored plenty of goals for the youth and reserve teams, I hadn't expected this so soon. Nicky Morgan was also in the squad and I felt that I was simply going along to make up the numbers.

When we arrived back at Chadwell Heath to train on that Friday evening, it was very daunting to find the youth team dressing room locked up and the only other room open was occupied by first team players. Although I had trained with first-teamers before, it was something quite different to be sat there, getting changed alongside them and listening to their banter. These were the same players I had travelled hundreds of miles to cheer on as a fan just a matter of months earlier.

After a five-a-side in the gym, I drove my car through the leafy country lanes to the Epping Post House Hotel, where the team was staying the night before our home game with Spurs. Naturally, Dicko, who travelled with me, and I roomed together and went down for dinner at about 7.30pm. I think our conversation went something along the lines of, 'well, it's great being here among the first team and eating steak and chips at a posh hotel, but I wonder what the lads are doing down at the Ilford Palais?'.

I thought about how I might otherwise have been seeing in the New Year with my new girlfriend, Lorraine. Yes, the same Lorraine who almost had a close encounter with a handful of maggots in our schooldays at Warren. We lost touch with each other after school and only met up again after a chance conversation I had with a friend called Jimmy Tuck, on a number 86 bus while on our way to training one morning in November 1982. Jimmy was a year younger than me but didn't get offered an apprenticeship by West Ham. It was fate, I suppose, that I should find myself next to Jimmy that day, because I'd passed my driving test in July and usually borrowed my dad's car for the drive to training.

Anyway, we were riding on the top deck when Jimmy turned and said to me: "Do you remember a girl named Lorraine who you used to go out with?" Even though our relationship had started some two years earlier and didn't progress once I left school, I replied: "Of course I do." Jimmy continued: "You want to see her now, she's a bit of a sort."

That was my cue to dig out Lorraine's telephone number when I got home that night and call her up. Her mum, June, answered the phone at their home in Marks Gate, Chadwell Heath, and passed the phone to her daughter. I said: "Hello, it's Tony," thinking that Lorraine would immediately remember me from two years ago. To which she replied: "Tony who?"

What a way to kick off the second stage of a relationship that, despite one or two rocky periods that all couples seem to go through at some stage of their lives, has lasted 13 years. Our relationship has provided many happy memories and produced a beautiful three year-old daughter, Chloe.

Even as we drove to Upton Park, Dicko and I never believed that either of us would actually play. There were about 15 or 16 players in the squad and once we heard that Goddard was injured, I said to myself that John Lyall would play Morgan up front alongside Clark. If I was really lucky, I might get on the bench.

Then, when we got to the ground, John pulled me into his small wood-panelled office and said: "Are you confident? Are you ready? Do you think you could do a good job?" I replied: "Yes, I feel confident." "Well," he added, "just go out and enjoy yourself. There's no pressure, you've just got to go out there and do your best. Everyone else will talk to you, just enjoy yourself."

Dicko was called in too and must have been as excited as me about making his home debut.

The first thing I tried to do was ring my mum and dad to tell them the news. But they had already left home and were on their way to the ground. So when they arrived they had no idea I was playing – my name wasn't even mentioned in the programme line-up. I didn't have the chance to contact all the people I would have liked to have been there, but as it turned out, my parents, brother, both grans, my dad's brother, Roy, and my old P.E. teacher Graham Penn, were all sat in the West Stand when the team was announced over the public address system before the game. Dad had been visiting his mother in Coventry the day before and when he heard that I had been called into the squad, he decided to take a chance and bring her down for the weekend, just in case I was given my big chance.

With Billy Bonds and Trevor Brooking both ruled out by injuries – Trevor played only the penultimate game of the season – Ray Stewart took over as captain for the day. Ray was always offering encouragement anyway, and the rest of the lads were brilliant to me and Dicko as I pulled on 'Sarge's' number eight shirt and he wore Bonzo's number four. The full line-up: Parkes, Stewart, Gallagher, Dickens, Martin, Devonshire, Van der Elst, Cottee, Clark, Allen (Paul), Pike.

As kick-off approached, I went into the little gym underneath the West Stand and set the pattern for what would become my pre-match routine for the rest of my career . . . kicking the ball up against the wall, practicing a few side-foot passes and stretching my muscles. I never went out onto the pitch to warm up that day and, apart from one or two rare occasions, have never done so.

I was aware before the start that the game was being televised by ITV. That added to my nervousness, which showed as I made about 10 visits to the loo – another habit that has remained to this day.

Tottenham took control of the early stages of the game. I recall Glenn Hoddle sending a couple of shots whizzing past the woodwork and it was case of hanging on. Then, with around 25 minutes gone, the ball was played down our right-hand side. I went towards it and was fouled from behind. Geoff Pike took the free-kick, curling the ball towards the far post. Joe Gallagher, our centre-half on loan from Birmingham, got his head to it and Spurs 'keeper Ray Clemence managed to touch the ball onto the crossbar. It hit the underside of the bar and bounced down. I did what I have always done instinctively throughout my career and followed up.

I jumped a few feet off the ground to head the ball into the South Bank net from around six yards out. In a situation like that you don't know what to do. Both of my arms were in the air as I turned and ran, waiting for the others to catch me. Paul Allen was the first to congratulate me, followed by the rest of my team mates. It was an unbelievable moment.

We built on our lead when Stewart made it 2-0 and I played a part in our third, which went all the way from Parkes to Pike, who scored to complete a memorable 3-0 victory.

I thought I had done well in adapting to the fast and furious pace of the First Division. I had cramp in both legs and felt very tired towards the end but in general I did well against the Spurs defenders. There were no sour grapes from any of them, no shirt-pulling or anything, and they said 'well done' as we walked off at the end.

I was very fortunate, because not many players can have experienced the pleasure my debut gave me. Many are unlucky – maybe their team is badly beaten and they get substituted, or give away a sloppy goal, or miss a great goalscoring chance.

Debuts can make or break some players. For me, everything went like clockwork. It really was Roy of the Rovers stuff, a fairytale come true. The only other occasion I could compare it to is my Everton debut, although by then I had experienced the thrill of scoring in front of a packed crowd many times.

The excitement surrounding my Hammers' debut continued long after the final whistle. The sponsors named me man of the match and presented me with a video game. I was interviewed for BBC and local independent radio, as well as the reporters working for national papers. Then Brian Moore interviewed me and

Trevor Brooking for ITV's The Big Match, which was shown later that night. I think that part of the day was more nerve-wracking than the match itself.

All of my family who had seen my debut, and Lorraine, who joined us when we got back home that night, gathered around our television for the highlights programme. We tucked into a Chinese takeaway and there were a few beer cans scattered around the place.

Seeing my goal go in, replayed from several different angles, was like re-living a dream. As I looked at the screen, I kept saying to myself, 'is that really me scoring?' It took ages for everything to sink in. But I felt a bit embarrassed when they showed my interview. Not quite as embarrassed, though, as I feel now whenever I watch a video of the interview. Those blond streaks in my hair take some living down!

Amid all the euphoria, the greatest day of my life was tinged with sadness. My two grandads, who had watched me play as a boy and predicted that I would go on to make it at West Ham, had both missed the moment I had always dreamed of. I've already described how grandad Griff collapsed on the forecourt at Upton Park before the cup tie with West Brom in 1980. Five years earlier, my dad's father had also passed away.

I'd like to think they were both looking down on me with a certain degree of pride and perhaps enjoying a little celebration toast of their own.

Claret & Blues

ON THE ROAD

JUST three days after my dramatic debut, I was scoring again on my second appearance, against Luton Town at Upton Park three days later. And to complete a remarkable week, I experienced the thrill of playing my first away game at Old Trafford of all places.

There was nothing memorable about my goal which put us ahead in the Luton match at Upton Park, watched by England manager Bobby Robson. The ball was bobbling around in the box, I took a swing at it with my left foot and the ball squeezed through the 'keeper Jake Findlay's legs on its way into the net. Although it was nice to continue where I'd left off against Spurs, we lost the match 3-2 and Paul Walsh stole the limelight this time with a hat-trick for the Hatters.

Three days later, I boarded the first team bus for the first time as we set off for Manchester to play a United side that included international stars like Bryan Robson, Steve Coppell, Frank Stapleton, Norman Whiteside and Arnold Muhren in the third round of the FA Cup.

As Alan Dickens was ruled out by injury, I sat next to Paul Allen and the prospect of playing against those big names in front of a full house at Old Trafford was a bit scary. I'd never even been to the stadium before, so it was a wonderful experience just to be part of the squad.

It was nice, too, to sample the luxuries that most first team players take for granted. On the bus, we were waited on hand and foot, with our own 'waiter' serving coffees and other snacks. When we arrived at our smart hotel for the evening meal, I remember having the choice of prawn cocktail or soup for starters, followed by fillet steak. After demolishing that, we could stuff our faces with chocolate gateaux. I'm not saying that I'd never had fillet steak before in my life, but this did open my eyes to the lifestyle of a professional footballer.

It still hadn't really sunk in what had happened to me in the space of a week. To be honest, I was a bit overawed by the whole experience. I didn't play particularly well on the day – we were beaten 2-0 – and the game seemed to pass me by. It was a wonderful experience but I knew that I still had a long way to go.

John Lyall did, too, because he pulled me out of the side after the visit to Old Trafford. I wasn't involved in any of our next three First Division games before coming on as sub. for the injured Sandy Clark in a 1-1 home draw with Southampton.

With Sandy having left for Glasgow Rangers in a £160,000 deal, I was back in the starting line-up for the next fixture – and was delighted after Dicko and I saved the game with a goal apiece in a 2-1 home win over Brighton & Hove Albion. We went behind soon after half-time but Dicko brought us level seven minutes from time when he came off the bench to send a stunning 35-yard left-foot rocket into the top corner. I'd never seen him hit the ball harder with his left foot – it was real goal-of-the-season stuff.

Then, a minute later, I chested the ball down and, turning to my left, struck a dipping shot from 30 yards that flew over 'keeper Gary Moseley's head and, once again, into the top corner. In normal circumstances, I would probably not have even thought of shooting from that distance or position on the field. I did so more out of desperation than in a genuine belief that I would score.

Afterwards, Brighton's manager, Jimmy Melia, was quoted as saying: "Those two players will never score two better goals." To a certain extent, he was probably right as far as I was concerned.

It's always a brilliant feeling to score a special goal like my winner against Brighton but, as I say, I was still learning the game at first team level. I didn't do that much in the game itself and, in fact, wasn't in the side for our next match at Liverpool. Indeed, I didn't start another senior game that season, making just four more appearances as sub. (in the days when a team could only use one).

Paul Goddard reclaimed his number eight shirt after recovering from the injury that gave me my debut, while the club signed big Dave Swindlehurst from Crystal Palace to replace Clark. I had to accept the fact that although I'd had a glimpse of the big time, I was still effectively in my second year as an apprentice.

I still continued to spend most of the week training with the youth team and only one day a week with the senior pros. I reverted to the youth team dressing room at Chadwell Heath but never had a problem with that. After throwing me in at the deep end for three games in a week at the start of 1983, John clearly didn't want to burn me out. If I'd struggled, my confidence could have dipped badly, so he sensibly took precautions to ensure that didn't happen.

Instead, he kept me on the fringe of the team by giving me outings as sub. – against Watford, Swansea and Sunderland. I'd come on for the last 10-15 minutes, so it was a gentle introduction.

The next big game for me was our last of the season, at Coventry City. The youth team was heading for its traditional end-of-season tour of Holland and John gave me the option of going on that or staying behind and possibly being involved with the first team. He wasn't promising me a game but I knew that even if I came on for the last 10 minutes, there was always the chance I might score.

As it turned out, I replaced the injured Geoff Pike and played for about half an hour, scoring twice for the first time in a game at that level, as we wrapped up a satisfactory campaign with a 4-2 win.

My gran was living in the Coventry area at the time and, along with my uncles,

Alan and Terry, went along to see me play there that day, and in subsequent seasons. Ever since that double strike on May 14, Highfield Road has always been one of my happiest hunting grounds.

With five goals in eight league appearances (only three starts), I was well pleased with my initial contribution on the field. My brace against the Sky Blues brought my goals haul, in all matches at youth (21 goals in 18 games), reserve (22 goals in 19 games, plus two as sub.) and first team level, to 48 in 46 matches (seven as sub.).

Off the field, life was equally good. I was courting Lorraine and the money I was now earning as a pro – quadruple the £25 per week I'd started the 1982/83 season on as a second year apprentice – enabled me to enjoy myself to the full. The three-year pro contract I'd signed the previous September gave me a basic weekly wage of £110, plus £100 for each first team appearance and an extra £200 win bonus, which I collected on six out of nine occasions. The contract also confirmed that my basic would increase to £135 per week in year two (1983/84) and £160 per week in year three (1984/85).

So, at the end of my first month as a First Division footballer, I would have been earning something like £500, plus bonuses, paid direct into my bank account. As a 17 year-old, still living at home with his parents, it was a big leap financially. I had more money than I knew what to do with. I handed over £100 to mum as my contribution towards housekeeping, but I was still left with more than plenty to spend on myself.

I passed my driving test soon after my 17th birthday and was grateful to mum for lending me her Chrysler Sunbeam to get around in. It was certainly a much better option than the bus, although I must admit I was looking for something a bit more tasty. My dad drove a Ford Escort XR3 – the 'in' car at the time – and with my increased earnings, I agreed to take over the payments and buy it from him. It was blue in colour and really looked the business with its white go-faster stripes and the XR3 flash across the side of the bodywork.

And to add a little more style, I had an illegal klaxon fitted that blasted out the Dukes of Hazzard theme tune at the flick of a switch. This seemed like the ultimate status symbol of youth to me and instead of getting a bus to a nightclub or pub on a Saturday night, I'd drive to the Ilford Palais or Room at the Top in Ilford High Road. Lorraine and I also enjoyed the atmosphere of the East End pubs, like Queens, Tipples or R.J.'s, around the Bethnal Green area. Sometimes we'd go out with John Cornwell and his girlfriend at the time.

In a matter of weeks, I'd gone from an apprentice earning next to nothing, to a young pro who was pulling in more than £500 a month, with a lovely girlfriend and a flash car. It was great!

But I'm not sure what Trevor Brooking must have made of me when I came across him going into training one particular morning. After roaring into the car park in my pride and joy of an XR3, I accidentally nudged the klaxon switch as I went to remove the keys from the ignition . . . and Chadwell Heath reverberated to the sound of the Dukes of Hazzard!

Trevor was strolling gracefully towards the dressing rooms as my mishap occurred, and I can only imagine what he must have thought about the cocky new kid with the flash car and blaring klaxon. For me, it was a moment of real embarrassment.

I also spent quite a bit on soul records and have amassed a large collection. My favourite albums were by Kool & The Gang, George Benson and Luther Vandross, although I also built up a collection of over 100 twelve inch singles that became very popular at the time. But I was never one for spending ridiculous amounts on clothes, a habit that remains today.

Above all, I was totally consumed by football. I'd lost touch with virtually all my old schoolfriends and, after a holiday in Spain, nothing could come between me and my determination to continue making progress with the Hammers as the 1983/84 season dawned.

There was a strong feeling of achievement when, as the new season approached, John Lyall invited Dicko and I to transfer from the youth to the first team dressing room permanently. I was allocated squad number 35 and when I returned to West Ham from Everton 10 years later, I asked for, and received, the same number. By then, of course, we wore squad numbers on our matchday shirts, but the number 35 wasn't available, so I settled for 27 instead, before reverting to nine this season.

Like the team, I usually take time to get into the scoring groove but the opening first team game of 1983/84, at home to Birmingham, was just 22 minutes old when I scored with a diving header following a corner. Within five minutes I headed a second, to set us on our way to a marvellous 4-0 victory – the first time in five seasons that Hammers had kicked off with a win.

What gave me just as much pleasure as scoring those two was being able to play alongside Brooking, who was outstanding, for the first time. He was still the top man at the club and I held him in awe.

For years, I'd marvelled at his skill from the terraces. Now I was playing alongside one of my heroes – me wearing the number nine shirt and him number ten. It was difficult to take in.

It's one thing to sit in the stands and admire a player, but to play alongside him, to benefit personally from his presence, awareness and superb skill, is something entirely different. Trevor's speciality was to drop his shoulder, let the ball run past him and beat players without even touching the ball. To see him do that, then receive a perfect pass from him, was just brilliant.

As a person, Trevor was always someone you could talk to. He wasn't one of those unapproachable old pros who would shun youngsters seeking his opinion. If I had a doubt in my mind, we'd talk about my position and the timing of my runs.

Trevor retired as a player – some say prematurely – at the end of the 1983/84 season, so it was disappointing not to have enjoyed more than one full season with him.

With Trevor back to his best after a season out following a pelvic operation, we made a great start, winning our first five in the league. I was by far the youngest in the side and, to be honest, hadn't even expected to start the season in the first team.

Derby County's £150,000 striker Dave Swindlehurst was the new target man John signed to replace Clark, so I always looked upon Paul Goddard as my main rival for the other place up front. Nicky Morgan was also around, but he was another target man, and never really made the breakthrough and when Swindles arrived, he moved on to Portsmouth for £50,000. Big and strong, Nicky was a good finisher in his own right, but lacked a bit of pace at times.

Despite competing with Goddard, I never had a problem with him. Sarge was a nice fellow and if ever he was looking over his shoulder at me, he never showed any feelings of animosity. He was always offering encouragement and would put aside time if you asked him to work on specific moves in training.

I don't suppose there are many youngsters coming into the game today who could count on that kind of support from established senior pros, which emphasises just what a good pro Sarge had always been. But he missed the first game against Birmingham due to injury and made only five appearances all season.

Although the team made a flying start, and I'd added to my first day double by setting up a goal for Swindles in our 2-0 win at Tottenham and scored a tap-in in a 3-1 home win over Leicester that kept us top of the First Division, I was beginning to feel the pace a bit.

Once again, credit to the manager for recognising the fact and for dropping me in favour of Sarge. John knew I had plenty of promise and ability to score goals but he didn't want me to burn myself out. He knew that it was wise to rest me every now and again at the start of my first team career, and I benefited from his knowledge and judgment.

I had an outing as sub. for the next game against Liverpool, then played six on the spin before being rested again. I didn't figure in either of the next two matches, but regained the number eight shirt for our home defeat by Southampton on Boxing Day and never looked back. I started all the remaining league and cup games.

Looking back on it, I think I got through those first half-dozen games on pure adrenalin and youthful exuberance. The pace of the game at top level is so much quicker and different than any youngster can ever hope to experience playing reserve and youth football. It's not only faster and tougher in the physical sense, the brain has to function quicker too.

The two goals I scored in the first match set me up for the next five or six. But I remember being ineffective in our home win over Notts County, and with Sarge coming off the bench to score one of our three goals, I said to myself: 'That's it. Sarge has come back in, scored straightaway, so it won't be long before I'm out of the side.'

I was starting to feel tired after games. When your confidence also begins to slide, you know it's time for a rest. I'm sure John Lyall read the situation very well.

Not that I was happy to stand down, even though I understood the reasoning behind it and didn't complain. As an 18 year-old, I wasn't very good to be around if we'd lost a game, or I'd played poorly. I wouldn't go out on a Saturday night if the result had gone against us. I really took results and my performances to heart. Football was the be all and end all for me then.

While I was still seeking consistency in the league, the night of October 25 provided me and the rest of the lads with the chance to, literally, bury the opposition. The first leg of our second round Milk Cup tie at Fourth Division Bury had ended in a 2-1 win for the Hammers, and no one at Gigg Lane then could have predicted what lie in store for the return at Upton Park a fortnight later.

West Ham absolutely tore poor Bury to shreds. I scored a first-half hat-trick and we were winning 5-0 at half-time. We fancied our chances of scoring seven or eight, so to demolish them 10-0 (to set a new League Cup record, later equalled by Liverpool who beat Fulham by the same score) was a bit special. Trevor and Dev scored two each, while defenders Ray Stewart and Alvin Martin got in on the act, and I added one more on an incredible night.

The crowd of 10,896 certainly got their money's worth, while I got the matchball for netting my first hat-trick for the club and also took away with me a copy of the club video. By chance, West Ham chose the Bury game to begin experimenting with their own video system. It's not exactly a masterpiece of technology – the commentator must have been a real Hammers' fan, because he kept referring to me as 'Coatee' – but despite the rather tacky production, it must be a collector's item and I certainly wouldn't part with my copy.

What was perhaps even more bizarre than the actual result was the fact that John signed one of the Bury players who suffered that Milk Cup misery! Nothing against Paul Hilton – he proved himself a very valuable squad member and worked hard as youth and reserve team manager before his departure on October 1995 – but the thought that we could sign anyone from a team we had just stuffed by 10 goals, simply didn't make any sense to me.

I know the result was an awful lot for Hilts to live down, but he's come through it well and proved his worth as a very honest player who gave the club 100 per cent at all times and played in any position asked of him.

Back in the league, the turning point of my second season came in the last week of 1983. After returning to the starting line-up for the Southampton game on Boxing Day, I scored the next day at Luton and then found the net again as we saw out the year with a brilliant 4-1 thrashing of Spurs at Upton Park. The highlight being Ray Stewart's 25-yard angled blockbuster that nearly burst the South Bank net.

Sadly, the new year was anything but a happy time for poor Dev. An innocuous-looking challenge by a Wigan defender during our FA Cup third round tie at Upton Park, ended his season and almost his career. I was as gutted as anyone to see Dev suffer badly ruptured knee ligaments – an injury that sidelined him for 19 agonising months.

Dev's loss was an enormous blow to West Ham and me in particular. He was a wonderful player, a real down-to-earth Londoner. As a player, he had so many qualities: electrifying pace, two very good feet and superb vision.

As a front man, it was great to know that I could come short looking for the ball and that Dev would inevitably find me with a well-weighted pass of typical pinpoint accuracy. Although he was predominantly right-footed, he was devastating playing wide on the left, with the ability to either go round his marker or cut inside on to his right foot.

We definitely had a chemistry between us. I knew what was in his mind and I'm sure Dev could read me like a book. He'd always look to play the ball into my feet, or into the space ahead of me. We'd set each other up with little one-twos in and around the edge of the box. It was a deadly combination that led to many goals for me and others.

It's a travesty that Dev didn't win more than eight England caps, and I have nothing but admiration for the way in which he fought back from that terrible injury to play a very important part in West Ham's best-ever season.

I played only one full season with Brooking, so it is for that reason that I have no hesitation in declaring Alan Devonshire as the finest I have ever played with.

I opened my account in 1984 with the winner at home to West Bromwich Albion on January 21 and was pleased to score in the next three league matches, too. It was another good afternoon for me at Highfield Road, where I netted what proved the winner, although I thought I should have been credited with both goals in our 2-1 victory.

We took the lead in the first half when I flicked on Neil Orr's near-post corner. The ball went into the net after brushing the chest of Coventry City defender Dave Bamber who, despite my claims for the goal, was dubiously credited with an O.G.

It wasn't until the end of the season that the full disappointment of being denied that goal really hit home in the Cottee household – I missed my target of 20 goals by one, and my dad missed a £500 pay-out from the bookies, having staked £20 on me reaching that figure for the season at odds of 25-1!

One of the low points of my first full season came on our return to the Midlands a week later, to face Birmingham City in the FA Cup. The fifth round tie was marred by West Ham fans invading the pitch twice to interrupt play in our dismal 3-0 defeat. The first time they came on, I didn't even get as far as the dressing room. I just sat on a wall at the side of the pitch while the police – assisted by Bonzo, who tried to urge the trouble-makers to stay off the pitch – got the fans back behind the fences they had at St. Andrews (and many other grounds) in those pre-Hillsborough days.

When our fans came back on for the second time, with only a minute of the match remaining, causing referee George Courtney to take the players off for seven minutes, I saw a Birmingham player actually 'chin' one supporter. I don't know if he got his just desserts, but it was a very depressing scene.

I'd experienced crowd trouble as a fan but it was the first time I'd been close to it as a player, and it was a bit scary. There were 109 arrests – 32 inside the ground – and it was reported that more than 200 seats were ripped out.

As the last surviving London club in the competition, we'd gone up to the Midlands with high hopes of maintaining a good Cup run but were well beaten on the field and hundreds of our 'fans' brought shame on themselves and the club – in front of the watching FA secretary Ted Croker.

There was speculation that the FA Commission would force West Ham to temporarily close the terraces at Upton Park, but the club was relieved to escape with only a suspended sentence.

The sight of hooligans rampaging across the pitch, then pissing up the back of the stand afterwards, in front of my 78 year-old nan, made it one of the blackest days in Hammers' history. Fortunately, in the main, West Ham fans have been very well behaved in the years since then, but it was a very sad day in Birmingham.

Another bad memory from that season was our 6-0 thrashing at Liverpool on April 7. We were battered into submission by the rampant Reds who were inspired by Dalglish, Rush and Souness. It was hardly the ideal cure for John Lyall, who missed the match because of flu. But it could have been worse, for Liverpool might easily have won 10-0!

Despite the Anfield debacle and a home defeat by Sunderland, who included my schoolboy favourite 'Pop' Robson in their side, my two goals in a 3-1 home win over Luton 10 days later lifted us to sixth place and within sight of a UEFA Cup place.

But we fell away badly at the end, drawing two and losing four of our last six matches. Trevor Brooking hadn't enjoyed his last visit to Anfield as a player but ninth place was still a respectable position for him to leave the club in.

There was a feeling of sadness in our dressing room when Everton visited for the last game of the season – Trevor's farewell appearance. Make no bones about it, he was one of the all-time greats and proved it time and again for West Ham and England over many years.

Having missed virtually all of the previous campaign, I think Trevor knew when we kicked off in August that this would be his swansong. He went out in style, playing outstandingly week after week, and I was just disappointed that I had only one full season alongside him.

I remember his overwhelming influence in a 2-2 draw at home to QPR on March 31, when he took on Rangers almost single-handedly. He was simply brilliant that day and although I scored one and had another disallowed, I ought really to have converted four or five of the host of chances he created for me.

That emotional finale ended with Trevor taking a lap of honour and then being carried around the pitch on the shoulders of his admiring hordes. The attendance was 8,000 up on the previous game, and it was just a pity from his and the fans' point of view that Everton – fielding most of the side that went on to beat Watford 2-0 in their FA Cup triumph – beat us with a 1-0 win thanks to 'party pooper' Kevin Richardson.

Trevor could probably have gone on and played another season or two. It's not as if he was reliant on pace, because he was never exceptionally quick and had so much skill that it didn't matter anyway.

Only Trevor knows whether he made the right decision to quit when he did, but he made his decision and went out at the top in style. Not surprisingly, he got the fans' vote as Hammer of the Year, although I was pleased to finish runner-up.

In my first two seasons, West Ham had finished eighth and ninth in the First Division and the side was brimming with quality players. I was very lucky to come into the side in these circumstances, whereas so many other youngsters find themselves being thrown in to a team battling against relegation, when confidence and morale throughout the squad is very low.

Trevor and Dev were obviously outstanding from an attacking and creative point of view, but I'd also like to particularly mention my partner, Dave Swindlehurst. 'Swindles' got his fair share of goals, but his prime role was that of target man. He was very good at bringing others into play with his first touch. It's important to work at a partnership and Dave and I talked a lot. Although I top-scored with 15 league and four cup goals, Dave helped me tremendously and weighed in with 13 First Division goals himself.

But then I was very fortunate to have played with, and benefited from, so many quality players in the early stages of my career.

Claret & Blues

MONEY TALKS

HE was like a headmaster figure, someone I respected and looked up to. He had looked after me on and off the field since I was a 14 year-old schoolboy, and made it clear that his office door was always open if ever a player needed his advice. But I still had difficulty communicating my true feelings to John Lyall.

Although I thought highly of him as a person and a football coach and manager, and he did very well for me in my career, I always found it hard to approach John.

For while John is renowned as one of football's gentlemen, he also had a tough side to his character – as I discovered when we met for contract talks in the summer of '84. Although he looked after his players, he also distanced himself from them and was somewhat aloof. He was never the sort to jump into the bath with the players and have a laugh and a joke in that way.

I still had one year left of my existing three-year contract but as John said at the time I signed my first pro contract: "If you do well, the club will look after you."

I was still 18 years-old, felt I'd done well and was only on £135 per week. I say 'only', and know it was a good wage, but I also knew that players like Sarge and Swindles were probably being paid four or five times what I was getting. I felt that was a little unfair, as Sarge had hardly got a look in all season while I had scored 15 league and four cup goals.

It was the first time I'd gone to see John about finances – all our previous discussions had been purely about football – and I admit, I entered his office with some trepidation. I had no thoughts whatsoever of wanting to leave West Ham, I just wanted a decent rise to put me on a par with some of the other players.

I remember going in with all these rough figures in my head, but I don't think I said anything I'd planned to say. Feeling nervous in this headmaster-pupil situation, it was all I could do to blurt out that I felt I deserved a rise – I didn't even mention figures. John just said: "Leave it to me, I'll get back to you."

Ten days went by before John phoned and asked me to come to the ground for further talks. Once again, I felt nervous and was almost shaking as I sat waiting outside John's old office in the West Stand while he finished his other business.

Once inside and sitting down, John took the initiative, saying: "The directors have done absolutely brilliantly for you, they've come up with a great contract, a really excellent one."

He sat down and put the contract down in front of me to sign. The deal was £400 per week basic, rising to £450 the following year, £500 in year three, rising to £550 in year four, plus extra for appearances. I looked at the contract offer and thought to myself: 'Blimey, I'm actually getting more or less what I had in mind here.' So I said to John: 'It looks quite good, but I'd like to have a little think about it. I don't want to rush into anything and would like to talk it over with my dad and Lorraine before committing myself."

At that moment, I couldn't believe John's reaction. He picked up the telephone on his desk, slammed it down on the table in front of me and said: "Here you go, ring your dad!"

John really took me by surprise. He wasn't exactly angry, although he was clearly put out and possibly surprised that I didn't agree to sign there and then. He wanted the matter dealt with and took exception to the fact that I wanted a bit more time to think things through and discuss them with two of the people closest to me. I declined the use of his phone and said: "Well, John, even if I do speak to my dad now, I'm not going to sign before thinking about it and speaking to my girlfriend first."

He said: "Right then, tell me tomorrow." "All right," I replied, "but couldn't I have a little longer to think about it?" John had the last word: "No, tomorrow lunchtime – at the latest."

To tell the truth, John's manner scared the life out of me. I thought the club's offer was a good one, compared to the money I was already on, but then I told myself that surely not every player signed his new contract there and then without first giving it any consideration. But reading books written by other West Ham players over the years, I think quite a few of them did in fact settle immediately for the amount John offered them.

Players' agents have been widely criticised but it is in precisely the situation I found myself, as an 18 year-old sitting down with his manager to negotiate his first new contract, that an inexperienced youngster needs advice and guidance. The agent is the buffer between player and manager and I know I would have appreciated one the first time I came to face to face with John Lyall over money.

Anyway, after chatting to dad and Lorraine over lunch the next day, I decided to sign the deal offered to me. But the way the matter was handled left a bit of a sour taste as far as I was concerned. I didn't think it was the best way John could have dealt with an 18 year-old prospect, who had just finished his first full season as top scorer and who, in the main, he had looked after well in the early days of his career. I didn't like the way he had tried to force me to sign on the spot.

I confirmed my acceptance in a phone call to John, who didn't show much reaction. I guess, having been in this situation a thousand times before, he knew he was in the driving seat. He knew he'd got me on a fair whack, if maybe not as much as Sarge and Swindles were on. My problem was that I had in effect progressed too quickly for the original contract I was on. I'd gone from youth team to becoming top scorer at a reasonably successful First Division side in the short space of months, which made my original deal seem out of proportion with my achievements.

One final aspect of that contract saga that rankled a bit was that John tied me to a new four-year agreement, whereas I only wanted to commit myself for the next three years.

Footballers are funny when it comes to their wages. They'll always speculate what their team mates are earning, but you'll very rarely get a player turn round and say: "Look, I'm on £500 a week!" It just doesn't happen in the game. No matter how much you might trust or like a player, no one wants to tell anybody exactly how much they're on.

But you will never stop players speculating about others. I weighed up all the factors . . . the fact that Paul Goddard cost a club record £800,000 in August 1980, which was a helluva lot of money in those days, and thought that he must have been on £500 or £600 per week. I looked at it and said to myself: 'Hold on a sec, I'm on £135 per week, I'm top goalscorer, Sarge has hardly played all season, and yet I'm on this sort of money'. That's why I felt fully justified in expecting more from the club.

I never begrudge a player whatever he earns. If players are good enough, or lucky enough, to earn £15,000 a week, as some players do now, then good luck to them. As a player and a person, you owe it to yourself and your family to get what you believe you are worth.

As a home-grown product who has progressed through the schoolboy ranks to the first team, it is that much harder to attain a higher level of income. You start off on peanuts as an apprentice, so anything you get once you break into the first team seems a lot of money by comparison, as it did to me.

But if you are transferred for a lot of money, then you can automatically command much better wages – as I did when I moved to Everton in 1988.

And a big money move also brings with it a good lump sum payment in the form of a signing-on fee. Nowadays, most clubs pay signing-on fees to existing players who simply sign an extended contract. But in my day at West Ham the club never paid signing-on fees. When I agreed my new deal with John Lyall in the summer of '84, it was simply a question of improving my monthly wage and bonus – there was no lump sum involved, which we could have done with as a deposit on a new flat Lorraine and I wanted to buy. John's argument was that it was better from the player's point of view to earn a better basic rate of pay than to take less in basic pay and receive a lump sum signing-on fee. So I was never in the position where I could stick, say, 10 grand into a building society, and possibly use it as a deposit on a property. We had to save almost everything I earned.

I'm not criticising West Ham particularly, because what I'm saying here applied to most clubs in the 70s and 80s. I think I asked John about the possibility of a signing-on fee, and he simply replied: "No, we don't do that here at West Ham." And I had no reason to doubt his word.

But like the vast majority of clubs today, West Ham do now pay their players a signing-on fee, which is right in my opinion.

Signing that new four-year contract was a major turning point for me. I was pleased with the money I was on, which was a lot, and although I've complained about not having a lump sum, in hindsight I suppose it didn't do Lorraine and I any harm to have to save up for the five per cent deposit on the flat we eventually bought, in Hornchurch for £42,000, in late 1985.

I'd lived with my parents until then, but by looking to get onto the property ladder and putting a slice of my increased earnings away each month, it made me realise that it was time to grow up and begin to stand on my own two feet. Until then I was like a kid playing in a man's game.

I was lucky that my dad, who is an insurance broker, gave me good financial advice. At 17, he encouraged me to start investing in a pension policy. I couldn't see the point, then, of saving money that I wouldn't see again until I was 65 years-old. But he explained to me about the special deal for professional footballers that enables you to draw your pension from the age of 35, when most players have to hang up their boots.

So from the age of 17 I put away a small amount of £10 per month, and upped the payments to £100 per month when I got my first rise, continually increasing the payments ever since. My outlook on life from a money point of view has always been: 'When I get to the age of 35, what do I WANT to do? Not what have I GOT to do'. There's a big difference, and I'm very grateful and lucky to have received such sound advice so early in my career.

Claret & Blues

CRAZY DAYS

ALTHOUGH he could be a daunting opponent across the negotiating table, John Lyall always did his best to ensure our training routine didn't become too predictable. He varied it as much and as often as possible and in the main I found training enjoyable. On some occasions, even bizarre.

One day, he told us all to stand in a line with our hands on the hips of the player immediately in front. "Then, on the word go," explained John, "I want the player at the front of the line to lay on the floor, the second player to lay on top of him, the third player to lay on top of them both, and so on."

With the appentices joining in with the pro's, there must have been 30-35 players involved, and we all looked a bit puzzled. But puzzled is not the word I'd use to describe the feelings of Phil Parkes and Alan Devonshire, first and second in the queue respectively!

Fortunately, I was at the back, and the pile of bewildered (and somewhat flattened) West Ham players was nearly sky-high by the time I threw myself on to the human hill that had formed on top of poor Parkesy and Dev, who could be heard screaming out for mercy! Big Phil was none too pleased and left the field muttering: "That's the most f-----g stupid thing I've ever done in 20 years."

John didn't attempt to explain the logic of this strange 'exercise'. Presumably he hoped it would boost morale and team spirit, although that's not the way Parkesy and Dev saw it.

Another day, John had all the senior pro's in the middle of the training ground. We hadn't even warmed up or anything when he said: "Good morning . . . now I want to see the last player out of sight."

We all stood there, looking at each other, bemused. 'What does he mean?' John repeated his command and then the penny dropped: we all had to run and hide!

It was an hilarious sight – all the players running in different directions, behind trees, the dressing rooms, behind the dug-out, under bushes, some of the thinner players even attempting to conceal themselves behind the goalposts! I think I crouched behind a tree, for what it was worth.

John made us repeat the exercise because he reckoned we'd messed about too much the first time and hadn't taken it seriously enough.

At the time I was young and critical of some aspects of training. I'd think to myself: 'What a load of rubbish, what has he got us doing this for?' To a certain extent games like hide and seek were stupid but once I'd moved to Everton, as an older and more experienced person in the game, I could see what John was trying to do. He was simply looking to change things around and liven up the day by getting the players to do things that were a break from the usual routine.

John also used to vary the time we started training. One morning we'd be told to arrive at 9.45am for an 10.00am start, the next day it would be 10.45am for an 11am start. He used to say that by constantly varying the start time, he got his players thinking more in the mornings about what time they had to be in for work.

Now, under Harry Redknapp, we report for training at 10.15am and start warming up 15 minutes later. At least no one is in any doubt when to arrive and can plan their journey to Chadwell Heath accordingly. By varying it, some of the players were probably thinking: 'Now what did he say . . . 10 or half-past?', and one or two would inevitably turn up late – or even too early, depending on how confused they were!

Steve Potts times his arrival at training as accurately as he does those last-ditch tackles for which he is famed. Pottsy turns up at 14 minutes past 10, thus avoiding any fines for lateness by a whisker.

Another favourite 'treat' of John's was to get us practicing diving headers – in the snow. One year, I recall him pulling this stroke the morning after the players' annual Christmas party – it was his way of letting us know that we were back to work, which didn't go down too well with some of the lads.

Or he'd have us swinging on the metal support bars behind the goals, as if we were on an army training course. Stupid really, but the crazy things we did then seem funny when I look back on them now.

We certainly had a laugh the day Mick McGiven, one of the first team coaches, brought out a rugby ball at training. The ground outside was hard and frosty, so we played in the indoor gym instead. Unfortunately it was more like 11-a-side than the usual five-a-side and, to our amazement, we were ordered to play with a rugby ball.

Now picture the scene . . . 22 footballers chasing around after an oval-shaped ball that was rolling everywhere. Players were getting hit by it in the stomach, it was crazy really. It was quite fun, but still very stupid.

I actually said to Mick: "What are we doing this for?" He came back with the classic comment: "Well, the pitch could be frozen on Saturday, so to help prepare us for the possible unpredictable bounce we thought we'd play today with a rugby ball."

Ridiculous.

Another time, we actually played rugby at Chadwell Heath, using proper rugby rules. Some of us, including Frank McAvennie, Mark Ward and myself, were none too keen and hovered around in the background not wishing to get too involved.

Then, the ball went to Wardie, who did no more than smack it over a high fence and into a nearby garden. He did it on purpose and as no one fancied themselves in the role of Superman, the rugby fiasco had to be abandoned. I don't think John was too pleased with Wardie, but Mark was certainly very popular with the lads, who much preferred the round ball we were all used to playing with on a Saturday!

When former Hammer Paul Allen returned to train with the Hammers for a while last season, while he found himself out of the reckoning at Southampton and trying his luck on loan at Stoke, he reminded me of the time John got one over on me during one exchange at Chadwell Heath. I could be a bit cocky and arrogant in those days and on this occasion I had a strop on about a session I wasn't too happy with.

I had a bit of a moan at John, who turned on me and, loud as possible in front of all the other players, snapped: "You're not even out of your nappies yet, pal."

I was still 18 at the time and must admit, I didn't have a response to him. John brought me down a peg or two that morning.

Claret & Blues

DISAPPEARING MAGIC

W ITH three key players missing – Brooking, who had retired, and Devonshire and Parkes, both injured for long periods – it was no surprise that West Ham slipped down the First Division in 1984/85.

Dicko took over Trevor's famous number 10 shirt, which brought unfair pressure on the youngster having to take over from one of the club's all-time greats, while Tony Gale became our only significant summer signing, moving from Fulham for a bargain £200,000 fee set by a tribunal. He was supposedly signed to replace Bonzo, who was thought to be nearing retirement.

Little did anyone, including John Lyall, know then that he would still be going strong some four years later, at the age of 41!

If the fans were comparing Dicko to Brooking, they likened Galey to the legendary Bobby Moore, which was a tremendous compliment to Tony. It was easy to see the comparison, because although he was never the quickest defender around, Galey's reading of the game was second to none.

A lot of defenders today rely on sheer pace and strength and very little else to get them through, but Galey used his brain to outwit opponents. He and Alvin Martin formed a wonderful central defensive partnership that served the club well over many seasons, but especially in 1985/86 when we finished third. Nothing got past them that season.

They were not only a very good defensive partnership, but also very creative. When Frank McAvennie and I were buzzing, a fair few of our chances stemmed from the fine supply we received from the back, where Tony and Alvin would find us either in space or with a well chosen pass to our feet. They never crudely hoofed the ball forward, that wasn't their style.

It was a great shame that Galey left West Ham somewhat acrimoniously – after being informed by the club that he was being given a free transfer just hours before his well-earned Testimonial in May 1994 (which I was delighted to be asked to play in). I can understand West Ham's reasons for deciding to release Galey. In him and Alvin they had two centre-backs who were both in their mid-30s, Steve Potts was well established as a good central defender in his own right and they had Simon Webster, recovering from injury, as cover.

Having said that, after releasing Galey, the club brought in another central defender in Adrian Whitbread from Swindon, as part of the deal in which the club cut its losses over the infamous Joey Beauchamp.

It was the timing of the decision to let Galey go that was wrong. It could have been handled more tactfully, but trust Galey to have the last laugh. After a spell training with Barnet and looking out in the cold, Tony received a shock call from Blackburn Rovers. In the space of a few days he found himself playing for Rovers against Celtic in a tournament at Hampden Park and against Manchester United at Wembley in the Charity Shield. After 19 years as a pro, he was playing at Britain's top two grounds for the first time.

And no one was more pleased than me when Galey experienced European football and picked up a well-earned Premiership championship winners' medal last May.

Ironically, a few days after celebrating the title success at Ewood Park, Galey heard that Rovers were also giving him a free. But I'm pleased to see him back in action for Crystal Palace, where he will surely do a good job in their First Division promotion bid.

I'm sure Galey has been missed in the West Ham dressing room. After all, his real nickname is 'Reggie', so-called because the lads reckoned he was as cruel (in wit) as another famous character operating in the East End, Reggie Kray!

Tony made his debut for the Hammers in a goalless draw with Ipswich at Upton Park. For the next game at Liverpool, John decided to go for a five-man midfield, bringing in Dave Swindlehurst and Bonzo. I found myself on the bench and after replacing Swindles in the 3-0 defeat at Anfield, I started all of the other league and cup matches in 1984/85.

Paul Goddard reclaimed his first team place from Swindles and apart from the second game at Liverpool, Sarge and I formed a regular partnership.

Not that there was anything regular about the team's form. I opened my account in our 3-1 home win over Coventry on September 4 but after winning the two fixtures either side of that one, at Southampton and home to Watford, we never managed three wins on the trot again all season.

Probably the only player who recalls our 3-1 home defeat by QPR on New Year's Day with any affection is Steve Potts, who made his debut that afternoon. After Dicko and myself, Steve was the next home-grown player to progress from the youth team to the first team and what a loyal and dependable club servant he has become.

Steve played right-back on his debut, and during most of his early seasons, mainly as cover for Ray Stewart. But he developed into a very good reader of the game and, after Tim Breacker arrived in 1990, it was perhaps no surprise to see him switch to central defence without difficulty.

Now the club captain, he would be the first to admit that he doesn't offer a lot going forward – as one goal in more than 300 games suggests – but I've always believed that a defender's main priority is always to stop the opposition scoring goals, which Pottsy does very effectively.

My only other reason for remembering the QPR game is that John chose to break with tradition by allowing the West Ham players to spend New Year's eve at home, rather than stay overnight at an hotel. We were warned to behave ourselves – one or two glasses of wine or a couple of beers was okay, but nothing more. In general, I think most players act professionally in these situations and, personally, given the choice, I'd rather be at home anyway, where I can follow my usual pre-match routine. Players who have children tend to want to be with their family, although there are others who prefer to get away because their kids might be waking up all hours of the night.

It's down to individual preference, of course, but the fact that we lost the game 3-1 was enough to convince John that, in future, we'd always stay overnight at an hotel the night before a Christmas or New Year fixture.

There is no doubt that the absence of several key players took its toll, because it's impossible to adequately replace the likes of Alan Devonshire and Phil Parkes. Dev had spent 14 months recovering from his serious knee injury before attempting a comeback against Wimbledon in the FA Cup. After home victories over Port Vale and Norwich in the previous two rounds, we found a visit to Dons' little Plough Lane ground something of a culture shock.

Wimbledon had not quite established their 'Crazy Gang' reputation by 1985 but their ramshackle home ground – they had to erect a temporary stand for the West Ham fans – was nothing like the standard we'd been accustomed to. I scored my first FA Cup goal in the 1-1 draw, but the replay was much more clear cut as we romped to an easy 5-1 victory.

The first goal of my hat-trick at Upton Park that night was one of the strangest I've ever scored. Dicko's cross-shot came at such an awkward height, I could neither head it nor volley it, so I simply got my chest to the ball and it just trickled over the goalline before a Wimbledon defender hacked it clear. There were a few protests but the goal was given and we were on our way to a sixth round tie with slightly more glamorous opponents in Manchester United.

Our Cup dreams vanished, though, at Old Trafford. West Ham asked the FA to postpone the tie because our squad was depleted by a flu virus and injuries, but they insisted it went ahead.

A pity that, because I was to blame for one of United's goals in a 4-2 defeat. I was told to go back and defend a corner at the near post, which wasn't the ideal place to have me because I have never been, or will be, a good defender. Anyway, when the cross was only half cleared, I failed to push up with the other defenders, as they do in these situations, and Norman Whiteside (who would later become a team mate at Everton) was left free to nod the ball home. The talented young Irishman went on to complete the first hat-trick of his United career.

At least we had the very small consolation of knowing that we went out to the eventual Cup winners, United going on to beat Everton in the Final that was memorable for Whiteside's wonderful winner and the first-ever occasion a player – Kevin Moran – was sent off in the FA Cup Final.

A bad winter created fixture congestion to the extent that we visited United just three days after slaughtering Wimbledon, but Dev had returned to action prematurely and had to spend another four or five months rehabilitation before making a proper comeback at the start of the following season.

In the league, our position was beginning to cause some concern. After I scored both goals in our 2-1 win at Coventry in our last game of '84, we won just one of our next

11 First Division matches – at Forest on March 30, where me and Sarge were on target in a 2-1 success. My goal was the first scored by a Hammer in a league game at the City Ground for 16 years, since Geoff Hurst's in March 1969.

Tom McAllister had taken over in goal from Phil Parkes and although the likeable Scot generally did well as cover, there is nothing like having your recognised number one 'keeper between the sticks. After a bad 5-0 defeat at Watford, who were inspired by Barnes and Blissett and took a 3-0 lead in 16 minutes, my double strike at Loftus Road couldn't prevent us losing 4-2 to QPR, where Tom suffered two cracked ribs and a punctured lung and had to be replaced by Ray Stewart.

That was John's cue to recall 34 year-old Parkesy for the critical end-of-season run-in that would determine our First Division fate. Signed from QPR for a then world record fee for a 'keeper of £565,000, at 6ft 4ins, Parkesy was a man-mountain. He was so huge, he seemed to fill the whole goal and very little got past him. He was an exceptional shot-stopper – the best I've come across – and I spent many an hour at Chadwell Heath with the other strikers, firing in shots at him from all angles but rarely finding the net.

I wouldn't say that Parkesy dominated his penalty area – he was what we call a 'liner', not one to rush to the edge of his box to catch the ball or punch it away – but he was still a fantastic 'keeper . . . and a real character too.

Whenever I think of Phil, the image is one of him sitting at the back of the team bus, with his huge hands clutching a glass of brandy and a big cigar after the game . . . win, lose or draw!

That was obviously in the days before alcohol was banned from the coach. Most of us enjoyed a few beers on the way back from away games or if you fancied a tipple, our physio Rob Jenkins was your man. He carried a hip flask full of whiskey or brandy and would keep Parkesy topped up on the homeward journey.

Rob didn't gain the qualifications that our current physio John Green and a number of others have but he was a great laugh and brilliant to have in the dressing room before and after matches.

Rob enjoyed a drink and always kept a few cans in the fridge in the treatment room at Chadwell Heath. Indeed, it was a pre-condition of Rob's that before he'd treat a player on a Sunday morning, you had to bring him in four cans of Heineken!

As well as looking after our alcoholic requirements, Rob used to assist Alan the chef on our coach journeys. Rob would put on his apron and walk down the bus dispensing prawn or ham rolls followed by trifle, washed down with a few beers. After a bad defeat at, say, Old Trafford or Anfield, the long trip home could seem like ages, so it was nice having someone like Rob aboard to cheer us up a bit.

Although he is no longer employed by West Ham, Rob still runs his own physiotherapy clinic opposite the Boleyn Ground and pops into the training ground to see his old mates – Ronnie Boyce, Harry Redknapp and Frank Lampard – from time to time.

With Parkesy back, we lost only four of our last 10 games, including a 2-1 defeat at Sheffield Wednesday on May 11. Lee Chapman scored both Wednesday goals although I was quite pleased to end a run of five games without scoring thanks to a good finish from a Bonzo pass – but the game and my goal meant very little afterwards.

My mum and dad broke the news that, just 40 miles away, men, women and children had been burnt to death in the tragic fire at Bradford City's Valley Parade ground. I saw the horrific scenes on TV that night and it was awful. My goal – indeed, anything in football at that time – just didn't seem to mean as much once I'd seen what had gone on at Bradford.

Our next game, at home to relegation-doomed Stoke three days later, was played on a heavily waterlogged pitch that clearly suited us best because we easily won 5-1. Despite nearing his 39th birthday, Bonzo grabbed two to show that he wasn't ready to hang up his boots for a while yet.

There were only another three days before our next crucial match, at Ipswich on May 17. Victory at Portman Road would secure our place in the top flight and I duly obliged with a rare headed goal from Sarge's cross in the 11th minute to clinch a precious 1-0 triumph. With our First Division future assured for at least one more year, you can bet that the relatively short ride home down the A12 was a pleasurable one!

Our last fixture, at home to Liverpool, became largely academic, so when I received my first call up to the England Under-21 squad, John Lyall asked if I wanted to miss the league match in order to represent my country in Finland instead. It wasn't a case of me putting England before West Ham but in his own way John advised me that it would be good for my career if I went with the England party.

It was typical of John's consideration for his players. Although I've said how difficult I found it to talk to him at times, especially where money was concerned, he had many qualities and a personal regard for his players.

With me missing from the side, John used the opportunity to give George Parris his debut in our 3-0 defeat. George – who I'd played against as a schoolboy – was another graduate of the club's youth policy and had waited patiently for his chance. Although not blessed with an abundance of skill, George made up for that with his incredible work-rate and he was versatile enough to play in a variety of positions. He always gave 100 per cent, never complained if he was left out, and every club needs a George Parris. Ironically, he made his debut the same day Frank Lampard – whose left-back position he would go on to fill – made the last of his 551 league appearances for West Ham, a remarkable record bettered only by Bonzo.

One of the main reasons we survived the threat of relegation in 1984/85 was the brilliant form of Paul Allen, who hustled well and created a lot on the right side of midfield. That was the position he occupied most, but he did occasionally fill in at right-back, which I happened to believe was his best position, although I know Paul would dispute that claim.

I could see why 'Ollie' got the Hammer of the Year award but after finishing runner-up for the second year running, I couldn't help thinking: 'I've scored 17 league and seven cup goals, so what more do I have to do to win this award?'

I don't know how other players feel about awards voted for by the fans, but I always take great pride in trying to win them. I'd scored almost half of our goals, finished way ahead of our next highest scorer, who was Sarge on nine, and without my goals, West Ham would have been relegated. I thought I had done enough to win Hammer of the Year that season but I didn't begrudge Paul the honour – I'd never do that.

Besides, I was delighted to be nominated in the top six for the PFA Young Player of the Year award. It's always a great honour to receive the recognition of your fellow players and although I didn't win – that honour went to United striker Mark Hughes – it was still a great achievement for me.

Unfortunately for West Ham, for the second season in succession the Hammer of the Year winner left the club. While everyone wished Trevor well in his retirement, the fans were up in arms about Paul's move to rivals Tottenham in the summer of '85.

Ollie had performed really well that season and, at 22, was obviously one of the Hammers' brightest prospects. The problem was that he had come to the end of his contract and no doubt fully expected a decent increase from the club, who had reportedly offered him a new four-year deal. I understand that he had problems reaching a new agreement with John and, as his contract was up, effectively became free to talk to other clubs.

West Ham valued Paul at £600,000, while Spurs boss Peter Shreeves was offering only £350,000. The matter was dealt with by the transfer tribunal who said Tottenham had to pay the Hammers £450,000.

I was disappointed that Paul left but could understand his frustration in not being offered the contract that he certainly deserved. I say that without knowing the full facts, the ins and outs of the whole thing, but if West Ham didn't come up with the goods to keep a young player of Paul's obvious talent, then that's a great pity. I don't know whether it was Paul's fault that his contract was allowed to run out, or John's, but it should not have been allowed to get to that stage.

West Ham's loss was definitely Tottenham's gain, because Ollie fulfiled himself at White Hart Lane where he won an FA Cup winners' medal in 1991 and a losers' one in 1987.

Of course, his transfer to Spurs was never going to be popular among West Ham fans, who didn't miss an opportunity to give him the most ferocious stick whenever the clubs met in subsequent seasons. He has had a wonderful career and it's by no means finished yet. Ironically, while he was going through a lean time at Southampton, which wasn't the best career move he could have made, I know how he would have fancied returning to West Ham.

One of the great aspects of being a professional footballer is the opportunity to visit different countries you might not otherwise get the chance to see. I was very much looking forward to our end-of-season tour of Japan and had filled my suitcase with a tennis racquet, frisbee, swimming trunks, sunglasses, sun lotion – you name it, I was geared up for tourism and a nice, relaxing break in the Land of the Rising Sun.

Except the management didn't see it that way. Our 17-day tour included six games – against Santos of Brazil, the Japan and Uruguay national teams and a trio of local Japanese sides – and very little time to take in the wonderful sights of Japan. Instead of suggesting to the players that they maintained fitness by playing tennis, we endured some silly training sessions that didn't go down too well among the players. When we weren't training, we seemed to spend most of our time travelling from one game to the next by Bullet train, some of the journeys lasting three hours. So with six games, six days spent travelling to each of them, plus two days taken up with the 15-hour flights between London and Tokyo, we ended up with just two days in which to relax and enjoy Japan.

There was one light-hearted moment though. We were travelling to one venue on the same train as the Brazilian fans, who were banging away on their big drums and making a hell of a racket throughout the journey. Our only, totally inadequate, response came from Bobby Barnes who, carrying his large ghetto blaster, turned the volume switch up a few notches, but it was still another victory for the Samba beat!

But our nightmare tour of Japan ended on a note that would ultimately have far reaching implications for British football in general.

Claret & Blues

EURO OUTCASTS

DURING our tour of Japan, I remember turning on the TV, in the room I was sharing with Paul Goddard, and coming across the American news network channel, CNN, that provided only brief coverage of events in Brussels.

Sarge and I were amazed by the scenes of crowds fighting and people throwing missiles at each other. From this brief bulletin, which showed no pictures of the game itself, it was difficult to fully appreciate what was going on and it was not until we returned to England that we all realised the full scale of the disaster.

English clubs and their supporters became the outcasts of Europe because of the tragic events which preceded the 1985 European Cup Final in Brussels, where Liverpool fans ran riot and, as a result, 38 Italians died and hundreds of others were injured. A concrete wall at the front of the terracing crumbled and hundreds of people spilled on to the edge of the pitch before kick-off.

It certainly wasn't the first time English hooligans had caused trouble on the continent. Leeds and Spurs fans had been caught up in trouble at previous European finals, but what happened in the Heysel Stadium that night was something much worse. In the aftermath of the disaster, questions were asked of UEFA, the Belgian authorities, policing methods and the lack of segregation at the end of the ground.

But most of the blame fell on the 'so called' Liverpool fans whose actions totally overshadowed Juventus' 1-0 victory – a Platini penalty – and manager Joe Fagan's last match in charge of the mighty Reds.

It was a huge blow to football in general and the English game in particular. On the home front, our national sport had been devastated, just a few weeks before Heysel, by the Bradford fire disaster which claimed the lives of 52 people.

Football was still in a state of shock after those tragedies when the disaster of Heysel struck and plunged the.game into a crisis. The repercussions of that evening were to have a profound effect on English football for a very long period. In banning all English clubs from Europe for five years, UEFA must have set us back at least 10 years in terms of our players' development and ability to compete against the more skilful continentals.

The facts speak for themselves: England failed miserably in the 1988 European Championships, losing all three matches. Bobby Robson bounced back to lead his country to the semi-finals of the 1990 World Cup, where we were unfortunate to lose to West Germany in a dramatic penalty shootout, but under Graham Taylor, England were embarrassed at the next European Championships (Sweden, 1992) and didn't even qualify for the 1994 World Cup in the United States.

Manchester United and Arsenal put England back on the European club map by winning the ECWC in 1991 and 1994 respectively, yet both clubs have suffered bad defeats in the European Cup since the ban was lifted, while Blackburn have also struggled in Europe.

Apart from missing out on the chance to compete against the cream of Europe – the Milans, Madrids, Barcelonas and Benficas – the five-year exile also deprived the managers and coaches of our clubs the opportunity to pit their wits against the very best. The clubs themselves paid a heavy price, financially, in lost gate revenue, TV income and all the many other commercial advantages playing in Europe brings.

And it wasn't only the most successful sides of the 1984/85 season – champions Everton, runners-up Liverpool, third placed Spurs, FA Cup winners Manchester United and Milk Cup winners Norwich – who suffered. As the ban lasted five years, there were many other casualties in the second half of the 80s.

When I was a kid supporting West Ham from the terraces, I dreamt one day that I would get the chance to play for the club in Europe. I had obviously heard and read of the magnificent performance at Wembley in May 1965, just a couple of months before I was born, when Hammers beat TSV Munich to lift the European Cup Winners' Cup. And I was glued to the telly, a heartbroken 10 year-old, when we were beaten 4-2 by Anderlecht in the final of the same competition in 1976.

As a player you set yourself some clearly defined targets: a place in the first team is the immediate aim, followed by success in one of the cups. That automatically provides a passport to European football. Being called up for your country is the proudest moment of any player's career, while only the fortunate few get to experience the thrill of being involved in a World Cup final tournament.

In May 1986 the West Ham players and our supporters should have been looking forward to the prospect of European involvement the following season. Having done so well to finish third, behind Liverpool and Everton, in the First Division championship chase, a place in the 1986/87 UEFA Cup should have been ours by right. We deserved a reward for our fantastic season.

Instead, we had nothing to look forward to – except the hope of having another flat out bid for the league title again the following season. We had been robbed of our big chance, an opportunity that many of us experience only once in a lifetime and I haven't sampled since.

But I still maintain that UEFA got it wrong. They banned the wrong people. The players, managers and coaches who had worked so hard to achieve success in England were paying a huge price for the mindless actions of a small minority of hooligans. I can't call them football fans. The idiots who disgraced English football at Heysel may have been wearing red and white scarves, but they were not true

Liverpool supporters. They simply associated themselves with the club, who of course received all the bad publicity that followed.

There were many genuine Liverpool supporters who travelled to Belgium, just as they had to numerous European venues over the past 10 years, and behaved impeccably. Even so, I still believe that instead of banning the clubs, UEFA should have expelled the fans, or the so-called fans. What the rampaging yobs did at Heysel had nothing whatsoever to do with the Liverpool players or management, so why exclude them from Europe? It wasn't Kenny Dalglish, Alan Hansen and Joe Fagan who were rioting, so why ban them? Why deny players one of the highlights of their careers?

More to the point, why punish other clubs, who have nothing whatsoever to do with Liverpool or their supporters, who had worked just as hard to qualify for the Euro cups in subsequent seasons?

What UEFA should have done is punished the people responsible for causing the trouble. They should have allowed the English clubs to compete in Europe, but banned their supporters from attending all European away games the following season or for five years, the length of the ban.

That decision would have been very tough on the majority of fans who behave like decent people, but it would have been a much fairer option than the one UEFA took and one that, with careful planning, would have been quite easy to implement. I'm sure true supporters would rather have seen their club compete in Europe, even if it meant they were prevented from travelling abroad to see the matches live.

To be fair to Liverpool, it shouldn't be forgotten that this wasn't the first time English fans had caused havoc on their travels. My own club's fans had ran riot in Madrid in 1980, which resulted in the Hammers having to play the return leg of their Cup Winners' Cup tie against Castilla at Upton Park behind closed doors. Hooligans from Leeds, Spurs and Chelsea had also caused trouble in Europe over the years, but it is unfair to tarnish everyone with the same brush.

I can only imagine the sheer frustration Everton fans, in particular, must have felt when, after having seen their favourites win the European Cup Winners' Cup Final against Rapid Vienna in Rotterdam just days before Heysel, they were robbed of the chance of seeing their team competing in Europe again in 1985/86.

Worse still, they were effectively banned from the European Cup twice, having won the English First Division Championship in both 1984/85 and 1986/87, while the ban was still in force. And we were feeling sorry for ourselves at Upton Park! No one suffered from the Euro ban more than Everton who, to add insult to injury, were the biggest victims of a problem created by the actions of a lunatic fringe who supposedly 'followed' their arch rivals across Stanley Park.

It was an absolute scandal that the players, who had worked so hard to bring success to Everton Football Club, were banned from contesting the European Cup . . . it was so wrong.

And what about the Everton fans who went to Holland, celebrated their team's 3-1 victory over the Austrians and behaved superbly?

Although I'm fully aware that some punishment had to be imposed, particularly as so many innocent people had died at Heysel, it rankled with me at the time of UEFA's ban that certain people – especially the players – were made to suffer for the disgusting behaviour of hundreds of idiots.

As the years progressed, particularly after West Ham's best-ever season when we finished third and would have qualified for the UEFA Cup for the first time in the club's history, my anger and frustration only deepened.

Ten years on from Heysel, I am still bitter about that ban, and have to accept the growing possibility that – thanks largely to a bunch of thugs calling themselves football fans – I may never play in Europe.

Claret & Blues

WHAT'S NEW?

I WAS holidaying in Spain when news reached me that West Ham had signed Mark Ward and Frank McAvennie – two players who would go on to earn their own place in Hammers' history in the months ahead.

To be honest, I hadn't heard of either player, although I understood that Frank was a striker, which concerned me to be honest.

For although I had banged in 24 goals the previous season, and Dave Swindlehurst had moved on to Sunderland in a £60,000 deal, Paul Goddard remained the senior forward at the club and I knew that three into two wouldn't go.

Wardie, who was released by Everton as a kid before finding his feet at Northwich Victoria and then getting his league chance at Second Division Oldham Athletic, was bought as Paul Allen's replacement on the right for a £250,000 fee.

But who would make way for our new 24 year-old £340,000 unknown signing from Scottish club St. Mirren? That was the burning question I wanted an answer to.

It was an unsettling period that concerned me to the extent that when I returned from Spain, I phoned John Lyall to try and seek assurances. My anxiety was prolonged a week because he was fishing in Norfolk, as he liked to do every close season.

But when John returned, I drove to his house at Toot Hill, near Abridge in the beautiful Essex countryside, and spent the best part of an hour chatting about the forthcoming season and where he saw Frank, Paul Goddard and myself fitting in.

John and his wife, Yvonne, made me very welcome at their lovely home that had been renovated by their son, Murray, who was a builder by trade. The sun beat down as we sat in their immaculately maintained garden, which John obviously took a lot of care over.

John was very open with me, explaining that Frank was, in fact, a midfield player but one who liked to attack as often as possible. He said that he had bought Frank to play 'in the hole' behind Sarge and myself, which made me feel much happier.

It is probably fair to say that throughout my early years at West Ham, at the end of each season I was nearly always unhappy about something or other. The year before, I had been concerned about my contract; now it was the signing of Frank McAvennie.

I had no idea then, or indeed after we'd played all our pre-season games, quite what his arrival would mean to the club and me personally.

For Frank wasn't outstanding in pre-season, as we struggled to get results against even non-league teams. John tried several permutations: Frank with myself; Frank and Sarge; Sarge and myself; but no one really impressed. I think the players went into the new league season thinking: 'Oh, it's going to be a long, hard season, it could go either way.' In fact, after one poor defeat at Leyton Orient, an irate Hammers' fan burst into our dressing room to tell us, in the strongest possible terms, just how bad we were!

It was our indifferent pre-season form, and not the fear of a repeat of the crowd violence of 18 months earlier, that made us rather apprehensive going into our opening league match at newly-promoted Birmingham City – the game that transformed our whole season.

We lined up with Parkesy in goal and a flat back four of Ray Stewart, Tony Gale, Alvin Martin and Steve Walford. Mark Ward was right midfield, Alan Devonshire (back from long-term injury) on the left, with Neil Orr the anchor man in the middle. Then there was Frank playing behind Sarge and I. So we played a 4-3-1-2 formation . . . until fate intervened.

Sarge dislocated his shoulder four minutes into the second half, which meant that Frank moved up front to partner me, with substitute Alan Dickens completing a four-man midfield. We reverted to our traditional 4-4-2 line-up and after that 1-0 defeat, apart from a couple of early hiccups, we never looked back.

Frank celebrated his home debut the following Tuesday with two early goals against QPR, while Dicko also found the target in a welcome 3-1 victory. A disappointing 1-0 setback at Luton was followed by a Bank Holiday Monday roasting at Manchester United, where we went down 2-0 in temperatures that soared into the 80s. It wasn't the ideal time to play United, who were on a club record run of 10 straight wins at the start of the season and strongly tipped to win their first title since 1967.

If anyone had said at that point that West Ham would go on and finish third, they would have been marched off by men in white coats and taken to the nearest 'funny farm'. We knew we had a good squad of players, but I don't think any of us realised the full potential.

We certainly worked very hard in training, practicing a lot of one and two-touch play that would stand us in good stead in matches. It was around this time that we used to put a lot of effort into devising a team pattern that involved what is known in the game as 'third man running'. In basic terms, player A (let's say Alan Dickens) would pass to player B (myself), B would pass to player C (Neil Orr) and C would pass to A who had continued his run.

Another move we spent hours perfecting also involved the central midfielders, Dicko and Neil Orr. John had them running with the ball and committing the opposing central defenders. When they were about to be closed down, Dicko or Neil would flick the ball in behind the opposing defence for Frank and I – who worked at making lots of diagonal runs – to run onto.

People must have looked at the number of goals Frank and I scored in 1985/86 and thought, 'what a partnership'. But it didn't happen by accident – we both worked very hard to make it work as well as it did. You don't just walk onto the pitch and hope a striking partnership clicks.

And I must say the team as a whole worked hard to bring the best out of Frank and I. They played to our strengths, which was great for both of us. This was a problem I encountered at Everton, where the team played a certain way but not to my particular strengths.

But at West Ham, particularly that season, everything was geared towards Frank and I scoring goals and making chances.

I was probably at my peak sharpness. I didn't have Linford Christie-type pace but I was quick, particularly over the first 10 yards. Frank was quick as well.

It was funny that we should hit it off so well, because Frank wasn't a target man. People have often said to me over the years that I always perform better playing alongside a target man – someone big like Graeme Sharp – but I always point out that the most successful partnership I have had was with Frank McAvennie, who was far from being a target man.

I think John was also fortunate in that he had so many intelligent players at his disposal. I don't mean intellectual in the sense that we were brimming with 'O' levels. Footballers can be as thick as two short planks, academically, but if you've got a football brain you can be the most intelligent person on the pitch.

We had the likes of Dev, Dicko and Wardie who had tremendous vision and skill. Frank and I were shrewd enough and good enough to work with our talented midfielders, and training exercises were immediately understood by the players and put to good effect.

Frank and I needed to get into positions where we were either one on one with their 'keeper, or well placed to get in shots at goal. I know that I need to be scoring goals or else I'm just not happy. The team can win six on the trot and be playing brilliantly, but if I'm not scoring I'm unhappy. Goalscorers are a breed apart, because it's probably the one position where, if the team is winning, we still come off the pitch, having not scored, feeling gutted.

I'd come off in the games against Luton and Man. United feeling very disappointed, because I hadn't played well and was subbed. And then against Liverpool at home, I stayed on for the full 90 minutes but still didn't play well. Frank delighted the Upton Park crowd again with both goals in a 2-2 draw.

I've always had a bit of a psychological problem about the start of the season and have a tendency to worry about whether I'm at peak sharpness.

After my chat with John in the summer, I was looking forward to the season but it was starting to get to me and I felt a lot of pressure. Frank blitzed off on the goal trail, scoring four in five games before I could get off the mark. I just wasn't getting myself in too many scoring positions and didn't feel sharp in myself, physically or mentally.

I can't remember whether John called me in or I asked to speak to him, but we had another meeting and we agreed that I hadn't been looking too sharp so far. John said: "Do you think it would help things if I gave you a rest?" I replied: "I don't know,

Above left: A shot from our best-ever season, 1985/86.
Above right: 'Over here!' – in action at Upton Park
during my first full season, 1983/84
Below: Going for goal in our 2-0 win at Tottenham,
September 1983.

Anxious moments during the last two seasons of my first spell at West Ham. The picture (right) sums up the frustration I felt as the Hammers went into decline after our tremendous achievement to finish third in 1985/86.

After six months in the international wilderness., Bobby Robson recalled me for this sub. appearance against Hungary in Budapest, April 27, 1988.

Don't I look pleased after completing my debut hat-trick against Newcastle United at Goodison, August 27, 1988.

*On our way to Wembley . . .
action from the FA Cup semi-final
against Norwich City at Villa
Park, April 15, 1989. But a
glorious sunny day ended in
tragedy with the death of all those
Liverpool fans at Hillsborough.*

Mac-nificent! Stuart McCall gave us hope in the 1989 FA Cup Final – the match that I believe should never have been played – but perhaps it was always destined to be Liverpool's day.

Above: Posing with the TVR I bought soon after I signed for Everton. I decided to change it for a BMW after a lucky escape one day!

Above: Going up to receive my magnificent man-of-the-match trophy after a friendly in Bilbao, October 1993. It didn't survive the journey home from Spain in one piece but I superglued it back together and still have it at home!

Derby day delight . . . Above: One of the epic matches in FA Cup history – I managed to nutmeg Bruce Grobbelaar here to earn a dramatic 4-4 draw with Liverpool in the fifth round replay at Goodison on February 20, 1991. But despite my heroics, I was left out of the second replay a week later!

Above: Who says I can't tackle? Mark Wright and I compete for a loose ball which I scrambled home for our first goal. Wardie made it 2-0 in our victory over the Reds in September 1993

but I'm very worried about my form, especially as I've done so well in the two previous seasons.'

We played at Southampton in midweek and John said to me: "I'm going to give Greg Campbell a game." It was a very amicable discussion and I could see John's point. Greg had been another member of our youth side, the same age as Dicko, George Parris and myself. He'd been a fringe player at the club, who hadn't really been the same after suffering a serious jaw injury against Watford in 1984.

I remember that night at The Dell, because Frank was absolutely outstanding. It was like a personal duel between him and their 'keeper Peter Shilton, who made a string of saves but couldn't prevent Frank scoring our goal in a 1-1 draw.

After about an hour, Greg, who had done quite well, was feeling tired because he hadn't played for a long time. I sat on the bench for an hour and the situation suddenly hit me. I thought to myself: 'He's playing in my number 10 shirt, in my position'. Even though John and I had agreed that giving me a rest might be a good thing, I was annoyed with myself for allowing another player to come in and take my shirt.

By the time I came on, I was really fired up, the adrenalin was pumping through my body and I had that desire back again. Without desire as a footballer, you have very little.

Without setting the world alight in those last 25 minutes or so, I did enough to convince John that I'd regained my hunger and he recalled me to the starting line-up for the following Saturday's visit to Sheffield Wednesday.

Having virtually grown up under John's influence, I was always a little bit critical of certain things he did – training exercises, signings he made and other managerial decisions. But when I moved to Everton, I appreciated a lot more what John had done for me, or tried to do for me.

I was still very young, only 20 years-old that season, and still very raw. And I admit it, I was very arrogant, confident in my own ability.

So from that point of view John's management was superb. He recognised the problem, we spoke about it, he made a decision to leave me out of the side at Southampton and got the right response from me.

A lot of football management is about how you handle players, and over the years I don't think I've been handled too well.

My big turning point was Sheffield Wednesday away on September 7. We were losing the game 2-1 – Frank had netted his fourth in three games – and it looked like being seven matches without scoring for me.

There were only two minutes to go when Alvin pushed up front and won a header. As the ball was dropping, I arrived late at the far post and only just managed to volley it from an acute angle. I didn't really connect too well but the ball sort of bobbled a few times, went through the 'keeper Hodge's legs and rolled across the line.

My first goal of the season was no classic but it lifted a huge burden from my shoulders. The relief I felt was unbelievable and that point-saving goal really inspired me to go on and score in six of the next seven matches.

Frank and I had shown encouraging signs of developing a partnership but it didn't really click until I got off the mark at Hillsborough and joined him on the goals trail. Strikers are always judged on their goalscoring return and I can be playing as well as anyone, but if I'm not scoring it's no use to me or the team.

Frank, such a happy-go-lucky fella, could do no wrong. He made a dream start to his West Ham career and everything he touched seemed to go in. I wasn't resentful because he's such a nice bloke and deserved all the goals he got because he always worked very hard for the team as a whole.

I've never seen a player enjoy anything quite as remarkable as the spell he had when he first arrived at Upton Park, he was sensational. Even if he didn't score, Frank would force the 'keeper to make a save. I'd been top scorer for two years without a serious challenge from a partner who could push me hard. But if you have two players, who are both scoring goals, competing for the top scorer's award – as long as it's good, friendly rivalry – then the team can only benefit. I looked at Frank and envied the flying start he'd made, but I was positive about it and just wanted to catch him up and then stay with him for the course of the season, which is how it turned out.

We enjoyed a comfortable 3-0 home win over Leicester, only our second victory in eight games, and at that stage, with only just over 12,000 fans at Upton Park, who could have envisaged the way the season would unfold and how attendances would rise to 31,000-plus capacity level by the following spring.

I didn't play that well at Maine Road but Andy Dibble – making his debut in goal – boobed for my goal after just seven minutes and we managed a 2-2 draw from a game we should have won.

Frank and I both scored in our 2-1 victory at Newcastle and there is no doubt in my mind that we as a pair, and West Ham as a team, were benefiting from the TV ban that season. The Football League had failed to renew their agreement with ITV, so there was no football on TV whatsoever until BBC covered our third round FA Cup tie against Charlton on the first Saturday in January 1986.

Frank, who of course hadn't played in England before, profited more than anyone because the opposition were seeing him for the first time and no one had seen anything of him, or of us as a team, on TV. Compare that situation to today, where Sky's lucrative deal enables them to show every goal from every Premiership game as often as they wish. We didn't have Andy Gray in his Boot Room telling the football world how wonderful West Ham's new signing was playing and analysing his strengths and scoring prowess in great detail. We were very much a surprise packet.

Even so, the pundits were still predicting that Manchester United would go on to win the title. If not, Everton, who were defending champions, or Liverpool, in the middle of their glory spell of the 80s, were the two most likely to break United's grip. And Chelsea were on the fringe of the championship chase.

Our title challenge didn't really evolve until around Christmas time, although even then I don't think many took us too seriously. After all, the best the Hammers had ever achieved was sixth place, in 1968/69 and 1972/73.

As winter approached, Frank and I were scoring more or less every game. After going goalless in our draw with Arsenal on my 100th league appearance, we got two apiece in a storming 4-1 home win over Aston Villa. My 58th minute volley, that sailed over Spink from 25 yards, gave me a lot of pleasure.

That set us off on a run of nine successive wins in the league, including a 1-0 win at Ipswich Town where my winner ruined 'keeper Paul Cooper's 500th appearance. Our run ended in a goalless draw at Luton on December 21, followed by our first defeat in 19 games, at White Hart Lane on Boxing Day, when Steve Perryman netted a rare winner.

In the Milk Cup, after comfortably dealing with Swansea City, 5-2, on aggregate in the second round, we were unfortunate to be drawn away to runaway First Division leaders Manchester United in round three. What our 1-0 defeat in the record books fails to show is that we played them off the park at Old Trafford that night and had a perfectly good goal disallowed.

Wardie took a free-kick in the 78th minute which, although unbeknown to us was indirect, still flew into the net via 'keeper Gary Bailey's hand. We all saw it touch Bailey before entering the net, except the Welsh referee, Roberts, who disallowed it. The West Ham players were enraged by the decision on the night but perhaps it was a blessing in disguise, because we were left to focus attention on the league programme.

Frank missed our 4-0 home slaughter of West Brom on November 30, as he had to fly off to Australia with the Scotland squad for a World Cup qualifier, but he amazingly played – and scored the only goal – at QPR a week later, having just stepped off a 24-hour flight back from Aussie! That spoke volumes for Frank's carefree attitude to life and the game itself and what he achieved in football that season.

CHAPTER 20

Claret & Blues

HOUSE PROUD

IT was in November 1985 that I signed a new, extended contract. I was only 18 months into a five-year deal but as Lorraine and I were about to climb onto the property ladder, by buying a flat in Hornchurch, I went to see John about the possibility of a new contract.

He was very pro buying property and would advise his players to invest their money in bricks and mortar. As I explained earlier, I never had a lump sum from a signing-on fee, which would have been useful as a deposit, so I looked to increase my monthly earnings so that we could afford the repayments on the £42,000 flat.

I explained to John how I had seen the place I wanted to buy and he was very good about it. He said: "You've done very well, so I will approach the board and see what they say." He came back and said what he always said in those situations: "The board have done brilliantly for you." He never took the credit personally, it was always 'we' or 'the club has done well for you.'

John's only stipulation was that I had to sign for the next five-and-a-half years, which I did on November 4, 1985. I still didn't receive any signing-on fee, but the slight increase in my basic was topped up by my agreement to receive appearance money each time I played for the first team. It wasn't as much as a grand a game, but it was a hefty sum – provided I maintained my form and managed to stay clear of injuries, which, happily, I managed to do.

I had nothing written into my contract about any additional reward for scoring 'x' number of goals, as more and more strikers insist on today. In 1985 it didn't cross my mind to ask for it, and I'm sure the club would have said 'no' anyway. It just wasn't the done thing in those days.

My improved earnings, together with the money I'd already put away in the building society for our deposit, enabled me to afford the large monthly mortgage repayments on the flat.

This time, there was no bad feeling surrounding our contract talks. I was pleased with what I was getting and John was as good as gold. I agreed to sign what the club offered me and it was all done and dusted very quickly in his office at Chadwell Heath.

That contract, which effectively had until 1991 to run, was the last I signed before leaving in the summer of 1988.

I'd lived with my parents at Collier Row until I moved into the flat, just off Upminster Road. Although I was obviously excited about buying our first home, it was another turning point in my life and it was strange at first not having my parents around me.

My dad nurtured my football career from a very early age but my mum's contribution over the first 20 years of my life should not be underestimated because she has been just as valuable to me. Mum could never do enough for me, whether it was making sure my clothes and football kit were washed, ironed and ready to wear, or cooking the tasty meals all youngsters take for granted, she waited on me hand and foot. I was living a five-star existence and know how lucky I am to have benefited from growing up in a happy, settled family home.

At first I lived alone at our new flat, although Lorraine visited me a lot, and then a modelling assignment took her to Japan for two months in January 1986. She did very well as a fashion model and I think earned more money on that trip than I did playing for West Ham the previous season!

It was just as well that I'd signed a new deal before she went to Japan, because I was spending sometimes an hour a day on the phone to Lorraine and the next quarter's bill came to a small fortune!

When Lorraine returned from Japan, she used her creative talent to decorate our flat – she has always been brilliant at decorating, which is much more than can be said for me – and actually moved in that April.

Apart from the flat, my other pride and joy was my 'B' reg Escort Cabriolet, which I bought from South Essex Motors at Basildon at five minutes past midnight on August 1, 1985. It was white with black stripes and spoilers. Cars have always been a big thing with me, and this one was my real pride and joy.

That winter of 1985/86 was one of the happiest times of my life. West Ham were riding the crest of a wave, Frank and I were scoring like it was going out of fashion, Lorraine and I had bought our first place to live and I was racing around in my dream-mobile.

All I needed now was a championship or cup winners' medal to complete my perfect world . . .

Claret & Blues

SO NEAR, SO FAR

WE will never know for sure just how much of an effect the bad weather, that swept across Britain in February and early March of 1986, hampered our efforts to bring the championship to Upton Park for the first time – but it must have been a big factor.

Yet there was no hint of the fixture pile-up that would be facing us in April as we gained our first league win of the year at Leicester on January 11 and then travelled to Liverpool a week later. It's not often that I've come away from Anfield having seen my team play well and feeling hard done by, but this was just such an occasion.

To lose 3-1 was a travesty of justice because we played them off the park at times and were holding Liverpool 1-1 until they were awarded a typically dubious penalty at The Kop end, following Alvin Martin's brush with Paul Walsh. Ray Stewart, who could be a bit fiery, protested so strongly that he was sent off and we never recovered from that bad decision.

One of our most thrilling victories of the season came on February 2 – a televised 2-1 home win over league leaders Manchester United in which Wardie scored a cracker. My winner, 14 minutes from time after a poor backpass by Whiteside, came 10 minutes after I'd hit the post from close range.

Not only did United lose top spot to Everton, they also lost their skipper, Bryan Robson, who gave United the lead but sustained ankle ligament damage in a centre circle challenge on me in the second half.

Apart from two cup replays against Ipswich Town on the 4th and the 6th of the month, we didn't play in the First Division again until mid-March, losing 1-0 at Arsenal and 2-1 at Aston Villa in the space of four days.

The record books show that West Ham contested the First Division championship race right up to the final Saturday of the 1985/86 season before having to settle for third place, but let's not forget that there was a double disappointment. For we had high hopes of FA Cup success that season, too.

BBC TV 'live' cameras were at Selhurst Park for the start of our Cup run on Sunday, January 5, when we beat Charlton Athletic (who had moved out of The Valley and were sharing Crystal Palace's ground).

Although I followed up Frank McAvennie's lob to volley the only goal from near the goalline in the dying minutes, it was Frank who attracted most of the attention. Jimmy Hill raved about his performance – remember, no one had seen us on TV before that season because of the ITV league blackout – and it was more or less after that showing in the Cup that Frank became a TV celebrity as much as a West Ham star.

It took three matches and five-and-a-half hours to resolve our fourth round tie with Ipswich Town and, once again, I was the only Hammer to find the target. A dreadful goalless draw at Upton Park was followed by a 1-1 draw at Portman Road, where I scored, before we returned to Suffolk just two days later for the second replay on February 6.

Those were the days when cup replays were arranged at short notice, without interference from the police, who have to rearrange their shifts to fit in with matches, or appeasing the demands of television, who have really taken a grip of football today.

The Ipswich pitch was covered in about an inch of snow and the lines had to be cleared before we could kick off using an orange ball. The tie was in extra-time when Town midfielder Mark Brennan made a costly error, leaving me to round the 'keeper and sidefoot the ball left-footed into the net for my fifth goal at Portman Road in five consecutive visits.

Having bounced back from two early season defeats at Man. United to beat them 2-1 in our home league game that the bad winter weather allowed us to play during February, we were not too downhearted when the fifth round draw paired us with United again.

Dev and I combined smartly to set up Frank for our goal in a 1-1 draw at Upton Park but, again, the headlines were dominated by yet another injury to England skipper Bryan Robson. And again, he limped off after a challenge on me, this time injuring his shoulder after only two minutes.

'Robbo' found out the hard way that season, not to mess with one of the game's hard men!

Having been knocked out of the Cup at Old Trafford in 1983 and 1985, it's fair to say that we travelled up to Manchester on March 9 thinking we'd blown our best chance of beating the holders.

Once again, the TV cameras were present and this time they were treated to a major shock as Hammers won 2-0 thanks to a bullet header from the edge of the area by Geoff Pike and a Ray Stewart penalty.

At this stage, we had very little title pretensions. Sure, we were going along nicely in the league, including that impressive home win over United, but I still thought that sixth place was a realistic target, especially when you considered the large number of games we had to fit in during March and April, due to the snow and frost that arrived in February. Fifth place would have been great, because the club had never done better than sixth in its history.

I couldn't see us winning the league at that point, but we were playing well as a team and after winning at Old Trafford, we underlined our qualities as a strong cup side.

So Wembley had started to enter our thoughts as we visited Sheffield Wednesday for the quarter-final on Wednesday, March 12 . . . only three days after our victory over United. They were undoubtedly that bit fresher on the night and had the game sewn up at 2-0 before my goal sparked a late rally, but it wasn't to be.

For the second season running we'd seen our FA Cup dreams shattered in the quarter-finals. And Sheffield Wednesday – who went on to play Everton in the semis – would return to haunt us again a year later . . .

By the time our cup run ended, we had lost our way a bit in the league. Opponents had done their homework and it was becoming more difficult for Frank and I to play as we'd done in the first half of the season. Teams – particularly at Upton Park – were beginning to man-mark us and play with a sweeper as extra cover.

We found it tough to beat both Sheffield Wednesday and Southampton at home by 1-0 margins, and lost our fourth away game in five, 2-1, at Nottingham Forest. I gave us the lead at the City Ground with one of my most satisfying goals of the season, where I received the ball on the edge of the box and turned Des Walker before curling a shot into the net.

But, just as we thought we had another precious point in the bag, Johnny Metgod struck a free kick from all of 35 yards that screamed in off the crossbar – one of the goals of the season – and Brian Rice snatched an agonising 87th minute winner.

The performance that broke that sequence of away defeats came at Stamford Bridge on Easter Saturday, a day that will live long in the memory of all our fans who saw it, for it was undoubtedly our most complete performance of 1985/86.

London derbies are always that bit special but this was even bigger than usual because both Chelsea and ourselves still had outside hopes of challenging for the title when we met on March 29.

You always take a lot of pleasure from beating your rivals and they don't come any sweeter than our 4-0 victory at Chelsea that day. Dev opened the scoring with a shot from 25 yards that found the top corner, a great individual strike, but our second was a wonderful team effort that actually began in defence.

Tony Gale headed the ball clear from our box to George Parris, who passed to me and went on a 'third man run'. I passed it inside to Dicko and went on another 'third man run'. Dicko controlled it and swept it out to the left wing. George, who had continued his run, wasn't the quickest around and I wasn't sure he would reach the ball before the defender as it drifted towards the corner flag.

But 'Smokey' – don't ask me why he was called that – did reach the ball first and crossed it with his left foot towards me, as I ran unmarked into the area. I finished off a magnificent team move by side-footing the ball past the 'keeper and into the far corner of the net at The Shed end.

We ran riot after going two up. Frank could have made it 3-0 himself but, unselfishly, rolled the ball across for me to slot it home.

There wasn't quite the same precision about my miscued shot that landed at Frank's feet late on but Frank being Frank, he volleyed it into the top corner to complete a brilliant win, which was captured on Match of the Day.

We absolutely played Chelsea off the park. We defended well, created plenty of chances and our finishing was superb. I think this was the result that made other people sit up and take notice of West Ham.

Not only that, but our players suddenly started to believe that perhaps we could go on and achieve a very good league position, maybe even challenge for the title.

A glorious Easter was completed when we beat another big rival, Tottenham, 2-1 at Upton Park with Frank and I scoring again to avenge our Boxing Day setback.

Easter killed Chelsea's chances, though, for after being hammered by West Ham, they went to QPR on Easter Monday and were thrashed 6-0.

So with Man. United also falling by the wayside after their early charge, Everton led the way from Liverpool, with West Ham in the Merseyside slipstream.

But we didn't only have to compete with the might of Everton and Liverpool, we had an horrendous fixture backlog to contend with if we were to really threaten to break the Merseyside stranglehold. A run-in of 13 games in 37 days – or almost three matches a week – was too ridiculous for any team to contemplate.

After Alvin – who had been sent off at Arsenal a few weeks earlier – scored the only goal of the game against Southampton, we proved more convincing 3-1 winners in our next home match, against Oxford United, who had taken the lead through Ray Houghton, the former Hammer who I knew we'd regret giving away.

Our third fixture in a week at Upton Park saw Chelsea come in search of revenge for their slaughter at the Bridge. We went into the game very confident, having stuffed them 4-0 just a couple of weeks earlier, and we were flying again early in the second half after Dicko made a great run and set me up for the first goal of the night – a crisp shot from the edge of the box that flashed past Tony Godden.

We had been very fortunate to avoid injuries but the loss of Tony Gale proved crucial. His replacement in the centre of defence, Neil Orr, came on and made a slip in a dangerous position, and we paid a heavy price as Nigel Spackman easily equalised.

I felt sad for Neil, who had been one of our unsung heroes, along with Pikey, in the central midfield holding role. His mistake was magnified by the importance of the match but the cruellest blow was delivered by Pat Nevin – later to become a good mate of mine at Everton – who headed Chelsea's winner 12 minutes from time.

It wasn't the end of the world because there were still seven matches to go, but we had to win our matches in hand and could ill afford to drop three priceless points at this stage.

We recovered well from the devastating blow of losing at home to Chelsea by winning 2-0 in front of the Match of the Day cameras at Watford four days later. Frank and I were on target again as our partnership continued to flourish.

If you had read the result of our next match, home to Newcastle, in the papers, you would have expected West Ham's star strikers to have hit the goal trail again. In a totally one-sided 8-1 victory, there was scope for both of us to have grabbed a hat-trick apiece, if not more.

Instead, the night belonged to Alvin, who achieved the rare feat of scoring against three different goalkeepers – Martin Thomas, midfielder Chris Hedworth and England striker Peter Beardsley. Everything we hit seemed to go in, with Ray Stewart, Neil Orr, Paul Goddard and an own goal adding to our tally.

Frank managed to find the net once, but the closest I came was a header that hit the post in the second half.

I came off at the end feeling mixed emotions: delighted that we'd won 8-1 and collected another three points, but gutted that I hadn't scored.

After the glut of goals that ripped Newcastle apart, I was back in business to score the winner in a drab home game with Coventry City, Again, they played with a sweeper so chances were few and far between. My goal was a scrappy one but nevertheless vitally important as we kept Everton and Liverpool in our sights.

The excitement was mounting in the dressing room and on the terraces. Whereas crowds of only 15,000 and 14,000 watched our first two home matches against QPR and Luton, rising to a modest 19,000 for the visit of Liverpool in September, we were now pullling in 27,000-plus at Upton Park to see us play Coventry, Man. City and Ipswich.

Everyone connected with West Ham believed we were in with a good shout of snatching the title.

In the last couple of weeks of the season, there wasn't time to train. We were simply playing matches, preparing for them or resting before the next game. Our schedule went like this: Saturday – play game; Sunday – day off ; Monday – play game; Tuesday – day off; Wednesday – play game; Thursday – day off; Friday – light training, five-a-side; Saturday – play game.

As the excitement grew, I don't recall nerves or too much tension creeping in. You feel tension when you are down at the bottom fighting a relegation battle but when you are challenging at the top, you get by on adrenalin a lot of the time.

The way the game has got so much quicker in the past 10 years, I don't think many teams today would have coped with the demanding run-in we faced at West Ham in the spring of '86.

As a team we had absolute confidence in ourselves. We didn't allow our gruelling fixture schedule to affect us because when you are winning consistently, you simply get on with it. We were playing off the cuff, not worrying about the opposition..

Not that Manchester City made it easy for us on April 28. We had to grind them down and won thanks to another Ray Stewart penalty in the first half.

Two nights later, Upton Park staged its final, dramatic, match of the season and more than 31,000 crammed in to see us face Ipswich for the fifth time in the season. The fans were at fever pitch and we didn't let them down.

Although Kevin Wilson silenced our fans by giving Ipswich the lead in the 63rd minute, we showed the quality and resilience expected of a side chasing the ultimate prize as we regained control of the game.

Dicko equalised with a great chip from 20 yards but the real drama unfolded in the last few minutes.

Ray Stewart clinched a memorable victory with another of his crucial spot-kicks, after Wardie had won a controversial 87th minute penalty for being upended by Cranson. Ipswich hotly disputed the decision by ref. Gerald Ashby and, looking back, it was dubious.

Their captain, England central defender Terry Butcher, vented his frustration afterwards by aiming a kick at the dressing room door. Ipswich were certainly not out to do us any favours, for they were staring relegation in the face. In fact, that defeat condemned them to the third relegation place, joining Birmingham City and West Bromwich Albion through the trap door.

After the game our fans rushed onto the pitch to congratulate us as we made our way up to the directors' box to throw our shirts and tie-ups into the crowd. Their chorus of "Bubbles" and 'We're Gonna Win The League" rang out around Upton Park on a highly emotional night.

We had three days to recover from the drama and excitement of the Ipswich game before what turned out to be the title showdown, at The Hawthorns on Saturday, May 3. We knew we had to win to keep alive our championship hopes, while hoping that Liverpool either lost or drew their final game at Chelsea.

If the Reds failed to win at Stamford Bridge, and we won at West Brom, the First Division title would have been won by either ourselves or Everton at Goodison Park the following Monday. It was that tight at the top.

We went to The Hawthorns fully believing that we could become league champions for the first time in the club's history.

There were no injury problems, it was our settled team and John Lyall didn't need to say too much beforehand. If I remember rightly, he said something like: "Forget about what's happening elsewhere, just concentrate on winning the game and if we're in a position to do something at Everton in the final game, then so be it. But don't worry about what's going on at Chelsea."

About 6,000-7,000 West Ham fans had travelled up to the West Midlands and packed into one end of the ground. Many of them clutched transistor radios to their ears, to keep a check on the Chelsea/Liverpool game.

I don't know where the information came from, whether a radio reporter had got his facts wrong or what, but I distinctly remember a loud roar from our fans about half-way through the first half. I thought to myself: 'Chelsea must have scored, so things are looking good for us'.

We got off to a flier when Frank headed us in front after nine minutes and after I made it 2-0 on 26 minutes, Madden pulled one back for Albion six minutes later.

We came into the dressing room at half-time still under the illusion that Chelsea were beating Liverpool. Nobody said a word to contradict our fans' reaction. Neither John, nor his assistants, mentioned a thing about the score at Chelsea. Our half-time team-talk concentrated totally on our game and what was required from us in the second half.

Our hopes suffered a body blow when 'Smokey' fouled Reilly, who picked himself up to equalise from the penalty. But the spot kick king himself, Ray Stewart, took over after Statham handled in the 69th minute to strike home his third match-winning penalty in six days.

As the final whistle blew, we were elated to have won 3-2 when the pressure was really on us to produce the goods.

But as we reached the dressing room we heard the devastating news that player/manager Kenny Dalglish had scored the only goal of the game for Liverpool in the 23rd minute at Stamford Bridge – precisely the moment the big roar went up at The Hawthorns. So much for Chelsea's 'goal', the Reds had clinched their fourth championship in five years, reaching an unassailable 88 points.

We'd done all we could at West Brom but we knew then that we could no longer win the league.

At Goodison on the Monday night, we had very little left to give. We had all felt dead-tired and once the title dream had gone, the adrenalin drained from our bodies and we were 11 weary souls at Everton. Of course we still wanted to finish second but it wasn't to be. They won 3-1, to finish two points behind their Mersey rivals, and my goal – a close range header from a rebound – was no more than a consolation. At least it took my personal tally to 20 and, although I didn't know it at the time, marked the first of many more goals I'd score at Goodison.

You have to give our fans absolute credit for the way they got behind us. Even after they'd experienced the agony the players went through at The Hawthorns, there were still 6,000 of them at Goodison on the last night.

The saddest part for me is that West Ham United deserved the championship that season because we played the best football over 42 games, entertaining crowds up and down the country with our own brand of exciting, attacking football. We were just four points adrift of the champions and won the same number of matches (26) as both of the top two. Obviously we weren't the best side on paper, because Liverpool and Everton finished above us in the final table, but I still maintain that West Ham played the best football.

And to emphasise how close we came to glory, the 84 points we amassed would have been enough to have clinched the title when Liverpool triumphed in the two seasons after the three-points-for-a-win rule was introduced in 1981/82. In 1991/92 Leeds United needed only 82 points to win the crown, while Manchester United equalled our 84 points haul in 1992/93.

We were third, but a very good third. In fact in the 14 seasons since 1981/82, the next best third place finisher was Man. United who managed 78 points.

After seeing the title slip away, it's only natural to reflect on where it was really lost. As I've said, the home defeat by Chelsea was the killer blow for me. But in general terms, I think you analyse things and say to yourself: 'If only I'd taken that chance, if only we'd drawn that one instead of lost, then things might have been different.'

But it's futile because you can't change anything in football, it all happens in a split second. Once you've missed a chance you can't ask the crowd to throw the ball back on for you to have another crack at it.

I felt that I'd done my best. I scored 20 league goals – my best-ever return – and also got six in the cups.

Frank had enjoyed an absolutely fantastic season, scoring 26 league and three cup goals.

To be honest, I thought he thoroughly deserved to be voted Hammer of the Year by our fans, so I was surprised to eventually win it myself. In the two previous seasons, I perhaps felt that I deserved to win it more than Trevor Brooking and Paul Allen. But when I did finally win it, I was a bit stunned because I felt Frank deserved that honour more than me.

But I was still very proud and privileged to have won Hammer of the Year (even though the trophy itself was actually smaller than my two previous runner-up awards!). It meant so much to me to be recognised by the fans who pay our wages.

Just as I had been thrilled earlier to receive my fellow players' winning vote for PFA Young Player of the Year award, which I received from Pat Jennings at a dinner held at the Grosvenor House Hotel in March. Having been delighted to be nominated among the top six when Mark Hughes won it the year before, this, and the Player of the Year award, is the ultimate accolade for any player.

At the end of the season I also won the Fiat Uno Young Player of the Year award and received a Fiat Uno turbo car from the sponsors. But after driving it around for a while, I decided it wasn't really my style and part-exchanged it for £5,500 cash, which I put towards another motor. Still, it was a great honour that I value very highly.

We considered ourselves hard done by at West Ham but I'm sure all the Everton fans reading this, who followed the Toffees at that time, will claim that the agony was even worse for them. To lose the title by two points is bad enough but to see Liverpool take the silverware instead must have been a real sickener.

Worse still, Liverpool piled on the misery by beating Everton in the FA Cup Final to clinch the double at the expense of their great rivals. I was there in person and disappointed to see Everton lose, having gone to Wembley that day with Lorraine to collect the Fiat trophy award on the pitch before the final.

And if Frank and I felt that we'd done our bit to help the Hammers to success, what about Gary Lineker whose two goals against us on May 5 took his league tally for the season to 30 (equalling Bob Latchford's 1978 return) and his overall haul to 40. It turned out to be his last league goal for the club before his big money move to Barcelona following the World Cup.

Thankfully, there was no marathon tour of Japan that summer. Instead, we attended a nice dinner arranged by the West Ham United supporters' club, at which the players were presented with inscribed 'Best Ever Season' trophies.

It was easily the Hammers' most successful-ever season and I was proud to be part of it. It was a wonderful achievement for a club that didn't have the financial resources to match the Liverpools, Evertons and Man. Uniteds.

Individually, West Ham has boasted some of the game's legends – Bobby Moore, Geoff Hurst and Martin Peters of the 1966 World Cup-winning team and of course all-time club greats like Billy Bonds and Trevor Brooking.

But in 1985/86 West Ham had their best team, the results and performances prove that.

It wasn't all about the goals scored by Frank McAvennie and Tony Cottee. We finished third because we were tremendous all over the park – at the back and in midfield, as well as up front.

This is how I rate West Ham's best-ever team:

PHIL PARKES: Magnificent all season. He came back after almost a year out and maybe that spurred him on. Parkesy was a collosus, filling the goal with his huge frame. The defence starts with the goalie and our defensive record that season said so much about what a great season he had.

RAY STEWART: I always felt that Ray was very underrated, for as well as being a good, steady defender, his distribution was good, too. He'd pick out me or Frank with a clever ball to feet, and 'Tonka' had a great shot on him. Ray will always be remembered as our undisputed penalty king. I know from painful experience that taking penalties is not as easy as it may look, but the great thing about Ray was that not only was he very reliable from the spot, but so many of his penalties were crucial. He could take them under extreme pressure. Alongside Liverpool's Phil Neal, Ray was the best of his generation from the spot. He scored six goals that season, which made him our third highest scorer – not a bad return for a right-back.

The left-back position was disputed by two players:

STEVE WALFORD: Played the first half of the season and, like Ray, was another dependable player. He was very quick but probably felt more comfortable playing centre-half. With a good left foot, he could cross a ball well. Defensively, if ever he did look like being beaten, 'Wally' mastered the art of tugging at his opponent's shirt to ensure that he still got to the ball first. I came across his technique in training, where Wally would just give you a little tug, but disguise it well enough so that the referee couldn't see anything wrong.

GEORGE PARRIS: My former youth team colleague took over Wally's number three shirt for the second half of the season – and did brilliantly, especially considering that he was predominantly a right-footed player. Despite his inexperience, 'Smokey' slotted into the back four very well and did a really good job.

ALVIN MARTIN & TONY GALE: Together, they were the best central defensive pairing in the country that season. Alvin would pick up the target man and deal with all the high balls, while Galey tended to stand off a bit and pick off the runs made by midfielders. Together, they had height, they could both read the game so well, and all they lacked was lightning pace. That didn't matter, though, because they were usually one step ahead of the opposition, in thought, anyway.

We conceded only 40 league goals all season, 16 at home and 24 away, which speaks for itself. The whole back four was so strong as a unit, everyone knew what they were doing.

Now for our four-man midfield:

MARK WARD: One of the best players I've played with. He got up and down the right wing, had real pace and supplied so many quality crosses for Frank and I. And for someone so small (he's only 5ft 5ins), Wardie was so strong. He used to have this saying: 'Pound for pound I'm as strong as anyone,' and he was right. You wouldn't want to pick a fight with him because he was so fiery. One of John's best buys, Wardie gave us width and pace in attack. One minute we'd be defending deep in our half, the next Wardie would lead the charge upfield and the ball would end up in their net. He had a powerful shot, too, and although he didn't score often, when he did they were usually long-range spectaculars. I particularly remember his great goal in the live league game against Man. United, when he scored a cracker from the edge of the box. The ball just flew across Gary Bailey into the net.

ALAN DICKENS: My old mate from our youth team days, Dicko was a West Ham supporter who loved to play for the club, but the crowd underrated him. His season revolved around the injury to Paul Goddard in the first game but once he got in the side, Dicko never looked back. He had talent to burn and made a helluva lot of chances and goals for Frank and I. Dicko would get the ball in the centre of midfield, run at defenders and commit them before slipping the ball in behind their back four for me or Frank to run onto. We had a great understanding.

NEIL ORR: It's fair to say that Neil wasn't in Dicko's class in terms of skill but he was a steady type of player who gave us a lot defensively. I think John paid Scottish club Morton £400,000 for him and although the fee raised a few eyebrows, he did a valuable job for us that season. You need players like Neil – someone who's going to hold in midfield, win the ball and then just pass it simple, invariably out wide. He gave us extra cover in front of the back four and I'm sure our defenders would agree with my assessment of his all round value to the side.

GEOFF PIKE: A very similar player to Neil, who came in to partner Dicko in the heart of midfield. A real terrier, he ran all day and would win a lot of important balls and then pass it simple to more creative players. Pikey read the game very well and was a very underrated player.

ALAN DEVONSHIRE: My favourite player who made such a great comeback from injury that season. His creativity on the left flank was second to none and, like Dicko and Wardie, Dev made countless chances for Frank and I. We probably missed a lot of them but it wasn't too costly because with great players like Dev around you knew that there would be many more chances to get it right. Dev was simply outstanding and it was a pleasure to play alongside him.

FRANK McAVENNIE: I have covered my strike partner in much more depth later in the book. Suffice to say, he was absolutely fantastic all the way through. We formed a truly tremendous partnership and really enjoyed ourselves too. We had our goalscoring rivalry but we were always pleased for each other no matter who scored.

PAUL GODDARD: It must have been so frustrating for him because he started the season up front with me and then, because of injury, lost his place to Frank. The club had so much success that he couldn't be a part of and we all felt sorry for Sarge. He was great about it, though, never moaned and kept training hard, showing what a great pro he was.

These are the 14 players, including myself, who played most of the season. In addition, Paul Hilton (two games), Greg Campbell (one start) and Steve Potts and Bobby Barnes (one sub. outing each), also played a small part in the best ever West Ham team.

There was quite a bit of press speculation towards the end of the season that I might be in with a shout of going to the Mexico World Cup with England. I didn't receive a call up and, to be honest, I don't think I'd have been ready for it. I was still just short of my 21st birthday and besides, manager Bobby Robson had plenty of good strikers to choose from with the likes of Lineker, Hateley, Beardsley and Clive Allen. It was probably a season too early for me, but it was nice to be linked with the squad all the same.

I was pleased that Alvin Martin was included in the squad, though. He flew the Hammers' flag in Mexico and did so well on his one appearance against Paraguay that no one could understand why he was left out of the team to play Argentina in the quarter-finals.

Lorraine and I were holidaying in Barbados at the time and I remember feeling devastated after seeing us cheated out of the tournament by Diego Maradona's infamous 'Hand of God' goal.

And I was doubly upset when Dancing Brave – by far and away the best horse I've ever seen – couldn't quite catch Sharistani on the line in The Derby at Epsom.

That seemed to sum up 1986 . . . so near, yet so far, on all fronts.

Claret & Blues

WHEN JOHN NEARLY QUIT

WITHIN weeks of almost leading West Ham to the First Division championship John Lyall threatened to resign as manager. The incident that provoked his shock ultimatum came on our pre-season tour to Holland when six players, including myself, broke his 11pm curfew.

All the team had gone out but were under orders to be back in time. Everyone was back before 11pm but Frank McAvennie, Mark Ward and I (otherwise known as the 'Three Stooges' by our team mates) got together and decided to slip out of our hotel in The Hague for a few more drinks at a nearby bar – even though John had warned everyone to go to bed.

The three of us were making our way down stairs, heading for the front door, when we noticed John and Mick McGiven still sitting in the reception area, effectively barring our way to the front door.

So we had the bright idea of sneaking out through one of the emergency exits. We were going down another flight of stairs when we bumped into Alvin Martin, Tony Gale and Steve Walford, who obviously had the same idea in mind.

We got to a self-closing safety door and as 'Wally' was the last of the six of us, we told him to keep hold of the door. Unfortunately, he heard the instruction too late, with the door slamming tight behind us.

So we were now trapped in the basement with a final flight of stairs to go down and, hopefully, an emergency exit door to freedom . . . or a night stuck in the basement! Fortunately, the door opened and we escaped to the nearest bar laughing our heads off.

Having enjoyed a few more pints, we rolled back into the hotel at around three o'clock in the morning, apparently undetected by the Hammers' management.

I'm not sure whether John had personally checked our rooms and found that they were empty, or he saw us arrive in the early hours, but a team meeting was called next morning.

He said: "I want whoever went out late last night to pay a fine. If you don't pay I'm going to resign."

We knew straight away which players he was referring to and immediately agreed to cough up £50 each to prevent our manager from quitting.

John was deadly serious when he made his threat and I have no doubt that he would have carried it out if we hadn't paid up. We didn't want to rock the boat any further by arguing with John about it, so after collecting £300 we deposited it with physio Rob Jenkins and the matter was never mentioned again.

That was typical of John's handling of the situation. He dealt with the problem there and then and the press or the fans never knew just how close he came to throwing it all in.

Another memorable incident from that Dutch tour involved Steve Walford, who gave the other players a big fright on the return flight to London.

Wally, feeling somewhat hungover, like the rest of us, from a heavy drinking session the previous night, suddenly began sweating and shaking and in desperate need of fresh air. He must have assumed that the pilot wouldn't entertain the thought of an emergency landing, so he started to make his way to back of the plane . . . and the exit door!

Honestly, Wally was on the verge of opening the rear door of the plane when he was swiftly leapt on by several players who restrained him in time to avert a disaster.

Afterwards, we all thought it was the funniest thing we'd ever seen, but if we hadn't spotted the state Wally was in and the panic he was about to cause, perhaps I wouldn't be here to tell the story.

It's easy to say now what West Ham should have done to build on our success in 1985/86, but the view I put forward here is one I held at the time . . . that John Lyall should have bought two new players.

I felt the two positions that needed strengthening were at left-back and centre midfield. George Parris did a good job for us at left-back, after he replaced Wally, but he wasn't really ideal for that position because he was right-footed.

I also felt we needed someone new to fulfil the midfield holding role, alongside Alan Dickens, that either Neil Orr or Geoff Pike had played the season before. Someone like Peter Reid or Steve McMahon – a quality player who could win the ball but play as well. Ball-winners who passed well and could contribute their fair share of goals, so that we wouldn't continue to rely so much on Frank and myself.

Two signings would have improved the team that had done so well in 1985/86. Whether John looked at it and thought we didn't need strengthening, I don't know. He may well have tried to sign players but, for one reason or another, was unable to do so.

The most successful teams tend to buy when they are still a success, when they are pulling in big crowds and can attract the star names, not when they are in decline.

And we definitely needed new options, because – as events later proved – we were playing a certain way and teams were getting wise to it. They were playing a sweeper to stifle Frank and I and forcing the team to modify its style.

We also had to bear in mind that, in our most successful season, we were very fortunate to avoid injury problems and the team picked itself from week to week.

Would we be so lucky again in 1986/87 or subsequent seasons? The answer was a definite 'no'.

So I was surprised that we hadn't made a signing when we lined up against Coventry City at Upton Park on the opening day of the season. A 1-0 victory, courtesy of Tony Gale's delightful free-kick, his first goal for the club, and a great 3-2 victory at Manchester United, where Frank scored two and Alan Devonshire the other, suggested that perhaps we could go on to do even better than before.

But a goalless draw at Oxford United and successive home defeats by Nottingham Forest and champions Liverpool, who battered us 5-2 with Kenny Dalglish the star of the show, brought us all back down to earth with a bump.

After the Liverpool game, I flew off to Sweden with the England squad and was delighted to earn my first cap in Stockholm. I came on for John Barnes seven minutes after Johnny Ekstrom scored what proved to be Sweden's winning goal.

I'll cover my England career later, but the call-up obviously boosted my confidence still further and I showed it at QPR three days later when I scored a hat-trick past David Seaman.

After maintaining our unbeaten away record with draws at Sheffield Wednesday, Watford and Norwich City, our 5-3 home win over Chelsea, after being 3-2 down, was undoubtedly the game of the season. My two goals proved good preparation for my second England cap, against Northern Ireland at Wembley the following Wednesday, but West Ham's next home game, against newly-promoted Charlton Athletic, resulted in a 3-1 defeat.

We couldn't find any consistency and the goals were drying up, especially for Frank, who after scoring five in the first 10 matches, added only two more in the First Division after that classic with Chelsea on October 11.

After scoring another hat-trick in the League Cup against Preston North End, I got the winner at Wimbledon in mid-November and scored again seven days later, when Aston Villa were the visitors in a 1-1 draw.

Form had been patchy but it dipped quite a bit after we were stuffed out of sight, 4-0, at Newcastle United on November 30. The fact that the game was shown live added to our embarrassment and it wasn't the ideal start to his league career for young Paul Ince, who made his debut as sub.

To add insult to injury, the Newcastle side that Sunday included Paul Goddard, who had been sold by West Ham to the Magpies earlier that month. Peter Beardsley tore us to shreds but Sarge had to leave the field with an eye injury.

As third choice striker at Upton Park, Sarge knew that a move was in his best interests and John agreed to let him go.

With Frank and I firmly established, it was unfair on Sarge - the club's record buy - to confine him to the subs' bench week in, week out. He needed regular first team football and John was good in that he saw the problem from the player's point of view and reluctantly agreed to let Sarge go, rather than insist on him seeing out the remaining year of his contract.

Losing a player of Sarge's quality from the squad was a real blow, but other problems were piling up in defence, where Alvin Martin (injured for two months), Ray Stewart (three months) and Tony Gale (one month) all had lengthy spells on the treatment table as winter set in. And midfield maestro Alan Devonshire missed an even bigger chunk of the season due to injuries which sidelined him for two separate periods.

I was apprehensive about how we'd cope, especially without our rock solid central defensive pairing, and my fears were confirmed as we conceded 11 goals over three consecutive away games, at Newcastle United, Manchester City and Tottenham.

One bright light in a winter of gloom was the form of new boy Ince. Extremely confident as a youngster who'd come up through the ranks, Incey had an arrogant streak in him. He'd been in a few scrapes as a schoolkid but John Lyall took him under his wing and saw Paul as our unpolished diamond.

Paul, who scored a diving header past Peter Shilton on his home debut against Southampton, had everything and I was extremely impressed by his ability from an early age. The only question mark against him was his temperament – he would moan at referees, managers, coaches and other players.

But in some respects Incey wasn't too different to me at that age. I was very confident of myself and arrogant to a degree. There is nothing wrong with these characteristics as long as they are channelled in the right direction.

I'm as pleased as anyone that Incey went on to achieve so much at Manchester United, where he won two league championships, an FA Cup winners' medal and a place in England's midfield. I know how hard it must have been for him to go to a big club like United with all the weight of expectation on his young shoulders. But after a settling in period of around 18 months, he really blossomed and became probably the best midfielder of his kind in the country before his shock £8 million transfer to Inter Milan last summer.

But Incey was still very much one for the future as West Ham struggled to come to terms with a spate of injury problems and individual losses of form.

One of the few enjoyable games of that winter was our 4-1 thrashing of Leicester City at home on New Year's Day, when I scored twice (and should have had more), but we were particularly pleased that Frank had ended a barren run of almost three months without scoring. Typical of Frank, though, he had never stopped running and working hard for the team during that lean patch.

Our FA Cup challenge began across East London at Leyton Orient, where, although the usually excellent Brisbane Road pitch was playable, it was bone hard as the temperature had dropped to something like minus six degrees centigrade. I've never felt so cold on a football field and for once wished I'd abandoned my habit of always wearing a short-sleeved shirt. My arms were red raw from the elbow downwards and I had to soak in the bath for 20 minutes afterwards to get the feeling back in my fingers.

I wondered how the supporters had managed to stand on the open terraces in weather that cold . . . but then again, I doubt that anyone was as foolish as me to wear a short-sleeved shirt!

The third round cup tie was special for me and John Cornwell in that it was the first time we'd faced each other in a first team game. John played midfield for the O's and there was a funny moment in the game when the ball broke loose and I found myself tackling my best friend. I use the word tackle very loosely, because we both ran about five yards to compete for the ball in what must have been the tamest contest seen in the game! I've never been known as much of a tackler, whereas John was always strong in the tackle – except on this one occasion, where no one came away with the ball and it just squirted out to another player.

Although we fully deserved to win the replay 4-0, the frozen Upton Park pitch was too dangerous and the game shouldn't have gone ahead.

In the league, though, we needed fresh faces to give us a lift and John finally entered the transfer market in January, when he signed Stewart Robson from Arsenal for £750,000. Weeks later he brought Liam Brady, another former Gunner, back from Italy and signed two relatively unknown defenders in centre-half Gary Strodder from Lincoln City and left-back Tommy McQueen from Aberdeen.

Before signing Robbo, John actually asked me what I thought of him. Stewart was quite a good friend of mine and, having played against each other at school district level, and later together for England Under-21s, I confirmed that I thought he was a good player. He had been recovering from pelvic and groin injuries – problems that would return to plague him throughout his days with the Hammers – but I knew that, given the chance, he would jump at signing for West Ham.

On his day, Stewart was undoubtedly a class player, although I felt he was a better centre-half or sweeper than a midfield player. Stewart was the type of player I had in mind the previous summer when I said we should have signed a ball-winner who could play the midfield holding role. But Stewart didn't fulfil that role for the Hammers, he was a more attack-minded player who liked to make forward runs. On paper, his partnership with the more creative Alan Dickens should have been a very good one.

Robbo made his debut at Coventry City on January 24, when I scored all three on my lucky ground in our 3-2 win. As usual there was a large representation from the Cottee family at Coventry that day – and one other interested spectator, Everton manager Colin Harvey. I didn't find out he'd been at Highfield Road until after he signed me some 17 months later.

John's decision to sign Brady from Ascoli for £100,000 surprised me, although I was looking forward to him creating a lot of chances for me and Frank. We certainly needed them because the supply lines had dried up. We either faced defences that operated a sweeper system or those that dropped deep to the edge of their own area, so that we couldn't exploit the neat through balls that had created so many chances the season before. I was fortunate that, as a more natural forward, I managed to maintain decent scoring form despite the team's struggle, whereas Frank found it harder to adapt. Not that he allowed it to affect his confidence or enthusiasm – he was still bubbly on and off the field and a credit to John for sticking with him.

I don't know why Liam and I didn't hit it off on the field, but he wasn't able to create the same number of chances for me that I'd been used to from Dev. To be fair, Liam was approaching the end of his career, after seven great years in Italy, but he had to play on the left-hand side of midfield in most games and had come into a struggling side, which is never easy for any newcomer.

I think it's fair to say that the two other buys, Strodder and McQueen, both tried hard but were not the quality players West Ham should have signed at the time. Tommy wasn't the left-back I had in mind to strengthen the team from 1985/86.

After the Coventry game we had a dreadful run of six league defeats in seven games, although one dressing room incident involving Tommy did at least bring a bit of light relief – although our quiet, Scottish full-back wasn't laughing himself. There were 15 minutes to go before kick-off in one game that spring when Tommy sluiced his face with water and then dried off on a towel.

What he hadn't realised is that another player had just used the same towel to wipe Deep Heat from his leg. So there was Rob Jenkins, our physio, throwing as much cold water as possible over Tommy's face to try and cool him down. Anyone who has used Deep Heat will know just how hot the skin becomes, and I'm sure Tommy had the most colourful tan in the team as we went out for that game!

Our progress in both cup competitions ended before March arrived. For the second season running, Sheffield Wednesday halted us in the FA Cup, this time in a fifth round replay at Upton Park, while we went down to Tottenham at the same stage of the Littlewoods Cup, too.

The first clash with Spurs at Upton Park ended 1-1. I counted that Clive Allen scored with one of his seven chances, while I equalised from the one chance I had on the night. I recall thinking to myself, 'If only I had that sort of service and chances created for me . . . '

But Clive totally stole the limelight in the replay, scoring a hat-trick as David Pleat's Spurs, with Hoddle, Waddle, Ardiles, Galvin and my old team mate Paul Allen playing delightful football in a five-man midfield, took us apart in the latter stages. I envied the service Clive got that season, but great credit to him for converting 49 goals to break Jimmy Greaves' record.

With three of our regular back four missing, John turned to Billy Bonds to try and help solve our crisis. Bonzo played in that 5-0 battering at White Hart Lane and in our warmly welcomed 3-1 home win over Arsenal on April 8, when Brady opened his goals account against his former club and the first of my two saw me reach the milestone of 100 goals for the club.

That win, followed by a 2-1 home victory over Spurs on Easter Monday when Frank got back on the goals trail with me, more or less ensured we stayed up. We had never really looked like being relegated, but had flirted with danger and after Brady and I scored in the 2-0 win over Manchester City in the final game of the season, there were only 10 points between the Hammers and the bottom three.

I'm not being critical of Billy in any way because I hold Bonzo in the highest esteem as a player and a person, but I thought that West Ham shouldn't really have to rely on a 40 year-old to help them out. John picked Bonzo and he did okay – the fans voted him Hammer of the Year ahead of Mark Ward – but it was a sorry reflection of our lack of strength in depth that he had to resort to bringing back the veteran defender when we really needed new, younger blood.

My frustration had deepened and looking back, I can see now just how confident I was in my own ability and how arrogant I'd become.

My feelings surfaced on the training ground towards the end of 1986/87 when I had an argument with Bonzo and Ray Stewart. It was a very windy day and we were playing a keep-ball session on a half-sized pitch. Bonzo's attempted cross-field pass to me was cut out and he (quite rightly) had a moan that as I was 50 yards away, and with a strong wind blowing against him, it was impossible to find me with the ball.

But in my own arrogant way I thought: 'If I could have reached my team mate with a pass from the position Bonzo was in, why couldn't he?' Anyway, the ball went dead and Billy and I, standing a few yards apart, exchanged a few choice words. Then Ray came over and pushed me away muttering words to the effect that: "I should grow up, get off my high horse and stop being so stupid."

I reacted by pushing back at Ray, who came towards me and gripped my throat with his right hand. I was shocked, because I'd always got on well with Ray and he'd never shown any indication that he felt I'd been behaving arrogantly. It was all very petulant, particularly on my part, and summed up my frustration at how badly the team had declined in the past year.

Without doubt, I was out of order to have had a go at a senior player. I was only 21 and yet I was having a go at Bonzo, who was nearly twice my age. Then Ray got involved and we stood there swearing at each other, although it never came to blows.

My attitude was that I was doing the business for the club and there were players around me who weren't doing the business. I had expected so much after our success of the previous season and hoped we would genuinely be challenging for the title again. Instead, we were fighting a relegation battle.

I'd played for England at the start of the season and playing for your country raises your expectations. You believe that everyone around you should be as good as yourself, and I was getting very miserable about things.

There were times in training when I'd be huffing and puffing when things went wrong. I've never been the best trainer anyway, only coming to life when there's shooting practice. But it's fair to say that I wasn't the best person to have around the dressing room at that time – and I was even worse the following season.

John never 'pulled' me on my attitude but I think he was aware that I'd become increasingly frustrated as the season wore on. I'd join the England squad and players there would be saying how wonderful it was to be winning this trophy or that trophy, or how they'd benefited from a big transfer (no doubt adding a few hundred pounds to their real wage to rub it in), and obviously it makes you think about your own situation a bit more.

I was young, ambitious and wanted to win things. I'd heard about how much other England players were on and thought to myself: 'I'm the one scoring the goals at West Ham, but people at other clubs are getting a lot more than me'. It's the grass-is-always-greener scenario and I developed a very selfish attitude.

I had made no secret of my ambition to play in Italy if the chance came along, and although I was linked with Fiorentina, nothing came of it. I certainly wasn't tapped-up by anyone that season but I was attracting more and more publicity and it seemed to make sense to employ an agent.

Trevor East, the former head of ITV Sport, introduced me to a fellow called Stuart Webb, who had been managing director at Derby County but was interested in working as a player's agent. We had a chat and agreed that Stuart would act as my agent in the foreseeable future.

Little did I know then how quickly our relationship would turn sour.

Claret & Blues

MISTAKES AND LESSONS

AT the end of our disappointing 1986/87 season, my frustration manifested itself in the form of a written transfer request that I handed in after talking to Stuart Webb, my dad and my girlfriend (and best friend) Lorraine.

We generally felt that if I was unhappy and unsettled – as I had been in one form or another in all but the summer of 1986, after our best season – then I should do something about it.

This was my way of showing John Lyall and the club how frustrated I was that their ambitions did not seem to me like they matched my own.

In my chats with Stuart, he painted a nice, rosy picture of a big money transfer to a top club that would considerably boost my earnings and also enhance my England prospects.

But I handled the whole messy business badly on two counts.

I handed in my request direct to secretary Tom Finn without even discussing it first with John.

And secondly, I naively allowed Stuart to announce the news immediately to the Press, who splashed it all over the next morning's back pages.

Quite understandably, John was livid. It was about a week after the last game of the season in May when he summoned me to his home for face-to-face talks that lasted three hours and could have gone on a lot longer.

He was right in that I should have told him, man-to-man, that I was fed up and thought a move would do me good. He was right, too, to point out that the matter should have remained private between him and me, with no need to involve the media. He said I was totally out of order, which was fair enough.

I was a bit bemused by the whole situation and definitely made some bad errors of judgment.

During our chat, John pointed out that the grass isn't always greener on the other side of the fence and said I should get my head down and work hard to improve my own all round game. He wanted me to work more for the team, instead of seeing myself purely and simply as a goalscorer – an argument I would hear more and more in subsequent years.

I pointed out to John that I wanted to win things and wanted West Ham to win things. They was my club and I wanted them to share the same ambitions as me.

John advised me to go away that summer and have a long, hard look at myself, so Lorraine and I flew off to my parents' apartment in Spain for three weeks in the sun to think things through more clearly.

When we returned to England, I met John again and he informed me that despite paper talk linking me with a £1 million move to either Fiorentina or Glasgow Rangers, no one had in fact expressed interest in me.

Despite Stuart Webb's confidence when I first handed in my request for a move, nothing materialised that summer.

John said I should think seriously about withdrawing my transfer request. It was clear to me that even if there had been a club willing to pay such a large sum to sign me, there was no way John was prepared to sell me then anyway. So I had to swallow my pride and formally write to the club withdrawing my request.

There was no extra incentive from John to stay at Upton Park – not that I deserved any. I remained on the same pay as before, deliberately lost contact with Stuart and then set about repairing the next bridge – with our fans.

Not surprisingly, West Ham fans were upset at me wanting to leave and I admit to being apprehensive when I ran out for our first home game since the transfer request business had died down – the Eddie Chapman Testimonial match.

When they announced, 'Number Ten, Tony Cottee' before the start of the game, the crowd booed. I was hurt by their reaction but I knew I deserved it because of my stupid actions – 'if only I could have turned back the clock,' I thought to myself.

But two minutes into the game, I scored a goal and the fans who had been booing me a few minutes earlier were now cheering me and singing, 'There's Only One Tony Cottee!'

I knew I had to win back the fans and score the goals that would get them fully behind me, as they'd been since New Year's Day, 1983.

So I thought it would be a good idea if I could get something in the papers along the lines of, 'I was sorry for what happened and was now very happy to stay at the club.' I thought it would clear the air with our fans and put the matter firmly behind me, so I phoned a local journalist, Jack Steggles, who was with the Daily Mirror, who agreed to pay me a small fee for my exclusive.

I drove to his house in Dagenham and spent the best part of an hour giving the interview which I hoped would help appease the fans and put the record straight. Somewhere in the conversation I mentioned the problem I'd had involving Billy Bonds and Ray Stewart at the training ground towards the end of the previous season, but the conversation mainly centred around me withdrawing my request and being happy to stay at Upton Park for the foreseeable future.

I (naively) looked forward to picking up the paper next morning and reading a nice headline saying something like 'COTTEE HAPPY TO STAY'.

Instead, I was flabbergasted to read the headline above Jack's piece which read 'MY PUNCH UP WITH BONZO'.

I was stumbling from one disaster to another. I couldn't believe it – firstly, because

I hadn't even had a punch up with Bill, and secondly because it was totally different to the piece I expected to appear.

Jack confirmed to me afterwards that the story he wrote was based accurately on our conversation, but the headline above it just glorified the row with Bonzo. It was one of my first bad experiences of the press, where the headline (written by a sub-editor, back at the Mirror offices) didn't fit the story.

I wasn't looking forward to going in for pre-season training that morning and my fears turned to reality when I bumped into a clearly angered Bonzo. He said: "Come here, you," and I followed him into the privacy of the referee's room. Holding a copy of the offending newspaper article in his hand, he snapped: "What the hell is this all about?"

I immediately said sorry for what had appeared in print and and tried to explain that I'd tried to put out a story about being so happy to stay at the club, but had been stitched up in the process. I think he finally accepted my explanation but warned me not to do anything like it again.

I've got to be honest, I nearly s--t myself because being called into a small room, for a face-to-face showdown with an irate Bonzo, was very scary. He's a big fella and although he didn't lay a finger on me, he made his point very strongly and certainly made me think twice about how to handle the press in the future. I'd learned a valuable lesson.

I also learned to treat some potential sponsors with a degree of caution, too, after a fella phoned me out of the blue at the training ground one day to ask if I'd be interested in receiving sponsorship from Mercedes. The mystery caller – I can't remember his name – explained that he was trying to recruit "Ten Top Footballers" and was offering a 280SL convertible worth £30,000 as part of the package.

I was quite excited by the call and after training one day, I even stopped at the local Mercedes dealership in Romford to admire the look of my next car.

But I needn't have bothered, because after a few weeks went by without any further contact from my 'sponsor', I read a snippet in one of the national papers warning of a bogus 'benefactor', who was not employed by Mercedes and had nothing whatsoever to do with the company, who'd been approaching professional footballers with a view to sponsoring them as a publicity stunt!

It's amazing some of the financial and sponsorship deals that some players encounter in their careers. In 1986, I was invited by an old business colleague of my dad's to become one of the Lloyds' names. He showed me around the Lloyds building in London and made it sound such an attractive proposal that I was keen to go ahead.

The only problem was that although I thought I had the £50,000 mortgage on our flat to use as collateral that wasn't acceptable, so I couldn't raise the £100,000 bond needed for the underwriting, and was unable to join Lloyds.

As it turned out it was a real blessing in disguise that I didn't because the Stock Market crashed, millions of pounds was paid out for natural disasters and everyone connected with Lloyds either lost almost everything or went bankrupt ... I was very lucky I didn't have £100,000 at that time!

Claret & Blues

FRANK AT WORK - AND PLAY

THERE was a myth that started in 1987 that Frank McAvennie and I didn't always get on and that there was an element of jealousy and friction between us.

So I'd like to put the record straight once and for all – that rumour was complete and utter rubbish.

Journalist Jeff Powell was talking nonsense when he claimed in the *Daily Mail* that Frank and I weren't seeing eye to eye and that a rift was developing among West Ham's two star strikers.

Do you know what? The same day that article appeared, Frank and I went straight from training to play a round of golf at Warley Park, Brentwood.

Now if there was any hint of friction between us, or we disliked or felt jealous of each other in any shape or form, do you really think that we'd spend all afternoon together on the golf course?

Apart from my first season when I played only eight league matches, I have top-scored for the Hammers in all but one of my six completed seasons at Upton Park. Of course, the exception was 1985/86 when Frank finished with 26 in the league and I got 20.

But the fact that Frank came out on top that season didn't matter to me. Take a look at the club videos from that season and you can see clearly that I was genuinely pleased for Frank whenever he scored and vice-versa. You could see the delight in our faces as we congratulated each other and those feelings came straight from the heart. There was no animosity.

Another prime example of our good relationship came in that memorable win at Chelsea, which I described in detail earlier. When Frank went through and had only the 'keeper to beat, there was no way he would have unselfishly rolled the ball across goal for me to tap in our third if we were not good mates. You just wouldn't do it.

Although I have always been a high profile player, I have never lived a high profile lifestyle. I like going out to the pub for a drink at times, and I also enjoy the occasional night out at a restaurant with Lorraine.

But to go clubbing at Stringfellows or Browns, with a blonde on my arm, just wasn't my scene. That was Frank's scene, he revelled in his image, and I don't blame him.

It's no good being seen out on the town with Page 3 girls when the team is losing, because people assume that that's one of the reasons why the team is losing. But it was different in 1985/86, because the team was winning consistently, Frank was in peak form on the field and quite right to enjoy himself as much as possible off it.

I thought it was great that he was getting most of the publicity – an appearance on Wogan, pictured regularly in the papers (and not always on the sports pages!) and generally milking his situation. He deserved all the acclaim and the glamour he attracted because he worked bloody hard for what we both achieved for West Ham that season.

Certainly, Frank didn't take liberties with his football. If he had been enjoying a few glasses of champagne the night before, he still reported in fit for training next morning and worked hard in every session John put on.

There was nothing we loved more than staying behind after the others had gone in for their shower, to practice shooting at the goalies, Parkesy and Tom McAllister, with Ernie Gregory barking instructions from the sidelines. We practiced all aspects of shooting: close-range finishing; shooting from crosses; shooting dead balls; hitting moving balls. We'd spend all morning just striking the ball at goal and have little competitions between us to see who could score most, just to add a bit of extra spice.

It was always good natured, friendly rivalry and we carried that from the training ground onto the field on matchdays.

I've never been the most enthusiastic trainer in the world – not like a Bonzo or a Dave Watson, at Everton, who trained as hard as they played – but lay on a shooting practice session and I'll be there doing it all day, every day. That was my extra training as I saw it.

I live and die for goals and could never get too enthusiastic after a good team performance if I hadn't contributed personally by getting on the scoresheet. Even after we'd battered Newcastle 8-1 I came off the pitch that night feeling dejected instead of elated, simply because we'd done the business as a side but I hadn't scored one of our eight.

In my early days goalscoring was the be-all and end-all for me. I saw my role at West Ham purely and simply as that of goalscorer. But I know that John Lyall wanted me to become a more complete player, someone who would close down the full-backs, chase back when we were under pressure and switch on when their 'keeper got the ball.

And I've no doubt that, from time to time, he would have made me aware of how much extra Frank did for the team as a whole compared to myself. I was criticised for not working hard enough in the team's cause and it's criticism I deserved.

Frank did do a lot more for the team and if you asked people who they would rather have in their side, even though I was more of a natural goalscorer than Frank, most of them would choose him because he offered a lot more.

He always covered a lot of ground, running across to try and shut down the full-backs as well as the central defenders.

I've scotched all rumours of a rift between Frank and I, but it has to be said, too, that Paul Goddard accepted being left out of the side with such dignity. I think we all felt for Sarge, who started the season but never got a look in after he suffered his shoulder injury in the first game.

Frank moved into his position up front and once Frank started scoring as prolifically as he did, and I got over my early season blues, there was no way John could leave either of us out.

Sarge was a quality player and give him credit, he kept plugging away and trained hard. He was fine with both Frank and I, there was never a problem or any animosity there, and I was pleased when he got the player/coach job at Ipswich Town, albeit for a brief time.

Claret & Blues

STRIKING OUT

ALTHOUGH I had made my peace with the club before the 1987/88 season began, it wasn't long before there was renewed speculation about me leaving West Ham.

And with rumours rife, and the Hammers showing no sign of recapturing the glory days of 1985/86, I felt that the time was right to have an agent working on my behalf.

After my unfortunate involvement with Stuart Webb, I turned to one of the most reputable players' representatives in the business in Jon Smith.

He was official agent for the England squad, handling the players' pool as well as Peter Beardsley's record £1.9m move from Newcastle United to Liverpool. I spoke to Peter about my situation and he had no hesitation in recommending Jon to me.

The funny thing is, I approached Jon about working for me just prior to an England Under-21 international in West Germany in September 1987.

But then I was sent off in the match and I wouldn't have blamed him for having second thoughts about taking me on! Little did Jon or I know at that early stage of the season just how busy he would be on my behalf over the next 11 months or so.

From the club's point of view, we couldn't have made a worse possible start, losing our first game 3-0 at home to QPR and seeing Alan Devonshire limp off after half-an-hour with an Achilles tendon injury that would rule him out for the whole season.

With central defenders Tony Gale and Alvin Martin also sidelined for long periods again, it was clear from the outset that we were in for another season of struggle.

My two goals in the home win over Norwich City opened our league account, but another six weeks passed before our next victory, at Oxford United on October 17, when I scored in the opening few minutes.

By then I was fighting a lone battle up front after my strike partner, Frank

McAvennie, had been sold to Celtic for £750,000. Although Frank had only contributed 11 goals the previous season, my 29 meant that we still amassed 40 goals between us, having smashed 55 the season before.

And even though Frank had still not scored in the first eight games of 1987/88, my four goals meant that we'd netted 99 as a pairing in just over two years – a brilliant return.

It was at this time that the Daily Mail published the article that I mentioned earlier, which ran with a headline that said: 'LYALL'S DILEMMA OVER FEUDING STRIKERS'. I don't know where Jeff Powell, one of the most respected national journalists, got his information from but it certainly didn't come from me or anyone who knows me well, and I'd like to think that no one connected with Frank fed him that line either.

Because the fact is, as I said before, there was never a problem between Frank and I. We never had a cross word, on or off the pitch, and anyone who says that we did is talking absolute rubbish.

But the article was damaging and obviously fuelled speculation that all was not well between West Ham's two star strikers and when Frank did leave in October, it was understood by a lot of people that one of the reasons was because we didn't get on.

I was surprised that Frank went to Celtic, even though he supported them as a kid and had always wanted to play for the famous Glasgow club.

Surprised and disappointed, because if either of the Hammers' front two would be moving on, I always reckoned it would be me first. I'd kicked up a fuss during the summer and even though I'd withdrawn my transfer request, the papers reported very early in the season that Arsenal had me in their sights as a replacement for Charlie Nicholas who, ironically, was also on his way to Celtic.

There were also reports linking me with Everton, who had apparently made contact with John, without taking the matter any further. With all the speculation about my future, plus our dismal start to the season, I still felt unsettled and unhappy again and yet there was no hint at that stage that Frank would be the one to move.

The rot set in when Frank left because John Lyall didn't have a ready-made replacement at the club and ultimately took six months to find me a new partner. In the meantime, I played alongside a variety of stand-in forwards, including Paul Hilton, who was reserve centre-half, and my old mate Alan Dickens, who was of course a midfielder. Other times, I simply battled away on my own up front, and felt pretty disillusioned doing so.

I couldn't understand what was going on around me at the club. A year earlier, John had let Paul Goddard go without signing a replacement as cover for Frank and I. Now he'd let Frank go without having a quality youngster to bring in or having lined up an alternative replacement.

Not that we were in a position to attract quality strikers, because we were languishing at the wrong end of the table right from the start of the season. And our problems weren't only confined to the First Division, as Barnsley came from two down to humiliate us 5-2 at Upton Park in extra-time of the Littlewoods Cup, second round.

I was devastated by the defeat at the hands of a Second Division club and the fans, clearly unhappy at seeing their big favourite allowed to leave without a replacement, turned the heat on John and the board afterwards by demonstrating outside the ground.

About the only ray of light I saw in a winter of increasing gloom came on November 21, when Nottingham Forest were the visitors. Billy Bonds made his first home appearance of the season at the age of 41 and stole the headlines with a typical swashbuckling display made all the more heroic by his head bandage.

But the game turned into a personal triumph for me, too, as I scored twice in an exhilarating 3-2 victory. My winner from about 12 yards out, an acrobatic overhead kick from Mark Ward's chest-high cross that flew into the top corner, is the best goal I've ever scored and I doubt that I'll ever better it. The fact that England manager Bobby Robson was watching from the stand made it even sweeter.

There was precious little else to feel happy about, though. The team badly lost its way over the Christmas/New Year period and I knew I wasn't performing well as an individual – for the first time in five years, I even failed to give my nan and uncles something to cheer as we drew 0-0 at Coventry City.

I had to try and put the frustration of my sending-off for England Under-21s – and the equivalent of a six month international ban – behind me and concentrate on West Ham's plight, but it wasn't easy. I became even more despondent with each new report about a striker who didn't want to come to Upton Park . . . Kerry Dixon (Chelsea), Mick Harford (Luton Town), Colin Clarke (Southampton), Peter Davenport (Manchester United), Paul Stewart (Manchester City) and Kevin Drinkell (Norwich City), all snubbed John in his attempts to sign a recognised striker to play alongside me.

The New Year brought still more gloom, as we slumped 4-1 at Norwich and then saw George Parris (broken leg) and Liam Brady (torn knee ligaments) stretchered off.

By the end of January, we were also out of the FA Cup, losing a bizarre fourth round tie 3-1 at QPR. After only 10 minutes, I remember looking around and thinking how tightly packed in our fans were in the corner at the School End. Then, as a number of fans climbed over the barrier to find breathing space around the edge of the pitch, the referee had no option but to take the players back to the dressing room.

There was no hint of the crowd trouble that had marred the fifth round clash at Birmingham four years earlier, this was simply a case of over-crowding at one end of the ground, where West Ham fans seemed to arrive late for the game, and there was some suggestion of forged tickets.

They brought on the mounted police to try and sort out the problem, while the players sat it out for 63 minutes. Bonzo, Wardie and myself watched the rugby league and half-time football results on a TV in the Rangers' kit room, before watching the horse racing!

It was weird because after being off for so long, we had to start our pre-match warm-up all over again. When we did get back on, QPR took the lead in the second half and although I equalised, we conceded two more, so that was that for another year.

At Liverpool the following Saturday, although we held on for a goalless draw, we were so overwhelmed that I hardly got a kick playing alone up front. Bonzo clearly realised how isolated I'd been that day because as we trooped off back to the dressing room he joked: "I'm Bill, in case you've forgotten!"

As transfer deadline day loomed, speculation that I would be moving intensified.

Everton emerged as the new favourites to sign me and actually offered £1.5m in February – only to receive a "hands off" response from John Lyall, who continued to draw blanks in his own efforts to sign a new striker.

Jon Smith informed me of Everton's bid in a phone call on February 23 and after a day off, I went in to see John about the matter before our next training session. When I told him that I'd heard of Everton's interest in me he seemed surprised how much I knew.

But, after admitting that Everton had made an offer, John said that I wasn't going anywhere at that stage and that we'd sit down and discuss it further at the end of the season.

Arsenal and Glasgow Rangers were also apparently in the frame and there were fresh rumours that I could be off to Italy, where Fiorentina and Inter Milan had, according to the papers, expressed interest, especially as the Italians had brought in a new rule extending their use of foreign players from two to three. I'd previously spoken to the Italian agent who handled the transfer of Gordon Cowans and Paul Rideout to Italy, but nothing came of it.

It was a boost to my confidence knowing that other clubs were keen to sign me, but the constant speculation did nothing to convince me that I had a future at Upton Park.

I saw John at various times over the next few weeks without really getting anywhere. My diary confirms that on March 4 he said he was "acutely aware of my situation and that if I still felt as unsettled at the end of the season, he'd discuss it again then." Which was just repeating what he'd said at our previous meeting.

On Saturday, March 5, we draw 1-1 at home to Oxford United and that was the worst I'd played in my five years at West Ham. The frustration was steadily building up inside me and I was unhappy that things appeared to be going on behind my back. Hardly a day went by when this newspaper or that newspaper wasn't reporting on a big money move to either Everton or Arsenal, but nothing was ever clarified to me.

I wanted John to be open and honest with me but then again, I understand that managers are often put in difficult situations. It wasn't up to John to do what was right for me, he had to do what he thought was right for the club.

He must have known how unsettled I was at that time but to be honest, if he'd come straight out and told me that Everton, or any other club, had come in and made a big bid for me, that would probably have made me feel even more unsettled than I was already.

I'm not one to show indiscipline, but I was not training as well as I should have. I wasn't disruptive in any way but then I wasn't doing anything to boost flagging team morale either. At that particular time, I'm sure I must have been a bit of a nightmare to be around.

It was on Monday, March 7 that Mick McGiven introduced a rugby ball into the training session, which I mentioned earlier in the book. That farce was followed next day by a game of 'piggy-back football'. Although I could see that the coaching staff were trying to break the monotony, especially as we were in the middle of a relegation fight, I couldn't help but wonder what these little games had to do with football. I mean, I've not carried too many team mates around the pitch on my back on a Saturday.

Trust Phil Parkes to come out with a good quote when he said: "We're doing piggy-back football, so we can get used to playing with the crowd on our backs!"

My growing feeling of discontent never caused me a problem with any of the players, though. I think players understand when one of their team mates is unsettled, because we're all unsettled at some time in our careers. In fact, I recall speaking to Alvin Martin and Mark Ward about the possibility of me going to Everton and what it would be like living on Merseyside. They both told me privately – and publicly, in the papers, after I'd left – that I'd do very well up there. I thought, if I'm going to be moving to Everton at the end of the season, I should find out in advance what lie in store.

Wednesday, March 9 – Jon Smith rang me to say that Arsenal might be keen on signing me at the end of the season. Apart from paper talk, this was the first clear indication we had that the Gunners were interested.

Friday, March 11 – There was a headline on the back page of one tabloid saying: 'I'LL SAVE THE HAMMERS' by John Fashanu. Fash was obviously hinting that he wanted to sign for West Ham, which of course he never did.

Saturday, March 12 – We played badly and lost 3-0 away to Charlton. I had an exchange of words with John at half-time, because he wanted me to track back with their full-back. I pointed out that if I was a forward, how could I possibly be expected to score goals if I was playing right-back or left-back at the time?

Monday, March 14 – Another chat with John, who called me in to tell me that I would be included in the England squad that was being announced the next day.

And, for the first time, he discussed with me the players he might possibly sign before the transfer deadline. He mentioned Fashanu, Lee Chapman of Sheffield Wednesday and Peter Davenport, and I felt good that he was considering my opinions on who to buy as my partner.

Of the three, I would have gone for Chapman, because I felt we needed a target man, someone with a bit of height who could hold the ball up. Davenport was smaller, while Fash of course played for Wimbledon who didn't have the best reputation in the game. It was ironic that, seven years later, I would end up playing a few games with Chappie at West Ham.

At that meeting, I also asked John whether I'd be going anywhere before the transfer deadline and he said: "No, you won't."

Tuesday, March 15 – some welcome good news, as Chancellor Nigel Lawson cuts taxes in the Budget, which meant I went from 60% to 40% tax rate.

Wednesday, March 16 – John phoned me to ask who I'd prefer to play alongside: Lee Chapman or Nico Claesen? I replied: "Claesen," because he was a quality Belgian international who had done very well for Spurs. I was pleased with that call.

Thursday, March 17 – My agent, Jon, rang to tell me what I already knew . . . that West Ham were about to sign either Chapman or Claesen on this, deadline day. Jon also said that he'd heard Everton were set to make a late bid to sign me before the 5pm deadline.

Friday, March 18 – I found out from Tony Gale that West Ham had signed Leroy Rosenior on loan from Third Division Fulham.

No disrespect to Leroy, who did very well in the closing weeks of that season, but I didn't think he had a pedigree in the game to compare with the other four players John had mentioned in our conversations about a new signing, or the other more proven First Division men who'd been linked with the Hammers earlier in the season.

To be fair, Leroy came in and did well for West Ham, scoring some vital goals that helped the club stay in the First Division, but I didn't think he was a good long-term signing.

I wasn't surprised that he started so well, because he had scored 22 goals for Fulham already that season, his confidence was very high and he had plenty to prove to everyone that he was worth his place in the top flight. The question was, could he sustain his glory spell the following season and beyond that? Unfortunately a succession of knee injuries hampered him throughout the rest of his spell, so West ham probably never saw the best of him as a player.

I knew very little about Rosenior before he arrived and even less about our other new signing prior to the deadline – a certain Julian Dicks. Talking to various people, I heard that the 19 year-old from Birmingham City was very highly rated by many people in the game, so he seemed a good signing for the future.

As it's turned out, Dicksy is probably the best left-back the club has ever had, with only Frank Lampard comparable.

But I undoubtedly felt even more frustrated that we hadn't brought in a big name player to play up front with me. Despite our earlier discussions on the subject, John never mentioned to me why he didn't bring in any of the four players we mentioned or why he went for Leroy instead. To be fair to John, it must have been very difficult to attract a big name to West Ham by that stage, because we were staring relegation in the face. It seemed a case of taking whatever was available.

Although Rosenior scored the winner on his debut against Watford, we managed to win only one of our last nine games and looking at our results, it's difficult to believe that we finally stayed up that year.

We owed a lot to Stewart Robson, who deservedly won Hammer of the Year in his first full season, always working tirelessly for the team. I was pleased for him and for Paul Ince, who was a shining light in midfield, while another youngster, Kevin Keen, developed well after being thrown in during our injury crisis. They were the few positive aspects to emerge from an otherwise very disappointing campaign.

Saturday, April 4 – Played Everton at home and, bearing in mind all the talk of me possibly going to Goodison, I was obviously especially keen to impress. As it happened, I did have a good game so it can't have done me any harm in the eyes of the Everton management.

Sunday, April 5 – The Sunday tabloids printed a story linking me with Glasgow Rangers again.

Monday, April 6 – My valuation is going up . . . I started the season supposedly worth £1 million, then I was worth £1.5m and now I was being tagged the £2 million man!

Friday, April 10 – Now I'm linked with Monaco of France.

The speculation was endless, and I honestly didn't have a favourite new club in mind at that stage. I kept an open mind on it although at the same time, it was very unsettling. None of the press speculation had been generated by me or my agent, but it was there all the same.

It seemed like my phone was ringing every hour of the day, with Jon calling to say that this club or that club were interested. I was still only 22 and found it very difficult to handle. Everything was beginning to get on top of me and I resigned myself to the fact that I would be leaving West Ham at the end of the season.

Claret
& Blues

BREAK POINT ON THE CARDS

MONTHS of pent up frustration exploded on the night of April 12, when our 1-0 home defeat by Arsenal left us just a point above the play-off zone near the bottom of the First Division.

I had gone closest to scoring when my angled shot rebounded off the inside of the post and rolled straight into the arms of Gunners' goalkeeper John Lukic.

We had conceded another sloppy goal, Michael Thomas shooting past Phil Parkes, and I reached breaking point as we got back to the dressing room after the final whistle.

Just as John Lyall started to go over what had gone wrong, I let fly with an outburst in which I complained about everything I could think of at the time. I don't remember my exact words, because I was so uptight and didn't let John or any of the coaching staff get a word in, but it went along the lines of: 'We didn't create any chances . . . all we ever do is let in rubbish goals', which is obviously the sign of a club threatened by relegation.

It was the kind of argument that happens in every team's dressing room from time to time, but it was the most upset I'd ever been after a game and I certainly let John know it.

The argument ended with me throwing my kit down on the floor and getting into the bath – while John was still talking to the rest of the team. I just sat there on my own in a daze. Everything had been building up for weeks and months, and it was not only football that was troubling me.

Lorraine and I had been going through a little bit of a rough time in our relationship – the sort of difficult patch that almost all couples experience at one stage or another – and with me and the team playing badly, plus all the transfer talk, everything just built up inside me.

I was an emotional wreck. Although I felt that I'd achieved as much as I could at West Ham, on the other hand I knew I wouldn't be leaving until the end of the season, so I was in no man's land to some extent.

After getting changed, I made my way through the car park to Jon Smith's car. We talked in his car for an hour, with me in tears at one stage. I was so frustrated and although Jon tried to reassure me that everything would be all right, I knew I'd hit rock bottom. That was the lowest point in my West Ham career and I honestly didn't know which way to turn.

Don't get me wrong, I was still very committed and desperately wanted the Hammers to stay in the First Division. I didn't want to leave the club doomed to relegation and would do all I could to ensure they stayed up.

And I think I did my bit in that respect, because I scored in three of our last four games that determined we would indeed beat the drop. I bounced back from the Arsenal defeat to score for the first time in 10 games as we drew 1-1 at home to Coventry City. My goal didn't stop us losing the next match 2-1 at Southampton, which saw the last of Billy Bonds' 793 first team appearances, but I scored our fourth goal in a thrilling 4-1 victory over Chelsea on Bank Holiday Monday, May 2.

With Leroy (two) and Hilts also on the scoresheet, we virtually made sure of avoiding relegation while at the same time condemning Chelsea to the play-offs and, ultimately, relegation.

Only a disastrous defeat by seven goals or more in our final game at Newcastle could have plunged us into the play-offs, and only then if Chelsea and Charlton Athletic both drew. But John still didn't take any chances and named Parkesy as one of our two subs, just in case Tom McAllister suffered an injury. This was, of course, in the days before reserve 'keepers were commonly named among three Premiership subs.

In fact, Parkesy wasn't needed as Newcastle won 2-1 and Paul Gascoigne and I played what proved to be our last games for our respective clubs before our big summer transfers.

I don't know what Gazza was feeling but it was a sad occasion for me. Although it was inevitable that I would be leaving West Ham, I still approached the game as best I could. I still loved West Ham and, after all that had gone on, it was sad to think that I'd be leaving shortly.

I didn't play very well at St. James's Park, but I kept the kit I wore that day as a memento and it still has pride of place in a frame on the wall at our home. Even though I'd played my last game for the club – or so I thought, because I couldn't have imagined then that I'd be returning in 1994 – I didn't feel that I wanted to wash my hands of the club I'd supported all my life.

That trip to the north-east was also memorable for a particularly tremendous card school that took place at our hotel in Newcastle the night before the game. My mate John Cornwell, who was playing for the Magpies at that time, came across to join me, Mark Ward and Tony Gale.

We always played three card brag and there was a lot of money flying around this time. At one stage, Wardie actually went £100 blind – which, to anyone who doesn't play brag, means he continued playing without looking at his cards. So, if I wanted to look at my cards, I'd have to pay double what the 'blind man' has staked in order to carry on.

After Wardie went £100 blind, and everyone else had stacked, I 'opened' with £200 and looked at my cards to find a pair of sevens, which isn't a brilliant hand, although it's usually enough to beat the blind man.

Then Wardie went £100 blind again, so I had to go another £200 open, and I was nearly sh---ing myself as I looked down at the pot of £800 – £400 of which was my money.

In the end Wardie looked at his cards and revealed eight high . . . and I breathed a huge sigh of relief as I scooped the pot!

I was even luckier a bit later in the game when after opening up, I looked at my first two cards, a pair of twos. There was only Wardie and I left in and with him appearing to have a strong hand, I said I'd 'see him'.

He revealed a prile of fives. Sensing defeat, I threw my cards onto the table face up . . . to reveal a prile of twos! I was so pleased I hadn't looked at my third card, otherwise I'd have easily lost my earlier winnings. It was certainly some card night!

As well as the players I've already mentioned, Frank McAvennie, Bonzo, George Parris, Dicko and Gary Strodder were also regular members of the West Ham Card School. We enjoyed some thrilling sessions over the years – and some of us lost quite a few bob, too.

I won't name him, but one player lost £2,000 in one card school on the way to an away game. At least he took it well and made us all laugh when he came in to training the following Monday and said: "I don't feel too grand this morning!"

It was a standing joke among the lads that the card school players paid for the horse Wardie bought for his young daughter, with Frank, myself and two others claiming to have bought a leg each!

Card schools are part and parcel of football and we certainly enjoyed them at West Ham. It's a good way to pass the hours on the way to away games, or at the hotel the night before a match. Sometimes, if we were in the mood, we used to play on the morning of a game – it can be a good way of relieving tension and I don't think it does any harm.

Just after the Newcastle game, I received the heartbreaking news from Bobby Robson that he was leaving me out of his 22-man England squad for the forthcoming European Championships in West Germany. Despite being immediately recalled to the squad after my three-match international ban ended, my hopes of going as cover for first choice strikers Gary Lineker and Peter Beardsley had effectively been shattered by my sending-off in Germany the previous September, which ruled me out of the England reckoning for most of the season.

It was a devastating end to a season to forget.

Claret & Blues

ON THE MOVE

AFTER all the problems that the 1987/88 season brought, I suppose I should have known better than to have thought that the summer would run any more smoothly. It was soon obvious that my eagerly anticipated transfer would drag on for a couple of months longer.

In between taking countless phone calls from my contacts at Everton and Arsenal, I was visiting Moorfields Hospital for treatment to a virus that badly affected my left eye. I felt a right idiot having to wear sunglasses to hide the blisters on the days when the sun was nowhere in sight!

I suppose all the hassle of the preceding months had taken its toll and manifested itself in a nasty eye infection that left me in considerable pain and discomfort for a week or so.

Apart from being a nuisance, the eye injury also harmed my chances of adding another England cap to my collection, as I joined the party late for training camp prior to the Rous Cup matches against Scotland and Colombia and didn't get on the bench for either game.

At least Wimbledon's shock FA Cup triumph over Liverpool cheered me up a little – though not for footballing reasons, as I've never advocated their long-ball game. I was pleased simply because I'd had a modest fiver on them to win the Cup Final at odds of 4-1!

Once the season had ended it became clear that my choice of new clubs would be between Everton and Arsenal, where contacts were designated to keep me informed of developments on the transfer front.

Hardly a day went by without a call from one club or the other, sometimes both, and then my agent Jon Smith was calling me regularly with further updates as the summer weeks went by. My contact at Goodison Park – an Everton player, who I won't name – would ring up and say: "Don't worry, Everton will be making an official bid for you before long, just be patient." My contact at

Highbury – a member of the backroom staff – was saying basically the same things.

Despite denials to the contrary, in nearly every major transfer, the buying club will have made contact with the player before they make their interest known publicly. It's obvious why they 'tap up' players, too, because there would be no point in a club going through all the rigmarole of going through the transfer process if the player they were willing to pay millions of pounds for, had no interest whatsoever in joining them.

So what normally happens is, you get a discreet phone call, asking simply if you would be "interested" in joining the club the caller is representing. Once that matter is established, the whole process continues from there.

On May 31, I went to see John Lyall to see if he could confirm what I'd read in the papers about Arsenal having made a bid for me. It was the best meeting I'd had with John to date, but he did no more than deny that report and reassure me that he would "keep me informed as soon as he received an offer from one or other of the clubs."

John made no attempt to sit me down and try to talk me out of leaving West Ham. He obviously realised by then that there was no point and that it was in everybody's best interests for me to go – as soon as he received the £2 million-plus he demanded for my release, and not before.

By then, the daily speculation about my immediate future no longer unsettled me as it had done during the season. I was pleased, flattered really, that two of the so-called 'Big Five' (Man. United, Liverpool and Spurs being the other three) were officially chasing me.

Although I'm not quite sure what Everton manager Colin Harvey, or Arsenal boss George Graham, would have made of the drunken antics of the young striker they were both about to bid a British record transfer fee of two million pounds for.

One balmy – or perhaps that should be barmy – night in June, John Cornwell, my brother Paul, our friend Michael Hockton and I, went to Southend for a night out that took in a disco, a casino and numerous drinks before we summoned a taxi to drive us back to Brentwood at five o'clock in the morning.

I was staying at my parents' house every now and again, as opposed to the flat, and we asked the taxi driver to drop us off about half-a-mile from their place, to give us the chance to try and sober up before we arrived home.

Anyway, we were walking along a country lane, at Bulphan, near Brentwood, when Michael declared that he was going to climb a nearby fence and go and 'chat' to a horse that was standing in a field at the side of the lane. The next thing we knew, John gave Michael a lift up onto the horse and he proceeded to ride it around the field, without a saddle, reins, stirrups or anything – only the horse's small coat to cling onto for safety.

You can guess the next bit . . . yes, I took up Michael's challenge to have a go myself. The first attempt ended in embarrassment, as he lifted me onto the horse and I fell straight off the other side and landed in the field!

I managed to get back onto the horse and ended up giving it a little gallop around the field. I said to myself: 'If only Colin Harvey and George Graham could see me now, riding a horse in a deserted field at half-past five in the morning, much the worse for drink'. I don't think either manager would have been too pleased at my Frankie Dettori impersonation, nor John Lyall for that matter, at the thought of his biggest asset coming a cropper in a field!

Fortunately, no one – including the poor, innocent horse – came to any harm and the four of us arrived home at 6am to crash out at the end of a wonderfully memorable evening that still brings a smile to my face whenever I think back to it.

The next couple of weeks were spent watching England's disastrous European Championship campaign unfold in Germany, where three defeats left Bobby Robson and his team's hopes in tatters. Everything went wrong and I thought to myself, perhaps it was a blessing in disguise that I wasn't in the party after all.

On Monday, June 27, I drove to the training ground for the meeting I'd arranged with John at the beginning of the month. I went there with a transfer request I intended to hand to him, because the situation had dragged on and on and, with no signing-on fee to lose anyway, I thought I might as well make my position perfectly clear. The only trouble was, John never turned up – and I don't know to this day whether it was a genuine misunderstanding or he simply forgot.

Undeterred, I went to the Boleyn Ground next day to hand in my request, as I knew that a board meeting was scheduled for Thursday, June 30. On the morning of Friday, July 1, John phoned me at the flat in Hornchurch and was very formal and to the point. He said: "Following your request, you are being placed on the transfer list and the club will notify all interested parties that we will be asking for a fee in excess of £2 million."

Whilst I was pleased that the club had finally accepted the fact that I would be going – Everton and Arsenal had already been contacting me unofficially anyway – I was apprehensive about the size of the fee. I couldn't understand why, when I'd put in for a transfer a year earlier, I was supposedly worth £1 million, and yet one year on, after my worst season for West Ham, my value had doubled. To me it seemed crazy, although I think Paul Stewart's £1.7m move from Man. City to Spurs made it a realistic fee, as he hadn't played in the first division and I'd established myself for five years and won four full England caps.

After receiving that phone call from John, my informant at Goodison contacted me and made it clear that Everton were basically making all the running and were going to offer £1.75 million for me. But my man at Arsenal said that, although they wouldn't be bidding at this stage, they would be there in the background waiting to come in through the back door, which was how they preferred to play it.

One paper reported that I'd signed for Everton, another that I had decided on Arsenal, while no one at West Ham said much more at that stage. I had a couple of nasty letters from fans, one in particular which I remember said: "If you don't want to play for the club, then f--k off and go somewhere else." I actually threw that one in the bin, but my dad retrieved it and kept it along with all the other mail I received from supporters.

They were entitled to their opinion although out of an average crowd of 20,000, I only received five unkind letters, which puts it in perspective.

With no sign of the transfer going through I grabbed a holiday in the Caribbean.

Although it was nice to take a break and relax in the sun, there was still no getting away from football. Jon, my agent, phoned while I was there and I also took calls from my Arsenal contact. The day after I returned to England, on July 17, both my Everton and Arsenal contacts phoned to say that the respective clubs had made offers to West Ham, although they obviously weren't as much as £2 million because neither bid had been accepted.

On July 19, I called John Lyall to ask if there was any news. He said that there were "a few things happening" but I had to go in and train with the other West Ham players!

This was something I hadn't even considered, because I knew in my mind that I'd played and trained for the club for the last time. It seemed pointless going back to Chadwell Heath for pre-season training and having to face the lads who knew full well that I wouldn't be playing for them next season.

It was a bit embarrassing for me but John's attitude was – and quite rightly – that I was still a West Ham player until told otherwise, and should therefore be training with the Hammers, like every other player on the club's books. And besides, as I was still under contract to them, they would be paying my wages until I moved on.

So I went in and trained that day, but spoke to John beforehand and he told me: "Everton were very close to offering what we want." Later on that day, things developed further when Jon Smith informed me that both Everton and Arsenal had bid £2 million, with West Ham saying they would decide "within 48 hours" who I could talk to.

In the meantime, I had to continue training with the other West Ham players, who had been back a week earlier than me, so they were that much fitter. At the end of my second day, which involved one 400 metre run, three 200 metres runs and four 100 metres sprints, I was completely knackered. It was stupid really, because there I was, on the verge of becoming the club's record transfer, risking pulling muscles by doing training my body wasn't prepared for.

When I went in on the third day, I was so stiff it was ridiculous. I couldn't even jog because my body still hadn't recovered from the previous day's running, so I just walked round the pitch.

At least I could see light at the end of the tunnel, because after training John said he'd had a call from chairman Len Cearns and would be ringing me at home later that afternoon.

At 3pm on Thursday, July 21, I received the phone call I'd been waiting all summer for. As agreed, it was John calling to say that I could talk to both Everton and Arsenal. At last, I was on the move . . .

Above: *My debut goal against Tottenham at Upton Park on New Year's Day, 1983, aged 17.*
Below: *Scoring against another North London club – my 100th goal for the Hammers against Arsenal, 1987.*

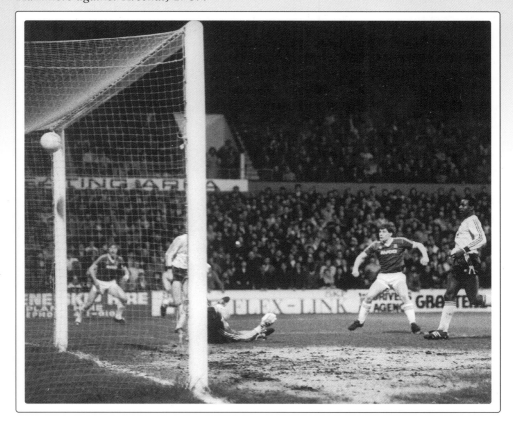

Above left: Me and my scrapbooks.
Above right: Me and two scousers –
Alvin and Wardie (in the days when
they both had more hair!).
Above: Holding the hat-trick ball at
Chadwell Heath following the FA Cup
replay against Wimbledon in 1985.
Left: With Sarge, one of the best.

Above: Celebrating with the Chicken Run after scoring
against Coventry, 1988.
Below: Sitting out the Birmingham riots, 1985.

Right: Fist
clenched
after my
second goal
in our
superb 4-0
drubbing of
Chelsea,
1986.

Left: *That's a shock – me in the bunker!*
Centre: *Believe it or not, I once I beat Steve Davis – after a 90 point start!*
Below left: *Essex 800 metres champion, 1981.*
Below right: *It's either six or out with me!*

Above: Collecting the Fiat Uno Young Player of the Year award from Ron Greenwood, 1986.
Left: The 'Three Stooges' with their Hammer of the Year awards, 1986 – I'm joined on the pitch by runner-up Frank and third placed Wardie.
Below: Completing a trio of trophy awards in 1986 – this time it's Pat Jennings who presents me with the prestigious PFA Young Player of the Year award.

Above left: *My last goal for West Ham in the crucial 4-1 win over Chelsea, May 1988 – or so I thought!*
Above right: *Scoring in the snow at Ipswich, FA Cup, 1986.*
Above: *In off my chest against Wimbledon, 1985.*
Right: *This goal against Coventry cost my dad £500!*
Below: *Another goal at Ipswich – to guarantee survival in 1985.*

One of 55 celebrations Frank and me had in 1985/86 ... and I was told we didn't get on!

Signing for Everton, July 26, 1988, with Jim Greenwood looking on.

CHAPTER 28

Claret & Blues

GEORGE GIVES ME THE BLUES

JUST 10 minutes after John Lyall phoned to give me the okay to speak to Everton and Arsenal, my phone rang again and it was Colin Harvey. He kept it short and sweet: "We've agreed the fee with West Ham. Are you interested in playing for Everton Football Club?"

I didn't ask how much Everton had offered West Ham. It was simply a case of me saying: "Yes, of course I'm interested," and agreeing to meet Colin for further talks the following Sunday, July 24.

Two hours went by before the phone rang again – it was George Graham, to say basically the same as Colin. I expressed the same interest in playing for the Gunners as I had Everton, although George said he was aware that I'd already made arrangements to meet Colin Harvey and was happy to speak with me later.

In the meantime, I was glad when John Lyall said I wasn't required to report for training that Friday, so I played tennis with my dad instead, and on Saturday evening I went to my parents' home, where they were holding a 18th birthday party for my sister Joanne.

It was quite frustrating having to wait two days from the time I spoke to both managers on the phone until meeting them in person. It was agreed at a meeting between Jon Smith, my dad and I on the Thursday night that when we met the club representatives, Jon would handle all discussions relating to finance – my wages, bonuses, signing-on fee, etc – leaving my dad and I to talk football with the respective managers. Jon was obviously fully aware of what I was earning at West Ham and felt confident he could negotiate a much better deal for me. He didn't promise me he would get me 'X' amount, just that he would get the best deal possible.

I was sure about one thing . . . we'd be going in style, for we were chauffeur-driven to Everton's Bellefield training ground that Sunday morning in the luxury of Jon's immaculate Bentley!

We arrived at 1.30pm and my first impression of Bellefield was that it was not much unlike the facilities at Chadwell Heath, although the buildings were a bit bigger, the place seemed to have more history about it and the actual pitches were in slightly better condition. Colin showed me around while Jon discussed my financial terms with the club's chief executive, Jim Greenwood.

Although Everton had finished fourth in 1987/88, Colin spoke of his quest to buy a striker to play alongside Graeme Sharp who, despite scoring 13 league goals the previous season, needed more support than the likes of Wayne Clarke (10 goals) and Adrian Heath (nine goals) had been providing. The club hadn't really replaced Gary Lineker, who scored 40 in the season before he left to join Barcelona in the summer of 1986, so Colin said he wanted someone new who could score 20 goals a season.

I was pleased with how the meeting went and impressed by Colin, who obviously cared very deeply about Everton Football Club and showed a big desire to recapture the glory days of the mid-80's.

After our talks at Bellefield, we were shown around Goodison Park – a magnificent stadium befitting a famous club like Everton – and then, at 5pm, we left Liverpool to head back south for the meeting, pre-arranged with George Graham, which was set for 10pm.

On the way back down the motorway, Jon explained the figures Everton were offering me, which were very good. In fact, taking into account wages and standard team win bonuses – although there was no individual goal bonus – they weren't far off doubling what I'd been earning at West Ham.

And the big difference was that their attractive financial package included the signing-on fee I'd never received in all my time with the Hammers.

I was naturally pleased with Everton's financial offer, although I had to keep an open mind and not get too excited at that stage. After all, I still had no idea how my meeting with George Graham would go and almost everyone was expecting me to sign for the Gunners anyway.

Arsenal offered the easiest option, because I could have continued living in Essex, near my family and friends, while a move to Everton represented a completely fresh start, moving 250 miles from home to a totally new environment. Signing for Everton represented a particularly big challenge for the reasons I've just given, which is why I sensed that the people close to me expected me to choose Arsenal, for geographical reasons more than anything else.

From a football point of view, I had other options to consider. Everton had enjoyed tremendous success in the mid-80s, winning the championship twice, the FA Cup and the European Cup Winners' Cup. Then again, they had a number of players who were nearing their 30s, so were they possibly entering a period of transition?

At Highbury, Arsenal had produced a tremendous crop of youngsters who had progressed through to the first team – Tony Adams, David Rocastle, Michael Thomas and Paul Merson – and, as proved in the years ahead, seemed the team of the future.

I was also spoilt for choice when contemplating my new strike partner – two big, successful target men in Everton's Graeme Sharp and Arsenal's Alan Smith. It was going to be a difficult decision to make.

When we arrived at the West Lodge Park Hotel, Hadley Wood, that Sunday evening, George Graham looked very smart in his suit and club tie, but after shaking hands and exchanging pleasantries, he immediately imposed himself on the situation by declaring that while he was happy to talk to my dad and I, he had no intention of speaking to my agent.

I was surprised and disappointed with George's attitude because he had been happy dealing with Jon and making arrangements with him prior to our meeting. I wish I'd known then what Frank McAvennie told me about his dealings with Arsenal nine months later. When George confronted Frank with his "I don't deal with agents" attitude, Frank simply responded by saying: "If you don't talk to my agent, you don't talk to me!" Apparently, George did reluctantly agree to speak to Frank's agent but, of course, nothing materialised there and Frank ended up re-signing for West Ham in March 1989.

We went into the room with George, who sat on the opposite side of the table to my dad and I. George was very overwhelming, such a powerful character, that I felt a bit nervous as he took the initiative, saying: "I know your family history, that your dad is in insurance, you've got a brother and a sister and that you've got a steady girlfriend."

He continued: "I'm looking to buy someone to play alongside Alan Smith, someone who is going to work hard, chase back if we need him to and generally work for Arsenal's good cause." I thought to myself, 'this is different to what Colin Harvey had said about wanting to sign me to score goals.'

Then George surprised me again when he added: "I want you to put on your club blazer and be proud to wear the Arsenal badge."

At this point I really wasn't too worried about club blazers. First and foremost I'd been a West Ham fan all my life, I was still officially a West Ham player and my strong feelings for the Hammers weren't about to fade because I was leaving them. They were my club so I was never going to feel a great sense of pride about wearing another team's club crest, especially that belonging to one of West Ham's main rivals Arsenal!

George underestimated mine and my family's affinity to West Ham and when the conversation moved on to money, he clearly hadn't done his homework there either.

I really needed Jon Smith present because it was his responsibility to sort out the finances of the deal and his experience of successfully negotiating Peter Beardsley's big move to Liverpool would have been invaluable to a nervous youngster like me.

Even so, I didn't need Jon or anybody else to tell me that what George was offering was laughable compared to Everton's offer.

Arsenal's offer amounted to just £3,000 more a year than I was on at West Ham. I said to George: "Yes, that sounds quite good . . . now what about my signing-on fee?"

George stunned me again when he replied: "Oh no, there's no signing-on fee – that's the package."

I looked at George and said: "You're joking. That's just £3,000 a year more than what I'm already on at West Ham!"

He said: "Oh, yeah, but you've got to look at the overall package. By living near London you're going to do really well from commercial spin-offs."

I said: "Well, that may be true, but it's not guaranteed income. Sponsorship and commercial opportunities will only come my way if I do well, nothing is certain.

"Look, you're paying over two million pounds for me, it's a record transfer, so surely you must appreciate that you've got to be offering me more than that. The increase in wages that I deserve for a player being bought for a record fee would be repaid to the club on the opening day of the season, when a capacity crowd would come to see your new record signing make his debut."

My dad also pointed out about the size of the fee – surpassing the £2 million Spurs had paid Newcastle United for Paul Gascoigne just a few weeks earlier – and that my earnings should surely reflect my valuation. John Lyall, having turned down Everton's earlier offer of £1.5m, insisted all along that West Ham wanted more than £2m for me, hence the fact that the fee both Everton and Arsenal had subsequently agreed to pay was exactly £2 million and fifty thousand pounds.

I was absolutely flabbergasted by George's offer. As he'd taken the trouble to learn all he could about me personally, including my family background, then why hadn't he found out what I'd been earning at West Ham? I couldn't believe it and felt not only very disappointed, but embarrassed.

For some reason, George wanted players to sign for him without offering the wages that other clubs were paying. It was a trend which continued throughout his managerial career at Highbury, with John Barnes, Frank McAvennie, Andy Townsend and Chris Sutton, amongst others, also turning Arsenal down.

Although money was not the be-all and end-all – I wanted to join the club who wanted me most – I obviously had to bear in mind the huge difference in the two financial offers. I told him that I didn't want to commit myself right away and would prefer to sleep on it and then arrange to meet him and Everton again the next day.

With the meeting with George concluded by midnight, Jon, dad and I drove back to Jon's house at Potters Bar where we spent the night. Jon couldn't believe it either when I told him what Arsenal were offering and after the three of us talked things over for an hour-and-a-half, we came to the conclusion that there was really only one option left . . . I virtually accepted in my own mind that night that I would become an Everton player.

I still felt the same when I awoke at 10.45am next morning. As I hadn't trained for a few days, I went for a three mile road run, accompanied by Jon and dad. I just about managed to win it, which didn't say much for my fitness considering that dad was 50 years-old and Jon was pushing 40!

After lunch, we set off for our meeting at Highbury which was scheduled for 2pm. As Colin Harvey had done at Goodison the previous day, George took me on a guided behind-the-scenes tour of the ground and I couldn't fail to be impressed by the famous marble halls that included the fabulous Herbert Chapman bust just inside the main entrance. Arsenal are a tremendous club, there is no doubt about that, but it wasn't for me.

Although Jon knew that he wouldn't be given the chance to talk directly to George, he joined us inside and had a private meeting with Arsenal's managing director and secretary, Ken Friar, in the hope of persuading them to increase their original offer.

As it happens, Arsenal did make a final offer which was much more realistic, but it was still considerably less than Everton's proposal which included a signing-on fee and I knew then, after an hour-long visit to the Gunners' North London home, that I wouldn't be going back there to sign for the club.

I couldn't understand what Arsenal were thinking. Why were they quite prepared to break the British transfer record, at a cost of more than £2 million, and yet not suitably reward the player they were buying? I'm not talking about me holding out for £10,000 a week, as some players are on today, but a wage relative to the fee they were willing to pay at that time.

Our second meeting with Arsenal officials on that Monday was simply to try and squeeze a bit more money out of them, but, despite their increased offer, they were never in the running financially.

So the ball was firmly back in Everton's court – and it was a sign of their enthusiasm to sign me that instead of asking us to travel back up to Merseyside two days running, their representatives readily agreed to travel down and meet us at the hotel by the South Mimms service area on the M25 at 6.30pm.

When Jon spoke to both interested clubs on the morning of Monday, July 25 to arrange second meetings, Everton knew full well that we'd be seeing Arsenal again first, so they must have felt quietly confident once they knew that our second meeting with them was still going ahead. They probably looked at the situation and thought, 'well he can't be too keen on joining Arsenal if he's still prepared to meet us again.' They were right – I couldn't wait to meet the men from Merseyside again.

The hotel was only five minutes drive from Jon's house and I knew in my heart of hearts as we pulled into the service area that I'd be an Everton player by the end of the night. There was nothing to choose between the clubs from a football point of view – they both had superb facilities, ambitious managers who wanted to win trophies and teams capable of challenging for the top honours. They were on a par in all respects except financially.

I thought it was a good sign when I saw that Colin Harvey and Jim Greenwood were accompanied by the Everton chairman, Philip Carter, one of the most influential and powerful figures in the game at that time, who hadn't been present at our first meeting the previous day. We split into two groups – Colin sat down in the lounge area with dad and I, while Jon went into a small boardroom with the two senior Everton officials.

We were talking generally for a while and then I said to Colin: "I know it's a silly question, but why do you want to buy me?" In response he said: "I want someone to score 25 goals a season for Everton."

I thought it was great to hear a manager saying he wanted to sign me to score goals, with no mention of blazers or wearing their colours with pride and honour. We carried on talking informally until Jon had completed his meeting, then we all met up in the lounge. Quite rightly, the Everton trio made themselves scarce for half-an-hour to discuss how things had gone from their point of view, leaving Jon to relay to me and dad what had been discussed.

He revealed that Everton had actually increased their financial offer, to include a loyalty bonus, which meant I'd receive a lump sum just for being at the club on June 30 throughout each year of my contract.

When Jon added everything up – my basic wage, signing-on fee, team win bonuses and now a loyalty payment – Everton's financial package was irresistible.

It wasn't a case of greed on my part, it all came down to common sense and taking the option that was so much more financially appealing. As a footballer, if you are lucky your career will last 15 years and in that space of time you have to try and earn what most people work to earn over 50 years.

I know that many reading this will be thinking to themselves that there is nothing to stop a player going out and doing a 'real' job when his playing days are over, but that's not quite as easy as it sounds. There are very few players who can continue to earn a decent living from the game once they quit playing – the obvious exceptions being those who go into football management (a very risky business in itself) or work in a media capacity, like Trevor Brooking, Gary Lineker, Alan Hansen and Andy Gray. And if, between the ages of 16 and 30 to 35, a player has remained active with a club, he will almost certainly not have learned a trade or gained the qualifications needed to get him a job once he's at the end of his playing career.

You also have to consider the high risk of injury. A prime example is John O'Neill, the Northern Ireland defender, who suffered a cruciate knee ligament injury on his debut for Norwich City against Wimbledon in December 1987, in a tackle with John Fashanu. O'Neill never played again, which shows how vulnerable footballers are.

It is for this reason that every player owes it to himself and his family to get the best possible deal, because you never know when you've played your last game.

So perhaps you can understand my decision to join Everton when I reveal that they offered me no less than SIXTY THREE THOUSAND POUNDS a year more than Arsenal!

And that was just the difference over one year. Take into account that I was signing a five-year contract, and the total difference over that period amounted to a staggering £315,000. Well, what would you have done in my position?

Much as I'd hoped all along that it wouldn't revolve around money – I wanted my decision to be based purely on football and the team's prospects – it was an inescapable fact that Everton and Arsenal were a million miles apart. I thought I'd be an absolute fool to turn down Everton.

Although I had made up my mind to sign for Everton, a decision that had the unanimous backing of Jon Smith and my dad, there was still one person whose opinion I valued and wanted before I went ahead and officially agreed to sign.

Lorraine and I had still not completely made up when the time came for me to make the biggest decision of my football life. While she was obviously aware that Arsenal and Everton were both in for me, she wasn't sure exactly how I felt about what I wanted to do in the future from a professional point of view. I knew in my heart and mind that it was the right thing to join Everton, but I wasn't going to uproot myself, move 250 miles north to a completely new lifestyle, without first consulting my best friend, the young woman I'd been closest to for the best part of 10 years. I had sorted out my football career . . now I had to get my head straight and sort out my personal life, too.

Lorraine and I had been living apart since March and only saw each other occasionally. But, I still loved her and the move to Everton was just the right challenge for us to start afresh. Although I would probably have signed for Everton anyway, I needed to get Lorraine's opinion and try and persuade her to travel north with me.

Jon arranged for Lorraine to be collected by his chauffeur, Marcus, and driven to the hotel that night, while we waited patiently with the Everton trio. When Lorraine arrived, she and I took a private stroll in the hotel grounds and talked about the future and what Everton were offering.

I had just turned 23 years-old and she was only 21, so it was an enormous step for both of us to consider. Could she leave her home, her parents in Chadwell Heath, her family, friends and job, to be with me in Liverpool?

I said to her: "I need to know that if I go, you'll come with me." I was putting Lorraine on the spot because it was such a big decision for a young woman to make, but she was fine about it and said that she would go with me.

That was all I needed to hear to settle everything in my own mind.

I walked back inside the hotel and went straight up to Colin Harvey. My exact words to him were: "I'd love to sign for Everton." I shook his hand and I've never seen anyone look as happy as Colin did that night. I then shook hands with Philip Carter and Jim Greenwood, who were equally delighted, and Jon produced a bottle of champagne to mark the moment.

I signed the draft contract document, with the official details to be completed at the club next day, and the Everton trio left to drive back up the motorway no doubt feeling well satisfied to have successfully completed the deal and to have proved wrong all those people who had expected me to stay south and join Arsenal.

That left one more difficult task to perform. I borrowed Jon's mobile phone and walked outside the hotel to personally inform George Graham that I wouldn't be signing for him. My call was answered by someone who said that George had already gone out for a Chinese meal. He passed the number on to me and when I dialled it I was greeted with: "Harro."

"Oh, hello," I said, "do you have a Mr. George Graham eating there tonight?"

"You like to book a table tonight?" continued the clearly confused Chinaman.

"No, I'm trying to find Mr. Graham," I repeated.

"How many people is it for?" he answered.

I was struggling to stop myself from laughing when, fortunately, the bewildered waiter at the other end of the line found someone who could understand and speak English. George did eventually come to the phone and I told him my decision before wishing him all the best for the season, which would prove a quite successful one for him and the Gunners! George took my decision very calmly but I think he knew from our meetings that he was going to receive a 'no' from me.

The formalities were completed when my uncle Terry, a solicitor, drove down from his Coventry home to South Mimms in his Porsche in record time – about an hour! – to run his eyes over the contract before I signed it. Jon contacted the media to announce that I'd chosen Everton and all five of us – Jon, Terry, my dad, Lorraine and I – borrowed a room with a TV just in time to see ITN's News at Ten announce that I had become Britain's most costliest footballer.

We all left the hotel and were joined by Jon's wife Janine and his brother, Phil, for a meal and more celebratory drinks at an Italian restaurant in Potters Bar.

It was four o'clock in the morning before I eventually crawled into bed feeling emotionally drained but, at the same time, relieved and very happy to have made a slice of British football history.

Claret & Blues

TRUE BLUE

I AWOKE at 8am on Tuesday, July 26, in a lively mood, considering I'd had only four hours sleep following the excitement of the previous night. There wasn't time to lay in at Jon's place because we had to be up early for the journey north to Goodison Park, where I was to sign the official contract forms.

We had a number of the morning papers delivered and reading through them, there was a general feeling of surprise that I had picked Everton instead of Arsenal. Jon had arranged an exclusive with The Sun who sent a reporter round for an interview and pictures in the back garden. Then Jon, mum, dad and I made off in the comfort of Jon's Bentley again for the four-hour trip north.

The press conference at Goodison was booked for 3.00pm and the reception that awaited me reflected the size of the transfer fee involved. The fans, who had gathered in numbers outside the ground, cheered as I got out of the car and walked in through the main entrance.

There were journalists and photographers everywhere and after doing lots of interviews at the press conference, where I was pictured with pen in hand on the contract, I went into Jim Greenwood's office to formally complete the paperwork in front of witnesses. As is tradition on these occasions, the photographers wanted me on the pitch for pictures posing in a club shirt with scarf held aloft.

Next stop was the clinic in Liverpool for X-rays, where they checked out my knees, ankles, chest and monitored my heart.

Then we moved on to the training ground at Bellefield, where I underwent a more thorough medical examination by the club doctor. This was a new experience for me and I admit to feeling a bit nervous as he poked and prodded at me and literally examined every part of my body.

Having just broken the British transfer record, I couldn't blame Everton for leaving nothing to chance. But having never suffered a bad injury or undergone an operation in my life, I knew I had nothing to fear when it came to passing Everton's medical.

Having been given a clean bill of health we headed for the Bold Hotel, on Lord Street, Southport, which would become home to me and Lorraine for the next seven weeks. It wasn't a very big place, but it was fine and we felt comfortable there.

After checking into my hotel room, we walked a short distance down the road to a lovely Chinese restaurant, where we were joined by my brother Paul, who had driven up in my car. At the end of a great evening Jon and all my family piled into the Bentley for a luxurious drive back down the M6, while I made my way back to The Bold. The club said I had to be ready by 9am the next morning, when Neil Pointon would be along to collect me for my first day's training.

As I laid back on my bed, it was as if I was in a dream world. There I was, 250 miles from home in a strange town, all alone in a place I had never seen before. The transfer saga dragged on for weeks but then, suddenly, it had all been completed so quickly.

I felt really content that I had chosen the right club and was starting not only a new chapter in my career, but my life. Briefly, I reflected on what might have been at West Ham . . . if they'd done this and done that, or bought certain players, perhaps we could have gone on to win trophies and sustain the success we had in 1985/86 . . . and, despite all the goals I'd scored, had I really done all I could personally, especially in the latter months of my time there?

These were the question going through my mind but I knew, deep down, that I'd done my bit to keep West Ham in the First Division. Now it was time to move on and start afresh, there was no point in looking back.

As I stared up at the ceiling it felt like I'd walked in through one door, closed it behind me and had entered a new room. It was a big, weird and wonderful experience.

I was full of excitement about coming to Goodison but, at the same time, a little concerned about the size of the fee Everton had paid for me. At the press conference I was asked how I felt about turning down Arsenal, and was I worried about the size of the fee. It did concern me because I didn't regard myself as a two million pound player – I knew that there were other players much better than me. Many people mistakenly assume that the player who costs most is also naturally the best, but that is by no means always the case. A player is only worth what someone is prepared to pay for him.

I knew that I was a good player – on my day, a very good player – but I wasn't the best player in the country.

I also knew from the moment I joined Everton that, in the eyes of the media, I was no longer Tony Cottee . . . from here on, I would always be referred to as the Two Million Pound Man – and it was a burden that would weigh very heavily on my shoulders.

There were a lot of big challenges ahead of me, starting with defenders who would be trying that little bit harder against the player who cost more money than any other in the Football League. The press would be watching my every move, just waiting for me to fall flat on my face, and of course the Everton fans had very high expectations, too.

The pressure was on . . .

Claret & Blues

GUINNESS AND BITTER

M Y initial impression was that training with Everton seemed easier than the previous pre-season work we did at West Ham. Whereas John Lyall always worked us hard on lots of cross-country runs when we reported back after the summer break, the routine at Bellefield when I arrived there on Wednesday, July 27 seemed comparatively relaxed.

The first person I bumped into was Pat Nevin, who cost £925,000 from Chelsea and would prove a valuable friend throughout my time there, as did the two other big signings that summer, Stuart McCall (£850,000 from Bradford City) and Neil McDonald (£525,000 from Newcastle United).

There are two dressing rooms at Bellefield and Pat was already sitting in the one I was shown into. We shook hands and at least I knew that I wasn't the only one concerned about the amount of money Everton had been splashing out that summer when he said: "I'm glad to see you . . . I was really worried about the big price tag on my shoulders!"

I was the last of the four major signings to arrive and I sensed that all eyes were on me because of my record fee. I don't know whether the other players expected to find me a typically chirpy Londoner or not, but I deliberately decided to ease my way into the club. I wasn't going to set myself up for any criticism at the start and purposely kept a rather low profile with the other players during the first few weeks. I just wanted to work as hard as possible in training, get to know how the others played and show how I liked to play.

My first full day as an adopted Evertonian ended with a visit to the supporters' club player-of-the-year award. These days, the event is held at the club itself but at that time it took place in the social club, just 200 yards or so from the main entrance at Goodison Park.

Big Dave Watson was there to receive the award on this occasion but all the players were in attendance. The place was packed to the rafters with happy fans who let out a great big cheer when me and the other new boys walked in. They seemed very pleased that I'd signed for Everton instead of Arsenal.

People have said to me that I became a favourite of the Everton fans when I scored my hat-trick on my debut against Newcastle, but I believe I won them over that night at South Mimms when I turned down Arsenal. Like supporters do everywhere, the Scousers like players who want to play for their club.

I had the best part of a week living on my own on Merseyside before I drove to London to pick up Lorraine and take her to our new home in Southport. I didn't feel too lonely, though, as Neil McDonald and his wife Lynn were also staying at The Bold, so we ate our meals together and kept each other company. Neil can take a while to get used to but I'd already come across him during my England Under-21 days and I happen to like him a lot, as a person and a player. We still keep in touch and speak on the phone regularly, although Neil was to be at the centre of one or two problems later in my Everton career.

Within a week of signing for Everton, I received a letter from John Lyall in which he basically thanked me for my services and wished me all the best at my new club. I thought I had left West Ham on the best possible terms with everyone – I shook hands with the players and staff on my last day there – but, nevertheless, it was still very nice of John to go out of his way to write that letter. I'm sure that doesn't happen when every player leaves a club and his thoughtful gesture was much appreciated.

Not so pleasing was a newspaper article, which appeared soon after I arrived at Goodison, written by the former Leeds United and England striker Allan Clarke. I suppose he was paid a handsome sum by a tabloid to rubbish me in print, describing me as a "waste of money, a player who couldn't head a ball," and so on.

It was a really nasty piece, totally uncalled for, and I thought that Clarke's younger brother, Wayne, who was still at Everton when that article appeared, would have been embarrassed by it, although it never came up in conversation. Allan Clarke repeated his bitter attack on me later in the season, just before the 1989 FA Cup final, through another of his scathing newspaper articles. Then, when Wayne was moved on during that summer, he too spouted off about me in print for no reason.

So I had an early taste of what the Clarke brothers were like. I think they were simply acts of jealousy on their part because, after all, I'd effectively been bought to replace Wayne in Everton's attack.

To me, there is nothing worse than an old pro who crawls out of the woodwork now and again to launch a spiteful and unwarranted attack on a current-day player. Emlyn Hughes had an even worse reputation than Allan Clarke for doing this through his tabloid column and it's sad when people like him feel the need to slate people in the same game as themselves.

The ironic thing is, Clarke was earning money – quite a few bob I expect – off the back of me and the transfer fee Everton had paid. Then again, perhaps Clarke needed me as the foundation of his articles, because later on, when I had my problems and was banished to the reserves, he too disappeared from the scene. What a shame!

Colin Harvey and his assistant, Terry Darracott, took training between them, with the senior pro, Peter Reid, also helping out. I'd only been around the place three days when I unwittingly reduced the players in a five-a-side game to fits of laughter.

Having started back pre-season later than all the others, my legs still felt like jelly in that first week at Bellefield. I received a ball and as I turned to run into space, I tripped over it. I was lying spreadeagled on the turf when skipper Kevin Ratcliffe piped up: "HOW much did we pay for him!"

The size of my wage packet was proving a constant source of speculation to the media and, no doubt, my team mates, too. I'd rather not be specific but, as I've already said, I was earning more than double the basic I was on at West Ham.

There were various amounts bandied around, from £200,000 a year to £300,000 which, in 1988, was a hell of a lot of money. Of course, these figures were nowhere near true but the speculation didn't die down for weeks. It became obvious that some of the more senior players, who had been at the club a long time, were keen to get a slice of the action themselves.

And they must have got a result, for within a month of my much heralded arrival I heard that FIVE players were given new, improved contracts.

At the time, I guess those five must have been as pleased as Pat Nevin was to see me there!

Our pre-season build up in my first summer at Goodison included three overseas tours – one aspect of Everton life that would prove very interesting and eventful as the years went by!

We visited Switzerland for four days and after one friendly we were given the all-clear to go out and have a few beers. I returned to our hotel and was in bed by about 1.00am, but Colin Harvey's sleep was interrupted in the small hours by the roar of a motorbike coming from outside his window.

It was Neil McDonald on a 'borrowed' scooter, tearing around the car park at four in the morning, slightly the worse for wear. Apparently the other lads thought it was funny but I was told that Colin wasn't quite so amused!

Next, we went to Southern Ireland and the wonderful town of Drogheda. We flew out from Liverpool on the Friday morning and after checking into our hotel and a few hours rest, we were taken by coach to the game. A big Irish fella, called Eamonn, who was our tour guide, had the lads in fits when he picked up the microphone and turned to address his passengers, which included chairman Philip Carter and the manager at the front of the bus. "I don't want to say too much, lads, except let's get this f-----g silly game out of the way and then we can get down to the real business!" Eamonn's love of Guinness was obviously not quite matched by his interest in football. As it turned out, we won the game 1-0 and while Ireland's favourite brew is not a particular favourite of mine, the rest of the lads assured me that it went down well. It was a very enjoyable trip – the Irish people were brilliant, so friendly and welcoming, that I've always enjoyed going back there.

Our third trip took us to Spain and a match against Athletic Bilbao, who were managed by Howard Kendall at the time. We lost that one 3-2, with six men booked and one sent off. Some friendly!

We arrived back in England the Wednesday before our opening First Division game, at home to Newcastle on Saturday, August 27. The excitement was building and, not surprisingly, I was at the centre of most press attention in the days leading up to the big kick-off.

If I learned one lesson early on in my time at Everton, it was not to stick my neck out and set myself goalscoring targets that would prove difficult to live up to.

I told the press I was aiming for 25 in my first season.

CHAPTER 31

Claret & Blues

ROAD TO GLORY

ONE of the funniest aspects of my Everton debut is that I didn't even know how to get to Goodison Park by car and had to rely on Neil McDonald to show me the way there!

I had obviously been to Bellefield before, but had never made my own way to the ground, so Neil and I agreed to meet in reception at The Bold and Lorraine and I followed his car to the ground.

A crowd of 41,560 packed into the magnificent stadium for the opening match against Newcastle United and I did my bit to boost the attendance by taking up the usual five complimentary tickets allocated to each player and then buying another 19 for mine and Lorraine's family and friends.

They were all staying at the same hotel in Liverpool and to mark my debut, I'd booked a little reception room for us all to meet in after the game. I had hoped it would be a celebration party but could never have dreamt it would turn out the way it did.

I was very nervous in the dressing room before the game and coped in my usual way – by going to the toilet numerous times. As the minutes to kick-off ticked by, I looked around the dressing room and felt confident that we would be challenging for the main honours.

Some key figures from the 1987 championship team were still there – like goalkeeper Neville Southall, midfield dynamo Peter Reid, defenders Dave Watson and Ian Snodin, wingers Trevor Steven and Kevin Sheedy and my new strike partner, Graeme Sharp – with the four new signings completing what looked, on paper, a very good blend.

The club had spent big and expected results. In the previous couple of seasons at West Ham, the priority was to preserve our senior status and try to win one of the cups. At Everton, I had joined a side that was fully expected to compete for the championship. It was exactly the challenge I was looking for and the events of that epic afternoon only enhanced my belief that we would be going places.

Just 34 seconds after kick-off, the ground erupted as though we had already won the title.

From the kick-off, the usual 30 seconds of frenzied football ensued before the ball was played back to Neil McDonald, who hoisted a big, high ball from the right-back position towards Sharpy, who controlled it on his chest and then hit it first time. Newcastle 'keeper Dave Beasant could only parry the ball in my direction and I latched onto it, sweeping it home with my left foot from the edge of the box.

I could spend the rest of this book trying to explain my feelings as I turned away in triumph, but I can't explain it. I'd scored 118 league and cup goals for West Ham but my first at Goodison on that glorious day gave me the biggest thrill since I scored on my debut for the Hammers five-and-a-half years earlier.

It's one of the oldest cliches in football, but it really was a dream start for me … and it got even better. My second goal came after about 31 minutes following a neat through ball from Peter Reid, which I hit first time across Beasant. I thought it was going to miss but was jubilant as the ball went in off the post.

By the time half-time came I really fancied my chances of a hat-trick. Newcastle were very disjointed and I was certainly getting the better of my marker, Andy Thorn, who'd just joined them from Wimbledon. Newcastle had big expectations, too, but we were swarming all over them.

It was just past the hour when I completed my fairytale hat-trick. Pat Nevin had the ball on the right and played it into the space. Again, I reacted quicker than every-one else and as Beasant came out, I flicked the ball up and over him, leaving me with the relatively simple task of rolling the ball into the net as a defender lunged in too late.

I just couldn't believe it as I ran, with both arms raised in triumphant salute, towards the fans at the Gwladys Street end. It was a wonderful feeling of elation.

And to cap a memorable day, I also had a hand in our fourth goal, a header scored by Graeme Sharp. It could have been five, six or seven-nil in the end.

Afterwards, I collected three bottles of champagne from different sponsors and met up with Lorraine and her mum and dad in the players' lounge. The rest of the Cottee contingent had already made their way back to the hotel, where the celebra-tions continued late into the night.

After the individual glory attached to my hat-trick, it was very satisfying to round off a brilliant day in the company of the family and friends closest to me. After all the drama and excitement, it was just as well that Neil knew the way to the ground, as I'd have hated to have missed it!

Our next league fixture was at Coventry the following Saturday, when I was delighted to score the only goal of the game, a header from a long cross by Neil McDonald. Four goals in two league games, it was going like a dream but, as I realised in the weeks ahead, the flying start brought enormous expectations and pres-sure that would prove difficult to handle.

We suffered a draw and three defeats before crushing Southampton 4-1 at home on October 8, having gone behind in the first minute. The two I scored were among my best in an Everton shirt. I was on target again in our next game at Goodison, a 1-1 draw with Man. United in front of the live TV cameras. It was this day, with all the media attention, that I realised I was no longer known as Tony Cottee. From this point the media dubbed me the 'Two Million Pound Man'.

My partnership with Graeme Sharp showed promise, although I had to change my style of play to fit in with the way we were playing as a team. At West Ham, the ball would be passed from defence, through midfield, to the forwards. Whereas at Everton, they favoured a more direct approach.

Nev would roll the ball out to one of the full-backs, who would look to ping it upfield to Sharpy, by-passing midfield. Everything revolved around Sharpy, so I wasn't expected to be involved in any of the build-up play, as I had been at Upton Park.

That was fine if the ball was chipped in to Sharpy, but if it was driven towards him at speed, I had to try and anticipate his flick-ons. As any striker will tell you, trying to anticipate where a fellow forward – under pressure from a defender – is going to head the ball, is very difficult. The ball can fly off at any angle and you have to try and predict, in a split second, where it will drop. Even then, you still have to react first and beat the defender to the loose ball.

That frustration materialised later in my first season but in the opening weeks of the 1988/89 campaign my new partnership with Sharpy was reaping rewards. I managed to score both our goals in the last 10 minutes at Oldham to clinch a 2-0 win in the Littlewoods Cup third round replay. I had no complaints about their much-maligned plastic pitch, especially as my second strike was a spectacular effort from 30 yards. I don't think the plastic pitches used at Luton, Oldham, QPR or Preston were good for football in general, because they offered the home team so much of an advantage, and I was pleased when the league banned astroturf pitches in the top two divisions. Having said that, smaller players always seemed to be better suited to artificial surfaces and I did score my fair share playing on them.

Unfortunately the fixture computer produced a quick return to Upton Park for our league meeting on November 26. I was apprehensive and it felt very strange walking into the ground, seeing lots of old friends and then going into the visitors' dressing room to pull on a different shirt. In many respects the crowd were good to me. I had expected a mixed reception and that's what I got.

There was inevitably booing from a section of fans, while others clapped me onto the pitch. I just wanted to get out there, play the game and get off again. This was one match I wasn't looking forward to and I didn't enjoy it one bit.

The Hammers already had the look of relegation candidates when I laid on the ball for Trevor Steven, who drove a low shot underneath Allen McKnight to give us a 1-0 victory.

I enjoyed the following week's 1-0 home win over Tottenham a lot more, not least because my eighth goal for Everton also marked my 100th in the league.

Eight days later I experienced my first Merseyside derby at Anfield. It was a strange weekend routine for me, because even though our live TV game with Liverpool was scheduled for the Sunday, we still stayed overnight at a nearby hotel – after having watched a local game on the Saturday.

Our destination on this occasion was Maine Road, where we saw Manchester City comfortably beat Bradford City 4-0 in the second division. Bradford were our opponents in the fourth round of the Littlewoods Cup the following Wednesday and I thought at the time that it didn't seem a very good idea, psychologically, to see them stuffed by City.

I can echo what many non-scousers have said over the years, that you never quite enjoy a Merseyside derby as a player if you don't come from the Liverpool area. The derby matches were usually too frantic, with not enough football played, for my liking, although I suppose that's what most people expect from any derby match. It was so fast and furious and I didn't enjoy the match itself.

Wayne Clarke, who replaced the injured Sharpy, scored our goal from the penalty spot. It ended 1-1 but we were unfortunate to have a goal disallowed and I've never come closer to winning at Anfield, either before or since.

The Everton/Liverpool derbies are unique in that both sets of supporters mix comfortably together and travel to the matches in the same cars. I remember travelling on the team bus to that particular game and seeing a dad with his three kids outside the ground. The dad and one of his sons wore Everton tops, while the other two boys were sporting the red of Liverpool. Once inside the ground, I spotted a group of around 1,000 Everton fans singing away in a corner of the Kop end — yet there was still no hint of fighting because their rivalry was intense yet still friendly.

Despite the fact that there are thousands of families on Merseyside with divided football loyalties, Everton fans obviously hate losing any game to Liverpool and vice-versa. As a fan, I never really liked Liverpool when I was younger, and once I was at Everton, I disliked them even more.

I don't mean that in a nasty way, because I admire what Liverpool as a club and their players have achieved over a very long period. I just didn't like them winning everything all the time!

For the players, it is also a strange kind of rivalry, because we often bumped into each other off the field. A number of us lived near each other in the Southport area, but once we were on the pitch, every player had a fierce determination to win.

At first it was hard for me to understand the strength of feeling and split loyalties among fans in the city of Liverpool. In my days as a supporter of West Ham, London derbies usually meant crowd trouble, especially with the likes of Spurs, Chelsea and Arsenal involved. But when it comes to derby games, the scousers certainly lead the way.

Anyway, I'd rather we had all stayed at home on the eve of my first Mersey derby, for the fears expressed about the wisdom of seeing Bradford before we played them proved well founded.

We definitely turned up for the cup tie in a complacent mood, having seen them crushed at Maine Road just four days earlier, and slumped to a dismal 3-1 defeat. We just turned up in Yorkshire expecting to coast to an easy win and got what we deserved.

Everton don't have a good record in the League Cup, having never won the trophy, and this was just the latest in a long line of disappointments. At least Colin Harvey admitted after the game at Valley Parade that he'd made a mistake taking us to see them play Man. City a few days before.

Things looked brighter in the league. An unbeaten run of 10 matches at the end of 1988 lifted us to fourth place going into the New Year, before our season turned for the worst at Nottingham Forest on January 2. Trevor Steven missed a penalty that could have put us one up. Instead, we lost 2-0 and began sliding down the table.

Arsenal brushed us aside, 3-1, at Goodison on January 14, their fans taking great delight in taunting me throughout the game with chants of: "We all agree, Merson is better than Cottee." I expected the stick for choosing the Toffees instead of the

Gunners in the summer and couldn't complain when their fans burst into chorus. I saw the funny side, although not as far as the result was concerned.

We didn't manage another win in the league until I netted the winner against Sheffield Wednesday on March 11. By then, our only hope of glory rested on the FA Cup, where we were making good progress.

After scraping a 1-1 draw at West Brom in the third round, after being absolutely battered, we beat them 1-0 in the replay. It was the same story in the fourth round at Plymouth, where we were under pressure before holding them 1-1. This time we comfortably won the replay at home 4-0.

Another away draw in the fifth round saw us visit Barnsley and, despite winning 1-0, it was more comfortable than the scoreline suggested.

Our quarter-final opponents at Goodison were Wimbledon, the Cup holders whose visit attracted much more attention than would normally have been the case due to an incident that had happened during our league encounter at Everton a month or so earlier, when Vinny Jones was sent-off for head-butting Kevin Ratcliffe.

BBC chose the tie – billed as a grudge match – for live transmission on Match of the Day that Sunday, but it turned out to be a rather timid affair. There was very little football played and Stuart McCall netted the only goal to send us into a semi-final clash with Norwich City.

The 1-1 draw with Wimbledon in February was a very heated affair. The 'Crazy Gang' were in their element but I've got no time for their direct approach and intimidating tactics. To me, there is no excuse for it but their success in winning the FA Cup the previous year obviously justified their antics.

Unfortunately, a number of other clubs – the likes of Dave Bassett's Sheffield United, Steve Coppell's Crystal Palace and John Beck's Cambridge United – followed Dons' rough and ready approach. Perhaps I shouldn't blame Wimbledon too much, because the origins of the long-ball game go back to Graham Taylor's Watford side in the early 80s, and the dubious appointment of Charles Hughes as the FA Director of Football.

To ask young defenders to simply kick the ball into the last third of the field as quickly as possible, is just pathetic and totally alien to how everybody else in the football world plays the game.

What people who have advocated the long-ball game fail to realise is that the direct approach will only ever achieve limited success – as Wimbledon did by winning the FA Cup and staying in the top flight, while Taylor's Watford finished runners-up to Liverpool in 1982/83. These sides can be very difficult to beat and intimidating to play against, but I'm totally against their philosophy.

It really annoys me when managers and coaches try to justify their long-ball theories by claiming that they don't have players good enough to play any other way. That's rubbish, a cop out. There are plenty of talented players around, but it's up to the managers and coaches to encourage them and spend more time getting them to do the right things.

After my first Christmas at Everton, my form definitely started to dip. I wasn't getting as many chances as I did earlier in the campaign and the team as a whole lost its way. After scoring against Middlesbrough on Boxing Day, I went six league and four FA Cup games without scoring, which gave the Press plenty to get their teeth into.

Without doubt, the pressure of being the 'Two Million Pound Man' and the lack of goals was beginning to weigh heavily on my shoulders around this time. Although I kept plugging away, I couldn't really see where my next goal was coming from. I was getting only one or two chances a game and, of course, I couldn't afford to miss them when we were creating so little as a team.

I wasn't getting the service I had been used to at West Ham, which, on the face of it, may seem surprising when you consider we had two class wingers in Steven and Sheedy supplying crosses. The fact is, Trevor didn't have a particularly good season – I think he knew he'd be on his way to Glasgow Rangers at the end of the season anyway – and when he or Sheedy did get into promising positions, they invariably looked to pick out Sharpy, who they'd played with for so long.

I felt as if I was being by-passed and the team wasn't playing to my strengths. Crosses were generally hit long towards the big man at the far post, few were delivered hard and low for my benefit. Not that Sharpy was cashing in either, because he, too, struggled for form in the early months of 1989 as the team slipped into the bottom half of the table.

Looking through my diary, I recall certain conversations with Colin about my problems. He said the obvious things . . . "keep plugging away, it's bound to take a while for you to settle down here". . . that sort of thing.

But after Christmas he had a go at me for travelling back down to London, which I was doing more or less every week. I wouldn't say I was pining for London, but it was a release for me and Lorraine to visit our families and friends at weekends. With seven London grounds to visit in the season, it was very convenient to stay over on Saturday night and spend Sundays with the people we had left behind, before driving back to Southport on Sunday night.

Colin was clearly concerned that the constant commuting back and forth was taking its toll on me. My argument, though, was that it did me good to get away from the pressures of being the player who was no longer doing what he was paid to do and had been bought to do.

When you are down on your luck and confidence, it often takes a slice of good fortune to turn things around again, which is what happened to me on Valentine's Day. I mishit a weak volley that Aston Villa's stand-in 'keeper Kevin Poole caught, then let slip through his legs after just four minutes. We eventually drew the game 1-1 but I was still very relieved to score, albeit one of the poorest shots I've ever attempted.

It had to take a flukey goal like that to end my drought – there was no way I was going to score a normal one the way things were going for me at the time.

After missing our 3-2 defeat at Derby due to a sore ankle, I returned to score the only goal in the next league match, again after four minutes, at home to Sheffield Wednesday. While it was good to get back in the scoring groove, I still didn't feel happy either with my own form or the team's performance.

Colin left us all in no doubt that this was the view he shared, too, after we played very badly and lost 2-0 in blizzard conditions at Newcastle. I was taken off with 13 minutes to go and in the dressing room afterwards he read the riot act. I was pleased to hear that night that my old mate, Frank McAvennie, had re-signed for West Ham, but my mind was on the following morning – when our day off was cancelled and we were ordered to report for training.

It was like a morgue at Bellefield. With no sign of Colin, his number two, Terry Darracott, or 'Tex' as we all called him, led us on an eight-lap circuit of the training ground – our punishment for the previous night's debacle.

As a player, I don't believe this achieves much, except get the players' backs up. It certainly messed up our routine because when we reported for training on the Friday, the day before Millwall visited Goodison, all we did was soak in the bath and have a massage. Our legs were too tired and stiff to train in the normal way after being given the runaround earlier in the week at St. James' Park and Bellefield!

Not that the soothing treatment did me much good – with Stuart McCall, I was dropped for the Millwall match, the first time in my Everton career (but by no means the last!) that I'd been left out of the side.

Equally annoying was that I found out in the morning papers, instead of direct from my manager. If Colin was going to leave me out, I would have thought he'd have the courtesy to inform me first before telling the Press. I would have respected him a lot more for that.

Colin gave no explanation for dropping me. As I've said, I read about it in the morning papers and Colin confirmed the bad news when he announced the line-up in the dressing room. I came on for the last five minutes of a tame 1-1 draw, but was recalled to the team for the trip to Middlesbrough two days later because Sharpy was unfit.

I scored in a 3-3 draw at Ayresome Park and then again in the next match at home to QPR – thanks to a backpass by Peter Reid, who was on loan to Rangers, having loaded the bullets for me from Everton's midfield earlier in the season.

But after losing 2-0 at Arsenal, I became the scapegoat again and was the only player dropped from the following home game, a 3-2 win against Charlton. After Highbury, I wrote in my diary: 'I played average but the service wasn't good.'

But it wasn't only my place in the Everton team that occupied my thoughts as the FA Cup semi-final beckoned.

CHAPTER 32

Claret & Blues

SLEEPLESS NIGHTS

AFTER staying at the Bold Hotel for our first seven weeks on Merseyside, we lived in rented accommodation for the next seven months. We looked at property in Chester, Manchester and Southport and in February 1989, finally found the house we wanted in the wonderful north-west seaside town of Southport.

The spacious four-bedroomed house in Birkdale was actually owned by former Northern Ireland manager Billy Bingham who, to complete a coincidental football triangle, had sold his previous house to Peter Beardsley! It was as though that house belonged to an adopted Evertonian because, of course, Billy had previously played and managed the Toffees before his second spell as Irish manager.

Our new home, which we moved into on April 17, was situated just half a mile from the famous Open golf course at Birkdale and we stayed there throughout the rest of my Everton years.

Living at Southport was one of the best decisions we ever made. It's within easy reach of Liverpool, about half-hour's drive, and the town is really a haven for Merseyside football folk. Gary Gillespie lived just four doors away from us, Peter Beardsley's place was just across the other side of the green, Kenny Dalglish and Steve McMahon were more or less opposite, Sharpy and Sheedy lived just a little way up the road and Ian Snodin also lived nearby. We were all based within two square miles of each other.

With its splendid promenade, superb golf courses and good schools and other amenities, it's a beautiful part of the country to live. I played the Hillside golf course once, as a guest, but I'm embarrassed to admit that in six years, I never played the championship course at Birkdale, which was just half a mile from our home. It's the equivalent of living in London and never going to visit the Tower of London . . . and I have never been there either!

With the FA Cup semi-final just five days away, I was obviously very concerned about being left out of the Charlton game, especially as Colin said that not only would there be changes for that match, but next Saturday's as well.

It was hard to swallow being dropped for the second time in a month, although I didn't believe I had an automatic right to a semi-final place. I knew I hadn't been playing well, but neither had the team as a whole, and it just niggled me that I seemed to be singled out for the blame. If there had been three or four changes, perhaps it would have been easier to accept.

I've got a lot of respect for Colin as a person and as a coach and tactician, and will be forever grateful to him for bringing me to Everton. But he undoubtedly had a problem communicating with people and, as I say, I was never told where I was going wrong or how he thought I might be able improve my game. Instead, he preferred to let his actions speak louder than words.

As we had the day off after the Monday night win over Charlton, and Colin wasn't at Bellefield that Wednesday, I had to wait until Thursday before I could speak to him about my unsatisfactory situation. He said that he'd expected great things of me and his other three major signings and if he wasn't seeing it, he'd leave me out. I was hoping to get a reassurance from him that I would be playing against Norwich in the semi-final on Saturday, but it wasn't forthcoming as I left his office no more reassured than when I entered it.

None of Colin's new boys had really taken Everton by storm though. Pat Nevin suffered an injury in only his third game and missed the next 12 in the league; Neil McDonald was actually dropped after six league matches and didn't start a first team fixture again until late December; and Stuart McCall, who held on to the number eight shirt for the first two-thirds of the season, found himself dropped or on the subs' bench in the latter stages of 1988/89.

I've always said that you can expect a new signing, or a youngster just promoted to the first team, to do well for the first half a dozen or so games. After that, he needs time to settle down and in the main, it takes most players the best part of a season to fully settle into a new team. Even after my spectacular start, I knew it would still take me the best part of a season to really settle in and get used to how Everton played as a team, the strengths (and weaknesses) of my new team mates and for them to learn what makes me tick.

My own form was very disappointing and I was definitely struggling to come to terms with Everton's style of play. It also took me a while to get used to the northern way of live, which is much more laid back in Southport compared to where I'd lived all my life. Everything is on a much smaller scale to London and it inevitably took a while to settle in. Having said that, I must say that the people up there were always fantastic to me and Lorraine – they couldn't have done more to make us feel very welcome.

The Everton fans were also very supportive of me. I think they could see that given the right service, I would score goals for their team. It soon became clear, though, that I joined the Toffees in a period of transition – a transitional period that would last throughout my time there.

The more I struggled to find form and score goals, the more the papers speculated on my future. 'What had happened to the Two Million Pound Man?' they kept asking. I couldn't wait for my first season to end because everything was beginning to get on top of me.

People also questioned whether I'd done the right thing by joining Everton, especially as Arsenal were on course for the championship. But I never regretted joining Everton, I just didn't know how I could find a way to regain form and the goalscoring habit.

Even though we had got to the semi-final, we were still not playing well and hardly deserved to be one step away from Wembley.

The semi-final against Norwich was set for Villa Park on Saturday, April 15, with Liverpool facing Nottingham Forest in the other semi at Hillsborough the same day. After my meeting with Colin on the Thursday, we travelled down to Birmingham after training the next day and all the players were still very much in the dark about who would be playing as our bus pulled up at our hotel.

But I think that every player should be told the day before a game whether he will be playing, so that he can prepare properly, especially for a match as important as the FA Cup semi-final, which most of us in the squad were experiencing for the first time.

So as I got off the bus, I walked alongside Colin and turned to him saying: "Look, am I playing tomorrow?" To which he replied: "Have a good night's sleep." "But does that mean I'm playing or what?" I continued. "Have a good night's sleep," he repeated, "I'll be naming the side tomorrow."

Colin's half-smile, although though not the absolute confirmation I was looking for, suggested I took it as a 'yes'.

My diary confirms that I had a 'nightmare sleep', although this couldn't be blamed on my regular room-mate, Pat Nevin. 'Paddy' and I struck up a very good friendship and had some interesting late-night political debates, bearing in mind that he is a Socialist and I'm Conservative. Funny that Pat should hold such strong left-wing views – I always thought he was our right-winger!

I'm not the most relaxed sleeper at the best of times – I tend to think more in bed than at any other time of the day – but in the last two or three months of the season, probably due to my lack of form, I hadn't been sleeping at all well, and I had another restless night before the semi-final.

My belief that I would play up front with Sharpy, at the expense of Wayne Clarke, was confirmed by Colin when we arrived at Villa Park, where the fans from Everton and Norwich made it a real carnival atmosphere.

The game itself was a bit drab. We went one up in the 26th minute when Ian Crook sliced Trevor Steven's cross onto the bar. Kevin Sheedy hit the rebound against the post before 'Paddy' finally tapped the ball into the net.

We went in at half-time winning 1-0 and had our usual team talk. I, and as far as I know we, was completely oblivious to anything else that was happening at Sheffield or anywhere else in the world.

In the second half, Gunn denied us a second when he made a great save from my header. Although we never really looked like adding to our lead, Norwich didn't look like scoring anyway. In the end we were fairly comfortable 1-0 winners and the game itself lacked the passion and drama normally associated with a big occasion.

When the final whistle went, some of our fans ran onto the pitch from the sides of the ground to celebrate and a few of them tried to lift me up in the air. I was mobbed and actually lost my shirt to a determined souvenir hunter. I eventually managed to pull myself away from the scrum on the pitch and walked towards our supporters who were fenced in at the end nearest the players' tunnel – opposite the Holte End.

I was going absolutely mad with joy. It's every player's dream to play in an FA Cup Final and after the difficult first season I'd had, it was overwhelming for me, emotionally, to be heading for a dream trip to Wembley – my first Cup Final.

I was clapping our fans, and they were still cheering me as I took off my shin-pads and threw them into the crowd. One last round of applause and I was off towards the tunnel to continue the celebrations in the dressing room with the rest of the lads.

As I got to the entrance to the players' tunnel, which is right in the corner of the ground, I was stopped in my tracks by a policeman who wore a flat cap, which meant he was a chief inspector. He put his arms around me in a rather aggressive manner and shouted: "People like you should be locked up, you're a disgrace."

I couldn't believe what the inspector was saying to me, as he didn't explain himself. "What the bloody hell are you talking about?" I said, brushing him aside. I was annoyed because, as far as I could tell, he seemed to be trying to stop me celebrating reaching my first ever Cup Final, which was crazy. Had throwing my shinpads into the crowd really provoked this reaction? I couldn't work out what was going on.

When I got back to the dressing room, everyone seemed really pleased, as you'd expect after winning the semi-final. We shook hands and congratulated each other. I'd imagine it was just like the scene in any other winning semi-finalist's dressing room.

But the mood was about to turn very, very black...

Claret & Blues

MERSEYSIDE MOURNING

IT wasn't until I took off my kit and walked through to the bath area, where I sat next to Kevin Ratcliffe, that I first knew of anything that had gone wrong at Hillsborough earlier on that hot, sunny afternoon of Saturday, April 15. Kevin said: "Have you heard that 20 people were killed at Hillsborough?"

I looked at him blankly, barely able to believe what I was hearing. It didn't really sink in at first because I was still on so much of a high at the thought of reaching the Final, although I thought that it did perhaps explain why the copper had been so upset when we clashed in the tunnel earlier. Perhaps he thought I was inciting the crowd, which I certainly wasn't.

Although Kevin had heard about the tragedy in Sheffield, we were not told collectively of the disaster. And I don't know whether Kevin had heard about it at half-time, but not mentioned it to anybody, or what. I certainly had no knowledge of the disaster, which unfolded just prior to kick-off at the Liverpool-Forest semi-final and forced it to be abandoned after six minutes, until he told me in the bath after our game.

As Lorraine had made her own way down to Villa Park, I went back to Southport with her in our car instead of travelling on the bus. As we drove along the motorway, which was jam-packed with fans heading back to Merseyside, the scale of the disaster suddenly hit us.

Radio announced that the Hillsborough death toll was 30; five miles further up the M6 and it became 40; another 15 minutes and the total increased to 50 and so on. We were tuned to the radio throughout our three-hour journey and the death toll kept rising. We just couldn't take in what was going on, it was so depressing.

It should have been the happiest day of mine and Pat Nevin's career, a first Cup Final to look forward to, but this was no time for celebrations. It's a curious experience of mine that whenever something good has happened to me, there has usually been something bad waiting around the corner. I'd experienced it with my goal at Sheffield four years earlier, when I learned afterwards of the horrific Bradford fire, and I could perhaps go back to my schoolboy days and relate similar feelings of turmoil when West Ham said that they would be offering me a contract, but not my best mate John Cornwell.

Football, like life, is full of highs and lows.

By the time we arrived home from Birmingham, the death toll had reached 75. I turned on the TV for regular bulletins as the full horror of Hillsborough gripped the nation. Lorraine and I had previously booked a table at a restaurant in Southport that night but we phoned to cancel it. We couldn't go out, not after what had happened at Hillsborough. The whole of Britain, not just the good people of Liverpool, was in a state of shock that so many innocent fans, including young children and women, could possibly die and suffer appalling injuries at a football match.

Match of the Day declined to show highlights of our semi-final, in fact they didn't show any football out of respect for those who'd died. The programme was devoted entirely to the Hillsborough disaster, showing the terrible pictures that brought home to us the full scale of the tragedy.

When I awoke on Sunday and read the papers, it was reported that 95 Liverpool fans had died on the Leppings Lane terrace. Lorraine and I discussed the possibility of driving over to Anfield, where fans were going to lay wreaths, to pay our respects, but decided not to. It was a difficult one, because we didn't want to appear patronising – an Everton player and his wife sharing the private grief of Liverpool fans – and, besides, I think it might have been a bit too much for us emotionally.

We were due to move into our new house the next day but the happiness normally associated with moving was tempered by the tragic events of that Saturday.

Everyone on Merseyside – be they Liverpool or Everton fans – was moved by the events of Hillsborough. Everywhere you went people spoke about the disaster. Although I never knew anybody directly involved in the disaster, or anyone who lost a member of their family on the Leppings Lane terrace, there was simply no escaping the awful feeling of sadness and sorrow that swept across Merseyside in the days and weeks following April 15, 1989 – the blackest day in British football history.

The horror of Hillsborough wasn't confined to Liverpool Football Club or its supporters. We knew that for every Liverpool fan who died, his or her loss would leave its mark on Everton supporters, too, because of the divided loyalties in so many scouse households. It was obvious that Everton fans who travelled to Birmingham for our semifinal would have known relatives or friends who went to the other semi-final. Sadly, some never saw them again.

Everton players were given the following Monday morning off and told to report for training later, at 1pm, in preparation for the following night's home game against Derby County. The mood was very low, no one hardly spoke a word, and after a quiet five-a-side we all went off home again. Quite rightly, the match with Derby was postponed as the city of Liverpool united in grief.

On the Wednesday, Everton reacted by announcing that they would be taking down all the perimeter fencing at Goodison – a move that would later become compulsory following publication of Lord Justice Taylor's report into football ground safety that did so much to change the face of the game in the wake of Hillsborough.

A catalogue of errors led to the loss of those 95 lives. One of the first mistakes was to allocate the greater share of tickets to Forest fans, bearing in mind that Liverpool attracted much higher average attendances.

I don't agree with former Forest manager Brian Clough who laid most of the blame on Liverpool fans who arrived late at the ground and, some, without tickets.

Of course, those people who tried to push their way to the front of the stand only added to the problems, but the police also made serious errors of judgment in the heat of the moment by opening the gates and allowing more fans to enter an already over-crowded area of the terracing.

There were communication breakdowns all round, and of course with the perimeter fencing in place to keep the fans penned in behind the goal, there was no escape route for the fans crushed at the front.

It's very unfair to blame any one person or group of people in particular. The sad-dest aspect of all is that it took the death of 95 Liverpool fans to make everyone realise how unsafe most of our football grounds were.

Not only did 95 innocent people die (later to become 96 with the tragic death of Tony Bland some three years later), let's not forget the others who survived the disaster but suf-fered serious injuries, or those who are still affected by it. It may be of precious little con-solation to their families and friends of the deceased, but the comfort today's supporters are accustomed to at grounds all over Britain is the legacy of Hillsborough. Now, most football stadia have finally come to terms with the 20th century and are ready for the 21st.

As a young teenager, I supported West Ham at grounds all over the country and stood on crumbling terraces. But, like all the other people, I never complained. No one turned around and said, this ground should be closed or that one should be shut, because they're unsafe. We supporters accepted the situation without question, because we knew no different.

The warnings of Ibrox, Heysel and Bradford were ignored for too long. Now, most of our Premiership and First Division grounds are superb. I think fans in general did some soul-searching and re-examined their behaviour at matches; police, aided by CCTV cameras and better stewarding by the clubs themselves, got a grip of the situa-tion; the old concrete steps were replaced by seats; fences were swiftly removed.

At least something positive came out of Hillsborough but while the rest of the world mourned and then got on with life, the wounds took much longer to heal in Liverpool.

The Everton players reported for training on the morning of Friday, April 21 and after the session the team bus headed for Anfield, where all the players and the manager walked on to the pitch. It was quite unbelievable to see all the rows of flowers that had been laid on The Kop and across the penalty area in front of the goal at that end. Outside, there was a massive queue of people waiting to lay their own wreaths and little mementoes.

We stood around the centre circle, heads bowed, in a minute's silence. If we're hon-est with ourselves, we have all stood to observe a minute's silence and not done so with quite the sincerity we would have if a loved one or someone close to us had died. But at Anfield that afternoon, I think we all related to what had gone on . . . it was a minute's silence in every respect.

The Liverpool fans clapped us off the pitch, and as we made our way on to the bus football was the last thing we felt like at the end of a very distressing week. I thought our game at Tottenham that day should have been postponed.

More importantly, I felt the FA Cup itself should have been abandoned at that point. I thought so at the time – it's not a view I put forward in hindsight, after we'd lost to Liverpool in the Final.

Although it would have been very disappointing to miss out on the Cup Final, I felt the heart and soul had already been ripped out of the competition. The magic and romance of the FA Cup had died along with those 95 fans.

I also thought it unreasonable of the FA to expect the Liverpool and Forest players to replay their ill-fated semi-final, which was switched to Old Trafford.

In 1993, the Grand National was abandoned after two farcically failed attempts to start the race at Aintree. The Jockey Club said 'that's enough' and the records show it as a 'void' race, which is what the FA should have said after Hillsborough.

If the football record books had read: 'FA Cup 1988/89 – competition abandoned', that would have been a far more fitting epitaph to the Hillsborough victims. Instead it says: 'Liverpool – winners' . . . a result just like there has been every other year.

Except that no other year was like 1989. By cancelling The Cup, it would have been a sensitive way for football as a whole to have shown its respects for the people who lost their lives and it would have ensured that in 100 years time people would associate the FA Cup of 1989 with Hillsborough.

I don't think anyone connected with Everton would really have minded being deprived of a Cup Final, much as we were hungry for success. After all that had gone on since semi-final day, all the gloss had been removed from reaching the big occasion in any case. There no longer seemed any point to it.

The Everton players didn't discuss the pros and cons of playing the Cup Final. This is just my personal view and I thought carefully about it as the days unfolded before Wembley.

We, at Goodison, were in a no-win situation, too. If we'd won the Cup, many people would have said that the silverware should have gone to Liverpool because of Hillsborough. And when Liverpool did win, everyone outside Goodison said they deserved to anyway.

On the morning of Saturday, April 29, the Everton players were given the option of attending the Hillsborough memorial service at Liverpool Cathedral. Not all the players went to the requiem mass and although I'm not at all religious – I'd only been to church once before – I felt it was something I really had to do, because I would have felt very guilty if I hadn't bothered to go. Scousers are such wonderful people and, as a cockney who'd been warmly welcomed into their hearts, something inside me said I should be there to pay my respects.

Seven Everton players attended, along with all the Liverpool players and officials. The service was televised live and a very emotional occasion it proved to be. When a lone choir boy sang Liverpool FC's anthem, 'You'll Never Walk Alone', it brought a lump to my throat.

Afterwards, we collected the other lads who had been training at Bellefield in the afternoon and made our way to London, this time to face Nottingham Forest in the Simod Cup Final the next day. I'd scored a few goals along the way but it was the competition nobody showed much interest in unless they got to the final.

As it happened, the Final was a tremendous game, with end to end football, excitement and seven goals. Unfortunately our three (of which I scored two) couldn't prevent Forest from taking the trophy 4-3 on a lovely spring day, with Lee Chapman scoring twice for them.

It was the first time in a couple of months that not only had I scored two well-taken goals, but I'd played well, too, which was reassuring after all the self-doubt that had crept in.

It's always nice to score your first goal at Wembley and, in fact, this was my first full game there. It was another schoolboy dream fulfiled, if not in the most glamorous of cup finals.

Back to the league, and our next match was the Merseyside derby at Goodison. I hadn't enjoyed my first taste of derby action at Anfield the previous December but this was one of the most entertaining goalless draws I've played in, with plenty of chances at each end.

The match – Liverpool's first since the horror of Hillsborough – was preceded by another minute's silence, but this was a night for 46,000 scousers to get together and show their unrivalled close-knit community spirit inside a football stadium.

Drifting along in mid-table, our remaining league matches were pretty meaningless, it was a case of ticking along until the Cup Final. For Liverpool, it was different because they were also locked in a two-horse race with Arsenal for the title and had a fixture backlog to contend with.

These were crucial times for West Ham, too, as they teetered on the brink of relegation. A run of four straight wins had raised their hopes of surviving the drop but my old club was still badly in need of more points when they arrived at Goodison on May 13 – a week before the Cup Final.

Stuart Slater set the Hammers buzzing with his first league goal for the club but we eventually overpowered them and won comfortably 3-1. I was very much aware before the game that if we won, it could be curtains for my old club. I'd supported and played for West Ham for the first 23 years of my life and while I had to act professionally and do my best for Everton, it would have been very easy not to have had a particularly good game that day. You don't just stop caring for your club after you've left them.

I kept in touch with people like Alan Dickens and Paul Ince during the season to find out how they were doing. John Lyall bought David Kelly to replace me and although he tried hard, Kelly found it very difficult to bridge the gap between third division, where he'd scored plenty of goals for Walsall, and the first division.

And I knew, too, that Allen McKnight was having a bad time in goal until he was finally dropped and they recalled the veteran Phil Parkes.

I was disappointed to see West Ham struggling near the foot of the table but to be honest, their plight didn't surprise me. The warning signs had been there in the previous couple of seasons, when we had flirted with relegation before escaping in a mad scramble at the end of each season.

I was still sad when the Hammers eventually lost their final game, 5-1, at Anfield and were relegated along with north-east rivals Newcastle United and Middlesbrough.

I couldn't help thinking (and no doubt the Hammers' fans felt the same) that, with all due respect to Kelly, John Lyall should have looked to have invested the £2 million he got for me in a proven First Division striker. David has done very well in the First Division, for Newcastle and Wolves, since he left Upton Park, and has been a success for the Republic of Ireland too, but there is a question mark against his ability to perform consistently well at Premiership level.

While West Ham had to try and pick themselves up and rebuild in the Second Division, all thoughts at Everton turned to the FA Cup Final.

Claret & Blues

WEMBLEY LET DOWN

AS we settled into the Bell House Hotel in Buckinghamshire on the eve of the FA Cup Final, I felt none of the anxieties about team selection that had troubled me in the build up to the semi-final. I hadn't quite regained top form but I knew I'd done enough to earn my place alongside Sharpy.

My old 'mate' Allan Clarke, brother of the player I kept out of the side, had another swipe at me in his newspaper column, claiming he'd warned at the start of the season what a waste of money I'd be and that he saw no reason to change his opinion. It was another pathetic article.

After another restless night, I woke at 8am and after breakfast gave my first-ever interview to Sky TV. The newly launched satellite channel was still very new to football and no one could have imagined then how powerful they would become four years later with the formation of the Premier League.

A cock-up with the players' pool earlier in the week saw a miss-mash of jackets and trousers arrive from Top Man. But as some of us couldn't find a suit to fit, we sent them back and hastily made arrangements for another company to supply our Cup Final outfits, so at least we all looked smart for the journey to Wembley.

It was still possible then to drive the length of Wembley Way and after the usual game of cards on the coach, the players sat back to watch the fans make their way towards the famous twin towers. As we got close, the giant double doors opened and our coach edged forward into the tunnel area. It was then that we discovered we had been allocated the away team's dressing room, which I thought at the time could be an unlucky omen, having always used the home dressing room.

After inspecting the hallowed turf, on what was a scorching day with the temperature approaching the 90s, we returned to the sanctuary of our dressing room. Maintaining routine, I stayed inside to go through my stretching warm-up exercises as kick-off time approached, rather than join the other players who had ventured out on to the pitch again to soak up some more of the atmosphere.

There were about 10 minutes to go when Colin's team talk was interrupted by two pranksters wearing large hairy masks. It was Terry 'Tex' Darracott and our club doctor, Ian Irvine, in disguise. The stunt had obviously been stage-managed with Colin's knowledge and approval and did much to ease the mounting tension and spark laughter among the lads, particularly as 'Tex' and 'The Doc' are both bald!

Once you pass through the tunnel the roar of the crowd hits you, the last thing the players want to do is line up for the national anthem and pre-match handshakes with royalty and other dignitaries. You just want to get on with the game.

We lined up with Neville Southall in goal, Neil McDonald at right-back, Pat Van Den Hauwe left-back, with Dave Watson and Kevin Ratcliffe in the centre of defence; Trevor Steven and Paul Bracewell centre midfield, Pat Nevin wide right and Kevin Sheedy wide left; Sharpy and myself up front. The only real debate before the game was who would be on the bench. Stuart McCall and Ian Wilson got the nod.

Everton started as brightly as the afternoon sunshine, spraying the ball around and showing plenty of good movement in the first five minutes or so. Liverpool had hardly had a kick when, all of a sudden, they won possession on the edge of their box and Steve McMahon hit a magnificent through ball to Ronnie Whelan. He squared it to John Aldridge whose first time shot found the net. I couldn't believe it, it was a real sucker-punch that knocked both me and the team for six.

It was still 1-0 to the Reds at half-time and the match was by no means a classic, more like a stalemate, when Colin introduced our subs midway through the second half. Wilson came on for Sheedy on the left, with McCall taking over in midfield from Bracewell.

As the final drifted into the last 10 minutes, we did what we had often done in these situations – threw big 'Waggy' into the attack. Dave's an inspirational figure and having failed to convert possession into goals, we needed his presence in attack.

It did the trick, as Sharpy touched the ball off to me and I knocked it out to Pat Nevin. He had a little run before laying it off to Dave, who hit a shot on the angle. Bruce Grobbelaar palmed the ball loose and I followed in hoping it would drop at my feet. I got very close to Grobbelaar and virtually had to jump over him on the goalline. But Stuart McCall had spotted the chance, too, and saved the day by toe-poking the loose ball into the empty net.

When Stuart made contact with the ball, I was actually standing on the goalline in what was, undoubtedly, an offside position. I couldn't do anything about it, because it was the momentum of my run that took me towards the net at the end where our supporters were – opposite the tunnel. I was just so relieved that I wasn't given offside because I don't think the Everton fans would have ever forgiven me.

All hell broke lose. The Everton players were jubilant; some of our fans were on the pitch celebrating (the fences were taken down after Hillsborough); and when I asked the ref how much time remained, he confirmed it as 23 seconds!

There was barely time for Liverpool to kick-off again than the referee blew to signal that extra-time would be needed.

The Final was a tale of two substitutes – Stuart McCall and Ian Rush, who came on for Aldridge. And extra-time was just five minutes old when the lethal Rushie put Liverpool ahead with a great shot into the top corner.

A few minutes later, we won a corner that was headed out to the edge of the box. Stuart controlled it with his chest and his volley nestled nicely in the corner. 2-2. Our fans were on the pitch again and most of us at that stage were probably thinking of a replay.

Except Rushie. Within a minute of scoring our second equaliser, John Barnes put a great ball in for Rushie to score with a header to make it 3-2 in the first period of extra-time.

We were very tired, mentally and physically, and had nothing more to give. The second period was a non-event and Liverpool held on to win the Cup.

As soon as the whistle went, it all became a blur for me. Personally, I knew I'd let myself down, because I hadn't played well and their skipper Alan Hansen did such a good job on me that I never had a shot in 120 minutes. I had a losers' medal in my hand before I knew where I was. I don't even remember going up the steps to collect it.

Even as I was walking off the pitch, totally dejected, Everton fans were coming up to me saying "well done' and "don't worry, we all love you," which was incredible. When I got to within 50 yards of the tunnel, tears began streaming down my face. The game had passed me by . . . I just thought I'd let myself down, I'd let the club down and I'd let the other players down.

Although most people wanted Liverpool to win the Cup after what had happened at Hillsborough, that didn't make defeat any easier for the Evertonians to swallow.

Afterwards, we made our way to the Royal Lancaster Hotel for what should have been a celebration party, but no one was in the mood for it. 'Tex', our compere for the evening, tried to lighten the mood by cracking a few jokes and leading a sing-song, and 'Ratters' said a few words on behalf of the players, but it was a big dampener.

My dad and brother, who have always been very honest with me, shared the disappointment and let me know how poorly I had played. Not that I needed telling at the end of such a dismal day.

At the time, I tried to console myself in the belief that, OK, so we hadn't won anything this season, but we would surely be back at Wembley or challenging for more silverware again next season. Really, it had all happened too easily for me . . . two visits to Wembley in the space of a few weeks, even though neither me nor the team had been playing that well. I was taking it for granted.

The lads went to Magaluf for a week to try and cheer themselves up, but I missed out because I was about to make my first – and last – start for the full England team.

Claret & Blues

NATIONAL PRIDE

AFTER six previous appearances as substitute – three during my time at West Ham and three at Everton – the disappointment of losing the FA Cup Final was considerably eased a week later when I finally made my full England debut against Scotland on May 27, 1989.

Starting the Rous Cup match in the number 10 shirt at Hampden Park, Glasgow, was the fulfilment of a boyhood dream that began many years earlier.

It is every player's ambition to play for his country and I have always pulled on the England shirt with great pride ever since I earned my first youth caps in the former Yugoslavia in September 1982, at the age of 17.

But, having been ignored by England at schoolboy level, my first involvement with the Football Association came in July 1981, when I was invited as an apprentice on a three-day youth coaching and development session run by the England youth coach, John Cartwright, at the Lilleshall national school.

The group of apprentices at that get-together included Stewart Robson (Arsenal), who went on to become my team mate at West Ham, and three youngsters who became future team mates of mine at Everton – Paul Rideout (Swindon Town), Trevor Steven (Burnley) and Ian Snodin (Doncaster Rovers). Although there were a number of others who later enjoyed good careers as professionals, including: Danny Wallace, Mark Walters, Mark Wright, Nigel Winterburn, Alan McLeary and Keith Stevens.

Later that year, I was selected in an FA Youth squad to play a Public Schools XI, along with fellow Hammers apprentices Alan Dickens and George Parris, but the game was postponed due to the bad winter weather.

The next get-together was in February 1982, although it was not until the mini tour of Yugoslavia in the first week of September that year that I represented England at youth level. John Cartwright, a real football purist who resigned from his job after a fall-out with the FA over policy, was replaced by David Burnside, and I was very pleased to be chosen, along with Dicko, after top-scoring in my first season of youth football at West Ham.

The tournament proved a personal triumph for me. I celebrated my debut in the town of Pula with a hat-trick in a 3-1 win against a Yugoslavian XI who replaced the withdrawn Greek team. Although the record books don't credit this match as an official international, no one could take away my three goals, scored with great pride in the white shirt of England.

I didn't find the net in our next game, a 1-0 victory over Russia, but netted once in a 2-0 win over Switzerland that ensured we met Yugoslavia in the final, which we won 1-0. Four goals in the tournament earned me the top scorer's award and a trophy I've kept in my cabinet to this day.

Not that Dave Burnside was too pleased when half-a-dozen of us London-based lads, including Alan McLeary and David Kerslake, turned up for one morning training session about half-an-hour late. We'd tried to relieve the boredom by going canoeing, only the windy conditions caught us out and most of us ended up overturning. No one got into more trouble than poor Dougie McClure – our 'hatchet man' in the no-holds-barred 'North v South' training sessions – who lost control and crashed into rocks.

He cut open his foot and had to have it bandaged before he could train again. To be fair to the manager, though, he didn't overreact to the act of indiscipline and there was never any danger of us being sent home in disgrace.

I'm sure that the success Dicko and I enjoyed on our first appearances for England youth had a bearing on the fact that, within days of returning from Yugoslavia, we were both awarded our first pro contracts by West Ham.

But things had changed quite dramatically between September '82 and our next England youth gathering three months later. Charles Hughes had been appointed the new FA Director of Coaching – and I use the term coaching very loosely – while the new manager of the England youth team was a certain Graham Taylor, who was Watford boss at the time.

Even then, almost a decade before he became the most ridiculed manager in the history of the national team, I couldn't understand why a 'long-ball' advocate like Graham was put in charge of the youngsters. But, then again, with Hughes, the principle long-ball preacher at the helm, that was obviously why he got the job!

And I didn't exactly get off to the best possible start with Taylor when Dicko and I reported to his first training session session at Lilleshall in the first week of November. I drove the two-and-a-half hour car journey to Shropshire but we arrived half-an-hour late and I don't think Graham was too amused.

Our preparations certainly won the approval of our fellow youngsters, though, as we unpacked the portable TV from my car and set it up in our room! The other lads in the squad, which included another future team mate of mine at Everton, Neil Pointon, then of Scunthorpe United, often sneaked round to watch the box. As 'experienced' visitors to the Lilleshall school, we knew they had no televisions there for the lads to watch, so we made a point of taking our own!

We needed the telly to take our minds off the football, which was proving far from enjoyable. It was patently obvious to me on the first day that the style of football we were expected to play – with the full-backs asked to punt long balls into the channels for the forwards to chase after – was totally alien to what Dicko and I had been used to at West Ham.

Nothing had changed when we all met up again at Lilleshall in April 1983 – by which time Dicko and I had both broken through into Hammers' first team, although neither of us were included in the original squad and only received late call-ups. It was obvious to me at this point that we didn't figure in Taylor's plans, and in fact he never picked me again.

To be fair to Graham, though, I found him a very honest man who was quite willing to admit his mistakes, albeit six years later. When I bumped into him at the FA Cup semi-final at Villa Park in April 1989, he stopped, shook hands with me and said: "It's nice to see you're still proving me wrong after all these years."

It was a nice comment and his admission that, to a certain degree, he'd made a mistake in not picking me, certainly moved Graham Taylor up in my estimations.

There was a big gap between my last training session with England youth, in April 1983, and my debut for the under-21 team, against Finland at Southampton, on October 16, 1984, by which time I'd already completed a full season as West Ham's top scorer in the First Division. Most of the lads in that 17-man squad were 18 months, and as much as two years, older than me – players like Chris Waddle, David Seaman and Trevor Steven. As I was the 'baby' of the squad, I hadn't expected to be involved on the night, so I was delighted when manager Dave Sexton sent me on as a sub. 10 minutes from the end.

I got on reasonably well with Dave, a softly-spoken ex-Hammer who was manager for all but one of my 10 under-21 appearances, but felt he had difficulty communicating and tended to over-complicate practice sessions.

I particularly disliked his use of 'shadow' play in training. For anyone not familiar with 'shadow' play, it involves a team of 11 players against the other six squad members who were not selected for the side. So once you were handed a bib – as I invariably was in my early days with the under-21 squad – you knew you wasn't playing in the team for the next day's game anyway!

We would play 11 v six on a full-size pitch, sometimes even 11 against . . . no one! We would practice the goalkeeper rolling the ball out to the full-back, who would knock it forward into midfield. The midfielder would pass it out to the wing, for the winger to cross the ball to a forward, who would 'score' in an empty net.

If only the game was always that easy! To me, it was stupid and so irrelevant to a game situation, but we did 'shadow' play at every training session with the under-21s.

A month after my debut against Finland, a 17-man squad travelled all the way to Turkey, stayed in a very poor hotel and ate the worst food any of us had ever tasted. And to cap a nightmare trip, I was the only one of the 17 who didn't even get changed, watching the game instead from the subs' bench, next to two burly Turkish security guards!

After a wasted trip to Turkey, I wasn't over-enthusiastic about going all the way to Israel for the next under-21 international at the end of February 1985. I think Dave Sexton was ill at the time, so Howard Wilkinson – another long-ball disciple at that time – took temporary charge of us and he and I soon fell out.

Ominously, I was handed a bib again and after a boring session where I was told to stand in front of the corner-taker and jump into the air to try and block the cross, we practiced set pieces for ages.

It was quite cold in Tel Aviv at the time but our relationship got even frostier when I simply tucked my hands into the back of my tracksuit bottoms to keep warm. Howard stopped the practice and turned to me and snapped in his broad Yorkshire accent: "Have you got piles, lad? – take your hands out of your bottoms!"

Fortunately for me, Howard didn't take the under-21s again while I was involved, although to be fair to him, like Graham Taylor, whenever I've met Wilko since then he has always acknowledged me and said "hello," and I certainly bear him no grudges. It couldn't have been that bad, anyway, because at least Howard gave me a run-out in Israel as sub!

I made my full debut, without scoring, a month later in a friendly against the Republic of Ireland at muddy Portsmouth, although I was relegated back to the bench for our next European Championship qualifier in Romania in April '85. I never seemed to be rated too much by the management of the under-21s and the fact that I was always younger than the other players contributed to me being more often a sub. than playing.

While to most people it might have seemed glamourous playing for England, albeit at under-21 level, and visiting all these far-away places as a young footballer, the reality of the situation was somewhat different, as I realised on that trip to Romania.

As under-21 players, we were treated very much like second class citizens compared to the full internationals who were invariably on the same trip as ourselves. We were all treated equally on the plane going over, eating the same food, but as soon as we landed, the difference was remarkable.

While the senior squad boarded their luxury bus for the short ride to their hotel, we were given a clapped-out version on wheels.

As the 'first team' settled into their five-star hotel beside the beach, four hours later – and usually after losing a fortune at cards! – we'd roll into our comparatively ramshackle hotel that seemed miles from civilisation in a run-down part of town.

Then, after playing our game in Brasov on the Tuesday, we all watched the full team play their big match in Bucharest the next night. Equality only being restored on the charter flight back to Luton, where we'd eat as much food as possible to make up for what we hadn't eaten in the previous four days!

But I found that the senior England players – big names like Bryan Robson, Ray Wilkins, Peter Shilton and Kenny Sansom – were always very good towards the under-21 lads and never belittled us in any way, which was hardly surprising because, after all, most of us were playing against them in the First Division week in, week out.

Perhaps this was the FA's clever incentive to all youngsters that they should aspire to make the senior grade as quickly as possible – and if so, it had the desired effect as far as I was concerned!

I played in Finland in May '85 after being given permission by John Lyall to miss West Ham's last match of the season, against Liverpool. John always encouraged me to represent England whenever possible, because he knew how invaluable the experience of playing in different countries, and against teams that used various tactical systems, would prove to be. I played up front with Chelsea's Kerry Dixon but we let in some sloppy goals and never looked like winning.

After the opening two games of the 1985/86 season, I was beginning to wonder if I would ever score for my country. Paul Allen, who'd just left West Ham for Tottenham, was our over-age player when we returned to Romania in September '85, but I didn't find the net that night or the next month against Turkey at Bristol City.

My search for a goal continued the following March, when my best and most enjoyable performance at under-21 level, against Denmark at Maine Road, saw me hit the crossbar but not the net.

I thought I'd played my last game for England under-21s in Manchester that night, because I was effectively too old, under UEFA rules, for the start of the next European Championship qualifying campaign. But there was still plenty of excitement in my football career at that time, with West Ham chasing the championship, Frank McAvennie and I in full flow . . . and newspaper speculation that my outstanding club form might earn me a surprise late call into Bobby Robson's squad of 22 for the Mexico World Cup in the summer of '86.

Nothing came of it, but I sensed that I was on the verge of another big breakthrough and couldn't wait for the 1986/87 campaign to start . . .

Claret & Blues

HOPE AND GLORY

IT was in the first game after the Mexico World Cup, on September 10, 1986, that I fulfiled another lifetime ambition – to play for the full England team. I hadn't really expected to get a game when the squad for the friendly in Sweden was announced, but top striker Gary Lineker, who had recently joined Barcelona, wasn't included and both Peter Beardsley and Mark Hateley withdrew due to injury, so I joined the party for the flight from Luton airport in a hopeful and very excited mood.

As I didn't know any of the senior players personally, I was pleased that my West Ham team mate, Alvin Martin, was also in the squad for what was the last of his 17 senior caps. Alvin had performed excellently against Paraguay in the World Cup and many believed he was very unlucky to have been left out of that ill-fated quarter-final against Argentina.

Alvin had enjoyed the experience of being part of the England squad many times before but to me it was very exciting – and nerve-wracking. After some of the less appealing experiences I'd had with the under-21s, this was a life of luxury by comparison.

The butterflies filled my stomach once we landed in Stockholm, so I was absolutely delighted when Bobby Robson included me among his five substitutes, and even more pleased when my big moment came 33 minutes from the end when I was sent on to replace John Barnes.

Sweden had taken the lead through Johnny Ekstrom seven minutes before I came on to play alongside Chelsea's Kerry Dixon. My full debut didn't end in fairytale fashion, though, as Glenn Hysen, later to join Liverpool, marked me and we were unable to equalise against the effective sweeper system used by the solid Swedes.

Even so, having just turned 21 years of age, it was a big thrill to have been involved at the very highest level for the first time and it was with tremendous pride that I fulfiled a promise I'd made to my dad when I handed him my red England shirt, which still has pride of place at my parents' home.

I retained my place in the squad for the next full international, against Northern Ireland at Wembley on October 15, which kicked off our European Championship qualifying campaign. With Lineker, Beardsley and Hateley – all older and much more experienced players than myself – available for this one, I accepted that my immediate aim was to establish myself as the fourth striker in the squad.

Once again, I felt very nervous in the build up to the game for what was my first visit to Wembley as a player. Our old national stadium may not offer the best spectator facilities in the world, but it has a special aura all of its own and it was a tremendous experience to savour the magic of a place steeped in character and tradition. The huge dressing rooms, with five-feet deep baths, are an experience in themselves!

Just being at Wembley is special but to be out there lining up in an England kit for the national anthem, is something else altogether. I know that England players have been criticised at times for not singing the national anthem with quite the same full-blooded passion and patriotism as our rugby and athletics internationals do, but I think I can explain why that is the case . . . we're singing the wrong song!

The Scots sing 'Scotland The Brave', and the Welsh sing their hearts out to 'Land O' My Fathers', so why do we in England persist with 'God Save The Queen?' Don't get me wrong, I'm pro the Royal family but is it any wonder that Englishmen don't display quite the same degree of pride shown by players from other UK nations when the anthem we sing is the one that embraces ALL the home countries?

I tend to believe that 'Land Of Hope And Glory' – a truly English song – would produce a much better vocal response from all English sports men and women wherever they are competing.

Anyway, 'God Save the Queen' didn't do the England team any harm against the Irish on this occasion. Dave Watson, a future team mate of mine at Everton, came in to replace Alvin from the start, while I had to bide my time on the bench until 13 minutes from the end when I replaced Peter Beardsley, another player I later met up with at Goodison. Northern Ireland played a typically British flat back four but they couldn't stop Lineker, who scored twice before Chris Waddle completed the scoring in a convincing 3-0 victory.

Although I was named in the squad for the next game, against Yugoslavia at Wembley in November, I didn't make the subs' bench and had to wait until February 1987 for my next involvement with England, in Spain.

I think Bobby Robson thought it would be better for me to play a full game rather than sit on the bench or miss out altogether with the senior team, so I returned to the Under-21 squad as one of their two official over-aged players.

The cold and snowy conditions in the northern Spanish town of Burgos suited us more than it did the Spaniards and after David Rocastle opened the scoring, I was delighted to end my under-21 goal famine at the ninth attempt. From a defensive point of view, it may have been a bad goal to concede, but my flick with the outside of my right foot was certainly intended as it wrong-footed their 'keeper and nestled in the corner of the net.

Just a couple of hours after our afternoon victory in Burgos, the senior team crushed their Spanish counterparts 4-2 in Madrid. As usual, Lineker stole the show with all four goals, but I was just as pleased for 20 year-old Arsenal central defender Tony Adams, who made his full debut at the Bernabeu that night.

I'd got to know Tony quite well at the under-21 get-togethers – he was based just a few miles from me, at Rainham, so we shared the driving to training and matches – and I was delighted for him when he made the big breakthrough in Spain.

Tony deserves a lot of credit for the way that he has proved so many critics wrong at international level. I thought it was sad the way the tabloid press castigated him after England's failure in the 1988 European Championship finals in West Germany, where he and the rest of our defence were pulled to pieces by Holland's Marco Van Basten. But Tony was still only young and relatively inexperienced at that time and certainly didn't deserve the disgraceful treatment he received from some sections of the media.

But I'm very pleased to say that Tony has come through all that and re-established himself at the heart of England's defence. He is as important to this country now – with Euro '96 on the horizon – as he has been for more than a decade at Arsenal.

Tony kept his place for the next full international against Turkey in Izmir and the Rous Cup match against Brazil at Wembley in May, while I had to be content being part of the squad for those games and the one against Scotland at Hampden as the 1986/87 season reached its climax.

It was a long wait until the next international against West Germany at the start of the following season – but I'd soon get used to long spells in the England wilderness.

Claret & Blues

AUF WIEDERSEHEN

THERE are very few aspects of my career that I regret but being sent off for my country is definitely one of them – a moment of sheer frustration and lunacy that almost certainly robbed me of more full caps and, quite possibly, a place at the 1988 European Championship finals.

I was banned for three England matches, effectively a six-month suspension in international terms, after being dismissed in an under-21 match against West Germany in Ludenscheid on September 8, 1987.

Just as he'd done in Spain seven months earlier, Bobby Robson decided to include me in the under-21 side as an over-age player. I wish he hadn't!

The match was very physical right from the kick-off and I found myself marked man-for-man by a big, powerful centre-back called Peter Zanter. He spent the best part of an hour pulling my shirt, kicking lumps out of me and using his elbow, although I wasn't the only English player who came in for the rough stuff.

We conceded a sloppy goal, scored by Labbadia, midway through the first half and the Germans made it 2-0 right after half-time when Karl-Heinz Riedle, who went on to star for the senior team, added a second.

But matters got much worse in the 58th minute as Zanter and I turned to chase a long drop kick from our substitute 'keeper, Tim Flowers. Just as I began to race after the ball, the German defender held my shirt at the back with both hands and then caught me with a kick on the ankle.

He got to the ball first and as he controlled it, something inside me just snapped. I'd been kicked all round the field by this guy, without any protection from the Norwegian referee Egil Nervik, and I'd reached breaking point.

I ran towards Zanter and, quite blatantly, forgot all about trying to win the ball and kicked him in the calf instead.

I can't defend my daft actions, other than to say that I'd suffered tremendous provocation for an hour that night, as did most of our players. Sheffield United's

Peter Beagrie, another future Everton team mate of mine, and Nottingham Forest's Nigel Clough, two of the game's 'good guys', were both booked as England, who also included Newcastle United's Paul Gascoigne and Neil McDonald, lost their composure.

And it's fair to say that a number of other things had been playing on my mind before the game itself.

I felt thoroughly frustrated that my international career hadn't progressed at quite the speed I'd hoped it would, and that I was playing for the under-21s instead of the full team, who were in action the next night at Dusseldorf. Lorraine and I were also going through a difficult period in our relationship, and I guess the young German master of gamesmanship was the final straw.

But I should have known better, and the referee couldn't get out his red card quick enough. I sat alone in the dressing room until the players trooped in at the end and apologised to them and manager Dave Sexton for letting them down.

My mum, dad and brother Paul had travelled to see the game and they obviously weren't too pleased with my indiscipline, but at that stage I still hadn't contemplated the full consequences of my sending-off. Sexton didn't make anything of it in the dressing room afterwards and I received no personal reprimand from either Bobby Robson or FA chairman Bert Millichip, who were watching from the stands.

But just before Paul and I went out for a drink to drown our sorrows with some of the other players, I phoned Lorraine to explain what had happened and, as I wouldn't be flying back to England until the following night, asked her to buy the morning papers – just to check their reaction to my dismissal.

Under-21 matches normally warrant a few paragraphs, with brief reference to the scorers, etc, and I suppose I expected the British press to simply report the fact that I had been sent off and leave it at that.

You can imagine how amazed I was, then, to arrive home and see that my 'shameful' incident had completely dominated all of the tabloid back pages, with one headline screaming 'COTTEE GOES POTTY'.

I couldn't believe that the story was given such huge coverage, especially as it happened at under-21 level, but the media had another feast, speculating that I would face a very heavy punishment from the FA, who made it known at the time that they were concerned that violence on the field could spark hooliganism on the terraces. The FA were in the mood to make an example of players sent off while playing for England.

Before facing the music from Lancaster Gate, I had to face my West Ham team mates at training later that week and naturally they had a good laugh at my expense. Frank McAvennie said laughing: "How can you get sent off, wee man?" And Mark Ward chipped in with: "You never make a tackle, so how can you be sent off!"

But the FA saw nothing to smile about. For the first time in their history, they voluntarily and internally imposed an international ban on an England player.

I hoped and believed I would escape with a one, maybe two, game ban, but they suspended me for the next three England matches, covering full and under-21 levels, and ruled that I had to miss the next two games, against Turkey and Yugoslavia, and couldn't be considered for selection again until after the match against Israel in Tel Aviv on February 17, 1988.

The next full international after Israel was against Holland on March 23, 1988.

So when I weighed up the full extent of the damage caused by my sending off, it was, effectively, a SIX-MONTH BAN – or Auf Wiedersehen!

It could hardly have come at a more crucial stage of my England career, with the '88 Euro Championships set for West Germany just three months after the Dutch visit to Wembley.

My sending-off cast a large shadow over my future England career as well as my temperament, although this was the first time I'd been sent off at any level of the game and I'd only been booked about half-a-dozen times for West Ham.

But through my own stupidity, I'd really wrecked my hopes of establishing myself as a regular in the full England team that season. By being ruled out of three consecutive games, I'd disappeared from Bobby Robson's 'shop window' at a very crucial time.

Robson actually recalled me for the game against Hungary in the lovely city of Budapest on April 27, 1988 – my last cap as a Hammer and Middlesbrough centre-half Gary Pallister's debut – and I came on as sub. for Lineker, but my worst fears were realised a month later when we visited Lausanne, Switzerland, for a friendly, which I didn't play in.

After the game the manager pulled me and three others aside in the dressing room to tell us the news we'd dreaded . . . that we wouldn't be on the plane to Germany. I was gutted because, apart from the matches I'd missed through the ban, I'd been a regular squad member since my debut back in September '86 and had got back into the squad to challenge the top three of Lineker, Beardsley and Hateley.

I was surprised, too, that England elected to go to the finals in Germany with only three out-and-out strikers, although Robson also had John Barnes who could play either wide on the left or up front.

I wasn't going to give up hope, though, and still had Italia '90 clearly in my sights.

CHAPTER 38

Claret
& Blues

CHICKEN RUN

O NE of the most pleasing aspects about my involvement with England was that it gave me the chance to see and benefit, at close hand, from the skill of Paul Gascoigne.

When Gazza and I were sent on as substitutes against Denmark in the 77th minute of the friendly at Wembley in September 1988, it was the the bubbly Geordie's full debut. Neil Webb's 28th minute goal settled it but all eyes were on the new, young midfielder who would go on to become a national hero.

Having made my big move to Everton that summer, and started the season in such flying form with four goals in my first two games, I was more confident than ever of starting my first game for England. England needed to put the disastrous '88 European Championships firmly behind them and with Gary Lineker injured, I had high hopes of starting against the Danes.

Unfortunately, it wasn't to be, as Bobby Robson brought in a big target man in Luton Town's Mick Harford, who was ironically wanted by West Ham as my partner a year earlier. Apparently, Bobby was concerned about the attack being too lightweight if I'd played alongside Beardsley – a point we certainly disproved at Everton three years later.

But I still had a lot of respect for Robson, as a manager and a man. When he disappointed me by leaving me out of his 22-man squad for the Euro finals in Germany, at least he let me down by telling me face to face.

And you couldn't argue with his record as manager, despite the personal vendetta he suffered at the hands of the tabloid press later in his term of management. Before he got the top job, Bobby transformed Ipswich Town into serious First Division title challengers and brought them European success.

Bobby used to make us laugh sometimes whenever he got his players' names mixed up – like calling Mark Hateley by the name of his father, Tony! And it was Bobby who coined the phrase "daft as a brush" in reference to the sometimes crazy antics of Gazza.

Although he wasn't involved when I gained my fifth cap as an 80th minute sub.

against Sweden in the opening World Cup qualifying game at Wembley a month later, in a disappointing goalless draw, Gazza was very much the life and soul of the party on the long trips to Saudi Arabia and Albania later that season.

We flew to Saudi by Concorde – my one and only experience of flying in such style – and passed much of the time on this and other long trips by playing seven card brag. The regular card school consisted of Peter Shilton, skipper Bryan Robson, Kenny Sansom, Chris Woods, Gazza and myself. We'd play for £5 a hand although the stakes doubled each time it went round to the dealer. Some times there would be a couple of hundred pounds in the kitty, which was paid out when we totalled up the scores on our return to Luton airport.

The stadium at Riyadh, where a Tony Adams equaliser saved us from an embarrassing defeat, was a tremendous space-age construction. Although I watched from the stands, it was a great trip to be involved in and I returned home to Lorraine more than happy.

Unfortunately my good/bad syndrome struck again when Lorraine informed me that nanny Cottee had died earlier that morning at the age of 80. She loved watching me play football and those trips to Coventry would never be the same again.

The wealth of Saudi was in stark contrast to the appaling conditions we encountered in Albania in March 1989.

I'd heard all sorts of horror stories about Albania before our visit and when we arrived in the capital, Tirana, our worst fears were confirmed. It was like turning the clock back 50 years – the war-time army bunkers were still in the fields! – and the city itself had just one set of traffic lights and about 10 cars. Strangely, most of the locals roaming the streets were wearing overcoats ... even though the temperature was 75 degrees!

The England management took the precaution of preparing and cooking their own food and sent two chefs on the trip, armed with fillet steaks, baked beans and the kind of food we were used to at home

I shared a hotel room with my Everton team mate Ian Snodin, who was included in the squad for the first time, and conditions were far from ideal. But trust Gazza to make light of the situation. Ian and I were suddenly aware of roars of laughter coming from the room Gazza and Chris Waddle were sharing. To relieve the boredom, Gazza had decided to aim a bar of soap at a chicken, some 50 feet below, which happened to score a direct hit on the bird's backside!

A few of us gathered in Gazza and Chris' room and were urging Gazza to try and repeat his trick. Then, just as he took aim with another bar of soap, in walked Bobby Robson who had heard all the commotion from his room. Bobby knew full well about Gazza's sense of fun and rather than spoil the fun by giving Paul a ticking off, he actually encouraged him to have another throw.

And Gazza proved he can throw a bar of soap with the same pinpoint accuracy as he aims a free-kick – by hitting the poor chicken up the bum a second time! Bobby and all the players were in fits of laughter at Gazza's prank, which certainly livened the trip up. The team spirit throughout the whole squad was very good, though, which is crucial to any team's hopes of success.

Gazza was up to his tricks again the day before the game, when we trained at the stadium. At the end of the session he and one or two other players stayed behind to entertain the 5,000 Albanian fans who'd come along to watch. But this time Gazza decided to play the role of goalkeeper and had the crowd captivated with a series of spectacular saves!

He saw much more of the ball than Shilts did in the match the next day, when England comfortably won 2-0 thanks to goals in each half by John Barnes and Robbo. I didn't even make it onto the bench in Athens, Greece, where we won 2-1, and after missing out on the return match with Albania at Wembley in April, I was recalled for the two Rous Cup matches against Chile and Scotland at the end of the 1988/89 season.

Although I was still getting over the disappointment of losing the FA Cup Final to Liverpool just three days earlier, I still felt sharp when I came on for Wimbledon's John Fashanu, who, along with Forest's Nigel Clough, was winning his first cap, with 20 minutes left. The attendance was a mere 15,628 and those who stayed away missed my first – and last – shot in an England shirt!

The Chilean 'keeper dropped a cross but the ball bounced a fraction higher than I would have liked and my volley was headed off the line by a defender. I never came any closer to scoring for the full England team than that.

One first I did achieve, though, was to start my first game for England, against Scotland at Hampden Park the following Saturday. I did quite well in the opening stages, and was pleased to be involved in the build up to Chris Waddle's 20th minute goal, but the effects of a long, hard season took their toll and I tired in the second half before being replaced by Gazza.

Two minutes later, Steve Bull came on for his debut . . . and scored the second in our 2-0 victory over the old enemy.

At that stage I still had Italia '90 in mind, although I knew I had to improve my form for the Blues first. I saw my transfer to a big club like Everton as the perfect springboard to international success but the signing of Mike Newell in the summer of '89 effectively ended those hopes.

It took me six months to re-establish myself in the Everton team, which left me no time at all to regain my place in the England squad and, more importantly, a seat on the plane to Italy. Instead, I had to be content with watching the World Cup on TV and what a memorable tournament it turned out to be.

The semi-final against West Germany – best remembered for Gazza's tears and the heart-breaking penalty shootout misses by Stuart Pearce and Chris Waddle – should really have been the final itself. It was a great game and I firmly believe that had England beaten the Germans that night, they would have gone on to win the final against an Argentina team that was a pale shadow of the side that played so well in Mexico four years earlier.

When I look back on my international career, I do so with a degree of frustration because I felt I should have played more often than I did, particularly when I was in top form for West Ham. I might well have doubled my collection of seven caps but, having said that, there are many players who obviously feel the same way as I do.

Quality players like Alan Hudson, Stan Bowles, Clive Allen and Joe Royle all won less caps than me, Frank Worthington (eight caps) and Rodney Marsh (nine) didn't achieve much more than me internationally and Billy Bonds – a legend at West Ham – was very unlucky not to have won even a single cap.

There are many more who can look back on their careers and justifiably feel hard done by, but no one can take away my seven caps and I'm very proud of that. Although the season had finished, I still had a very important 'match' to look forward to … My wedding!

Claret & Blues

ALL CHANGE

BEFORE Lorraine and I tied the knot, we travelled up to Newcastle for another special wedding – that of my best mate John Cornwell and his bride, Sandra, whose evening reception was held at United's St. James's Park ground on June 3.

We stopped at Southport to collect our belongings before driving on down to London on Monday, June 5 to visit our families. It was on that afternoon that I switched on the radio to hear the shock news that West Ham had sacked John Lyall.

After suffering relegation on the final day of the season, I suppose I knew there was a chance that West Ham would maybe ask John to 'move upstairs' and bring in a new, younger manager to work under him. The most obvious choice would have been Billy Bonds, who could have come in and learned the ropes under John, who had 34 years' experience of the Hammers under his belt. To me, that seemed the most sensible thing to do.

So I was absolutely astounded to hear that they had sacked John and intended to bring in a new manager from outside the Upton Park 'family'.

There was quite a bit of transfer news at the time, too, where Everton were concerned. On June 9 Trevor Steven completed his predictable move to Glasgow Rangers for a fee of £1,525,000. Martin Keown joined Everton from Aston Villa for £750,000 on June 12 and, more significantly as far as I was concerned, on June 14 they signed Mike Newell from Leicester, who got Wayne Clarke (valued at £450,000) as part of the deal.

Despite the previous season's disappointments, Sharpy and I still had the makings of a good partnership. At the time, I considered that £1.1m was a lot to pay for Newell if he was only going to sit in the reserves. Or was he?

The following night I went out for a meal and a chat with Jon Smith and my dad, with nothing specific in mind other than to recap on the disappointments of the previous season and look forward to improved fortunes in the coming campaign.

Fired up for action . . . or is
that London yearning?

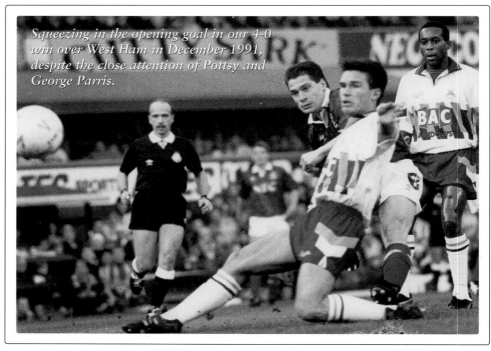

Squeezing in the opening goal in our 4-0 win over West Ham in December 1991, despite the close attention of Pottsy and George Parris.

Right: *Running into space and trying to predict the knock-down.* **Below:** *Why do they make us wear these shirts?*

Left: *Fan-tastic! It's time to celebrate with the fans after beating Liverpool 2-0 in September 1993.*
Below: *High jump! Spectacular action against Aston Villa, with Paul McGrath lunging in.*

Above: *Match of the Day – Lorraine and me on our wedding day, June 24, 1989.*
Left: *Holidaying in Miami, June 1990.*

Above: My two girls!
Right: Happy families in Orlando, summer '95.
Below: Me and 'Gorgeous' – my nickname for Chloe.

One of the most satisfying goals from 1994/95, my first against Everton at Upton Park in February 1995. 'Waggy' and Nev don't seem to share my pleasure!

Christmas cracker! Celebrating after scoring against Ipswich Town on Boxing Day, 1994.

Right: On the ball at Highbury.
Left: Action from the 1995/96 season.

Ruud Gullit – probably the most famous player I've played against – and me on his Upton Park debut, September 1995. I managed to give Chelsea's Dutch master the slip this time but there is no disputing that he's world class.

So I was very surprised to hear Jon say that he understood Everton would start the following season with Newell, instead of me, in the side. Even though I hadn't set the world alight with 13 league and five cup goals, which was reasonable but obviously not as many as they should have expected from a £2 million player, I still didn't think that Colin would drop me, his most expensive asset, after only one season.

But I put any doubts about my Everton future on hold as June 24 dawned, the sun shone very brightly and I walked down the aisle of St. Giles and All Saints Church in Orsett with my lovely bride, Lorraine. About 150 people turned up at the church and we had the best day of our lives. With most of the Everton players away on holiday, and bearing in mind the wedding took place in Essex, the only representative from of Everton was Neil McDonald. John Cornwell flew the black and white Newcastle flag but his real role was that of usher, with Paul as my best man.

After a night at an hotel near Gatwick airport, we flew off to the Seychelles for what was intended to be a three-week honeymoon. But two weeks into our holiday, I got a call from Jon Smith saying that after originally giving me permission to extend our break by a few days, Colin Harvey had been on to say that he now wanted me back for training, so we flew home a week early.

Meanwhile, Everton had been busy in the transfer market again, signing Ray Atteveld from Dutch club FC Haarlem for £250,000, Norman Whiteside from Manchester United for £750,000 and Stefan Rehn from Swedish club Djurgardens IF for £400,000.

So in the space of a year, Everton had signed nine new players, although a few left the club during this time. Apart from the departures of Steven, Clarke and another striker, Adrian Heath, who had previously left to join Espanol in Spain for £500,000 in November '88, Van Den Hauwe moved to Tottenham for £575,000, Neil Adams moved on to Oldham Athletic for £100,000 and Ian Wilson joined Turkish club Besiktas for £200,000, while Peter Reid had already joined QPR permanently on a free the previous February. I was disappointed about his departure because I had really been looking forward to playing with him. Reidy was particularly helpful when I first came to the club and as a midfield workhorse who could also play as well, I felt I would benefit a lot from having him around me.

I hadn't seen the best of Steven in an Everton shirt, while Van Den Hauwe was keen to get back to London. 'Psycho Pat' was a real character and also an excellent player but he had his moments. He'd go missing on odd days and suddenly reappear at training as if nothing had happened. It was inevitable that Colin would move him on eventually.

Pat and Julian Dicks, of West Ham, are the two players I've made a point of keeping well away from in training matches!

It was clear that Colin wanted to be his own man and rebuild the side after Howard Kendall had guided Everton to the championship in 1987. Of the title winners, only five first team regulars remained by August 1989: Southall, Ratcliffe, Watson, Sheedy and Sharp, while Paul Bracewell was transferred to Sunderland the following month in a £250,000 deal.

Our pre-season involved a monster tour of Japan, Malaysia and Thailand, including a game against Manchester United who we beat 3-1 in Japan, before beating the Japanese national team by the same score. After two games in that country, we were due to fly to Thailand but were delayed 10 hours at Tokyo airport. With so much time to kill, it was no surprise to see a number of the lads drift off to a bar, while myself and a few others played cards.

After about five or six hours, I wandered around the departure lounge and met up with the other lads, who had got talking to a touring American football team. Anyway, we moved on to the next bar by which time our lads were certainly the worse for wear. The booze was starting to take its effect as Stuart Mac and Kevin Ratcliffe got involved in a heated debate about football in which they not only questioned each other's contribution but also examined Everton's problems as a whole.

It got very heated at one stage and, being relatively sober after only a couple of beers, I stepped in. Stuart was my friend but I was really saying "cool it" to both of them when 'Ratters' turned on me and said: "Well, what are *you* going to do about it? . . . what are *your* plans this season?" He took me completely by surprise with his obvious inference that I'd had a crap first season at the club and had let everyone down.

I said that obviously I was looking to do a lot better than last season, or words to that effect, but I was a bit taken aback by the attitude of the club captain.

I knew I'd let myself down but I hadn't been aware of any ill feeling towards me by other players. Obviously the beer had fuelled the arguments but it wasn't a very pleasant situation to be in.

Ratters and I had both said our piece and it soon fizzled out, but it was about this time that I got the feeling – and events proved me right – that there was a bit of friction developing between the more senior players, who had enjoyed so much success under Howard Kendall a few years earlier, and the younger ones Colin Harvey had brought in. Especially as another five players had arrived that summer.

It is never good for team spirit to have a 'them and us' situation in the dressing room but I could see it beginning to creep in on that pre-season tour and it didn't augur well for the future.

When we finally arrived at our hotel in Thailand, at around 11pm, a few of us, including me, fancied a drink. Colin gave strict instructions that no one was to go out but Sharpy, Sheeds, Stuart Mac, Norman Whiteside and I slipped out through the fire exit to avoid detection. In fact, it wasn't so much a case of sneaking out through the back door, more like legging it, as the fire alarm went off as soon as we opened the exit door!

We caught a taxi into the main part of town where one of the locals spoke of a nearby bar that stayed open to well into the early hours. So we got back into our smallish taxi . . . the driver, five players and our new tour guide. He sat on one player's lap in the front seat, while I lay stretched out on the back across the laps of the other three players.

I don't know why, but our car was forced to stop at a road block, where armed police were checking every vehicle. When the policeman opened the back door and saw me laying there with my head at one side of the car and my feet at the other, he was speechless. Thankfully he saw no reason to use his gun and waved us on to enjoy the rest of evening in one of the dingiest bars I've ever been to.

It must have been gone three o'clock in the morning when we returned to our hotel – with our manager none the wiser.

We had another enjoyable outing the night before we played the Thai national team in Bangkok. Colin thought it might be a good way of improving team spirit if the players went out together for a few drinks.

He said it would be OK for the lads to have a couple, but two led to three, then four and when we were on our fifth bottle of beer, he made a decision that everyone had to leave the bar.

Rather than walk back to the hotel, the players commandeered four locals who rode tourists around town on one of those big four-seater bicycles called Tuk-Tuks. So there we were, four teams of four, racing through the streets of Bangkok, each of us urging our own 'driver' to put his foot down that little bit harder, whilst leaning across the road to try and push the rival team's bike off course. My team came in first and we were busy posing for the pretend 'team photo' when the others arrived!

On Friday, August 11 we played Malaysia in what was our last pre-season friendly before the opening First Division match at Coventry City eight days later. In the preceding friendlies, Colin had tried different attacking permutations – Sharpy and Newell; Newell and me; Sharpy and me. Now he announced before our last friendly on tour that he wanted to play his "strongest team" against Malaysia and as I wasn't picked, this was the first clear indication I'd had, since the chat with Jon Smith, that I would be left out in favour of Mike Newell.

The following Wednesday, as is traditional at Everton, we trained on the Goodison pitch. We played three games of 20 minutes each way and I was in outstanding form, scoring twice, hitting the bar and really buzzing. I thought hopefully I'd done enough to clinch a place in the team at Coventry, I couldn't have done any more.

Then the next day, he played me alongside Sharpy in a warm-up game, which was another encouraging pointer to selection. Friday was a normal session – head tennis followed by a five-a-side – and as we travelled down to the Midlands I still felt I had a good chance of playing the next day.

I was in my hotel room when, at 1pm on Saturday lunchtime, I heard a knock at the door and it was Colin. I could tell he was very nervous as he informed me of his decision to play Mike Newell instead of me. He admitted that I'd done very well in training all week and had almost changed his mind. At least this time Colin had gone about dropping me in the right manner, instead of me finding out via the press, which I respected him for.

That didn't make me any happier, though, watching from the bench as we lost 2-0. I got on for 'Newelly' 15 minutes from time but it was too late to make any difference.

After the game, as I chatted to my parents outside the ground, I encountered one of the few times that any Everton fans had openly criticised me to my face. Two scousers stood there complaining: "Look at him, we paid two million pound for him . . . "

    I didn't react, it's not in my nature to have stand-up arguments with supporters, but some choice words from my mate, Michael, soon put them in their place.

Claret & Blues

IN THE COLD

BEING dropped is one of the worst feelings a footballer can ever experience, and the disappointment, the hurt you feel inside, really cuts deep. Of course you want the team to do well, because if they keep losing one game after another, you could find yourself fighting a relegation battle and if the worst comes to the worst and the team goes down, then everyone suffers.

But if the team struggles in the odd game, then there's a fair chance that the player who has been left out can benefit from defeat. For some of us, it can often be the only way back. The manager will usually keep playing a winning side – no one can blame him for that – but if the side slips up at some point, that could be the signal for a change or two.

So I have to admit it, there were times when, for selfish reasons, I hoped the team wouldn't play very well.

And any player in that position who says otherwise is a liar.

Either that, or he has no self esteem and cares little about his own career.

It's human nature. I can't sit there on the subs' bench or, worse still, in the stand and watch a player, in this case Mike Newell, take my shirt and play in my position and not feel bad about it. I certainly didn't want to stand by and watch Newelly play a blinder in my place, which would only prolong my absence from the side.

Sure, in the dressing room beforehand I would have been there wishing all the lads the best of luck, including Newelly. But deep down, if I'm truly honest with myself, I was hoping that he wouldn't succeed at my expense.

Having said that, I would never have wanted to win back my place as a result of injury to a team mate, but loss of form is another matter.

Any player who has pride in himself would surely think the same as me in that situation. Who can genuinely be happy or satisfied kicking his heels in the reserves while the first team's winning?

Newelly did very well at the start of 1989/90. He scored on his home debut, a

2-1 win over Tottenham, which was the start of a great run for him. He actually scored in seven matches out of eight as the team soared to the top of the table by mid-September and Mike was called up for the England squad.

I didn't get on in the Spurs game, so afterwards 'Tex' asked me to join him and the other squad players for four laps of the pitch and a few 'doggies'. A totally unenjoyable experience that only rubbed salt into my already gaping wounds.

But that was nothing compared to the humiliation I felt next morning when I was getting ready at home and the 'phone rang at 9.20am. It was Mick Lyons, the reserve team manager, telling me that I would be playing for him that night, at Coventry. I replied that it was the first I'd heard about it and as I was already going into training that morning, I would clarify the situation with Colin personally.

It hadn't even crossed my mind that, just three days into the new season, I'd be playing reserve team football. I went to see Colin for an explanation and he said: "It's club policy that if you don't play for the first team on Saturday, you play for the reserves in midweek instead."

I asked him why he hadn't had the courtesy to inform me the night before, at the Tottenham game, when all the other reserves knew they were being sent to Coventry. He couldn't answer my question and I informed him there and then that I didn't want to play. I said: "I've come in here this morning expecting to train. Now you're telling me you want me to go back home and return later to catch the coach to go and play for the reserves at Coventry? Well I'm not doing it, you should have told me earlier."

The situation was deteriorating rapidly. I just couldn't contemplate the situation I found myself in. I was still the most costliest player in Britain, yet I was now being treated like a kid and ordered to play in the reserves.

I wrote in my diary: 'Within 30 seconds of my meeting Colin, he told me that he didn't want me.' I don't think he actually said so in as many words, it was obviously the impression he gave that led me to write what I did.

Colin had basically had enough and the conversation ended with me saying I'd put in a transfer request in the morning, as I slammed his door shut behind me.

I think the way the gaffer looked at it, he had given me a chance, I hadn't proved myself, he had now bought Mike Newell who he was happy with, and he didn't want unhappy players. If I didn't like being in the reserves, I could go somewhere else.

His attitude disappointed me because I felt that what he should have done at the end of my first season, was call me in, sit me down and work things out together. We could have discussed the problems I'd had settling into the side, face to face, and come up with a plan to put it right the following season.

To me, it seemed crazy that the same manager who rated me so highly a year earlier that he paid a British record fee, was now turning round and saying I was no longer wanted. I couldn't comprehend that the club had invested so much money in me and yet were now quite willing to let me leave so easily.

Jon Smith tried to make me see sense and phoned, soon after I'd seen Colin, to advise me to go along with the manager's request, but I told him that I wasn't prepared to. Quite understandably, Jon didn't want me to be cast in the role of rebel but he came up against the stubborn side of my nature. I'm not always right on these occasions but I vowed to stick by my principles.

As the communication lines between the manager and I continued to deteriorate, it became a battle of wills. The day after I should have played for the reserves at Coventry, he called me in and told me I would be fined two weeks' wages. I verbally repeated my wish to leave and left it to Jon to speak to Colin, who said he would discuss the matter with the chairman.

Apart from the closest members of my family, I didn't discuss my situation with anybody else, so it was a little surprising to wake up next morning and read in the papers that I'd been fined two weeks' wages – apparently the information came from the Professional Footballers' Association, who I had spoken to on the Thursday for advice on my position. As usual, the PFA backed their member and made a statement to the effect that I'd been fined too heavily, suggesting that a week's wages would have been more appropriate. The *Daily Mirror* reported that I would be fined £6,000 – supposedly two weeks wages – which would have been funny had my position not been so bleak. I remember thinking: 'I wish that was what I was earning!'

I was completely bombed out of the squad for the next game, home to Southampton, and to add insult to injury, Newell scored again in our 3-0 victory.

On the Monday prior to our midweek visit to Sheffield Wednesday, Sharpy told me that he had an injury and wouldn't be fit to play. Colin did at least acknowledge my presence at the club when he asked: "Are you in the right frame of mind to play tonight?", to which I responded positively. He put me back in the side alongside Newell but in a poor game, I didn't manage a shot at goal and was taken off with 10 minutes to go. We led 1-0 at the time but Wednesday equalised with 30 seconds left. Even though I'd told Colin I was OK to play, on reflection I probably wasn't in the right frame of my mind to play well.

With Sharpy fit again, I was totally left out of all five games in September, and on the 7th of the month received my weekly pay slip that showed I'd been deducted a week's wages . . . even though the club had not confirmed in writing that I would be fined. (They obviously intended to deduct a further week's salary the following week.).

So, having failed to tell me in good time that I would be playing in the reserves, the club had again fouled up by not informing me of my fine in writing – all I had was Colin's verbal communication. Gordon Taylor and Brendan Batson at the PFA advised me that I should either settle my differences with the club, possibly persuading them to reduce the punishment to a one-week fine, or take the matter before the appeal committee.

My diary shows that I went to see Colin again on the Monday after the Man. United game, where he showed me a copy of the letter Everton had supposedly sent to me, but had never arrived. To which I pointed out that I should have got that before money was deducted from my wages. He also said that he'd "try to sort things out within the next 10 days," as he didn't wish to keep an unhappy player.

I left it that the matter would be discussed at the next board meeting, and on September 13 I duly received Everton's letter informing me of their fine. The following day I wrote to the Football League to say that I would be appealing, because firstly, the fine was too harsh, and secondly, the club hadn't followed PFA procedure by deducting my money before I'd received written notification of their intended action.

In the meantime, I just sat their in utter frustration as Newell continued to hit the goal trail and the team returned to the top of the table in the third week of October. My football was confined to the reserves – nothing matches at top grounds like Old

Trafford (in front of 200 people) and Nottingham Forest's City Ground.

For the first time in my so far successful career I was banished to the reserves and felt like an outcast. It was very difficult to handle because this was a completely new experience for me.

But there was no way, deep down, that I wanted to leave Everton. I'd signed a five-year deal and was just settling in after a year.

On the other hand, I hadn't moved 250 miles, lock, stock and barrel, to settle for reserve team football. It wasn't that I thought I was too big or too good to play for the reserves, I just-felt that Colin was out of order to banish me to the reserves just three days into the new season. After a week or 10 days, fair enough, but Colin knew that his decision would knock me for six and lead to a lot of unnecessary problems.

Unless you are coming back from injury, where a run in the reserves can be a good thing, dropping down into the Central League was soul-destroying. To go from experiencing the thrill of playing in front of 20,000-30,000 people every week, and the buzz of scoring and celebrating with the crowd, to playing in front of two men and a dog, it's a world of difference.

No matter how positively you try and approach the reserve game, telling yourself how determined you are to score goals and prove the manager wrong, it's so hard to get going when the ground is empty and the majority of the players you are playing with and against are of inferior standard or just as de-motivated as yourself.

And I knew full well that, with Newell doing so well, even if I did score two or three goals, there was no way back into the first team. I either had to wait for him to lose form or the team to start struggling.

On September 26 I had another meeting with Colin, where he confirmed that I was available for transfer, but that the club had not put a price tag on my head. Wimbledon and Portsmouth had apparently enquired about me but I told him I had no interest in joining either club.

There was also speculation that I could be going to Arsenal, Chelsea or Tottenham, and Jon Smith spoke to them all, but there was nothing doing. Arsenal clearly wouldn't take me after the way I'd snubbed them before; Chelsea weren't that keen; and with Spurs it was a case of, 'if we move so and so on (Paul Stewart in this case), we might find an opening for you'. Tottenham was the one club that I was persistently linked with, but it was always just talk.

A brief respite came in the Cup tie against Leyton Orient at Goodison, where I came on as sub when we were losing 1-0 and sparked a recovery that salvaged a 2-2 draw in the second leg and ensured an aggregate win after our earlier 2-0 advantage at Brisbane Road.

I must have impressed someone that night because I was nominated as man-of-the-match by one of the sponsors, but after having only played for 18 minutes I decided that they should surely be able to find another, more appropriate, winner and therefore declined to collect the traditional bottle of bubbly. To underline just how poor the performance was, we had to sit through a video replay of the game at training the next day.

On October 5 I had to attend the appeal hearing in Manchester – me, accompanied by a couple of PFA representatives, with Colin and Philip Carter, the Everton chairman, putting the club's case. But I knew within 10 seconds of the hearing starting, as the disciplinarians on the committee took Everton's side, that I never had a hope of winning the case. The bottom line was that I was told to play reserve team football and had refused to do so, which made me the guilty party.

To be honest, I was pleased in a way to put the whole matter behind me after six weeks of turmoil in which I'd been dropped, fined two weeks' wages and generally lost my way. At least there was some light at the end of the tunnel as Colin commented to Jon Smith, who had travelled up for the hearing, that if I continued to play as I did when coming on against Orient, then I'd soon get back in the side.

Indeed, I returned for the next game, a 2-1 home win over Millwall, and was pleased to set up a couple of goals in a 3-0 defeat of Arsenal at Goodison a week later. Colin took me off again with 15 minutes to go in the Cup win over Luton, but told me not to worry as I'd be starting the next match.

A timely boost for me came on October 28, when I scored my first goal of the season in a 1-1 draw at Norwich. It was an embarrassing goal really, because a defender headed the ball into the air and as it came down I totally mishit my volley, sending the 'keeper the wrong way. It must have bobbled five times before going in – one of the worst shots I've ever hit – but I was still absolutely delighted to get that one under my belt.

It was the Friday before the Norwich game that Everton signed Peter Beagrie from Stoke City for £750,000. 'Beags' is a tremendous character and also an excellent player, although I was a bit puzzled by Colin's quote that he'd signed Peter because he would have regretted it if he hadn't signed a very good player like him. Which was strange, because surely he should have been saying that he'd signed him because he was bought to play in a specific role – on the left wing.

Beags was Colin's tenth signing in little over a year and he was heavily criticised for spending as much money as he did on new players. Most of those players have gone on to do well at other clubs, which proves that Colin knew a good player when he saw one, and he signed a lot of excellent players, but what he didn't do was buy players, like me, to fit into the established team pattern.

On November 5 we were blown apart at Aston Villa, in front of the live TV cameras. David Platt scored twice and played exceptionally well as Villa romped into a 3-0 lead at half-time. We were shocking and an angry Colin decided to take off Norman Whiteside, before turning to me in the dressing room and saying: "And you're coming off as well." I sat there thinking 'here we go again . . . the team's losing 3-0 so the manager, in his usual wisdom, decides to take off his striker'.

Just then, Dave Watson chirped up and said he was injured and couldn't play on, so Colin told me to put my boots on again because I was staying on! It was farcical, another blow to my confidence, and things went from bad to worse as we went six down. Beags' shot was deflected in and I managed to add a second near the end but there was no disguising the fact that it had been an absolute nightmare from beginning to end.

I managed to keep my place for the visit of Chelsea the following Saturday but another setback was lurking around the corner. With 25 minutes to go, I saw the number seven board thrust in the air, to indicate that Pat Nevin would be coming off. But this was swiftly replaced by number 10 and the crowd vented their disappointment by booing the decision to substitute me.

I was as bemused as the 33,000 crowd and as I approached the bench, I asked: "What the bloody hell was that for, we're losing?" Colin told me to "shut up and sit down," an obvious frank exchange of views that the press picked up on after the game.

All through my Everton career I could never understand why, if we were either drawing or losing, they usually substituted me – a natural goalscorer who, even if I wasn't playing too well, needed possibly only one chance to change things around.

My row with Colin in August had been simmering and we seemed to be at odds with each other from time to time since then. I asked him the Monday after the Chelsea game why I had been taken off. After he justified what had happened by saying that he brought on Sharpy to try and turn things around, I responded by adding that if the team wasn't going to play to my strengths, there was no point in playing me.

The way Everton were playing – the full-backs bypassing midfield and hitting long balls into the target man – was totally alien to what I'd been used to at West Ham. It's probably fair to say that if that's the Everton way, then it should have been up to me to fit into that style of play. But there was definitely a conflict of opinion because I insisted to Colin that, given the service, I would produce the goods.

On the Friday before the Wimbledon game, Sharpy knew he was playing the following day, so with Newell in good form, it was obvious that I would be left out – not that Colin said a word to me about it. I spoke to the gaffer again after our home draw with the Dons and he said let's leave it another fortnight to see if there were any further developments.

After Nottingham Forest knocked us out of the Cup, I was sub again for our league match at Forest, but returned to the starting line-up at home to Coventry City at the start of December. Despite our 2-1 defeat at Spurs, I was pleased with my well-taken goal but after keeping Newell out of the side for five games, I was out in the cold again at the turn of the year.

I mentioned earlier about a growing divide between the older, more senior players, and the younger brigade, and the problem deepened when we went to Spain for a four-day golfing holiday – ironically designed to improve team spirit! – after the Tottenham game. With all the local courses waterlogged following torrential rain, the players were grounded and bored at the hotel, where we did little else to pass the time but drink.

This only led to more sniping and the unbelievable situation, at one stage, where a fight between an older and a younger player seemed inevitable.

Strong words were exchanged, with one set of players blaming the other for the team's poor form, and the mood of unrest continued throughout our stay without, fortunately, getting any worse.

Actually, there was a funny situation one night after we'd left the bar and a few players – including Stuart Mac, Neil Pointon and Kevin Sheedy – gathered in Sheeds' room. Considering we'd all had a few, it was perhaps foolish to continue talking football and risk reopening old wounds.

But as we got back onto the subject, I had to ask 'Sheeds' a question that had been bothering me for some time: "Why, whenever I come short to receive the ball, do you almost always ping it over my head to Sharpy? Are you deliberately not passing to me?"

He explained – and I could see his point of view – that it was not a deliberate snub on his part and that having played with Sharpy for so long, it seemed the natural thing to try and find him with his passes.

I had to ask Kevin outright, though, because I definitely had the feeling – and it wasn't paranoia – that I was deliberately being ignored on the pitch.

The discussion must have gone on for another half hour, with Sheeds assuring me that he had nothing against me personally, and an amicable agreement to try and work on improving what we had been discussing.

Then the door swung open. It was Colin, somewhat anebriated, who added fuel to the fire by saying: "Come on, Sheeds, be honest, you don't want to pass to TC, do you?" It was pure coincidence that Colin should come into my room at that precise moment and say what he did. At least we all saw the funny side.

I've got to say that, individually, I got on well with every player at the club – there was no one I disliked. But I did feel that when the senior players got together in a group, particularly when they'd had a drink, there was a lot of resentment towards the younger players.

One of the younger newcomers who got caught up in the crossfire more than most was Neil McDonald, who the older players singled out for criticism. They claimed he was miserable and unwilling to mix with the older pro's but to be fair to Neil, he had a lot of problems with his young daughter having to enter hospital. I think he bottled a lot of things up and, sure, he would come into training some days a bit moody. But it was unfair to make him the scapegoat for the general attitude shown towards the younger players.

There were cliques everywhere – the older players, the younger players and then a group in between which included the likes of Dave Watson, Norman Whiteside and Neville Southall who basically didn't get involved with either group.

I'm sure that Colin was very aware of the lack of team spirit and tried to construct his own team by shipping out the rest of Howard Kendall's successful, though ageing, side. There is no doubt that he would have eventually sold Ratters, Sheeds and Sharpy, too, but he couldn't quite get there quick enough.

CHAPTER 41

Claret & Blues

ON THE LIST

SICK of being made the scapegoat for the team's ongoing struggle, I finally put in a written transfer request after being left out of the squad for the home game against Luton Town on New Year's Day, 1990. But when I handed it to Jim Greenwood, it wasn't really a demand for a move, because I didn't want to leave the club. It was more like a protest at the way I was being treated and, despite our differences, I still wanted to play for Colin and Everton.

We were comfortably settled in our house after seven months and the last thing I wanted to do was uproot again so soon after coming to the north-west.

And it wasn't as if money was the motive behind putting my request in writing – I would have sacrificed three years of signing-on fees that were due in the remainder of my contract. I was just fed up banging my head against a brick wall.

Five weeks of more reserve team football under Jimmy Gabriel went by – and further false speculation about a possible move to Tottenham – before I returned at the expense of the injured Mike Newell for our home game against Charlton Athletic on February 10. It was a very poor game, 1-1 at half-time, but that didn't concern me as I came in late at the far post to force the ball in off the bar following a deflected cross from Sheedy in the second half.

There was some debate about who should be credited with the goal but I was adamant. As a striker, I believe that you should claim the goal even if you only get a hair to the ball, and I was definitely having this one. I said so immediately after the game and, just to make sure, I even made a point of seeing Colin on Monday to confirm that the club had awarded it to me. It was possibly one goal I wasn't fully entitled to but I desperately needed a break and that goal had the desired effect.

To a certain degree, the pressure had been lifted by my transfer request. I felt that I had nothing to lose anymore and tended to have a more carefree attitude. If things didn't sort themselves out at Everton – as I hoped they would – then I would be moving elsewhere at the end of the season.

I started all of the remaining 13 league games as well as a three-match marathon with Oldham Athletic in the fifth round of the FA Cup. In the first game at Boundary Park, where I was playing up front with Sharpy, we went 2-0 up, with me scoring one of them. But after half-an-hour, Oldham manager Joe Royle took off winger Neil Adams, put Paul Warhurst on at the back to make a third defender, with the two full-backs pushing into midfield. The switch was a tactical masterstroke by Royle, whose Latics side came back to draw 2-2, and I remember thinking at the time how shrewd he had been to act so swiftly in the game.

It was Oldham who ended Everton's FA Cup challenge that season. After a 1-1 draw in the replay at Goodison, in which Whiteside was sent off and I was one of five booked, my goal couldn't prevent us from losing the second replay at Boundary Park 2-1. Oldham played some wonderful football that season, doing the Second Division proud by reaching the Littlewoods Cup Final (where they lost to Forest) and the semi-finals of the FA Cup (beaten in a replay by Man. United, who found it tough to beat Palace in a replay of the final).

Back in the league, we were cruising in mid-table but I was playing better than I had all season and feeling much happier with myself. The goal against Charlton in February was only my fourth of the season, just to underline what a poor spell I was enduring, but it considerably boosted my confidence as I embarked on a run that yielded nine goals in seven matches.

One of my most pleasing performances was in a live TV game against Forest on April 4 in which I scored twice, was denied a hat-trick by the post and won the man-of-the-match award. The team climbed to third in the table but slipped back to sixth as our rivals across Stanley Park regained the title, nine points clear of Villa.

My sparkling end-of-season form convinced Colin that I was capable of being his number one striker and after another chat at the end of the season, I was happy to agree to withdraw the transfer request I'd tabled at the start of the year.

As I've said, I never wanted to leave in the first place and was delighted to come off the list once it was clear my future lay with Everton.

Our summer tour took us to Beijing, China, for two days and then on to one of my favourite places, Hong Kong, where I visited the Happy Valley racetrack, one of the best horse racing tracks in the world. We played against a Hong Kong XI, who featured my former West Ham team mate Steve Walford and John Spencer, who later joined Chelsea.

The lads flew on to Hawaii for a further seven-day holiday, but I came home after Hong Kong to prepare for the holidays in America and the Caribbean that Lorraine and I had previously planned. While we were on the Dutch-Caribbean isle of Curacao we enjoyed watching the 1990 World Cup which, after an awful start to the tournament, saw England get stronger and stronger. If they had won against Germany in the semi-final I am convinced they would have beaten Argentina in the final, too.

I was a little bit disappointed not to have been there myself because if ever I was going to play in a World Cup, it would have been Italia '90. But after starting the season on the fringe of the England team, I was a million miles from it by the time Bobby Robson named his 22-man squad.

Italia '90 will best be remembered for Paul Gascoigne's tears and his emergence as a world class performer. I could never understand why Gazza had not been given his chance earlier because he was, and still is, the best player England has produced for a long time. I got to know him quite well with the England squads and he's a tremendous character and a lovely lad.

If only the press would get off his back and let him get on with his football career. The pressure on him must be intolerable and I really feel for him at times. People have got no right to interfere with his private life. The only thing we should read about him is his football contribution. But, unfortunately, as with most superstars, all people want to do is dish the dirt, which is sad.

Why is it that the English always tend to slag off their best players – and let's make no mistake, Gazza is our best player. We should be encouraging and praising him and when he's fit, we should build the England team around him.

When England are successful, it gives the whole nation a big lift and there was definitely a new air of optimism as the 1990/91 season approached.

Claret & Blues

DOWN AND OUT

HAVING made my peace with the club and got fresh assurances from Colin Harvey that I would be first choice again from the start of 1990/91, I was really buzzing in pre-season.

Then it all went horribly and mysteriously wrong for me on our three-match tour of Southern Ireland. In our warm-up games, I played in friendlies against Cork City, Athlone and Swindon Town in Dublin, but I started to feel intense pain in my lower stomach region.

I also felt hot and generally under the weather. As soon as we arrived back in Liverpool, I drove to see our club doctor, who suggested it was probably a hernia, which explained my stomach pains but not the other problems I was experiencing.

I went right off my food, which is most unlike me, and after two days I had to go to bed feeling very sick and coughing up blood. I was feeling delirious as Lorraine took me by car to Southport Hospital, where the doctor feared that I might have malaria (possibly contracted on our previous year's tour of the Far East) or meningitis. They performed a lumber puncture, and put me to bed, where I stayed for six days. In that time I lost over a stone in weight, dipping under 11 stones, and was repeatedly sick.

Colin visited me in hospital and was disappointed to hear the doctor's prognosis that I'd be out of action for six weeks with a mystery virus that no one in the medical professional could explain. Apparently there are dozens of viruses that the experts know very little about and I happened to have one of them

I continued to convalesce at home but another three weeks passed before I was able to resume light training. With more time needed to get match-fit, this was the last thing I needed when I should have been concentrating on re-establishing myself as first choice striker.

I could only watch as we lost our opening home match to Second Division champions Leeds United 3-2. I was watching from the directors' box and when I went out to see the second half, after my cup of tea, I was surprised to see Neville Southall sitting by the goalpost by himself.

Apparently the management hadn't realised what Nev had done until after the game, when he was duly fined for his sit-down. It was one of the most eccentric things Nev did, although I can remember another amusing story from the training ground.

It was around that time that Nev got bored during one particularly drawn out training routine which involved taking loads of free-kicks and corners which excluded Nev. After a while, a few of the lads started laughing loudly and I turned around to see that Nev had climbed up onto the crossbar at the other end of the field and was laying across the bar with his head resting on one hand! It certainly broke up the tedium of the training session and had everyone in fits of laughter.

Our defeat by Leeds was followed by two more, at Coventry City and Manchester City. I managed to make it onto the bench for the 1-1 draw with Arsenal, although I still wasn't fit, and after not being involved at Sunderland, I was on the bench again as we went down 3-2 at home to Liverpool.

Colin had signed Mike Milligan from Oldham, who struggled all season to settle in, and Andy Hinchcliffe from Manchester City, who also needed time to find his way at the club. It became a difficult first few games for them both.

Once I was given the all-clear to resume playing, I got off to a flier, scoring a hat-trick on my first appearance, a 5-0 League Cup win at Wrexham, and then two goals in our first league win of the campaign, at home to Southampton.

Although I had regained favour in the closing weeks of the previous season, Colin was still perming any two from three upfront. One week I'd be playing with Sharpy, the next with Newell. There was still no sign of a settled partnership forming.

Comparing Sharp and Newell, I'd say that they are both excellent target men. Sharpy was probably better at holding the ball up, but Newelly was definitely the quickest of the two. I think if I'd had the chance to play with Newelly over a longer period of time, we might have clicked a bit better but it never happened.

The frustrations I felt were probably shared by those two lads, too. It couldn't have helped their game much either to be playing alongside me one week and someone else the next.

Although I'd scored five goals in my first two outings, there was still no way I was fully fit – I got through those matches on pure adrenalin. The virus had really taken a lot out of me and it wasn't looking good for the team either. With only one win from our first 10 league matches, we were languishing in the bottom three as autumn merged into winter.

And any hopes of an improvement in team spirit suffered another blow when Kevin Sheedy and Martin Keown were involved in a fight while most of the lads were out for a Chinese meal, followed by a drink in Southport. I actually missed our traditional night out this time because I was playing in the reserves at Blackburn Rovers the next night, but everyone on Merseyside was aware of the incident. It took place in the Carlton Bar, and left Sheeds needing four stitches in his head. Their fracas, covered fully in the press, once again highlighted the ill feeling that had developed between young and old in the Everton dressing room.

People were beginning to question Colin's position – I know I was asking more questions of him when he took me off with 20 minutes to go of our third round

Rumblelows Cup tie at Sheffield United. To me, it was another stupid example of taking off a striker when the team is losing 2-0. Pat Nevin, who came on for me, got one back but it didn't stop us from going out of the competition.

It was only half a dozen games since I'd been a hero with a hat-trick in the previous round and a couple on my first league appearance. I was again left feeling utterly frustrated.

But Colin Harvey had a far bigger problem to face just around the corner.

We had the day off after our cup defeat at Bramall Lane and it was around 11am that morning when the 'phone rang at our house. It was John Keith, of the *Daily Express*, to tell me the shock news that Colin had been sacked. I knew we'd had a bad start to the season but I couldn't believe the board's decision.

I know we had our differences, but I was very disappointed and felt sorry for Colin, who, after all, I liked as a person despite problems football-wise.

I felt that I'd let him down in that he'd signed me for a British record fee and although I'd done reasonably well, I hadn't set the world alight.

Whether other players asked themselves whether they could have done more, on the field, to have kept Colin in his job, I don't know. I can only speak personally and if you do think anything of your manager, you must feel some guilt when he is sacked.

I felt disappointed, too, that Everton were booting him out when, given a couple more changes and a bit of good luck, we would have had a decent side.

Colin was Everton through and through, the club was his whole life. While there was growing concern about our league position, and the fact that we were out of the Littlewoods Cup, I don't think he had any inkling that he would be going.

I phoned him at his home that afternoon, basically to commiserate and wish him well in the future. He sounded shocked but dismissed his plight by saying simply: "These things happen."

Whatever differences we had, I will always be very grateful to Colin Harvey for taking me to Everton and giving me the chance to play for one of the biggest clubs in British football.

There was all sorts of speculation about Colin's likely successor but I had no doubt in my mind about the man I would have appointed – Joe Royle.

I'd been impressed with how he'd performed with virtually no money to spend at Oldham the previous season, taking them to the FA Cup semi-final and Littlewoods Cup Final, and I fancied the opportunity of playing under him at Goodison. He was of course a big Everton favourite in his own right and when Colin was sacked, it seemed as if the door had opened for Joe.

While the speculation intensified, the players had to get on with it and try and pick up the pieces. Jimmy Gabriel was appointed caretaker manager and picked the team for our home game against QPR on November 3.

On the morning of the game I picked up the papers to read a critical outburst by Jimmy, who claimed that the players had let Colin down badly. He said he would be making changes, leaving out the players who had failed Colin.

I arrived at Goodison on Saturday to discover that the "changes" threatened by Jimmy amounted, in fact, to one change: I was out in the cold again.

To say I wasn't too pleased is putting it mildly. I stormed into Jimmy's office and threw the offending newspaper article down in front of him. I was fuming: "What do you mean by this? How can you just point the finger at me, there are 10 others in the team?"

He was all apologetic but I was still dropped and had to sit back and watch the lads produce their most convincing performance of the season to beat Rangers 3-0, with Newelly, who came back at my expense, getting one of the goals.

Although I liked Jimmy as a fella, I obviously didn't relish the thought of him taking over from Colin full-time. The sooner the club brought in a new man the better, as far as I was concerned.

The following Tuesday, I played (not too well) for the reserves against Manchester City. There was an awful lot of talk before the game that City's boss, Howard Kendall, could be returning to Goodison.

Sure enough, that same night, Kendall was re-appointed Everton manager.

Even more incredibly, Colin Harvey was named as his new assistant.

Both decisions caught all the players and the media by surprise. When Colin first went, no one even considered Kendall a possibility.

His return was warmly welcomed by the senior pros, who had worked with him before and only had good words to say about him.

But while they were looking forward to working with him again, I was sceptical. I'd seen how he'd brought in old Evertonians, Alan Harper and Adrian Heath, at Man. City and thought then that he obviously liked having familiar faces around him.

The big question on my lips was how he would take to younger, newer players like myself.

My fears soon proved well founded. When Howard arrived at training next morning, he went round shaking hands with all the players who had played under him in his previous spell in charge, virtually ignoring the rest of us. Although he spoke to the team collectively, his only one-to-one contact was with the older players.

It was the start of another unsettling period for players like myself, Peter Beagrie, Stuart McCall and one or two others who had been in and out of the side under Colin Harvey. Instead of getting better, I could only see more problems ahead . . .

Above: The four new signings from the summer of 1988 – Stuart McCall, Neil McDonald, myself and Pat Nevin.
Above right: Action from my first game for Everton against Torino.
Below: August 27, 1988, against Newcastle, 34 seconds gone . . . 1-0!

Above: *Celebrations with Sharpy after my first goal.*
Below: *My hat-trick goal in the second half of that game against Newcastle.*

Time to salute the Gwladys Street end after my third debut goal against Newcastle.

Above: *A rare headed goal wins my second league game at Coventry – my happiest hunting ground.*
Right: *A 'Buddy Holly' against Southampton, October 1988.*
Below: *Reidy chases after me, but Casey doesn't look too pleased.*

Above: *A poor volley from me against Villa goes through the 'keeper's legs for my first goal in 10 games.*
Below: *Semi-finals here we come . . . time for a piggy back!*

Above: *My bobbler at Norwich which sent Bryan Gunn the wrong way.*
Right: *Happy days on the bench at Forest with John Ebbrell!*
Below: *Kick the ball, not my head, next time, please! This one found the net against Southampton.*

Above: *A headed fourth goal against Sunderland in the ZDS Cup, 1991.*
Below: *Anyone want a smelly shinpad!*

What an eventful game against Notts County in 1991 . . .

Above: *My worst-ever miss!*

Right: *Jumping for joy after my goal in the 1-0 win.*

Below: *Unfortunately, my overhead kick hit the bar, with Peter Beardsley (now Newcastle) and Craig Short (now Everton) looking on.*

Claret & Blues

NEW BOSS - SAME OLD STORY

A NY hopes I had that a new manager would give me a much-needed fresh start at Everton were soon shattered – in my very first communication with Howard Kendall.

Ironically, his first game in charge was our league visit to Sheffield United, where Colin's reign had ended in the Littlewoods Cup defeat 10 days earlier.

The only change Howard made from the side that had beaten QPR the previous Saturday was to recall one of his old favourites, Kevin Sheedy, at the expense of Peter Beagrie, who joined me on the subs' bench.

Beags got on for the last 15 minutes, while I watched it all from the side as we managed a point from one of the worst goalless draws I've ever seen.

In the dressing room afterwards, Howard ran through each member of the team, praising them in turn . . . "Nev – brilliant; Kevin – great performance; good game Sharpy . . . "

He'd congratulated every single player, offering them nothing but praise on working hard for the point. Then he turned to his subs. "Peter, next time I tell you to warm up, warm up as if you look like you want to get on. I want to see you running past as if you're desparate to get on the pitch.

"And as for you," he continued, pointing straight at me, "until you get you're finger out and start trying in reserve games, and you start trying in training, you'll never get in my team."

I just stood up, shook my head in total dismay and got in the bath. My first conversation with the new boss and he'd totally slaughtered me. My worst fears were being confirmed.

To a certain extent, what Howard was saying was true but if he felt that way, why didn't he simply call me into his office to make his views known?

By singling out Beags and I like that, he unnecessarily humiliated us in front of all the other players, and I didn't respect him for that.

Although I started the next match, a home draw with Tottenham, I occupied the bench again for our defeat at Wimbledon and I was in and out under Howard just as I'd been under Colin. It was the same old story.

Howard quickly made up his mind that I wasn't his type of player and although he didn't say that at the time, two years later he admitted to me that he hadn't fancied me when he first returned to Everton.

And the communication problem I'd suffered under Colin, remained under Howard, too. We barely exchanged a word to each other when he first arrived, avoiding each other, and it was a cold, non-existent relationship.

I can never understand why, when I was bought for £2.05m, Everton didn't work to get the best out of me for the benefit of the club and myself. I might as well have been a Two Pound player as far as the management was concerned. My confidence had been destroyed and I couldn't understand it.

To be fair, once Howard arrived, he improved team spirit. His more relaxed, jovial approach to training lifted the lads and made them laugh more.

When Howard did pick me, I scored goals, most notably when he brought me back for a Zenith Data Systems Cup tie against Sunderland at Goodison in January 1991. I scored all four goals in a 4-1 win to make a point, even though few people took the competition very seriously.

But that didn't deter Howard from substituting me with half-an-hour to go, against non-league Woking in the FA Cup fourth round, the following Sunday, when we scraped a fortunate 1-0 win.

I was sub. for the next game, home to Sunderland in the league (even though I'd just put four past the same defence in the ZDS!) and came on for Beags in the 58th minute of our league match at Liverpool. That was followed by our first game against Liverpool in the FA Cup fifth round. Once again, I wore the number 14 shirt at Anfield, coming on in a tight, uninteresting 0-0 draw that was shown live on TV.

If the viewers didn't exactly get good value that afternoon, no one who saw the replay at Goodison the following Wednesday could have any complaints. It was one of the epic matches in FA Cup history, one of the most thrilling games I've ever been involved in.

Even though the game was at home, Howard liked to take the lads away to an hotel the night before, so we stayed at a place on the Wirral. It was also around this time that Howard declared that he didn't mind if the players had a couple of glasses of wine or half a lager the night before a game. Apparently it was a policy he reintroduced, because the players were afforded this unusual privilege in their successful era under him.

Even though I'd come on for Sheeds at Anfield, I didn't for one moment think that I would start the game and, sure enough, I was on the bench again, this time with Stuart McCall.

The game swung one way, then the other. Liverpool went one up after 32 minutes through Peter Beardsley, before Sharpy equalised just after half-time. Liverpool went 2-1 up with a brilliant goal from Beardsley, but Sharpy equalised again almost immediately. There were 13 minutes left in the second half when Rushie scored his usual Merseyside derby goal to make it 3-2 to Liverpool.

There must have been about 10 minutes left when Howard shouted at me to "go and have a warm-up." I ran up and down the line for a couple of minutes before he called me back to the bench and said: "You're going on, just run around and see what you can do for us." Just before stepping on to the field, I glanced up at the electronic scoreboard and saw that we'd entered the 84th minute. I thought to myself: 'Is he sure, what on earth does he expect me to do in six minutes?'

In normal circumstances as a substitute (and I should know), you really need a good 15 minutes to get your second wind, to get used to the pace of the game.

I came on for Pat Nevin and immediately ran straight to the centre of the pitch. I just thought I had to get involved and get into the box, where I could score a goal.

Three or four minutes went by, during which I had only one touch – a simple lay-off. The clock kept ticking over and Liverpool seemed set for the quarter-finals when Neil McDonald got the ball in the right-back position. As he drilled it into the box, it deflected into the ground off a Liverpool player and the ball just skidded through. Stuart Mac, who got on at half-time, managed to stick out a leg and just flicked it behind the Reds' defence, catching everyone off-balance.

Where I'd just come on, and my mind and legs were probably a bit fresher than the others, I reacted quickest. Mike Newell was actually in front of me when the ball was deflected, but I ran in front of him to get to the ball and finished well with my left foot.

The feeling I had when that goal went in, knowing there was only a minute left to play, was unbelievable. I ran towards the corner flag to celebrate with the fans behind the Gwladys Street goal.

In the first half of extra-time I put a chance over the bar and when John Barnes scored a cracker to make it 4-3 to Liverpool, I think everyone thought that it was asking a bit much to equalise for a fourth time.

The game went into the second period of extra time, and Andy Hinchcliffe got the ball. He cut in from the left and sort of lost control of the ball, as Jan Molby eased it back to Glenn Hysen. For some reason, instead of whacking it clear, Hysen stepped over the ball and let it run – I don't know whether he thought Bruce Grobbelaar was behind him.

I read the situation, followed the ball and although it was at a difficult angle, and on my left foot again, I took a swing at it, connected very well and the ball went through Bruce's legs before nestling in the corner.

I ran to the corner flag again, it was a brilliant feeling. I felt that if I'd stayed out there all night I would have got my hat-trick . . . four . . . five, who knows? It was one of those unforgettable nights when it all went right for me for a change.

People have often asked me, what was it like to play in that game? I tell them that I didn't play in it, I only came on as sub, with six minutes to go! It was, undoubtedly, one of the best games I've ever been involved with and I don't think you'll see another 4-4 between Everton and Liverpool. It was a one-off occasion that will probably be impossible to emulate.

After a classic like that, how could we have decided it on penalties? That's why I'm totally against cup ties being decided on pens, when replays are so much fairer. The three games we had against Liverpool, and other marathon ties over the years, are an important part of FA Cup romance and drama. That's what the competition is all about and we should do all we can to preserve it.

Howard was pleased for me afterwards. This time I got a pat on the back and a few words of praise, instead of a rollocking, and it made a nice change.

Our enthralling 4-4 draw with Liverpool caused massive repercussions across Stanley Park, where Kenny Dalglish sensationally announced he was quitting as Liverpool manager within 48 hours of the first replay. The Everton players first heard the shock news as we were warming up at Bellefield – a fella, whose garden backed onto the training ground, popped his head over the fence and shouted very excitedly: "Dalglish has resigned."

We all thought he was joking but we knew it was the truth once a few press boys arrived as we finished the session. It was unbelievable to think that my two goals had possibly contributed to his resignation.

There were a lot of rumours about why he suddenly decided to walk away from the job, but it seemed to me that, basically, Kenny had felt the pressure building up and could no longer live his life as he wanted to.

Kenny was simply the latest managerial casualty on Merseyside in the early 1990s, but he would by no means be the last. Indeed, after a period away from the spotlight, he re-emerged at Blackburn Rovers where, backed up by Jack Walker's millions, he added to his incredible list of honours by leading them to the championship in 1995.

The following Saturday at Goodison, I started my first league game in quite a while. I made the most of it by scoring an early goal but couldn't prevent us losing 2-1 to Sheffield United.

Four days later, we again stayed overnight at an hotel before the second replay with Liverpool at Goodison. It was about 4pm on the afternoon of the game when Howard 'pulled' me and dropped his latest bombshell. "I know you did well for us in the last game against them," he said, "and I've tried really hard to get you in the team tonight, but I can't. I've got to pick a side to win the game tonight and I can't get you in it."

I looked at him, totally dumbfounded, and said: "You're joking." I'd scored two goals when I came on against Liverpool in the first replay, I'd scored and played quite well in the next game against Sheffield United . . . and now I was dropped again. What more could I do to win a place in the side?

To be fair to Howard, he said he was picking a team to win the game and they did just that, 1-0, but from a personal point of view I didn't know where to turn. I suppose a few people might have thought that I would have welcomed a trip 'home' to West Ham for the quarter-final, but it was only the second time I'd been back since leaving, and I wasn't particularly looking forward to it.

Billy Bonds had taken over from Lou Macari a year earlier and the Hammers were flying at the top of the old Second Division at the time, looking a strong bet for promotion. I was very apprehensive as we arrived at our Essex hotel the night before the game.

As usual, the lads enjoyed a few glasses of wine, to help them relax and put them in the right frame of mind the night before the big game. It was an unusual approach and to be honest, by the end of the season it was getting a bit out of hand. Players, including myself, were having a few too many drinks.

There would be four bottles of wine, between four or five of us, on the table with our evening meal, so by the end of the night we'd had around a bottle each, which was unprofessional. We didn't really think about it at the time, because we weren't drinking to get pissed – it was social drinking. If you're sitting down with the lads for a couple of hours, and there are four bottles of wine on the table in front of you, it's very easy to get through them.

I don't think our consumption of wine had any bearing on our 2-1 defeat at Upton Park though. I don't want to take anything away from West Ham, because they played tremendously well and deserved their victory and in Stuart Slater they had the star of the show. He had probably his best game for the club and Howard actually told the press afterwards that Stuart would be worth £3 million.

Bearing in mind it was a passionate, highly-charged cup tie atmosphere, I had to expect the hostile reception I got from the West Ham fans when I came on as sub. I'd got a mixed reaction when I returned to Upton Park for the league game more than two years earlier, but this was much more hostile. I thought their actions were designed more to put me off my game, rather than serve as a criticism of me as a player.

Without a doubt, I was hurt a little bit by the treatment the fans gave me. I'd expected to go back and get a tremendous reception, because I felt I'd scored a lot of goals and done my best for the club. But, being realistic, most players who go back to their old clubs get a bit of stick. Why should it be any different for me?

I admit, it is off-putting when the fans behave in that way towards you. As much as you try and switch off, you are very aware when you receive the ball and the fans boo you, that they are trying to put you off your game – and it invariably works. It can make you more inhibited on the field but I think as I've got older I've learned to live with the fact that if opposing fans boo you, you've got to take it as a compliment really. They are booing you to put you off your game, which means you must be a good player, or otherwise why do it? The players who get stick from fans are invariably the best players, or the ones who score goals.

After the game, which the Hammers thoroughly deserved to win, I walked down the corridor to the home dressing room, poked my head in and wished the players all the best in the semi-final. I genuinely thought that if Everton couldn't win it, then l hoped West Ham would.

Little did we know that night that the infamous Tony Gale sending-off against Nottingham Forest in the semi-final was going to cost West Ham a place at Wembley. I watched the game on TV and that decision by Keith Hackett was one of the worst I've ever seen. To send Galey off in that situation – with him, Gary Crosby and the ball heading towards the corner flag, and players running back to cover – was totally crazy. Hackett got it wrong. He ruined the game, which turned into one of the most one-sided semi-finals, he ruined Tony's big day and he ruined West Ham's season.

After the cup exit, my sole intention was to get back in the side and stay there in the two months or so that remained of the season. Two nights after playing at Upton Park, I started at Barnsley in the ZDS Cup and was pleased to score the only goal of the tie. I scored in our 4-3 league win at Southampton the following Saturday but – surprise, surprise – was dropped for the ZDS Cup northern area semi-final, second leg, against Leeds United at Goodison.

It was like an action-replay of the Liverpool cup tie as I came off the bench, towards the end of the second half, to score a late equaliser, then netted again in extra-time. John Ebbrell made it 3-1, and 6-4 on aggregate, to take us back to Wembley to face Crystal Palace in the final.

I was concerned, though, that I was now being dubbed 'Super Sub' by the press – a nickname I most certainly didn't want. Thankfully, Howard started to pick me regularly that spring, when I started all of our last 11 First Division matches, scoring seven times.

The fact that only 12,000 Everton fans attended the ZDS Cup Final showed just what they thought of this much-maligned competition, although a large turnout from South London ensured a healthy attendance of 52,000. The majority of fans went home happy with Palace's 4-1 victory in extra-time, but all we had to show for it was another Wembley losers' medal and a collection of bumps and bruises from a hard-fought encounter. Like the fans, I suppose we viewed it as 'just another game'.

There was an amusing incident at our hotel the night before the game, when Howard wandered into the restaurant and asked if the meal was all right. To which Mike Newell piped up: "Dunno, boss, but the wine's magnificent!"

A few weeks before the final, Howard made his first signing since returning when he bought Polish international winger Robert Warzycha from Gornik Zabrze for £500,000 – he looked real quality from the first day we saw his incredible pace and shooting ability in training. He got off to a great start by scoring on his debut at Leeds in the ZDS Cup and also both goals in a 2-2 draw at Aston Villa.

But, yet again, Everton never got the best from a player of obvious talent. The following season, Robert claimed the unwanted record of being substituted 25 – yes, TWENTY-FIVE – times! It's not surprising that his confidence slumped and he ended up joining a Swiss club.

Stefan Rehn was another example of a quality player who failed to fulfil his undoubted class in an Everton shirt. He played numerous times for Sweden, starred for Gothenburg after joining them for £400,000, and has won the player of the year award since returning to his country. But at Everton this central midfielder's confidence was destroyed once when, within 15 minutes of coming on as sub. Stefan was actually substituted himself!

Another foreign player who didn't develop at Goodison, but who has since done very well after leaving Merseyside, is the Dutchman Ray Atteveld, who had a very brief loan spell with West Ham before joining Bristol City for £250,000 in March '92. Last season, he went close to a call-up to the Dutch national squad.

I felt I finished the season even stronger than the previous one. Even though we lost at home to Wimbledon on April 10, my volley from outside the area was my best goal of the season. I scored against Chelsea in the next match, at Tottenham in a 3-3 draw and after netting the winner at home to Luton, one of their defenders, John Dreyer, commented that I "had to be as good as any forward in the country when he performed like that."

Interestingly, on the day we played Derby County at the Baseball Ground, there was a lot of speculation that the Derby striker Dean Saunders could be joining Everton at the end of that season. It was being billed as a 'Cottee v Deano' showdown, so I was obviously delighted to score twice in our 3-2 win.

My performance earned me a call up to the England 'B' squad, which I was delighted at, but in the Derby game I was pulled down for a penalty and fell very heavily on my chest. I hadn't broken any ribs but I still had to come off after only 23 minutes of our last game at QPR with breathing problems.

The injury also forced me out of the 'B' squad to play Switzerland at Walsall which was bitterly disappointing because it was the first time since the summer of 1989 that I'd been in contention for any England honours. Graham Taylor had taken over from Bobby Robson and it would have been an opportunity to show what I could do.

Alas, I should have known, after the ups and downs I'd experienced all season, that something would crop up to throw another spanner in the works.

It would have been a nice way to round off another difficult season. I'd scored 24 goals in all competitions from only 27 starts. And my 10 goals in the First Division came from 20 starts and made me top scorer at the club, so I was pleased with my return.

The club had recovered from its early season blues to finish ninth, and, as had happened at the end of the previous season, I was looking forward to the start of the next campaign.

So were my old club, who had finally got themselves back into the First Division, where they belonged. I said when John Lyall was sacked that Billy Bonds was the right man to bring in – preferably to work under John to start with. I couldn't understand in a million years why they chose Lou Macari instead.

He had preached the long-ball game at Swindon, whereas West Ham had always been renowned for playing good football, and he had no experience of management at top level either. The West Ham board moved outside the club and it backfired on them in a big way – as it did when Everton brought in Mike Walker years later – and from a distance I couldn't understand it.

Bonzo got the job seven months too late, but at least he took the Hammers up at the end of his first full season as manager.

Claret & Blues

HOWARD'S WAY

IN the summer of 1991 Howard Kendall took the players on the first of his legendary pre-season tours – and they were certainly different to anything I'd been used to.

It was the first time in my career that I'd ever heard of footballers being told off for NOT going out drinking with the lads!

I said earlier how much Howard believed in the players socialising together to build team spirit and would openly encourage us to go out of the hotel for a few drinks to pass the many hours of free time we had on this particular 10-day tour of Switzerland.

One night, everyone went down the town for drinks except Pat Nevin and Andy Hinchcliffe, who both decided that they would have an early night and go to bed to read a book.

I was rooming with 'Paddy' and rolled in during the small hours having enjoyed the evening. I had as much of a lay-in as possible, bearing in mind we were due to train that morning, so Pat went down with Andy for breakfast.

About an hour later, Pat returned to tell me that Howard had approached them at breakfast, asking where they'd been the previous night. When they said they had both stayed in, Howard had a bit of a go at them for not doing their bit to improve team spirit by joining the rest of the lads, and the staff, at the bar!

Howard was the master of one-liners. While we were in Spain to play Real Sociedad, Peter Beagrie ran into trouble on the back of a moped that belonged to a local lad who offered him a lift. I can remember Beags disappearing into the night, on the back of this bike, it looked just like John Wayne riding off into the sunset.

Anyway, in the morning, Martin Keown came to mine and Pat Nevin's room to tell us: "Keep it quiet, but Beags crashed on the bike and needed 63 stitches in his arm!"

We were travelling home that evening to Manchester airport and to try and hide the full extent of the damage from the press and photographers we knew would be waiting to welcome us at Manchester, Beags wore a long-sleeve jumper. Unfortunately Mark Ward, our new signing who was sat next to him on the flight, was unaware of the moped episode and kept knocking into Pete's injured arm, which was causing him a lot of discomfort.

As we walked through the arrival lounge, Beags noticed the photographers with their cameras poised to get the picture follow-up to their papers' morning stories of our winger's misdemeanour. He turned to Howard for advice. "What shall I do, boss?" Howard's reply was: "Smile!"

It was while we were in Switzerland that Martin Keown had a close encounter with an Everton 'fan'. The lads went out onto the pitch for a warm-up – including myself, as it was pre-season – only to find about a dozen Everton followers having a kickabout into one of the goals. Martin went up to a couple of them and politely told them that they'd had their fun and could they please now get off the pitch so that the players could warm up properly.

After an angry response from one of the 'fans', Martin told him more forcefully to get off and turned his back. The 'fan' then kicked Martin very hard up the back-side and, as Martin turned to confront him, a few of the players, myself included, sprinted over to prevent any further aggro.

Martin did very well not to retaliate 'Cantona-style' and the 'fan' was ushered off by his friends. It just goes to show the intense provocation some players have to put up with nowadays, and it was no surprise when the same idiot was pictured in the papers after being deported following an England game a couple of years later. Football could really do without thugs like him.

I think we actually returned from that tour less fitter than before we went. There was just too much time to fill between games and, of course, we filled it with frequent nights out visiting local bars.

At least I had something special to celebrate – the news that Lorraine was expecting our first child.

The tour was also Stuart McCall's last with Everton, before he joined Glasgow Rangers for £1.25m. Howard had been playing Kevin Sheedy in centre midfield in pre-season games, so when Stuart told a few of us that this was his farewell trip, we knew he'd be on the move.

To me, losing Stuart Mac was a big blow, the start of all Everton's problems, and a mistake. When a club is in the position of selling its best players, you have a recipe for disaster brewing, which proved to be the case in the next few seasons.

Stuart was happy at Everton, he didn't want to leave, and it was only the lure of Rangers that tempted him to Scotland. His Everton career had ran parallel to mine, because he'd also been in and out of the side under both Colin and Howard, despite his Cup Final heroics.

Having been disappointed to see Stuart go, I was also sorry when Graeme Sharp joined Oldham Athletic for £500,000 that summer. I had originally been bought to play alongside Sharpy and, through no fault of his or mine, we never really gelled as a partnership. Sharpy was joined on his way to Boundary Park by Mike Milligan, who rejoined the Latics for £600,000 after a poor season.

I felt Howard bought well that summer. When Dean Saunders chose Liverpool instead of Everton – much to the obvious disgust of all Evertonians – it paved the way for us to bring Peter Beardsley across Stanley Park for just £1m.

And in a double deal with his old club, Manchester City, Howard signed my old mate from West Ham, Mark Ward (£1m), and Alan Harper (£200,000), who had proved his worth as a utility player. Wardie is a great little player and a real character, and I really enjoyed my time with him at both West Ham and Everton.

After losing our opening game 2-1 at Nottingham Forest, Wardie scored twice on his Goodison debut and I got the other as we defeated Arsenal 3-1. With me and Beardsley up front, Wardie wide left, Robert Warzycha on the right, and Sheedy and John Ebbrell in midfield, no wonder the press quickly labelled us the 'Mini Marvels'.

Beardsley was tremendous, even in training. He doesn't drink so he'd never come into training the worse for wear. His enthusiasm for the game was superb, a great example to every young player. Kevin Keegan has said it, and I go along with his view, that Peter will probably play until he's 40 years-old, as he looks after himself so well. I was honoured to have played alongside such a great player.

Things very quickly turned sour for me, though. After the win over Arsenal, we failed to win any of our next six matches in the league and I was subbed against Man. United, Sheffield Wednesday and in our 3-1 defeat at Liverpool. For some reason, I had a very sluggish start to the season even though Howard had put me in the side from the outset.

I was on to the bench for the home game against Norwich City – but didn't even get that far against Crystal Palace in the first week of September, when my Everton career slumped to a new low. On Thursday, September 5, I was named in the reserves at Manchester City where, despite the inclusion of several players of first team experience, we were stuffed 4-1, although it could have been 8-1 – we were that bad.

Soon after arriving at Bellefield the next morning, we heard a rumour that the reserve team might be playing in an 'A' team game at Morecambe that night. The 'A' team being the equivalent of Everton's third team. Howard spoke to us and confirmed that after the poor performance at Maine Road the previous night we would, indeed, be 'enjoying' a night out at Morecambe.

I arrived at the Northern Premier League ground to find a stand that held about 300 people and a pitch more suited for grazing cows. It was a bit different from the stadium I'd played at a week before – Anfield!

It was our new youth team manager Dave Fogg's first game in charge of the 'A' team and he must have wondered what it was all about with the so-called 'Famous Five' – Peter Beagrie, Neil McDonald, Ray Atteveld, Eddie Youds and myself – not exactly relishing the match. It was degrading for me, the club's record transfer, being forced to play for the third team, while Neil showed his feelings by throwing his team sheet in the bin!

My anger turned to laughter, though, when I saw 'Scan' – an ex-Everton apprentice, run out to play for the other side. A couple of weeks earlier, 'Scan' had been cleaning the windows at our house in Birkdale with Roly Howard, the manager of non-league Marine, who was our regular window cleaner!

The other Everton lads had a good laugh at my unexpected meeting with my window cleaner but despite winning 2-1, with me scoring one, it couldn't disguise the fact that Morecambe was the lowest point of my career.

Eight days later, I returned to the first team fold at Sheffield United but after a run-out as sub., I was again left out of the squad for the next two, at Man. City and home to Coventry City.

For me, it was back to the reserves, although a goal on my return to the first team, albeit in the ZDS Cup against Oldham, earned me a recall for the First Division home game with Tottenham on October 5. I've usually done well against Spurs and this occasion was special in that I scored a first-half hat-trick, which set me buzzing again.

I was still on a high when we arrived home but, as I've said many times before, when something good happens, there is inevitably something bad just waiting around the corner. Sure enough, two hours after the game we got a phone call to say my nan had slipped over and broken both hips.

Before our next league game a fortnight later, Howard made a new signing, paying Luton Town £600,000 for 19 year-old Matt Jackson. He soon had a good chance to get to know everyone as Howard organised a game in Spain, followed by four days relaxing in Magaluf, to fill a free weekend in early November.

The friendly was against a Spanish third division side based in Bilbao. Their pitch was a mudheap, not helped by the torrential ran that had fallen since we arrived the previous day. Despite my goal, it was a largely forgettable game, although there was one amusing incident in the second half that made us laugh.

One of the Spanish defenders hacked away a clearance that skidded off the muddy surface and into the dug out, where the ball hit Howard on the head. It was difficult to concentrate on the game for a minute or two as we tried to stop laughing at the sight of the muddy ball mark left on Howard's forehead!

My hat-trick against Tottenham had restored confidence and I scored against QPR and Wolves, in the Rumbelows Cup, before the end of October, but I was back on the bench for the visit to Luton on the first Saturday of November. It was a quick return to Kenilworth Road for Matt Jackson, who had played only nine games for the Hatters before his big move. Matt became a great friend of mine and I've been pleased to see him develop his career. He was signed shortly after Howard sold another good mate of mine, Neil McDonald, to Oldham Atheltic for £500,000.

Howard's next move in the transfer market came just a few weeks later, after I scored in our 2-0 home win over Wimbledon, when he moved Eddie Youlds on to Ipswich Town for £300,000 and, more significantly, transferred Mike Newell to Blackburn Rovers for £1.1m.

In subsequent years Howard was repeatedly criticised for selling Mike but at the time I thought it was a good decision. Newelly wasn't playing well at the time and, just as he'd run out of patience with me, so Howard lost faith in Mike.

Where I thought Howard went wrong was replacing Newell – not with a big target man, who would have provided a good option to Beardsley and myself, but with another smallish striker in Maurice Johnston, who cost £1.5m from Glasgow Rangers that November. The failure of 'Mo' to make a big impact would ultimately play a big part in Howard departure.

So, in the space of three months, the club had undergone a total change of strategy as far as its strikers were concerned. Howard had sold two target men, in Sharp and Newell, and replaced them with two small men, Beardsley and Johnston. Everton fans had always been brought up on big target men – their famous number nines, like Dixie Dean, Dave Hickson, Fred Pickering, Joe Royle, Bob Latchford and then Graeme Sharp – and this was a strange decision.

Mo made his debut up front alongside me against Notts County on November

23, with Beardsley in his favourite 'floating' role just behind us, and three in mid-field. It was probably one of my best games for the club, as I rattled the crossbar with an overhead kick and scored a tremendous goal. The 'Mini Marvels' were back!

In the Rumbelows Cup it was not so good, though. In our heavy home defeat by Leeds United in the fourth round, we completely lost our shape – as I was quick to point out to the manager.

Howard had decided to play with only three at the back, with the full-backs pushing on, but it wasn't working at all well. We had no width, no shape and we were losing 2-1 by half-time. Howard decided to invite the players to air their views on where we thought we had been going wrong in the first half. "Has anybody got any suggestions?" he asked, looking around the dressing room. I chipped in with a comment: "I think we're unbalanced, particularly on the left side, where Mel Sterland and Rod Wallace are ripping right through us."

Howard seemed to agree with me, but I hadn't done myself any favours as he turned to me and said: "Right, get your kit off, we'll change it around and go back to 4-4-2."

Me and my big mouth! I was the only player to say a word when Howard sought our opinions and I'd well and truly shot myself in the foot this time. I came off at half-time (along with Kevin Ratcliffe), although the switch didn't exactly work wonders as we went on to lose 4-1.

We dished out a hammering ourselves at Goodison on December 7, when Mo, Beardo, Beags and I scored in our 4-0 victory over West Ham. I was pleased to get the first goal, especially as I'd been getting a lot of stick from the fans behind that goal. After I scored I gave them a little sarcastic wave which, on reflection, I suppose I shouldn't have done. It wasn't meant maliciously, it was my way of saying to them that I could still score goals. And I needed every goal possible to try and re-establish myself in the side.

West Ham were poor on the day and, to be honest, I was very fearful of their survival chances even at that relatively early stage of the season.

A hamstring problem ruled me out of our next game, at Oldham, and when fit, I was annoyed to be confined to the bench at Arsenal just before Christmas.

When I did get back in, at home to Sheffield Wednesday on Boxing Day, I missed four or five really good chances and, as we lost 1-0, the press focused sharply on my misses.

Beardsley scored a cracker to defeat Southend United at home in the FA Cup – I had a good chat with John Cornwell, who was on their bench, after the game – which earned us a fourth round trip to Chelsea. As I'd been in and out of the side at the turn of the year, I only played at Stamford Bridge because Mo was injured.

The BBC covered the game live on the Sunday afternoon and Chelsea took the initiative when Clive Allen scored in the second half. There were about 20 minutes to go when I raced through on to a good chance, but succeeded only in driving my volley straight at their 'keeper, Kevin Hitchcock.

I was starting to worry that it wasn't going to be our day when we were awarded a penalty. Kevin Sheedy had been our regular penalty-taker that season but as he wasn't on the field, and I'd taken them before, I grabbed the ball and put it down on the spot. As I did so, Dennis Wise came up to me and, with a superb piece of kidology, said to me: "You're gonna miss this, you're gonna miss this."

I said: "No I'm not, I'm gonna score."

"I bet you a fiver you don't," continued Wisey, as the ref ushered him out of the area. "All right, you're on," I said.

I ran up, and although I didn't hit the ball poorly, I didn't strike it very well either, and it went at the perfect height for Hitchcock, who held the ball to his stomach. I just wanted the ground to cave in and swallow me up. I was aware that the match was on TV and that our whole season hinged on that penalty kick. Looking back, It was perhaps surprising that Peter Beardsley didn't take it. We were nowhere in the league again, already out of the Rumbelows Cup and now out of the FA Cup as well.

It was a personal disaster for me and I shot off from the ground quickly without stopping to pay Wisey his fiver. Although I think most of the Everton fans respected me for taking the penalty – there certainly weren't too many other takers on the day – the press slaughtered me and viewed the penalty miss as the final nail in my coffin at Everton. They thought it was more or less certain that I'd soon be on my way, part of another shake-up at Goodison.

The actual taking of a penalty is something a player has to be comfortable with. I'll take them if no one else wants to, but right through my career I've never felt really comfortable about taking them. I don't enjoy taking penalties, in the way Ray Stewart and Julian Dicks do. I think part of it's down to the belief that a penalty isn't a proper goal to me, because you don't score them in open play.

It began to look as if I may never score for Everton again. I was forever in and out of the side but it seemed as if Howard had dropped me for the last time when he left me out of the squad to face QPR at Goodison on February 8.

The reason, this time, was that I seemed all set to join Tottenham in a swap for Paul Stewart. Jon Smith told me the day before the QPR game that the deal was very much on, with Spurs manager Terry Venables keen to take me back to London.

And Howard confirmed as much when he told me: "It looks as though you'll be going to Tottenham and with all the speculation going on, I'm leaving you out today."

At that time, I would have relished returning to London and linking up with England's top striker Gary Lineker at White Hart Lane. I don't know whether Venables doubted my suitability to play alongside Lineker – who was not a target man – but, whatever, the strong speculation about a move came to nothing.

However, I was soon heading back to London – for a most eventful afternoon at West Ham . . .

CHAPTER 45

Claret & Blues

BOND BOMBSHELL

I KNEW full well before our visit to West Ham on February 29 that my old club were struggling badly at the foot of the First Division – and secondly, the troubles they'd been having over the fateful bond scheme.

The game itself saw Mo score early on but I didn't make it past half-time. About 10 minutes before the interval, I turned to chase a ball played over the top. I was running with Steve Potts – we always had a good duel and he was always so difficult to play against because of his pace – who just got to the ball first and went to knock it back to Ludek Miklosko.

As he did so, I over-stretched to try and cut out his backpass and planted my studs in the ground. My knee extended out the wrong way and it immediately felt very sore. As Ludo cleared the ball upfield, I jogged back towards the halfway line and as I got there, my knee 'locked' on me. I hobbled on until half-time, when Les Helm, the physio, advised me to apply an ice pack and rest it.

I watched the second half from the dug out and play had resumed only 10 or 15 minutes when a West Ham fan ran to the centre circle with a corner flag in his hand and then planted it on the centre spot. A few more fans came on, then a few more and before we knew it, there were hundreds on the pitch.

I didn't hang around to see what was going on, for I knew they were protesting about the bond scheme and, possibly, at the poor way their team had been playing on the day and most of the season.

Gary Ablett, signed from Liverpool for £750,000 in January, added to Hammers' misery by making it 2-0 and pushing them further into relegation trouble when the players went back on. I was more concerned with my knee at the time, but I managed a drink with my parents in the players' lounge before making my way through the main reception area at Upton Park where the press tend to congregate after matches.

Basically, the journalists wanted to know my views on what was happening to my former club. My response wasn't rehearsed in any way, it was simply my honest opinion straight from the heart, as someone who'd grown up a West Ham fan. I said something like: "I can't believe what was going on out there, it's very sad and unless the players can rise above it, then the club would be relegated."

I talked about the intimidating atmosphere among the crowd and how you could sense something was going to happen. The fans were clearly restless and had more or less accepted that the team was going down.

I went on to criticise the board, who had taken a lot of money in transfers but hadn't replaced players like myself, Incey, Wardie and Stuart Slater. The question had to be asked: where's the money gone?

And I also gave my view on the controversial bond scheme. I made the point that it wasn't fair to ask the ordinary working man to pay out and finance what was a very costly scheme to pay for the Upton Park ground redevelopment.

It was all very much off-the-cuff stuff, I just said what I thought as if I were a supporter of the club, as opposed to a player. Julian Dicks also spoke out against the bond scheme and we were both quoted in the Monday morning papers.

A couple of days later, Howard called me into his office and told me that the club had received a letter of complaint from West Ham secretary, Tom Finn, who basically said that there were enough problems at the club without ex-players chipping in with their opinions. Howard advised me not to get involved but I told him that I had simply given honest answers to the questions I'd been asked.

I didn't say what I did to the press at Upton Park that day to win back popularity with the West Ham fans but, in my own way, I think I did just that. They seemed to respect me for saying what they all thought themselves, but I certainly didn't set out to win their approval again. I spoke from the heart, as a lifelong Hammers' fan, and after that I definitely got a better reception from them as a result of my comments over the bond fiasco.

It was a very sad state of affairs. I didn't bother replying to Tom's letter. I ripped it up and threw it in the bin – not out of disrespect, but because I saw no point in prolonging the issue.

After the interest from Tottenham came to nothing, former Spurs manager David Pleat was next to enquire about me, phoning Howard to ask if he could take me on loan to Luton Town. I have a lot of respect for Pleat as a coach but, without wishing to sound disrespectful, I didn't think that leaving a big club like Everton for a move to Luton would benefit my career in any way, so I asked Howard to thank him and politely tell him 'no thanks'.

If I was going to leave, I wanted to go to a club of my choice – and certainly not one of Luton's size, in the Second Division.

My knee still felt sore but Les advised me to try and battle on and, if it was still causing me concern at the end of the season, he'd recommend an operation.

As spring arrived, Lorraine had already beaten me into hospital – to give birth to our first child on March 25. Chloe Lorraine Cottee weighed in at 6lbs 7oz at Southport and Formby General . . . which meant she immediately became an official 'Sandgrounder,' the nickname of the local non-league football club and the term given to everyone born in Southport!

It was a wonderful and very emotional experience and, to be honest, I was so busy crying as Lorraine delivered our beautiful baby daughter that I completely forgot to ask the nurse if the baby was a boy or a girl! Chloe has become such a wonderful part of our lives and her arrival was the highlight of another disappointing season for me, football wise.

The problem with my knee restricted me to just two more outings between the West Ham game and the end of the season – a sub. appearance at home to Southampton on April 1 and a start against Sheffield United, when I had to come off before the end. I'd finished with just eight league and two cup goals – my worst ever season and the only time in all my six seasons at Everton that I didn't finish overall top scorer, that honour going to Peter Beardsley who managed 20 in all competitions.

Peter was obviously outstanding but another player who I felt deserved much credit for his contribution that season was Martin Keown. Along with Paul Parker (Manchester United) and Danny Maddix (QPR), I rate Martin one of the best man-markers in the game and he certainly did a very good job for us in 1991/92.

As soon as the season ended I entered a private hospital on The Wirral for the inevitable operation on what proved to be a torn cartilage. In a way, I was pleased that they had found something wrong and that I had plenty of time to recover and fully rehabilitate before the start of the following season.

After a nice, quiet week away from it all in Bournemouth – we didn't go abroad with Chloe still so young – I returned home to watch TV coverage of the disastrous European Championships from Sweden. To this day, I still cannot understand why England manager Graham Taylor substituted Lineker in a desperate, last effort to salvage a result from their final game against the Swedes.

Unfortunately, I knew from experience what Gary must have been going through as he saw his number come up. I will never be able to understand any manager who, with his team losing, takes off his leading goalscorer – in Gary's case, the second highest scorer for England after Bobby Charlton. It just defies all logic to me and that decision by Taylor must rank as one of the worst, most craziest, in football history.

Although my knee never quite felt as good as it did before my operation, it still felt OK and I was confident of starting the season in good shape. Then, four weeks before the start, I noticed a lump on the outside of my troublesome right knee, which was diagnosed as a cyst.

Even so, I went on our pre-season tour to Germany which proved more eventful for what went on off the pitch rather than the four games we played on it.

I was rooming with Peter Beagrie who, like me, had been in and out of the side a lot, so he seemed very interested in a move when it became known that Everton had already agreed to accept Southampton's offer of £750,000.

With Beags apparently set to go, we had a few 'farewell' drinks one night but, as I was tired, I went back to our room a bit earlier than Peter. But I was awoken at 2am when our door swung open and in staggered Beags and Howard, who were both fairly the worse for drink.

Beags was actually due to fly home for talks with Southampton next morning but after having a few with Howard, he declared that he'd made his peace with the manager and wanted to stay at Everton after all. I'm not too sure that Peter did the right thing, though, when he phoned his wife, Lynn, in the early hours of the morning to tell her the news!

As it happened, when Peter awoke next morning, he changed his mind again and did in fact go and talk to Southampton. But his on-off move was off again when he failed to agree personal terms with the Saints!

It was very hot in Germany at the time and I recall a very poor training session the morning after another night out at the local pub. Howard made us do a keep-ball session, man-to-man, which means you had to follow your designated partner wherever he went and vice-versa.

Unfortunately, no one wanted to run because of the heat, so the game was played at walking pace and was soon abandoned! Not surprising really, because Peter Beardsley was the only sober one amongst us – and that was only because he doesn't drink!

Howard and I were still having our disagreements and one morning we exchanged words while we were doing our warm-up exercises. We were stretching our hamstrings but I was struggling to touch the floor, as I've never had a good stretch anyway. Howard said to me: "Put some effort into it, lad." To which I replied: "I can't go down any further." "Well at least put some expression on your face," he continued." I snarled back: "Oh, that means I'll be doing the exercise better because I'm pulling a funny face, does it!"

It was a stupid exchange but Howard and I did have a love-hate relationship.

After returning from the intense heat of Germany, we completed our pre-season preparations with a visit to Woking – a friendly arranged as a 'thankyou' to them for their valiant efforts in the FA Cup at Goodison back in 1991. My knee was still a bit sore, so I was among the subs, but I came on and changed the game.

Not that I made it to the final whistle, though. About 10 minutes from the end, I was nudged in the back and my knee buckled under me, forcing me to hobble off. This time, I didn't want to take any chances so I was admitted to hospital where they removed the cyst and also trimmed my cartilage, which I'd torn for the second time.

With the start of the season just days away, the timing of the injury could hardly have been worse. More so, in that Howard had signed another new striker in Paul Rideout for £500,000 from Glasgow Rangers.

His other new signings that August were Barry Horne, a competitive midfielder from Southampton, for £675,000 and Predrag Radosavljevic, from St. Louis Storm (USA), for £317,000. With a name like that, no wonder we all called him 'Preki!'

On the way out of Goodison that month were former skipper Kevin Ratcliffe, who joined Scottish club Dundee on a free, and my old mate Pat Nevin, who moved across Merseyside to Tranmere Rovers for £200,000.

I was very disappointed when Paddy left the club after asking for a transfer, not least because I'd lost my room-mate of four years! Like the rest of us, Paddy had his problems with Howard and inevitably moved on to Tranmere where he has since re-established himself in the Scotland squad.

I always enjoyed playing with Pat. He had tremendous skills and could put a cross just where you wanted it. Unfortunately, being a winger, Paddy was an easy scapegoat when results went against us and, like me, was just unlucky he went to Everton in a transitional period for the club.

The start of the 1992/93 season marked a major turning point in English football. Sky TV, in partnership with BBC, signed a record-breaking £304 million five-year television deal that secured the satellite channel exclusive rights to live coverage of the newly-formed FA Premier League and the Beeb a revival of their popular Saturday night Match of the Day highlights programme.

To me, the only real difference was in the name of the league, with the remainder of the Football League clubs left to compete in divisions one, two and three. A significant, and very worthy, change though was the quality Sky introduced to football TV coverage that had become rather stale and predictable under the BBC and ITV banners.

With their varied camera angles and action replays, use of interesting statistics, and introduction of thought-provoking tactical and discussion programmes, Sky have helped to take football towards the 21st century. They have ploughed an awful lot of money into the game in Britain and deserve great credit for the original way they've presented the sport.

Other changes saw the introduction of a third substitute, the half-time break extended from 10 to 15 minutes and referees wearing green shirts instead of the traditional black.

What hadn't changed at all was my luck.

CHAPTER 46

Claret & Blues

SWEET AND SOUR

I WAS a bit concerned about the condition of my knee and after the second operation I wondered whether it would ever be the same again. All I could do was
work hard in training . . . and watch the first seven games from the stand.

After Barry Horne scored on his debut in the 1-1 home draw with Sheffield
Wednesday, we surprised a lot of people by winning 3-0 at Manchester United, but
it merely gave false hope of a return to the glory, glory days. Two defeats and two
draws in our next five matches provided a more accurate indication of the season-
long struggle ahead.

I managed to get in a couple of reserve games at the start of September before
making my first team return in the midweek thriller at Blackburn Rovers, who'd
made a flying start, on September 15. Alan Shearer gave them the lead after 12
minutes but we were inspired after Mark Ward unfortunately broke his leg in a late
challenge in the first half.

I scored our equaliser, a fortunate goal, and John Ebbrell made it 2-1 before
Shearer equalised. Our winner came in the 81st minute when Beardsley found
Warzycha on the right and as his cross came over, I was standing unmarked on the
six-yard line to tap home the winner.

I wasn't really fit, getting through the game on adrenalin as much as anything,
but it was a great way for me to bounce back after all the problems with my knee.
But my roller coaster career at Everton was soon to take another nosedive as we
gathered at our hotel prior to our league match at Oldham Athletic on Sunday,
October 4 for a live game.

Howard had developed a policy of announcing his team by walking from the
front to the back of the team bus, pointing to each chosen player in turn. It was a
bit like a school teacher taking roll call as he slowly moved down the aisle of the bus
. . . "Nev – one; Alan Harper – two; Andy Hinchcliffe – three; John Ebbrell – four;"
and so on, until he reached the card school table, which included Matt Jackson, Peter

Beagrie, Mo Johnston and myself. In fact, I was sitting next to Mo when Howard looked at me and said: "I'm sorry, TC, you lost the toss of the coin this week . . . you're number 14!" And then he added: "Mo, you're number 10."

Of all the times I'd been left out, this was the most ridiculous way of finding out. I would have appreciated it a bit more if Howard had pulled me aside to tell me the bad news, as he had done in the past, rather than announce the team in this fashion, but nothing really surprised me any more.

At least Howard maintained this method of naming the side and, to be fair, he reversed the roles for the following week's Coca-Cola Cup win over Rotherham United when he dropped Mo and recalled me.

Not for long, though, as after our home draw with Coventry City and 2-0 defeat at Arsenal, I was demoted to the reserves at West Bromwich Albion. I didn't play particularly well at The Hawthorns but I was determined to prove a point and, after going two goals down, I hit back with a hat-trick to win us the game 3-2.

The following Friday, I was cornered at Bellefield by several members of the press who were eager to get my side of the story on being banished to the reserves. As I've always done, I answered their questions as openly and as honestly as possible and the gist of it was that I'd become fed up being made the scapegoat for every poor team performance and couldn't understand why Everton had paid £2 million for me and didn't play to my strengths.

I also complained about the lack of chances being created and put forward Leeds United's Gary McAllister as the ideal type of midfield player whose service I'd really benefit from. What I said to the reporters wasn't premeditated, they'd simply caught me on an off day, feeling thoroughly frustrated once again.

When I got home I guessed that my comments would make very good copy for the press and, sure enough, when I read the papers next morning – when the first team were due to play Manchester City at home – they'd had a field day, my comments splashed all across the back pages of the tabloids.

My criticisms were aimed at Howard – not the other players – for failing to play a creative midfielder in one of the central roles that were occupied by Barry Horne and John Ebbrell. They were both very good, hard-working players, and every team needs a player like them, but the point I was trying to make to the press was that they were too similar and that we only needed one or the other in the side – not both. I wanted Howard to make room for the more creative midfielder we lacked at the time.

When I arrived at the ground for the Man. City game, Howard manipulated the story so that it looked as if I had used the newspapers to personally criticise my own team mates. He came into the dressing room and asked the midfielders: "Do any of you have a spare ticket for TC to use?" That was his subtle way of telling me that I wasn't in the side again that day – but the matter didn't end with our 3-1 defeat that saw us slide to 20th place.

The Sunday papers carried quotes from Howard saying that I had committed the ultimate crime of slagging off my own team mates and if I had not said anything, he would have played me against City. That Sunday we had company and decided to go down to the local pub for a lunchtime pint. We rarely visited the local, so you can imagine my surprise and embarrassment when the first face I saw when I walked in was Howard's.

He gave me a big smile, shook my hand and said: "Well, what a surprise." I tried to spare my blushes by offering to buy him a drink but, quick as a flash, he quipped: "No, save your money, you're going to need it!"

It certainly cut the ice between us and when he called me into his office the following morning, we were both laughing all the way up the stairs about our chance meeting in the pub.

The Monday papers reported that I was going to be fined two weeks wages – again, ridiculously estimated at £6,000!

As it was, Howard gave me two options: firstly, to face a fine of a week's wages and train with the youth team for a week; or apologise to my team mates for supposedly criticising them in print and take them all out for a Chinese meal and drinks at my own expense.

I chose the second option, hoping it would prove cheaper. I apologised to all the lads at the training ground – even though I stuck by what I'd said – but I fully accepted that I deserved to be punished for publicly criticising my manager.

The bill at the Chinese restaurant in Southport came to £1,000 – and that didn't include the champagne that Wardie had to pay for because of a separate incident! It was the most expensive outburst I've ever made and it was certainly a case of more sour than sweet that night!

I paid an even heavier price, though, because I wasn't involved for the first team again until I was substituted with 15 minutes to go in our 1-0 defeat at Ipswich Town on November 28.

And on November 7, while Paul Rideout was scoring our winner at Nottingham Forest, Everton's first victory there since April 1982, I even suffered the humiliation again of being told to play for the 'A' team against Oldham Athletic, along with fellow first-team squad members Mo, Beags, Preki and Andy Hinchcliffe. The game was played on a school playing field and we changed in portakabins. It wasn't an enjoyable experience, despite the fact that I scored after 30 seconds and we won 5-0. At least I didn't find myself playing against my window cleaner this time!

What pleased me, though, after my public show of discontent was the strong level of support I received from the Everton fans, many of them writing or telling me in person how much they shared my opinions on mine and the team's problems. Their support helped to clear my own mind and was important to me.

With my five-year contract up at the end of the 1992/93 season, I needed to be playing regularly and playing well if I was to earn a new one, but I was so far out in the cold it was unbelievable. It was devastating to see the first team go off to an away game while I stayed behind at Bellefield to train with the reserves and without sounding too big-headed, I felt I deserved a first team place.

I tried to work hard in training but despite going into each reserve game full of good intentions, it was very difficult to motivate myself playing with youth team players in front of 200 people at Goodison. In the meantime, I still went to watch all the first team games at home but with Howard rotating his three strikers, Beardsley, Rideout and Johnston, I couldn't get a look in.

During that period of disillusionment, I always thought I had an ally in Colin Harvey, which is ironic considering our previous differences when he was manager. But Howard said to me from time to time that Colin really rated me and Colin himself offered me words of encouragement.

Ever since the age of 17, I'd invariably spent Christmas and New Year's eve staying overnight at an hotel with the team. And whilst it was nice to have plenty of free time over the holiday period as 1992 came to an end, I would obviously much rather have been involved with the first team.

My recall didn't come until after Rideout was injured at Crystal Palace on January 9, 1993 and then suspended, and I was back in the side a week later for our home clash with Leeds United. It could hardly have gone better for me, as I dived full length to head home Beardsley's cross and then followed it with a more customary tap-in to win the game 2-0.

Having already been knocked out of the FA Cup by Wimbledon after a replay at Goodison, we had no game scheduled on fourth round day, so Howard took us off to Ireland to play Derry in a friendly. It was an awful night, pouring with rain, but for some reason – whether it was the buzz I got from scoring twice against Leeds, I don't know – but I was really on form.

We weren't playing well as a team, though, and as we came off at half-time one down, Howard had a right go at us. He accused us of not trying hard enough to put on a show for the fans who'd paid good money to see the game. Then, he paused in mid-sentence, pointed at me and said: "With the exception of HIM!"

For the first time in ages, the manager had actually acknowledged my contribution and the fact that I was giving everything and doing something right. We ended up winning the game 3-1 and the pints of Guinness went down very smoothly that night and in the next couple of days before our return to England.

Before the Leeds game, I really couldn't see myself being at the club beyond the end of the season. And while I was disappointed that we went out of the Cup to Wimbledon, I wasn't unhappy about not being involved in either game with the Dons. I thought that if anyone was going to come in and buy me before the March transfer deadline, it would help my prospects if I wasn't cup-tied.

It was academic, though, because after my double against Leeds, I scored twice again in our next league game – a revenge 3-1 league win at Wimbledon in front of a pathetic crowd of 3,039, one of the lowest ever for a league match at senior level.

The game was more memorable for the picture that appeared in next morning's papers. Midway through the first half, Ian Snodin, who scored our third goal, put in what can only be described as a very strong tackle on Wimbledon defender Roger Joseph. As expected, several Dons players came rushing in to remonstrate with 'Snods', who was still on the ground, and in the end there were 16 players in a melee – not unusual for a game involving Wimbledon's 'Crazy Gang.'

But there was actually a funny picture of 'Snods,' who caused all the trouble in the first place, crawling out from under the legs of the other players, completely unnoticed by everyone, which we pinned up on the noticeboard at Bellefield to everyone's amusement!

The game at Selhurst Park was Martin Keown's last for Everton before his £2 million transfer to Arsenal. Just as I was disappointed when we sold Stuart McCall, so I was disappointed when we lost Martin, who was our best defender.

It was sad, and astounding, that a massive club like Everton was cashing in on its best assets, just as West Ham had done to their detriment when they let go quality players like Paul Allen, Paul Goddard and Frank McAvennie during my time there. It was around this time that rumours of cash-flow problems and a boardroom takeover began to circulate and it was obvious to me that Martin was being sold to balance the books.

Everton didn't replace Martin, simply switching Gary Ablett from left-back to centre-half alongside Dave Watson. At this stage, David Unsworth had still to establish himself in the first team, although he was a tremendous youth prospect with a good left foot. He weighed about 14 stones – the same as he did while a first-year apprentice! – but I don't think Howard was too sure about him when playing him occasionally at left-back.

One positive decision Mike Walker made when he arrived two years later was to immediately switch 'Unsy' to the middle of defence, where he has done very well and gained England recognition.

My confidence was in full flow at Sheffield Wednesday where, although we had a poor day as a team, losing 3-1 with Nev sent off for handling the ball outside his box, I was delighted to score a special solo goal. I turned three defenders on the halfway line before going on a Stan Collymore-style run and chipping Wednesday and England 'keeper Chris Woods from 25 yards.

My next goal came on March 3, a 2-1 win at Goodison that completed the 'double' over Blackburn Rovers. Howard was singing my praises by this time although in all our talks, he always made the point that he didn't care whether I was scoring goals, as long as I was working hard for the good of the team.

He used to say to me: "If you get that part of your game right, the goals will come naturally." He didn't just want a goalscorer, like Gary Lineker, but someone who would become a good all round player.

I think he had a point when he looked back at games we'd lost, when I hadn't scored, and asked himself: "What am I getting from Tony?"

But, in my own single-mindedness, I kept insisting that my number one priority was always to score goals, as I'd done since my young schooldays, and not be concerned too much about working on other aspects of my game. Instead of moaning about lack of service, I should have rolled up my sleeves and worked harder myself to put things right.

In hindsight, I appreciate now the point Howard was trying to drive home when he was manager, and I can thank him for making me a better all round player and for making me more aware of team responsibilities.

Mark Ward, one player who always ran himself into the ground for the team, marked his comeback after six months by scoring the winner in our 1-0 live TV win at Coventry City on March 7.

I was so pleased for Wardie, having seen him in hospital in obvious pain from a broken ankle that required a metal plate to help mend the bone. Wardie's injury looked horrific when I visited him in hospital but, typically, he showed tremendous character to battle back from it and has since done very well for himself.

Wardie was messed about when Mike Walker arrived, but he got a move to Birmingham City and I was so pleased for him when, as player/coach, he helped to win promotion from Division Two in his first full season with the Blues.

When we got back to Bellefield, where we had parked our cars, after our win at Coventry, most of the lads decided to go for a quick beer at the local pub. It was good to see the whole team socialising together but we were still on our first drink when we suddenly heard tapping at the window. We looked up and, to our surprise, saw Howard and Colin's faces at the window. They hadn't come to catch us in the act or anything, but simply had the same idea as the players!

Howard enjoyed mixing with the players socially, he was never aloof from them, and that was one of the great aspects of his management. He strongly believed in team spirit and enjoying a few beers with the lads.

There is no doubt about it, Howard was a very popular manager with most of the lads. If you were one of his players, then I can't think of another manager you would prefer to play under. But I always felt that I was battling to become one of his players. I eventually achieved it but it took a long time.

To underline the growing harmony between Howard and I, before our next game, at Chelsea, he asked me to arrange for my agent Jon Smith to meet him at our hotel. I wasn't in on the meeting but it was the first indication Howard had given that he wanted to sign me on a new contract at the end of the season.

I must have enhanced my chances of a new deal by scoring twice in our 3-0 home win over Nottingham Forest, who made the strange decision to play Nigel Clough as sweeper and for all their creative football, they looked a team doomed to relegation. They had plenty of talented players but perhaps fell into the trap of believing they were too good to go down, which clearly wasn't the case as the final league table proved.

We weren't doing an awful lot better in the league ourselves, although successive wins against Ipswich Town and Middlesbrough helped to ensure we finished 13th.

Our talented Yugoslav, Preki, scored in three of our last six matches but he was yet another who never quite fulfilled his potential at Everton. He played mainly on either right or left midfield but would have been better operating in a floating central role, if only Howard could have found the chance to play him there more often. Instead, it was Portsmouth who saw the best of him after he joined them a little over a year later.

Although I played as well in the second half of the season as at any other time in my Everton career, reclaiming the top scorer's tag with 12 league and one Coca-Cola Cup goal, I have to be honest and say that, if the opportunity had come along, I would still have welcomed a move back to London. I couldn't allow the last 19 games, in which I played so well and scored 10 goals, to erase my overall feelings of disappointment and frustration that had plagued most of my five years at the club.

For the first time in my career, I'd reached the stage where my contract was about to expire. I wasn't determined to leave but I knew, deep down, that if a London club had come in for me I would have been tempted. West Ham were not a serious option at that stage, though, despite having just won promotion from the new Division One. The Hammers had been up and down in recent years but I hadn't honestly considered the possibility of going back to Upton Park. I just couldn't imagine it, even though they had been looking for a goalscorer and I know my name had been mentioned by the fans.

If I was going anywhere, Tottenham seemed a more likely possibility, simply because I'd been linked with them constantly in the preceding few seasons.

Claret & Blues

NUMBERS GAME

WITH a question mark still hanging over my future at Everton, I was as determined as the rest of the lads to enjoy our end-of-season tour to Mauritius, where we went to play friendlies against the national team and Aston Villa.

It was a memorable trip, particularly the 12-hour flight from Heathrow. Being an end-of-season tour, the drinks were flowing as soon as the lads boarded the coach from Liverpool to London.

And by the time we took off, there were some merry souls at the back of the business class section of the plane. Howard was holding court with players from Everton and Villa and by the time we reached Zurich the plane and the players needed refuelling. It was funny to see Paul McGrath asleep on Howard's lap at one stage, but he had the right idea and eventually everyone went to sleep for a couple of hours.

About one-and-a-half hours before we were due to land, the lights went on and it was time for breakfast. I soon noticed Ron Atkinson walking down the aisle of the plane from the first class section to where we were. Even after 10 hours in flight, Ron still looked immaculate in his trousers and shirt. As he approached Howard to talk to him, he was met by a hostess pushing a trolley full of breakfast. He shuffled into the row of seats in front of Howard and knelt on one of them.

Unfortunately, Ron had picked the seat which had been vomited on by one of our players. It was covered up by a tracksuit top but even so, I don't think 'Big Ron' would have been too pleased if he had known what we all knew!

My contract situation still hadn't been resolved when Lorraine, Chloe and I flew off to America for a holiday in the summer of 1993, but while speculation about my future continued, the press had a major story to cover when Peter Beardsley was sold to Newcastle United for £1.5m.

It was a move that shocked most of the football world, but it never surprised me.

Peter is undoubtedly one of the best players of his generation, we all know that, but in the struggling Everton team that we were, his role was causing complications. Everton have always been at their best playing the 4-4-2 formation but with Peter in the side, they had to adapt the formula.

When he was playing up front, Peter rarely stayed there for long because he preferred to drop deeper and play a more 'floating' role. And when he was picked in midfield, he would push forward and tend to leave space behind him.

Howard was widely criticised for selling Beardsley and while I understood why he sold him, what I couldn't understand was the club's failure to re-invest the £1.4m they got for him in another quality international.

So, in the space of 18 months, Everton had sold their best midfielder (McCall), their best defender (Keown) and now their most creative player. And in all three cases, hadn't replaced any of them.

I can't praise Peter highly enough and he didn't want to leave Everton. I don't think he would have left if it hadn't been for a club like Newcastle United, where he'd first made his name.

There were no secret reasons for selling Peter. From the couple of chats I had with Howard in Mauritius, I got the impression that he had problems accommodating Beardsley in the 4-4-2 system he wanted Everton to play. Of course, Peter went on to perform brilliantly for Newcastle, but he had more players there who could complement his style than were around him during his time at Everton, and that was the big difference.

Howard told me in Mauritius that I would be his number one striker in season 1993/94 and Beardsley's departure only underlined my importance to the manager and the club at the time. While I was in America I still asked Jon Smith to check around and see if any other clubs were interested in signing me, but when I returned to England he was honest when he said: "If you turn down Everton's offer of a new three-year contract, there are no guarantees that anyone else will come in for you."

Everton were offering me quite a good rise in my basic wage and signing-on fee, so I had to weigh up my options and question whether I could afford to risk turning them down when I met Howard and Jim Greenwood to discuss the situation. I'd heard all sorts of rumours of what money other players were on at Everton, but our first suggested figure was laughed at. Everton were not going to increase their offer, so after that meeting Jon made a few phone calls, including one to Tottenham, but didn't get a commitment from anyone.

I still belonged to Everton and really enjoyed playing for them – when I was in the team. I still felt as if I had something to prove to some people at Goodison and wanted to win a trophy before I left, so I was eventually pleased to sign my new three-year contract on July 7.

Lorraine was very happy for us to stay on Merseyside, too. Never at any time has she put any pressure on me to do one thing or another in football terms and whilst we would both have been happy to have gone back to London at that time, we were both equally pleased to stay in Southport, where we had a lovely home and nice friends.

Being the wife of a professional footballer may seem glamourous to the outside world, but in reality that often isn't the case. Many of them are housewives with children to care for and husbands who are away on long tours. They very often don't have much choice other than to revolve their own life around their husband's.

As the new season approached, I felt that despite the sale of Beardsley, Howard wasn't far off building a decent squad. We were on our pre-season tour of Switzerland when he had a bid of £3.2m for Duncan Ferguson turned down, 'Fergie' making the move from Dundee United to Glasgow Rangers instead.

Howard was also linked with numerous other players, including Sheffield Wednesday's Mark Bright, but without success, and I was disappointed that his only new signing was Graham Stuart, an £850,000 buy from Chelsea, who had a difficult start to his Everton career.

At least it made a change for me to be worrying about who would be playing around me, instead of being concerned about my own place. Although Howard left me out of one of our Swiss tour matches and another pre-season match at Hearts, he went out of his way to reassure me that I was still his first choice striker.

The Swiss tour reminds me of another amusing time when Howard sensed that we were all dehydrated and totally unenthusiastic after a good drink the previous night – none more so than striker Mo Johnston, who found himself in the role of goalkeeper, except that he decided to approach the job laying down! It was comical to see Mo laying across the goalline, watching helplessly as his opponents scored one goal after another in one of the most low-key five-a-sides I've ever been involved in!

Undoubtedly one of the game's great characters, Mo reminded me very much of Frank McAvennie, the way he performed on and off the field. Mo came to Goodison with a reputation as a colourful, cavalier character from Scotland who liked a drink or three. But I never saw a wayward side to him – he drank no more or less than the rest of us when the beers were flowing.

Confirmation that I would be Howard's first choice striker came in the form of the number nine shirt, handed to me by our kit man, Jimmy 'Gonzo' Martin – so-called due to his resemblance to the Sesame Street TV character! It was at this point that the Premier League adopted the squad numbering system tried in the previous summer's European Championships. Commercially, I can see the sense in players wearing a regular number and their name on their back, but it can be confusing for fans and if we're not careful we'll end up looking like American footballers, with number 98s running around the field. If you asked most players and supporters, they would prefer to revert to the old days of one-to-11.

But as the new season dawned, I was just glad to be wearing the number nine on my back, instead of the 12 or 14 shirt I'd worn far too regularly for my liking in previous seasons.

Claret & Blues

OUT OF THE BLUE

AFTER signing my new contract, you can imagine my surprise when, just a few hours before our first game of 1993/94 at Southampton, I received a phone call out of the blue.

It was 11am on the morning of the game when I took the call in the hotel room I was sharing with my new regular room-mate, Matt Jackson. I won't reveal the name of the caller, an agent, but he said: "Hello, I know we haven't spoken for a few years, but I'm ringing on behalf of a representative of Chelsea. I wondered if you would be interested in joining them?"

I informed him that had he phoned a couple of months earlier, I might well have been interested but, as it was, I'd just signed a new three-year deal with Everton.

I ended the conversation by saying that if, at any time in the future, Everton wanted to sell me, I'd be delighted to talk to Chelsea if, in fact, they are interested.

I would have enjoyed playing for Glenn Hoddle, who took over as player/manager at Stamford Bridge after I signed my new contract. I'd seen and admired Glenn at close hand from my England squad days and rated him one of the best midfielders England had produced in the past 20 years.

Indeed, it was a travesty that he was capped only 51 times for England – in any other country he would have been capped 150 times.

The call from the agent caught me completely by surprise and, to a certain degree, it put me off my game at The Dell that day.

Even so, we made a flying start to the season, following our 2-0 victory at Southampton – where Peter Beagrie showed Saints what they were missing with our first goal – with successive home wins over Manchester City and Sheffield United.

I normally start the season slowly, so I was delighted to score a hat-trick in the 4-2 win over Sheffield United. My new partnership with Paul Rideout clicked from the start, with Paul holding the ball up very well for a big target man. We enjoyed excellent service from Beags, on the left, and Mark Ward, on the right, while John Ebbrell and Ian Snodin won the ball well in midfield and quickly got the ball wide.

But we soon came back down to earth with three straight defeats, at Newcastle United, where I missed two good chances, and Arsenal, as well as at home to Aston Villa.

My winner at Oldham Athletic got us back on track and on September 18 the old West Ham connection of Wardie and I, combined to sink Liverpool 2-0 at Goodison. We'd played the Reds off the park but, unfortunately, our victory was overshadowed by the fracas involving Liverpool players Bruce Grobbelaar and Steve McManaman after our first goal.

But a week later all the headlines deservedly belonged to Norwich City striker Efan Ekoku, who scored four in his team's shock 5-1 win at Everton. Mike Walker's City team were really playing well at that time but, having taken the lead and been pegged back to 1-1 at half-time, no one could have envisaged how Norwich eventually tore us apart in the second half.

It was neither the first time nor the last that season that we'd give away bad goals. In our next game at Tottenham, Paul Rideout scored a brilliant diving header and I put us 2-1 up from the penalty spot, yet we still managed to concede two goals in the last two minutes to lose 3-2.

The game turned on Howard's decision to take off Beags when we were leading 2-1 and then me after it went to 2-2. A few arguments broke out in the dressing room after the game as Howard sought opinions from the players around him and, of course, I chipped in with a few comments that brought disbelieving looks from my team mates.

I said to Howard: "I can't believe that you took off both Beags and myself when we were level."

Howard replied: "What are you on about, we were winning 2-1?"

I said: "Don't be silly, my penalty goal made it 2-2!"

But Howard still wouldn't have it and I started to get really annoyed as I repeated the stupidity of taking Beags and I off while it was 2-2. I was ranting on and on . . . until Barry Horne, sitting next to me, muttered under his breath: "Shut up, Tone, you're wrong, you're wrong!"

For some reason I'd convinced myself that I'd scored the equaliser from the penalty spot but, in fact, I had put us 2-1 ahead. I thought Howard had taken off Beags when the score was 2-2 and when I came off Spurs had made it 4-2, when it was really 3-2.

So, in fact, the situation was even worse than I thought when I first started having a go at Howard during the heated dressing room inquest! I've often had players – particularly defenders! – come up to me and ask the final result, but this was the first time in my career that I'd lost track of the score!

I made myself look a right prat in front of all the lads but when I got home and watched a video of the game, Gary Mabbutt made me feel a lot better when he told the TV interviewer: "When Tony Cottee equalised from the penalty spot . . . "

At least someone else was on my wavelength!

With no league matches due to international week, Howard took us away to Spain to play his old team, Athletic Bilbao, followed by a four-day break in Magaluf.

Unusually for a friendly, I played very well and, even more surprisingly, scored a cracker with my left foot. Stuart Barlow scored our other goal in a 2-0 win and afterwards I was presented with a magnificent man-of-the match trophy, a sculptured footballer mounted on a wooden base.

Not wishing to carry the large trophy around and risk damaging it, I asked 'Gonzo' if he would look after it for me on the way home. Gonzo put the trophy in the kit skip and, after enjoying our brief holiday in Magaluf, I was looking forward to collecting my award again when we reported to Bellefield prior to out next league game at Swindon.

I asked Gonzo for my trophy but could detect from his sheepish look that there was something wrong. "I'm sorry, TC," he explained, "but we've had a bit of an accident and I'm afraid it's a bit broken."

When Gonzo showed me the full extent of the damage, I was dismayed to see that the footballer figurine had been snapped off at the knees and had lost both arms and his head!

It turned out that we had packed so many bottles of champagne and red wine into the skip, to smuggle through customs, that the weight had completely smashed my trophy.

Gonzo, Howard and the players thought it was hilarious – but all was not lost. I somehow managed to Superglue the pieces back together and that marvellous memento from Bilbao still made it into my trophy cabinet at home!

It was around this time that Mo Johnston, the player we'd bought from Rangers for £1.5m, was transferred to Hearts on a free. Mo was a good player but, almost as soon as he arrived, he had some problems with Howard, despite scoring some crucial Merseyside derby goals. It was a free transfer that would give Howard big problems.

The Spanish break might have been fun but it didn't bring about much improvement on the field. Only a draw at Swindon Town, who were struggling to beat anyone in their first season of top flight football, was followed by a home defeat by Manchester United – Lee Sharpe scoring a great goal – a win at Ipswich Town and then successive defeats against Coventry City and QPR.

We fared better in the early rounds of the Coca-Cola Cup, easing past Lincoln City 8-5 on aggregate and then overcoming Crystal Palace in the third round replay. It was on the night of our 4-1 victory at Selhurst Park that Paul Rideout earned his new nickname. He went up for a high ball with Eric Young and landed face down in the mud. It wasn't funny as I ran across to tilt Paul's face to one side, so that he could breath properly in the vital five seconds until Les got to him.

Thankfully, Paul recovered and after his experience of wallowing around in the mud, the lads decided to call him 'Cabbage.' Nicknames are of course part and parcel of every football club and mine was 'Stumpy'. It was Martin Keown's response after I nicknamed him 'Bob' (Brain of Britain), which was a nicknamed Tony Adams told me about. In fact, while mentioning the Arsenal skipper, I can claim to have lumbered Tony with the nickname of 'Rodders'. Tony used to turn up for the England Under-21 games and where he was so tall and used to have his hair a bit scruffy – just like Nicholas Lyndhurst who plays Rodney in the TV comedy classic Only Fools & Horses – I dubbed him 'Rodders'.

Martin got his revenge on me, though, when he finally came up with the nickname 'Stumpy' – an obvious reference to my undeniably short legs!

Perhaps 'Grumpy' would have been a more apt nickname for yours truly after the penalty nightmare I experienced in the FA Cup at Chelsea the previous season came back to haunt me in the autumn of '93. I squandered the chance to earn us a 2-2 draw at Coventry – normally one of my luckiest grounds – when I thumped my spot kick against the inside of the post and it flew off for a throw-in.

I vowed then that I'd taken my last ever penalty, only to tempt fate a few weeks later when we faced Manchester United at home in the fourth round of the Coca-Cola Cup. Mark Ward had agreed to take over the spot-kicker's role but had been substituted (thanks, Howard!) just 10 minutes before the pen. was awarded.

Actually, I thought Stuart Barlow was going to take it as he raced over to pick the ball up and place it on the spot . . . only to walk away and leave it to someone else. I looked around to see if there were any volunteers and there weren't. Instead, they were all looking at me, so I shouldered the responsibility of trying to cut the two-goal deficit . . . and watched in horror as Peter Schmeichel dived to his right and palmed the ball away.

I used the side-foot technique that proved successful at White Hart Lane at the start of the previous month, but this time it was to no avail and our Coca-Cola Cup bubble had burst.

I put that disappointment behind me to some extent by scoring the only goal in our next game, at home to Southampton on December 4, and was surprised in the dressing room afterwards when several bottles of champagne were brought in for the lads to drink.

As I'm not a champagne drinker, I didn't indulge on an occasion that was hardly worthy of celebration, but for Howard Kendall, the bubbly had already gone very flat.

The emotion of scoring – I've just got my second goal against Leeds in January 1993.

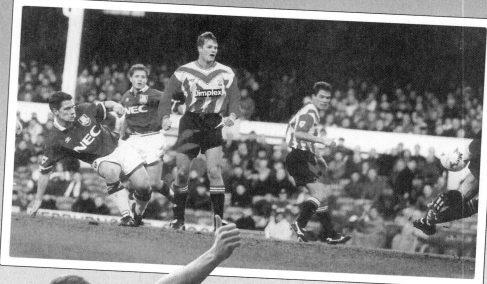

Above: *The last Everton goal by an Everton player for Howard Kendall in December 1993.*

DAILY POST SPORT

DERBY SPECIAL Top reports and pictures of the Cup thrills at Goodison

The greatest

erby stars
alute to a
up cracker

Left: *Thumbs up from the No.10.*
Right: *Reading the Liverpool Daily Post after the greatest derby game ever – the 4-4 draw in 1991.*

Above: This goal won second place in the Match of the Day Goal of the Month competition. I chipped Sheffield Wednesday's Chris Woods after beating three players.
Below: Another favourite goal of mine – a thunderbolt against Southampton in 1988.

Left: *A hat-trick goal, from the spot, in a 6-2 against Swindon in January 1994.*
Below: *Another hat-trick goal against Sheffield United in August 1993.*

A happy England player back in 1987.

Above: Who'd want to travel to Turkey with the under-21s and sit next to these two?
Below: Some familiar faces on show before we played Romania in 1986.

Have you been tangoed?

Above: Glenn Hysen calls for offside on my full England debut against Sweden, September 1986.

Left: In action against Chile at Wembley, May 1989.

Right: In serious mood against Scotland on my one and only start for the full England team, May 1989.

Claret & Blues

GO FOR JOE

I HAD left the champagne behind in the Everton dressing room and was driving along the Formby by-pass when the shock news came over the radio confirming that Howard Kendall had resigned.

Howard had given the players no indication whatsoever, either before or after the game, that he was about to quit, although Colin Harvey told me at Bellefield on the following Monday morning that the manager had earlier confided in him that he would be going after the Southampton match.

Obviously, Howard and I had our differences but, hand on heart, I can honestly say that I was genuinely disappointed and upset when he left the club. As a person, I liked him a lot and always got on well with him. Howard was a manager you could enjoy a laugh with, he wasn't at all aloof, and, unlike Colin, I found it easy to talk to him.

Without doubt, Howard was the most successful boss in Everton's history and if you were one of 'his' players, he was a great manager to play under.

I'd been fighting to become one of Howard's players for three years but, typical of what happened to me throughout my Goodison career, I was back to square one again once he'd gone.

I believe there were two main reasons why Howard decided he'd had enough. Firstly, the criticism he received over Mo Johnston, who cost £1.5m from Glasgow Rangers but, less than two years later, was allowed to leave for Hearts on a free transfer.

In hindsight, Howard should have waited until a club came in with a sensible offer for Mo, who still had plenty of time left on his contract. But, on the other hand, he was supposedly among the highest paid players at the club, so Howard could probably have argued that he had acted in Everton's best interests by reducing the wage bill. After all, Mo had started only seven league games the previous season and hadn't featured in a single match in 1993/94 before he left.

The second and main reason why I think Howard resigned was because he had been denied the £1.5m needed to buy another striker, Dion Dublin, who was playing in Manchester United's reserves at that time. I could understand the board's scepticism about splashing that much money on a reserve player, especially after having lost the same amount on Mo, but they should still have backed their man.

By not putting their faith in Howard's judgment, the board had effectively undermined his role and made his position as manager untenable. In the circumstances, I don't blame Howard for quitting but his departure only added to the club's mounting problems.

There was uncertainty everywhere. In the dressing room, where the players were apprehensive about who would replace Howard, and also in the boardroom, where the public and lengthy wrangle for control between Peter Johnson and Bill Kenwright brought more bad publicity.

The chairman at that time, Dr. Marsh, called a short players' meeting at Bellefield on the Monday after Howard left, basically to ask us to keep doing our best and confirming that Jimmy Gabriel would take control as temporary team manager until further notice, with Colin remaining as assistant manager.

Jimmy indicated to the press that, if results went well, he might be interested in taking the job permanently . . . but after six defeats and one draw in our next seven matches, and only two goals scored, he declared that he had absolutely no intention of taking it on!

The confidence and spirit among the players had slumped to a new low as we fell to 16th place over the Christmas and New Year holiday period. Jimmy was okay to manage our reserves, but he wasn't up to the task of managing senior players and internationals, who were becoming increasingly disillusioned.

We went to Chelsea on January 3, 1994, on course for an unwanted new club record having already equalled the club's worst blank spell of six games, for the longest league sequence without scoring a goal – and it didn't look good as we went two down by half-time. Colin went berserk in the dressing room, questioning everyone's attitude and commitment, but he got the right response. I scored within 10 minutes of the restart and then Stuart Barlow made it 2-2 . . . only for us to concede two more silly goals towards the end of another miserable afternoon at The Bridge.

Speculation continued to surround the appointment of Howard's successor, with Bobby Robson among the main contenders for the job, but in my opinion I thought there was only one choice. Joe Royle should have been given the job when Colin was sacked more than three years earlier and this time there were no other serious contenders as far as I was concerned. The whole club was in a mess and it needed someone like Joe, who knew Everton FC through and through, to pull us out of trouble and point the way forward.

Alas, instead of appointing the former Goodison centre-forward and crowd favourite, who had taken unfashionable Oldham Athletic from nowhere to the Premiership and two Wembley finals, the board turned to Norwich City's Mike Walker.

Make no mistake, Walker – who was appointed the day before our 1-1 FA Cup third round draw at Bolton Wanderers on January 8 – had worked wonders in his previous 18 months at Carrow Road, guiding them into Europe which included a memorable UEFA Cup victory over Bayern Munich with an attacking, entertaining brand of football.

Everton is not Norwich City, though, and I don't think Mike appreciated what he was letting himself in for when he left East Anglia, where City were not expected to compete consistently for the main honours, to Goodison, where success was almost demanded of the manager and his players.

Although he spoke to the players as a group, Walker never took the trouble to speak to us individually, which would have been a good idea bearing in mind our perilous position near the foot of the Premier League. I couldn't understand why, as the new man at the helm, he didn't sit us down and speak to us, one by one, to try to establish exactly what had been going wrong at the club and to discuss how, together, we could possibly put it right.

A 6-2 home victory over relegation-doomed Swindon Town, in which I scored a hat-trick, couldn't paper over the cracks. We led 2-0 but were pulled back to 2-2 and only took full control after they had Andy Mutch sent off. With Paul Rideout injured, Walker brought in Brett Angell, his new £500,000 signing from Southend United. Brett had played one game on loan, as sub. in the 5-1 debacle against Walker's own Norwich City the previous September, but he had paid half-a-million for a striker who had spent a long time recovering from a bad thigh injury and who was untried at top level.

A more accurate picture of our problems came in the replay against Bolton at Goodison, where we took a two-goal lead but lost 3-2 in extra-time. The result captured all the third round headlines, although Bruce Rioch's enterprising side proved themselves by winning at Arsenal and then beating Aston Villa at home in subsequent rounds, having knocked out Liverpool in the third round of the same competition a year earlier. Ironically, their amazing Cup run of '94 was ended at the quarter-finals – by Joe Royle's Oldham.

I think the new manager made a few mistakes when he first arrived that didn't help his cause at Everton. Declaring that he'd long been an admirer of the Liverpool style of play wasn't the the most diplomatic thing to say, and then shutting the gates on the press, until after we'd finished training, only got their backs up. As a manager, you must look after the press, as Howard did, to keep them on your side.

I also felt sorry for characters like Roy Wright, a die-hard fan who'd do anything for you, who were made far from welcome at Bellefield, despite the fact they'd been going there ages. You need people like Roy at the training ground and we've got plenty of characters who come regularly to Chadwell Heath to create a good atmosphere.

I think Walker was trying to do things his way but he was upsetting people and making basic errors.

It was also quite obvious, soon after Walker arrived, that he was more of an office manager than a tracksuit boss. He took some of the early training sessions himself, before appointing Dave Williams as his assistant, but never looked comfortable in the role. Whereas Howard would walk on to the training ground and simply put on an enjoyable session off the cuff, Walker found it difficult and too often he and Williams lacked the ideas to sustain the players' interest.

Our daily warm-up consisted of the first team squad of, say, 16 players gathered in a circle. Depending on what the call was, we either had to run with the ball to the middle of the circle and pass it to someone else, or leave it completely. When another player wants you to leave, or 'dummy' the ball, he usually shouts 'over', followed by the player's name, because a simple call of 'leave it' will result in a free-kick to the other team.

But instead of calling 'over', as we did at West Ham, and as many other clubs do, the new management duo introduced silly alternatives like 'Sid', 'Jack' and 'Fred', depending on what you were asked to do at the time. The players were so busy laughing as they shouted these ridiculous names that the session often deteriorated into a shambles.

I also found it embarrassing having a Premier League coach explain to me and the others what they wanted us to achieve by a 'third man run' . . . the very same routines I'd been fully familiar with in my earliest days as an apprentice at West Ham.

It was schoolboy stuff and one day Dave Williams pulled me into his office to question my attitude during training. He asked why I hadn't looked interested in his sessions and I replied that I found them utterly boring and predictable. I suppose in a way he was right to have a go at me because, as one of the senior players, I should really have been setting a better example, but I just felt that if you treated people like schoolboys, they tended to act like them.

Sadly, with the arrival of Dave Williams came the inevitable departure of Colin Harvey. Colin had been a good ally for me under Howard Kendall and as with his sacking as manager, I was sad when the club released him. After helping Andy King at Mansfield I'm pleased to see Colin now assisting my old team mate Graeme Sharp at Oldham.

My problems with the new regime continued after I came off at half-time in our 1-0 defeat at Manchester United. I'd aggravated the ankle I twisted during the win over Swindon Town the previous Saturday and with no match scheduled for FA Cup fourth round day, I was expecting to rest the injury.

If we had had a league game scheduled, I would possibly have risked the ankle but there was no point in doing so in a friendly at Southend United, organised as part of the Brett Angell deal. There were several others squad players struggling with injuries but, for some reason, Les Helm, the physio, insisted that only I had to travel on the team bus with the rest of the lads.

I was livid and wondered whether Les disbelieved me when I told him my ankle was sore? I felt adamant that I shouldn't be asked to go all the way down to Essex when I had no chance of playing in the game but with Mike Walker having gone back to Norfolk for the weekend, he was uncontactable, despite my vain efforts to obtain his phone number from Jimmy Gabriel.

I very nearly didn't turn up for the bus and although I thought better of it, I made the journey in silence, completely ignoring Les. I was still fuming when we finally arrived at the Swallow Hotel, Waltham Abbey, a few hours later. Feeling disgusted, the first thing I did on arrival was phone my dad and ask him to come to the hotel to collect me.

I spent the rest of the afternoon drinking at a pub with my brother and when Dad finished at his office, he returned to drive me back to the hotel. I'd blanked Les throughout the journey south and was nowhere to be seen when he went looking for me that afternoon to do some physio work.

As I obviously wasn't playing at Roots Hall, I had a few more beers in the bar before watching the match and then boarding the coach for the long drive back to Merseyside. We arrived home at 3.00am and for me, still nursing a sore ankle, it was a completely wasted trip.

Mike Walker called me into his office after training the following day to ask what had gone on. I told him my version of events and wasn't reprimanded for my after-noon session in the pub. The matter ended amicably with Les and I shaking hands and agreeing to forget about our dispute.

To prove that I hadn't been feigning injury, I sat and watched the following Saturday's home game against Chelsea from the stands. We won 4-2, with Paul Rideout scoring twice and his new partner, Brett Angell, netting his first senior goal for Everton in a 4-2 victory.

Even so, I was still disappointed not to be immediately recalled when I was declared fit for the following Saturday's game against Ipswich Town at Goodison. As the team's leading goalscorer I was very surprised to be left on the subs' bench, espe-cially as the alternative was to play two big, six-foot-plus strikers together up front, which didn't seem much of a blend to me.

After that dismal goalless draw with Ipswich, I found myself sub. again as we faced Arsenal in the third match at Goodison on consecutive Saturdays – but forced myself back in the reckoning when I came on 20 minutes from the end to net our equaliser in a 1-1 draw. We moved one place up the table, to 14th, with a very wel-come 2-1 home win over Oldham Athletic but I reached a huge personal turning point of my own the following Monday, March 7.

As soon as West Ham announced that they would be staging the Bobby Moore memorial match, I hoped that I would be invited to play in the Premiership Select team managed by George Graham . . . and was delighted when the Arsenal boss proved he held no grudges against me for turning him down all those years ago by picking me to play alongside Man. United's Brian McClair in the first half.

Once again, I was a bit sceptical about the reception I would get from the fans, even more so after Manchester City's former Arsenal star, David Rocastle, was booed when his name was read out over the P.A. system. But, to my delight and relief, I received a loud cheer, which really took me by surprise after the stick I'd been given on the night of Everton's FA Cup quarter-final at Upton Park two years earli-er.

The night got even better for me when I scored after 25 minutes and although I knew beforehand, along with all the other players, that George would completely change the team at half-time to ensure all 20 Premier League club representatives got at least half a game, I had thoroughly enjoyed myself.

As I clapped the West Ham crowd before going off – a gesture really to thank them for clapping me onto the pitch at the start – I soaked up the atmosphere of a typical night under the Upton Park lights and thought to myself: 'I really miss this'.

Although Lorraine stayed at home in Southport with Chloe, the rest of my fam-ily were there for the Bobby Moore memorial game and I know that they were as proud and honoured as I was when I was chosen on such a poignant occasion. In many ways it was just like old times and for the first time since I'd left to join Everton, I thought that it might be nice to go back to West Ham if ever the oppor-tunity presented itself.

I remember the day Bobby died of cancer. I'd just arrived home from training on Wednesday, February 24, 1993, when I turned on Teletext and saw the big headline 'BOBBY MOORE DIES'. I stared at the TV for a good 20 seconds in total disbelief, unable to take in what I was reading. I kept asking myself: 'do they mean THE

Bobby Moore, the most famous player West Ham and England has ever produced?'

The two occasions when I met Bobby were both during my time at Everton, when he was at Goodison as a member of the Capital Gold commentary team. Spurs were the visitors one night when we bumped into each other after the game and Bobby said "hello" and "well done". He was very pleasant, asking if I'd settled okay in the north, and although he kept it short and sweet, I thought at the time that it was very nice of him to go out of his way to speak to me and offer those few words of encouragement.

A few days after his death, I picked up the Daily Mirror and saw a picture of a woman weeping at the main gates at Upton Park, where supporters had laid wreaths and hundreds of other mementoes out of respect for the legendary 'Mooro'.

I studied the picture very carefully and although the woman's name did not appear in the caption, I was amazed to see that it was in fact my mum, who, unbeknown to me, had gone there to pay her own tribute to her former Hammers idol.

Although the Bobby Moore memorial game had whetted my appetite – apart from the game itself, West Ham also chose that night to officially open their new South Stand, named after their most famous son – my immediate concern was Everton's worsening position in the Premier League. A 2-1 defeat by Liverpool at Anfield was followed by an even poorer 3-0 drubbing by Walker's old team in front of the Sky TV cameras at Carrow Road.

Norwich absolutely stuffed us on the night but while I and the rest of the players were growing increasingly concerned with our plight, the manager remained confident that we would pull through the deepening crisis. A defiant Mike Walker told the press: "There's no way that we're going down."

In February, Mike had followed his signing of Angell by taking Gary Rowett from Cambridge United for £200,000 and before the transfer deadline day in March he re-entered the transfer market with another foray into the lower divisions to sign Joe Parkinson from Bournemouth in a deal that amounted to around £700,000. His biggest deal, though, saw Everton pay Arsenal £1.6m for Swedish winger Anders Limpar, although some of that fee was offset by the sale of Peter Beagrie to Manchester City for £1.1m.

I was personally disappointed to see Beags go because, on his day, he is good enough to play for England. But, like me and numerous others, he was regularly in and out of the side at Everton and never quite fulfilled his potential there. Limpar was very much in the same boat as Beags at Arsenal, where George Graham continually left him out of the team despite his obvious skill.

Anders is a world class player but he was going to take time to settle in and time was something we were running out of at that crucial stage, with relegation fast becoming a distinct possibility.

The manager's confidence was further undermined by our 1-0 home defeat by Tottenham on March 26 – the game immediately after the transfer deadline – which saw us drop to 17th place. In the week preceding that game, I thought I was about to become a Spurs player myself after receiving a late-night phone call from Jon Smith, who had just got home from watching England play Denmark (coach Terry Venables' first game in charge) at Wembley.

Jon called at 11pm to say that he'd been speaking to Steve Perryman, Ossie Ardiles' assistant at White Hart Lane, who said Tottenham were "very interested" in signing me. They were struggling in the wrong half of the table, too, at the time and were on the look out for a goalscorer before deadline day.

Lorraine and I were quite excited about the thought of moving back to London but, not for the first time (although certainly the last), speculation that I could be signing for Tottenham came to nothing. We never heard another thing from Perryman or anybody else at Tottenham, and Mike Walker never mentioned anything about it to me either. In the end, Spurs signed Liverpool's Ronny Rosenthal instead.

Walker decided to drop both Paul Rideout and I for the next game, at Aston Villa, where Angell played up front on his own in a goalless draw. April began with an abysmal 5-1 defeat at Sheffield Wednesday, where I came on as sub. to score our goal, followed by an equally depressing 3-0 home defeat by title-chasing Blackburn Rovers. I was a little apprehensive about returning to West Ham for what was for us such an important game on April 9, but I needn't have worried.

Fortunately, the Hammers had virtually secured their own place in the Premier League with victories over Ipswich Town and Spurs over the preceding Easter holiday period, so my winning goal did them no real damage – but did me and Everton a power of good.

Before the game, as I went to look at the pitch, as I do before all away matches, I bumped into Ronnie Gale, the scout who introduced me to West Ham as a 13 year-old. I said I'd see him later for a chat but as I came back to walk down the tunnel towards the dressing room, I spotted Ronnie again, sitting in the pen behind the dug-out, so I sat down beside him.

Whether it was intuition or not, I don't know, but he looked me straight in the eye and said: "You want to come home, don't you?" I said: "Yes, I do, can you have a word at the club and see if it's possible?"

I would like to make it absolutely clear that my private conversation with Ronnie in no way affected my commitment to Everton in the remaining five games of that season. Indeed, as it turned out, my winning goal at Upton Park ultimately ensured our survival. I knew I wouldn't be going anywhere in the short-term, because the transfer deadline had passed three weeks before and, besides, we had a relegation battle on our hands.

There was no way that I wanted to leave with Everton relegated. I was just taking a realistic long-term view, bearing in mind that I saw no future for me under Mike Walker's management and the fact that I had enjoyed my return to the East End for the Bobby Moore memorial match.

A week after the win at West Ham, we returned to the capital to play QPR, but my delight at scoring the opening goal turned to despair as we lost 2-1. That goal was my 99th for Everton and it still hurts me today that I never reached the magic century in a blue shirt.

We looked like a relegation side in a dour goalless draw at home to Coventry City, which saw us slip down to 18th. Worse followed at Leeds United a week later where, on a ground where Everton had not won for 43 years, we slumped 3-0 and slipped into the bottom three for the first time.

So, it all hinged on the final Saturday of the league season – our home game against Wimbledon on May 7. Swindon Town had already been relegated, Oldham were virtually down, and Everton were favourites to join them through the Premier

League trap door. We had 41 points – one less than Sheffield United, Ipswich Town and Southampton immediately above us. So we went into the critical decider knowing that even if we won, and the three others above us did, too, we would still be relegated for the first time since April 1951.

I travelled into Goodison for the Wimbledon game with Paul Rideout, who told me that the Dons' team coach had been set on fire by arsonists outside their hotel overnight. If this was Everton fans' way of putting the 'Crazy Gang' out of their stride, it didn't work.

Wimbledon took the lead after only four minutes when Dean Holdsworth scored from a penalty after Anders Limpar had inexplicably raised his arm to the ball. It was the first bizarre incident in an extraordinary match and the last thing we needed on an afternoon of high stakes and rising tension.

Our nightmare continued 20 minutes later, as Gary Ablett misskicked into his own goal. You could hear a pin drop in the crowd of 31,000 – the capacity being reduced due to redevelopment work at the Bullens Road end.

At least we got one back before half-time, Graham Stuart converting from the spot in the 25th minute (mac to check) after Limpar was controversially adjudged to have been fouled inside the box.

If there was a doubt about the legality of our first goal, there was none whatsoever concerning our stunning equaliser. Barry Horne chested the ball down and, from 25 yards, thundered a rasping shot against the inside of the post and into the net. It was his first goal since he scored on his debut back in August 1992 and what a time to score it!

The ground was electric when, with just nine minutes to go, we conjured a miraculous winner from nowhere. Stuart played a one-two with me and although I didn't get a good touch on the ball, he still managed to sidefoot the ball towards goal. It was probably one of the weakest shots 'Diamond' has ever hit, and 99 times out of 100 Hans Segers would have saved it. But not on this, the most dramatic of all days. Just before the ball reached Segers, it took a slight bobble and went over his hands into the net.

Goodison Park erupted in a collective cry of relief and euphoria. Some fans ran onto the pitch to celebrate the most unlikely of match-winners but even after surviving the last few minutes to win 3-2, we were still not sure of our fate.

That moment of tremendous relief came after I'd pushed my way through the hordes of supporters on the pitch towards the players' tunnel, where Wimbledon striker John Fashanu confirmed that we had indeed survived. Southampton and Ipswich Town had also stayed up by drawing at West Ham and Blackburn Rovers respectively, but the cruellest luck went the way of Sheffield United who were relegated thanks to Mark Stein's late winner for Chelsea.

There was a lot of rejoicing in our dressing room afterwards but I saw no reason for champagne. The bubbly is great after you've won something but a big club like Everton should never have got itself into that dire position, where we missed relegation by just two points. If the Toffees had been relegated, it would have been an absolute disaster, financially, for a club of that stature.

In the weeks and months following that unbelievable epic match with Wimbledon, rumours of match-fixing allegations began to emerge. Wimbledon's Segers and Fashanu, and Southampton 'keeper Bruce Grobbelaar, were charged in connection with a Far Eastern betting ring who had allegedly staked thousands of pounds on the outcome of several Premier League matches that season.

In respect of Segers, the focus of press attention turned to our drama-filled match against the Dons, but I can assure everyone that none of the Everton players, and as far as I know, anyone else at our club, were aware of any supposed match-fixing at the time, or any other impropriety involving that end-of-season fixture. We were not approached by anyone seeking to fix the result of the match or to offer back-handers.

Sure, it was an horrendous mistake by Segers for the third goal but I clearly saw the ball bobble up and over his hands – there is no way he deliberately intended to pull his hands out of the way of the ball. If the authorities prosecuted every 'keeper who made a bad blunder like the one Segers did, we'd have no goalkeepers left, because they are all human.

As for Fash, when he congratulated Ian Snodin and I on staying up as we walked down the tunnel at the end of the game, he didn't look like a man who'd just earned himself a fortune as part of a match-fixing syndicate. I knew Fash from our England days and he was genuinely pleased that we'd avoided the drop.

I just hope that the whole business surrounding match-fixing claims is finally laid to rest and that all the players implicated in the scandal are completely cleared of all charges.

On paper, I'd had my best-ever season for Everton, finishing top scorer for the fifth time in six seasons with 16 league and three Coca-Cola Cup goals, but I knew, after all the problems I'd been through with Colin Harvey, Howard Kendall and then Mike Walker, that the time was right for me to move in the summer of '94.

Claret & Blues

TALK OF THE TOWN

AS soon as the season finished I was strongly linked with a possible move to Ipswich Town. I don't know where the rumours came from – probably through people linking me with their general manager, John Lyall, and then putting two and two together and making five – but I could never see me going to Portman Road. I never got excited about the thought of going there and my agent Jon Smith, together with his brother Phil, agreed that it wouldn't be in my best interests to go to Suffolk.

West Ham would have been a different proposition, though. I was delighted to go back to Upton Park the day after our final game against Wimbledon to play in Tony Gale's testimonial. One of the reasons why I was so looking forward to going back there to guest for the Hammers against the Republic of Ireland XI is that my old strike partner, Frank McAvennie, was also down to play.

Unfortunately, Frank didn't make it to the ground and it was only last season – when he did turn up for George Parris' testimonial against Ipswich Town – that I discovered the truth behind Frank's absence on Galey's big day. When Frank ribbed me for having to miss George's game due to a calf strain, I reminded him about the time he missed Tony's match, only to be informed by Frank: "Well, I DID make it down to London – but I didn't get as far as the ground!" Typical Frank.

Once again, I enjoyed my return to West Ham, but I missed a good opportunity to pave the way for a permanent move back there while on a family holiday in the South of France a few weeks later. Lorraine, Chloe and I were at Cannes airport when we bumped into the England Under-21 squad who were on their way home from the annual Toulon international tournament. I got talking to Liverpool's Jamie Redknapp – but resisted the temptation to ask him to try and have a quiet word with his dad for me!

After our holiday in France, Lorraine and I enjoyed another break and had a lovely time in Bermuda, and when we returned home I occasionally phoned the Everton

Clubcall number to check whether there was any summer transfer news. One day, I heard them report that I was looking to move because "my wife was unsettled in the north," which was unfair on Lorraine and totally untrue.

Having said that, we would have welcomed the chance to move back south at that stage.

My dad told me that he'd heard, via a friend of a friend, that Ipswich Town were interested in signing me. Whilst there were a couple of plus points to joining Ipswich – my obvious respect for John Lyall and the fact that I would be that much nearer mine and Lorraine's family – I didn't really want to go to Portman Road for footballing reasons.

Mike Walker was a firm believer in the Continental approach to football but I still couldn't understand why Everton arranged THREE pre-season tours abroad that summer. It's okay for a team that has a European campaign to look forward to, because there would be obvious benefits in facing teams who play a slower style of football and use a sweeper system. But that didn't apply to us then and I thought we would have got more from playing the likes of Stockport County and Bury, from the lower divisions of the Endsleigh League.

We spent nine days in Germany, seven in Sweden and three in Italy – doing the wrong things, eating the wrong things and drinking the wrong things. It seemed crazy to me, but there was one amusing situation in Sweden.

Mike Walker wasn't keen on the lads going out for a drink but one night we decided to take the matter into our own hands and broke his 11pm curfew. Six of us lads found a secluded grass area, at the back of the hotel, where we were regularly supplied with beers by a willing waiter.

At 11.30pm, four of us strolled back to the hotel – not via the main entrance, where there was a chance the manager might be, but by jumping over the ground floor balcony. Just after midnight, I spotted the other two – Barry Horne and Gary Ablett – from the balcony returning to the hotel with some takeaway food and more bottles of beer.

They both had their hands full and as they reached a walkway, Barry dropped a couple of bottles. Although Gary heard our shouts and took our advice to re-enter the hotel via the balcony route, for some reason Barry didn't, and carried on towards the main entrance.

He sauntered into the reception area . . . and immediately came across Mike Walker. But as he struggled to keep hold of the bottles of lager, Barry kept a straight face and simply said to Mike: "Morning!" The manager glanced down at his watch, which revealed the time of five-past twelve, and casually replied: "Yeah, just about."

Barry continued on his journey back to the players' rooms, where we gratefully received what he and Gary had brought back for us and had a good laugh about his meeting with the manager.

There was nothing funny, though, about my performance in the friendly against Dutch side Vitesse Arnhem in Germany. We were coming to the end of a niggly game, which Everton led 2-0, when the Dutch pulled one back 15 minutes from time despite a blatant offside that wasn't given by the German referee.

My frustration boiled over seconds later, as my strike partner, Brett Angell, was clattered hard from behind by a towering defender. He must have been 6ft 3ins tall but something inside me snapped and I raced over to him and, stupidly, kicked him in retaliation for what he'd done to Brett. The Everton subs were laughing their heads off as the big Dutchman ran for cover, all the way to his team's dug-out!

I didn't wait for the red card, walking straight off to the changing rooms to reflect on the red mist and an act of petulance that was the last thing the club needed after Gary Ablett had also been dismissed against Cologne the previous day. I just hoped that the official wouldn't file a report of the incident to the FA, who would have banned me for three matches for violent conduct. It was a pathetic thing to do and I apologised to the lads afterwards.

After returning home to provide the opposition in Frank Bunn's testimonial match at Oldham, we flew off again, this time to Italy for another tournament that, if nothing else, proved that football isn't always a game of two halves. The tournament was decided on one day and we qualified for the final by beating Torino 2-0 in the first game, played over just 45 minutes. We then had to sit it out for a further 45 minutes while Torino and Lazio (without Gazza) drew their match and played another 15 minutes of extra-time and penalties. So by the time we played Lazio in the final, rigormortis had set in on the Everton players and, not surprisingly, we were walloped 4-0! Now you know what I meant when I said that the tour served no useful purpose from a football point of view.

It wasn't the best possible introduction either for our new £2.2m signing from Tottenham, Vinny Samways, although I was very pleased to see him arrive. We'd been crying out for a creative, ball-playing midfielder like him but Mike Walker's mistake was in not following up this excellent signing with the two or three other new buys we needed, particularly in defence where we'd given away too many silly goals the previous season.

Walker seemed quite laid-back as the 1994/95 Premiership season approached, but most of the players at the club, especially the senior ones like myself, were under no illusion about the size of the task ahead. Sadly, we were to be proved right.

The summer of '94 ended in a blaze of glory for Brazil, who captured the imagination of supporters world-wide to win the World Cup in America. Although they beat Italy in a penalty shootout, I was delighted that the South Americans had regained the trophy after missing out on it for too long. You couldn't fail to have been impressed by the brilliance of their striking duo, Romario and Bebeto.

I enjoyed the tournament as a whole and was particularly pleased by the introduction of the new FIFA rule which outlawed the tackle from behind. Referees went card-crazy in the opening matches but once the players all knew where they stood with the officials, we saw fewer and fewer yellow and red cards as the finals progressed and much more entertaining matches where the ball-players were allowed to outshine the hard men, who knew that tackles from behind would be severely punished.

As ever, I was watching developments at West Ham with interest and felt utterly dismayed by the attitude of their new £1m summer signing from Oxford United, Joey Beauchamp, who, within two days of pre-season training, decided he didn't want to be at the club.

From a distance, I just couldn't believe Beauchamp's attitude. He was a million pound player, obviously got a big wage increase and had the chance to play for a great club like West Ham in the Premiership. He should have been in seventh heaven but, instead, he didn't want to leave his comfortable Oxfordshire home and family to travel to London. Billy Bonds and his assistant, Harry Redknapp, who had guided the Hammers back into the top flight in May '93, must have been tearing their hair out in disbelief and disgust as all their hard work came to nothing. As two former Hammers players who always wore the club badge with undisguised pride, Beauchamp's pathetic behaviour must have seemed beyond belief.

My agent, Phil Smith, handled the Beauchamp transfer to West Ham and related to me some of the problems the club had to deal with. They even offered to let him continue living in Oxford but the move still broke down and I think Bill and Harry did the best thing by getting rid of him as quickly as possible – to Swindon Town.

I don't know whether the amazing, but sad, Beauchamp episode had a bearing on Bonzo's decision, soon afterwards, to quit as manager but it couldn't have done anything for his enthusiasm for the job. To be honest, I always had the feeling that Bill could jack it in at any time, simply because he has always been such a home-loving man who enjoys spending as much time as possible with his wife and daughters.

As a player, he was a born leader who had potential managerial qualities, having learned an awful lot under Ron Greenwood and then John Lyall. He'd seen and done it all, but I always felt, from the moment he succeeded Lou Macari in February 1990, that it wouldn't take that much to make him quit, because of the time and total commitment the job demands.

Bill had been through an awful lot as manager at Upton Park – two successful promotion campaigns, and a miserable relegation season after the dreaded bond fiasco that had knocked the stuffing out of not only the fans, but the players and management too. I am pleased, though, to see that after severing his links with the club, Bill re-emerged to take over as youth team manager at QPR.

There was never any friction between Bill and I, despite the training ground dust-up that happened years earlier, and, in fact, he wished me all the best when I spoke to him soon after I rejoined the Hammers. I had phoned Phil Smith's office and Bill just happened to be there, so Phil told him it was me calling and we had a little chat. Bill said: "I wish you well, Tone, the fans there deserve success," which was nice of him.

Bill's sudden departure, just 10 days before the start of the season, certainly increased the chances of me returning to Upton Park. As I said, there was no problem between us, but Bill would have had reservations about bringing me back. He will have remembered my somewhat surly, arrogant attitude before I left in 1988 and wondered, quite justifiably, if I could regain the hunger and enthusiasm to give 100 per cent for West Ham again. I had been unsettled at various times during my six years at Everton, and I'm sure he could have re-signed me for as little as £750,000 at one stage, but Bill was not prepared to take that gamble. The door opened a little wider for me when Harry Redknapp became the number one . . .

In the meantime, I was still an Everton player, albeit one whose confidence was low after just three goals in 10 pre-season friendlies. My form continued to suffer in our opening league game, a 2-2 draw against Aston Villa, at Goodison in which Paul Rideout and Graham Stuart scored for the Blues.

Mike Walker got my back up again by declaring before the game that everyone had to go onto the pitch for a warm-up. Gary Ablett and I were the two players who never went out and we both said we were happy not to do so. Walker said again: "Everyone goes out today," to which I replied: "I've never been on for a warm-up in 12 years." He answered "Well, today's the first time." Gary and I walked onto the pitch for two minutes, had a chat and went back in! Why upset two of your senior players' routines before the first game of the season? Everyone prepares for a game differently and we didn't appreciate being told otherwise.

That was followed by a disappointing midweek defeat at Tottenham, where the night belonged to Spurs' match-winner, Jürgen Klinsmann, who capped his home debut with a spectacular overhead kick, followed by his celebratory, self-mocking dive that also involved several of his team mates. The idea was sparked by Teddy Sheringham and I would like to have seen Jürgen continue to do it throughout the season, because it was original and brought a smile to our game.

I was a big fan of Klinsmann and thought that Ossie Ardiles made the bargain signing of the season when the club got the German striker from Monaco for a fee of just £2m. Okay, I know he was paid a fortune in wages, but Tottenham must have recouped that threefold, through increased commercial, merchandising and season ticket sales on the back of 'Klinsmania'. I warmly welcomed the arrival of Klinsmann, as I have those two other world class players, Ruud Gullit and Dennis Bergkamp, who joined Chelsea and Arsenal respectively at the start of the 1995/96 season. We want world class internationals in the FA Carling Premiership, not inferior foreign players who contribute little to our game and only take up team places that would otherwise have gone to British lads.

I certainly don't class Klinsmann as a one-season wonder, because his 29 goals for Spurs says it all about how much he did for them, transforming a mediocre side into one that reached the FA Cup semi-finals and challenged for a European place. I thought he was quite within his rights to invoke the clause in his contract that enabled him to leave (for Bayern Munich) after one season – and Tottenham had no grounds for complaint after his magnificent contribution.

We suffered our second defeat in the opening three games when we were crushed 4-0 at Manchester City. I don't recall us managing even one shot and skipper Dave Watson aptly summed up our state of disarray when he turned to Mike Walker in the dressing room afterwards and said succinctly: "Gaffer, you know we're s--t don't you!" The manager gave him a puzzled look but it soon became obvious that there was transfer activity afoot.

World Cup fever had also gripped Goodison Park over the second weekend of the season, with reports insisting that Walker was about to sign two stars from USA '94, Nigerian Daniel Amokachi and the Brazilian Muller. The fans must have been pleased to see that their club were apparently poised to splash out almost £5 million on two internationals, but I can't say that I shared their enthusiasm once it became known that the two incoming superstars were both strikers! Paul Rideout and I both feared for our futures at Everton, particularly myself because I hadn't been playing as well as Paul or scored the goals he had.

'Ridders' was definitely the best strike partner I had at Everton and we developed a great understanding on the pitch together. Although he was a target man he also had a great touch and was a good team player. One of the best headers of the ball I've seen, I'm surprised it's taken so long for Paul to be fully appreciated by the fans and management at the club. Anyway, Paul decided to sit tight amidst all the speculation but I was becoming unsettled.

I expressed my concern after training the following Monday, when the usual press men gathered for interviews at Bellefield. I admitted that, if the club were about to bring in Amokachi and Muller (who visited Goodison for talks but couldn't agree terms), then my future at Everton looked very bleak.

My comments made an ideal preview piece in Tuesday's morning papers and, at training before our home game against Nottingham Forest that night, Walker summoned me to his office for a word about the newspaper coverage. He wasn't happy that I'd given the interviews, saying that if I had something to say I should have said it to his face, which was a fair point, I suppose.

He went on to tell me that he was leaving me out of the side that night and that was the final straw as far as I was concerned. I'd had enough of being made the scapegoat – first under Colin Harvey, then Howard Kendall and now Mike Walker – and I made my feelings clear. I didn't bother to ask him to explain why he'd decided to leave me out, even though Gary Ablett, Joe Parkinson and I were the only two players dropped after the Maine Road farce. Walker decided to drop his striker, his top scorer from the previous season, despite the fact that our defence had let in four goals!

I just told him straight: "I've had all this before and at the age of 29, I don't need it any more – I want out. If any clubs come in for me, please let me know."

He said: "Fair enough, if that's how you feel," and made no attempt to try to make me want to stay at the club or reassure me that I had a future there. But I've got to give him credit for not attempting to stand in my way and confine me to reserve team football. He knew that I'd reached the end of the road at Everton and basically told me to ask my agent to try to sort something out with another club.

Amokachi was paraded on the pitch (after signing earlier that day) before the Forest game, confirming that at least one striker had arrived, and I sat in the stands and saw us beaten 2-1 after my mate, Paul Rideout, scored his third goal in four matches.

I obviously called Jon and Phil Smith and asked them to try to get me a move back to London – and West Ham in particular. I trained on Wednesday and Thursday of that week, and on Thursday evening there was a breakthrough. I was driving my sister-in-law, Sharon and her children, who'd come up to visit us, back to Lime Street station when I received a call on my mobile phone from Phil, who said: "I've just had a very good conversation with Peter Storrie at West Ham. They're interested in doing a swap deal, with David Burrows going to Everton and you moving to West Ham."

It was just the news I wanted to hear.

Claret & Blues

GOING HOME

I HAD heard so much transfer talk that had come to nothing in the past that I didn't allow myself to get over-excited by Phil Smith's phone call, but then everything happened so quickly.

Phil phoned me back at 6pm to report that "things might be moving" and by 10pm he called again to say "the deal's done and Jim Greenwood has given you permission to talk to West Ham." I couldn't believe it, and refused to get excited until I'd spoken to Harry Redknapp. Even though it was getting late, Phil said he would try to arrange for Harry Redknapp to give me a call at home. I waited excitedly by the phone until it rang again at 11.15pm. I'd never spoken to Harry before, but he sounded very happy and upbeat.

He said he'd been after me for quite a while and made it quite clear that he wanted me to re-sign for the club. Although I was aware of their situation, he made the point that, with Trevor Morley out with a cartilage injury, he needed someone to lead the line and to score goals.

I had expected Ipswich Town to have made all the running for me, and I heard from a local journalist that they did, in fact, make a cash bid that was rejected by Everton. The deal with West Ham seemed to suit all parties, because Mike Walker wanted a new left-back and I was surplus to requirements because of Amokachi's arrival.

My conversation was a very friendly one and from the moment I spoke to Harry, both Lorraine and I were very pleased that we now looked set to go back to London. Over the previous six months – from the Bobby Moore game, then going back there soon after for the league match – I had really re-discovered my love of West Ham and felt very good about going back there permanently.

Phil Smith said that he could arrange a meeting with Peter Storrie at the Toddington motorway services on the M1 for the coming Sunday, but Harry Redknapp couldn't be there, or I could wait and meet both Peter and Harry together at the Swallow Hotel, Waltham Abbey on the Monday. I wasn't too worried about the money side of things, I wanted to know exactly how Harry viewed the future at Upton Park and how he saw me fitting into his plans, so we agreed to meet them at 4pm on the Monday.

With no Premiership games scheduled for that Saturday, I honestly thought I'd played my last game for Everton . . . except Walker had other ideas. When I went in on the Friday to train with the reserves, I fully expected the manager to pull me aside to confirm that my move to West Ham was going through. But he said nothing to me before the session, so I asked to speak to him afterwards and, once again, he surprised me.

Walker had left the transfer negotiations to Jim Greenwood and, in typical laid-back style, said: "It seems as if something might be happening but I'm not too bothered whether you go or not."

Even more amazingly, he then pointed out that as I was still a registered Everton player, I would be playing for the reserves against Liverpool – in the mini derby – at Goodison the next afternoon, Saturday, September 3, 1994.

I said to him: "Don't you think it's a bit silly for me to be playing in a competitive match and risking an injury that could possibly wreck the deal?" West Ham had also expressed their concern about me playing in the game, but Walker was insistent and he had the backing of Jim Greenwood, so I had to accept their decision to make me play one more game in the famous blue shirt.

I hoped to stay out of trouble and simply see out the game in one piece with no heroics, so imagine my reaction when I picked up the team-sheet in the dressing room before kick-off and saw that Liverpool's number five was a certain Julian Dicks, the former Hammers 'hard man!' The match was only a few minutes old when I got chatting to Julian while the ball was up the other end of the field. He'd obviously read all the reports of my proposed move in the papers and acknowledged as much when he said: "It looks like you'll be going back to the Hammers then?" We had a little laugh about it and I said: "Yes, so please don't kick s--t out of me today!" Rumours had also circulated that Julian might also be on his way back to Upton Park soon after a summer dispute with Reds' manager Roy Evans, so I added: "From what I've heard, we could be team mates again soon."

To give Julian his due, he gave one of his most friendly performances and, as one of Liverpool's three centre-backs, hardly made any physical contact with me in a 1-1 draw.

When the final whistle went, I was very moved by the reaction of the fans. What began as a section of fans showing me their appreciation turned to a standing ovation, as most of the 6,000 crowd in the main triple-tier stand clapped me off the pitch at Goodison for the last time as an Everton player. It was a wonderful end to my Everton career and I was genuinely choked with the reception I got.

With lots of jobs needing to be done, Lorraine and Chloe stayed at home while I made the long motorway journey to Waltham Abbey alone. Before I set off, we had discussed my move at length and, as ever, Lorraine was fully supportive. We were both pleased we were going home and I was also happy for the rest of my family, who regularly travelled 250 miles up and 250 miles back every other week to watch me at Goodison through the good times and the bad times. My impending return to the Hammers would certainly make their Saturdays more pleasurable. I phoned to tell them the good news and sought their opinions. My mum and dad were as pleased as us at the thought of me going back to West Ham, although my brother was more sceptical. Paul has a lot of friends who are Hammers' fans and, quite naturally, he wondered whether I was doing the right thing by going back. Frank McAvennie had not managed to recapture his glory days when he returned to Upton Park in March 1989, while Howard Kendall couldn't reproduce the tremendous success he enjoyed as manager of Everton when he returned in November 1990.

But, if I had any doubts in my mind, I could point to Peter Beardsley's phenomenal return to Newcastle United and the success Mark Hughes enjoyed second time around at Manchester United, but there were never any worries on my part. And this time, unlike my previous record-breaking transfer in 1988, there were no nerves either.

I called into Bellefield on my way south, to say my 'goodbyes' to the players, management and staff. I kissed the two canteen ladies, Mary and Lynn, as well as Mary, the secretary and while I was excited about my move back to West Ham, it was still a sad last day for me at the training ground. I gave my tracksuit top and t-shirts to Jimmy, one of the lads on the groundstaff who'd arrived at the club just six months before me. He seemed 'made up', as they say in Liverpool, and it was a shame to say farewell after six years. I collected my boots, tucked them inside a bin-bag, threw them in my car and drove out through the gates for the last time.

The lump in my throat had disappeared as I drove down the M62, connected with the busy M6 and continued south on a journey I knew like the back of my hand. One big chapter of my life had closed behind me, another was about to open ...

I arrived at the Swallow Hotel in plenty of time for the scheduled 4pm meeting and met up with Jon and Phil Smith in reception. West Ham had pre-booked a small boardroom, so we made our way into there once Peter Storrie arrived with Harry Redknapp and his assistant, Frank Lampard. We chatted across the table but the formalities turned to laughter when the Hammers' managing director asked if my wife was from around here. "Yes, she's an Essex girl," I said, realising immediately that I'd done Lorraine a massive injustice! Despite all the jokes we've all heard about Essex girls and their white shoes and dyed blonde hair, I'm sure they are no worse or better than women from any other part of the country, it's just the stigma that's attached to the phrase 'Essex Girl'. Besides, Harry and Frank spared my blushes when they chipped in together, saying: "That's all right, we're both married to Essex girls!" and we all burst out laughing.

We still had to discuss my personal terms of the transfer, though, so we left Peter, Jon and Phil to continue their discussions while Harry, Frank and I returned to the lounge area to talk football, which was fine by me. Harry came across as a very bubbly, likeable character who obviously cared passionately about West Ham and I couldn't fail to have been impressed by his enthusiasm. His brother-in-law, Frank, seemed slightly more reserved and kept asking me if I would still have the hunger and desire to do well for West Ham.

It was a very valid point, because it would have been very easy for me to have taken the soft option by going back to Upton Park, where I knew I'd be around family and friends, and picking up my money each week of my new contract without putting in too much effort. But I kept answering that I did still have that hunger to score goals for the club I'd supported almost since birth.

My only real decision in whether or not to rejoin West Ham hinged on money, but I knew full well before I even got to the hotel that I would have to take a pay cut to play for the Hammers again. The financial structure of Everton and West Ham is so different but, to be fair to West Ham, they pushed the boat out for me.

Although I had to face up to accepting more than a 50 per cent cut in the sign-ing-on fee I'd received at the start of each year of my Everton contract, plus a cut of £10,000 a year in my basic pay, I was still very happy to agree to Peter Storrie's pro-posal. I knew that it was the club's best offer, so there was no need to haggle, and once Jon, Phil and I weighed up their various incentive payments on offer, the deal was done and dusted by 6pm.

The three-year contract I agreed to sign gave me all the incentive necessary to play as well as possible, score as many goals as I could and ensure the Hammers survived in the Premiership. Quite rightly, I would not have been rewarded if I hadn't per-formed well as an individual and the team had gone down – and why should I have done?

As it turned out, with the various incentives in the overall financial package, my earnings in season 1994/95 did not fall far short of what I'd achieved at Goodison the previous season, so it worked out well for all concerned.

As far as I know, the swap deal involving myself, valued at £1m, and David Burrows, who was valued at £1.5m, meant that the Hammers also received an addi-tional £500,000 on top from Everton. They possibly feel that they got better value from the deal, too, because 'Bugsy' spent only six months back on Merseyside before moving on again, to Coventry City.

One of the extra incentives West Ham offered me was to try and set up a car sponsorship deal, and I was very fortunate that Eddy Grimstead, the large main Honda dealer in Romford Road, came forward to provide me with a brand new Honda Civic.

Although I didn't actually complete the paperwork of the signing until 5pm the following day, Tuesday, September 6, 1994, the club had already arranged for me to undergo a medical by their qualified physio, John Green, at the nearby Holly House private hospital. When they mentioned the name I thought it rang a bell and, sure enough, my good/bad syndrome struck again. I asked the receptionist if my best mate, John Cornwell, was in for treatment to his damaged knee and I found the room where John was laying, flat on his back, looking in terrible pain after the oper-ation to repair the cruciate ligament he tore playing for Southend United reserves against Sutton.

I'd been in this state of mixed emotion numerous times before, of course, and my delight at rejoining the Hammers was tempered somewhat by the sight of my best friend in such a poor condition. John had done very well to make the grade in pro-fessional football, reaching top flight standard with Newcastle United after West Ham rejected him when we were both schoolkids, but he had to face the worst blow of all when, at the age of 30, his injury finally forced him to retire from football in February 1995. He now runs a country pub in Essex and, of course, we remain in close contact.

The medical West Ham gave me was much more thorough than the one I had when I left the club to join Everton. This time I even had to take an Aids test, which I was pleased to pass with flying colours.

A long day was finished off perfectly with an Italian meal, attended by my dad and brother, as well as Jon and Phil, coincidentally at the same Potters Bar restaurant where we'd gone to celebrate my first move all those years earlier.

Before I made my second 'debut' for the Hammers, it was time to reflect on the previous six seasons with Everton, where I thought I'd achieved as much as I possibly could at the club. There is no doubt in my mind now that Everton had peaked at the end of the 1986/87 season, when they last won the championship. That brilliant team started to break up and I joined them in a period of major transition.

When I joined them in the summer of '88, everyone wanted to join Everton, but in the years that followed it didn't help that we started to sell some of our best players (McCall and Beardsley to name only two) and then it became increasingly difficult for the managers to attract top quality players.

I had my disputes with all three of my managers but I can still honestly say that I really enjoyed my time at Goodison. It was a wonderful experience for me to play at one of the top clubs in the country.

I've been asked many times whether I ever regretted choosing Everton instead of Arsenal and the answer is 'no'. Okay, the Gunners deservedly won lots of trophies in that time, and good luck to them, but I could have joined them, broken my leg and never played a game under George Graham. And I maintain that Arsenal's style of play wouldn't have suited me You can never look back in football.

From a personal point of view, my going to Everton was also the best possible thing Lorraine and I could have done. The move north cemented our relationship, we were married during my time at Everton and our daughter, Chloe, was born in Southport.

The fans were always great to me. Even when I left to rejoin West Ham, I still received many letters from people thanking me for my efforts for the club and wishing me all the best in the future, which was very nice of them.

My only real disappointment about my six years at Goodison is that I never won anything. They won a trophy in 1987 and had to wait until 1995 for their next piece of silverware . . . so it was with very questionable timing that I joined the Toffees in 1988 and left them in 1994!

Some people said to me I must have been an idiot leaving Everton in the season in which they went on to win the FA Cup. But if I'd stayed, who's to say that they would still have won it? I could have missed an open goal in the semi-final, or anything else could have happened to change things.

Having said that I very much regret not winning a medal at Everton. There are many good top quality players who have never won a major honour in their careers.

Looking back, there were situations with my three Everton managers which, if I had my time there again, I'd handle differently. But hindsight is a wonderful thing – you can only do and say what you feel is right at the time. Howard Kendall, in particular, was a good influence on me even though his Everton team never reaped the benefit of that advice at the time. Howard kept drumming it into me about becoming more of a team player, someone who'd work hard outside the penalty area, but I didn't want to listen to him at the time. My only concern was scoring goals. Sadly for Everton, by the time Howard's advice finally sunk in, I became a West Ham player again.

My six years on Merseyside not only improved me as an all round footballer, but changed me as a person, too. I grew up at Everton and am now much more appreciative of the life I've got. As a youngster, everything came very easy, it all happened so quickly from the time I made my debut as a 17 year-old to becoming the record transfer, but at Everton I had to cope with new problems. I think I peaked at Everton on my debut, when I scored that incredible hat-trick, and from then on I was on a gradual downhill slope.

It rankled with me that I left Everton having scored 99 goals, because it would have been so nice to have completed the magical ton. But I can still take satisfaction from the fact that I elevated myself into the club's all-time top ten goalscorers list, alongside immortal greats like Dean, Latchford, and Sharp. My actual goal ratio remained more or less the same as it was at West Ham – one every 2.2 games – I scored six hat-tricks and, probably the best statistic of all, I was leading scorer for five out of six seasons.

Some critics claimed that I was a waste of money but if I let anybody down at Everton, it was only myself. The team didn't play to my strengths often enough and I didn't play to their strengths either.

I left feeling that I could have improved on my goals return had I not been in and out of the side at frequent intervals. In one quiet reflective period, out of interest, I compiled the table below. It shows just how many times, during my six seasons at Goodison, I was substituted, started the game on the bench or was dropped completely. Cup games are shown in brackets.

Season	Substitute	Taken Off	Dropped
1988/89	1 (0)	4 (0)	2 (0)
1989/90	2 (4)	5 (1)	4 (1)
1990/91	9 (5)	5 (3)	5 (1)
1991/92	7 (2)	6 (2)	4 (0)
1992/93	1 (1)	0 (0)	3 (0)
1993/94	3 (0)	2 (0)	1 (0)
1994/95	0 (0)	1 (0)	1 (0)
Totals	23 (12)	23 (6)	20 (2)

Key:
Substitute = On the bench at the start but came on at some stage.
Taken Off = Started the game but was withdrawn at some stage.
Dropped = Left out of the next game as a direct result of my last performance (not including injuries).

But I will still always look back on my Everton career with a lot of affection. Despite all my ups and downs, I am very grateful to have had the chance to play for such a great club.

Claret & Blues

RED MIST ON THE MERSEY

IT was like going back in time on my first day back at Chadwell Heath as I looked around the training ground at so many familiar faces. I'd played with two members of the coaching staff, Frank Lampard and Paul Hilton, and the youth team manager, Tony Carr, was my first-ever manager at the club when I was a schoolboy.

Ronnie Boyce, Ronnie Gale, Stan Burke and Eddie Gillam, the kit man, were all still there, along with Shirley, the cook, and not forgetting little Charlie on the gate. They all made me feel so welcome and it really did feel like I was coming home. Alvin Martin and Steve Potts were the only two players still at West ham from my previous time with the club, but I knew most of the others anyway, having played against them before.

The only person I had to get to know was Harry Redknapp!

I was pleased that Eddie managed to persuade one of the YTS lads to give up his number 35 training kit – the same number I had when I left the club. As I joined after the start of the season, my favourite number nine shirt had already been allocated to Trevor Morley. Peter Storrie offered me Burrows' number three shirt but he sensed that I didn't consider myself a left-back and, besides, I think he had an inkling that he might need that shirt for somebody else, so I ended up with the number 27 shirt.

It was ironic that my second Hammers' debut should take me back to Merseyside, to play at Anfield, a ground where I'd never won. We came close to breaking the Liverpool jinx, drawing 0-0 at half-time and really taking the game to them in the second half, when we created a host of chances.

But our hopes of springing a shock result virtually vanished in the 55th minute as I chased a through ball from former Reds midfielder Mike Marsh. Rob Jones, who came in on the blind side, caught my heels and brought me down for what I believed was a definite free-kick.

I was very annoyed that referee Paul Danson didn't award me the free-kick and as Jones took possession of the ball and started to bring it forward, the red mist came down and I lunged at him. I'm sure I didn't make contact with Rob – if I did, it was only my arm on the follow through – but it must have looked a bad tackle to everyone else, especially as it was right in front of the linesman and the dug out.

With the tough new FIFA directives in operation, I feared the worst and as Danson fumbled with his pocket, I saw two cards appear. My hopes that he would produce the yellow one were dashed as he pulled out the red as the Liverpool fans bayed for blood. Hands on head, I thought to myself: "Oh my God, what have you done. You idiot!"

I walked five yards to the touchline and then, as I didn't want to to appear that I'd deliberately intended to harm Rob, who was still rolling around, I walked back on to ask if he was okay.

There is no doubt in my mind that if I hadn't been sent off that day we would have won. It was stupid and impetuous of me and I didn't need anyone to tell me that I'd let myself down. I'd also let down my new manager, my team mates and, not least, the fans and myself. I was just relieved that at least we managed a very creditable goalless draw.

No one had a go at me as I offered my apologies to Harry and the lads. In fact, chairman Terry Brown came in and said "unlucky," which was very generous of him. Deep down, he must have been wondering what on earth he and the club had let themselves in for! The worst part about it was that I knew I'd miss three games due to suspension – and it could have been worse if my sending-off in Germany, pre-season, had come in to effect, too. I hadn't said anything about that to anyone when I first re-signed for West Ham and just kept my fingers crossed that it wouldn't come through. Thankfully it didn't, although Gary Ablett did face a three-match suspension for being sent off in Sweden shortly before my episode in Germany.

I clearly had to take stock of the situation, though, because after going seven years between my sending-off for England Under-21s in Germany and that pre-season incident with Everton, I'd now been dismissed twice in two months. Of my three sendings-off, this was the most embarrassing.

Lorraine and I spent that Sunday packing up all our belongings at our home at Birkdale. We'd actually put the house up for sale the previous March – perhaps the writing was on the wall for me at Everton then? – but in the end we rented it out to Vinny Samways, who moved in on the Monday morning. Fortunately, we still owned the first flat we bought in Hornchurch – it had been rented from us during the intervening six years by family and friends – and, luckily it became vacant at just the right time to provide us with a familiar roof over our heads.

On the Thursday morning before our next game, at home to Aston Villa, we had a training session in which I could do no wrong. Everything I did came off and I scored a lot of goals. More significantly, as we walked off towards the dressing rooms at the end of the session, Harry came up to me, put his arm round me and said: "You were magnificent today, you're whole attitude to training was great."

People will say that, at the age of 29, I shouldn't need words like Harry's to boost my confidence, but you do. That was probably the first time since my days with John Lyall, when my manager had really recognised my efforts and said something to me that made me feel good.

Harry's comment proved inspirational as I crowned my second home debut with our late winner, following Tim Breacker's cross. In the space of a week I'd turned from villain to hero. It was a great thrill to score in front of the West Ham fans again, especially after what had happened at Liverpool.

After a dismal Coca-Cola Cup first leg defeat at Walsall, which brought about a team meeting later that week, my suspension ruled me out of the home game against Arsenal (which I saw from the Sky TV box), our impressive 2-1 win at Chelsea and our more convincing 2-0 second leg victory over Walsall which saw us through on aggregate. We made it three wins on the spin against Crystal Palace at home and felt very hard done by at Manchester United, where we lost after doing enough to gain at least a point.

After our deserved win at Stamford Bridge, Peter Butler moved on to Notts County in a £300,000 deal. A typical Yorkshire terrier who was supremely fit, 'Butts' always gave 100 per cent even if he lacked the creative talent of Ian Bishop and John Moncur. His departure created the chance for me to take over his weekly column in the local Recorder newspaper!

Before our next home game, against Southampton, Harry made a tremendous signing when he brought Julian Dicks back from Liverpool for a bargain fee, spread over several seasons and based mainly on appearances. Julian had had a very unsettled year at Anfield but there is no doubt that, on his day, he is one of the best left-backs in the country and one of the game's genuine characters.

Apart from his impact on the field, Dicksy also took charge of the ghetto blaster we play our dance music on in the dressing room before matches. A heavy metal fan, Julian got fed up with our choice of music and decided to bring along tapes of Def Leppard and other loud bands.

It didn't bother the other lads too much, because they always go out on to the pitch to do a warm up prior to kick-off. Only Julian and I stay inside the dressing room beforehand, so my ears started to take a real pounding from then on and I find myself looking for a quiet corner somewhere!

Dicksy is amazing in that he hardly bothers to warm up before a game. He certainly doesn't go through the long stretching process that someone like Timmy Breacker does each time. He'll content himself with kicking balls up against a wall and then simply sit around sipping a Gatorade or can of Coke, listening to his music.

Dicksy is the same before training. He'll go out on to the pitch and ping a ball 60 yards, without even having done any warm-up exercises, and yet still not pull a muscle. It's incredible really, but he gets away with it.

Julian, or 'Norm' after the character in the TV programme Cheers, completely took over the ghetto blaster and if he didn't approve of the tape supplied by one of the other lads, I've seen him turn it off and rip it up in front of the player who brought it along. It was a little game that one or two of the other lads, like Don Hutch, did as their way of showing what is, and what isn't, acceptable musically!

It was around this time that tempers flared on the training ground and Matthew Rush and Alvin Martin were involved in a dust-up. The incident would have been swiftly forgotten by all the players and everyone else who saw it, except that there were about a dozen fans watching us train that day and someone thought they were on to a scoop. In fact, I believe a reporter, who was obviously informed of what had happened in the morning, turned up later that evening on Alvin's doorstep seeking quotes!

It was a fight between two players, but nothing more than I'd seen happen before and I'm sure it goes on at training grounds all over the country from time to time.

The incident was blown up out of all proportion and Harry summed it up well when he commented: "I've seen better fights at a wedding!"

Rushie and Alvin shook hands the following day and all was forgotten, except the fact that Alvin still had the battle scars, so I suppose Rushie 'won' on points!

My return to Goodison for the league game on Tuesday, November 1, was probably a little too soon for my liking. Everyone was so friendly towards me and I was delighted to hear, while I was kicking-in with Ludo Miklosko, a standing ovation from the 28,000 crowd, which was very nice.

But that was where the charity ended that night, as Gary Ablett headed Everton in front in the first half and they clung on for a 1-0 win. It was Everton's first victory of the season but manager Mike Walker's days were numbered and I was not surprised when he was sacked after they drew the next game against his former club, Norwich City. Ironically, they had gone a few games unbeaten when Walker was given the axe, so you could perhaps question the timing of the decision, if not the decision in itself.

The day after I went on record as saying that I hoped Everton would finally appoint Joe Royle as manager, I was delighted when they did just that. He should have been given the job four years earlier, but that's history, and Joe immediately restored confidence throughout the club. He steadied the ship, ensured they comfortably stayed up and guided the Toffees to FA Cup glory.

And no one was more delighted than me when Dave Watson lifted the Cup after Paul Rideout had headed the winner in the final against Manchester United. I don't know whether I thought it would be sod's law, or what, but I decided early on in the competition to have a bet on Everton to win the Cup. I spoke to Matt Jackson after he'd scored the winner – a cracking 25 yarder with his left foot, and don't ask me how he managed that! – at Bristol City in the fourth round, and he confirmed that they'd been totally outclassed by City but still managed to win the game. After Everton thrashed Norwich City 5-0 in the next round, I was tempted to have a dabble when I discovered they were priced 8/1 before facing Newcastle United in the quarter-final. I decided to hold back on the bet, thinking it would be a tough game, but after they went and won that 1-0, I had to put my money on before the semi-final against Tottenham, ignoring all those who claimed it would be Jürgen Klinsmann's year.

I phoned William Hill's with the intention of putting on a tenner at odds of 4/1 . . . only to be informed by the girl at the other end of the phone that they were, in fact, still 8/1, so I told her she'd better make it £20 instead. It turned out that the girl in the betting office had misunderstood what I asked her, so about a week after Everton's superb 4-1 semi-final victory over Spurs, I received a bill from William Hill saying that I owed them £20. They claimed that I'd backed Everton and Crystal Palace to reach the FA Cup Final, which I knew I hadn't. I hadn't even mentioned Palace, who lost to Man. United after a replay.

So I phoned William Hill's head office to query their bill and point out that they'd made a mistake. Luckily for me, every phone call is taped and once they played it back, it confirmed my bet of £20 on Everton to win the Cup outright and I duly collected my winnings in May.

After losing at Goodison, we continued our dodgy spell by making hard work of Leicester City at home, losing at Sheffield Wednesday and then going down to both

Coventry City and Bolton Wanderers (Coca-Cola Cup) at Upton Park, before another away defeat at QPR at the start of December. The Leicester game was a nightmare for Hutch, although after my problems at Liverpool, who am I to criticise any player for being sent off in the way Hutch was against Leicester. As it happened, Hutch and I started up front together earlier in the season, but then missed each other for long periods as we both served separate suspensions.

There is no doubt in my mind that Don has every attribute a quality player needs. It's incredible the things he does with a ball in training, he's got plenty of skill, is a good finisher and has excellent vision. Sometimes the fans are critical of him, probably because of his laid-back style and the fact that he doesn't charge around the pitch like some others who catch the eye with their all-out effort. But he's not a lazy player and I can pay Hutch no bigger compliment than to compare him to Southampton's Matt Le Tissier, another very creative and gifted individual who can win matches on his own.

As the club's record £1.5m signing, I know from experience how being the big-money signing can weigh heavily on your shoulders, but he's still only young and, I'm sure, will go on to prove a real bargain signing in the seasons to come.

To those who sometimes question Hutch's contribution, I say look at the 11 goals he scored from 25 games in the 1994/95 season and see where we'd have been without them. It's not for me to tell Harry what he should and shouldn't do, but Hutch's best position is as an attacking midfielder and to get the best out of him I think we need to give him a free role, like the one Le Tissier thrives on at Southampton, and build the team around him.

The 3-1 cup defeat by Bolton was one of the low points of the season, particularly for the fan I bumped into after the game, who handed me his season ticket and asked me to "give it to Harry!" The irate fan went on to question my own motives for coming back and then, when I explained that I loved the club, he asked why I'd left in the first place! it was one of those conversations that was leading nowhere, so I handed the gentleman back his season ticket and made my way to my car.

That fan wouldn't have been any happier with our 2-1 defeat at QPR, had he seen us play at Loftus Road just before Christmas. Just before this game, Harry signed experienced 'keeper Les Sealey as cover for Ludo. The tall, young American, Ian Feuer, had been on the bench until then but he needed regular first team experience so it was decided to loan him out to First Division Peterborough United. Given a little bit of luck and half a chance, I'm convinced that Ian will be Ludo's long-term successor, but 'H' felt that the dressing room was rather quiet and lacking in noisy, bubbly characters – Julian excepted of course.

But Les – or 'The Cat' – immediately changed all that. Les has enjoyed a lot of success with various clubs throughout his career and takes great delight in telling us how many times he's played in major games at Wembley with Man. United and how many medals he's won. A typical chirpy cockney character, Les dishes out lots of stick to the lads but he can take it in return. I'm sure any fan who has sat near the dug out at Upton Park will confirm what a loud voice Les has got, and we can often hear his shouts above that of Harry's or Frank's. None of the subs like sitting next to him on the bench because of the ear-bashing they take!

Les has West Ham in his blood – his uncle, Alan, having scored both goals in the glorious 1965 European triumph at Wembley – and even though he never played for the first team that season, I thought he was an important signing and a tremendous addition to the club.

Les used his sharp wit when he met chairman Terry Brown for the first time in our dressing room before the 2-2 draw at Leeds United. He said: "Hello, Les, I'm Terence Brown, the chairman." To which Les replied: "Hello, Mr. Chairman, you can call me The Cat!" Terry Brown and the other board members regularly pop into the dressing room before the game, but, as is tradition at West Ham, they tend to keep a low profile and don't interfere and try to tell the players what they should and shouldn't be doing.

Danish international Marc Rieper made his debut, on loan from Brøndby, at Elland Road, but the afternoon belonged to Jeroen Boere whose two headers earned us a 2-2 draw. A typical, old-fashioned centre-forward, 'Yosser's' presence up front proved important at times, because, although we all like to see West Ham play neat, entertaining football, he provided a vital option and he did well for me.

It was a baptism of fire for Marc, against big Brian Deane, and he made a steady start to his West Ham career. It's always a risk bringing a foreign player to the Premiership, but 'Rieps' has the qualities needed for our football. All he needed was the time to settle and it wasn't until well into the new year, after Alvin, who'd been playing tremendously well, pulled his hamstring, that the big Dane really emerged.

Rieps was outstanding in our thrilling 2-0 home win over champions-elect Blackburn Rovers later on in the season, scoring a header himself, and afterwards Rovers' boss Kenny Dalglish asked Harry about his future. With a tremendous piece of kidology, Harry said, quite casually, to Kenny: "Yeah, Rieps, does okay but he's a bit indifferent at times."

Two days later, to stave off any further enquiries from Rovers, Harry signed Marc on a new three-year contract and paid Brøndby £1.1m for him!

Michael Hughes was another key signing, arriving just prior to Christmas on loan from French club Strasbourg. A tricky winger who can play either on the right or left, Hughesie immediately won over the fans on his debut at QPR and was good for team spirit too. Hughesie was always promising to get me extra tickets for friends and family, only to have to turn round and apologise because he'd forgotten to say that he'd already promised the same tickets to another player!

Hughesie was instantly admitted to our card school, but please spare a thought for me – the only Englishman – trying to play three card brag with an Irishman (Michael), a Dane (Rieps) and a Dutchman (Yosser)! That's a recipe for disaster and at times it was hilarious trying to work out what were genuine bluffing attempts and those where the lads had out-bluffed even themselves! I've tried to explain to all three of them another game, 'Hearts', but it went over Hughesie's head!

There was little for me to smile about, though, as Christmas approached. The team hadn't won in six games while I hadn't scored in 10 Premiership matches, since my triumphant return to Upton Park. Harry was as good as gold, telling me to keep plugging away, and at least I was contributing in other areas for the good of the team. If I had gone 10 games without scoring at Everton, I would almost certainly have been dropped, but I finally learned what Howard Kendall had been trying for so long to make me realise. I just kept working hard even when the goals weren't going in for me and Harry – and the fans – recognised that.

I had a word with my dad and also Ronnie Boyce, who knows my game inside out, and he, too, offered words of encouragement. Boycey said that, as far as he could see, I wasn't doing anything different to normal, but just wasn't getting much luck in front of goal. I wasn't getting an abundance of shots on goal, so it wasn't as if I was missing a lot of chances.

Funnily enough, Dale Gordon, who has suffered horrendous injuries since he's been at Upton Park, tried to reassure me after training one day when he commented: "Don't worry, you'll score a hat-trick and then you'll be flying again." Within a couple of weeks of making that remark, I scored all three in our home victory over Manchester City – my first-ever hat-trick in the league at Upton Park.

It was a mixed Christmas/New Year for the Hammers, though, as we were held at home by Ipswich Town on Boxing Day, lost by a single goal at Wimbledon and battered Nottingham Forest 3-1 in the final game of '94. That set us up nicely for a daunting visit to Blackburn Rovers where we outplayed the title-chasers for long periods, showing great character to bounce back from Alan Shearer's early penalty. I equalised with an instinctive left-foot shot on the turn, which clipped Colin Hendry's heel and spun away from Tim Flowers into the corner. Mattie Holmes should never have had his goal disallowed for offside, but Dicksy headed us in front and for an hour we more than matched Rovers. Unfortunately, we didn't hold the lead for long enough and once Blackburn got level, they took control and went on to claim a 4-2 victory. At least we gave the champions one of their hardest games of the season.

Claret & Blues

FAN-TASTIC FINALE

OUR first win of '95 came at Wycombe Wanderers in the third round of the FA Cup and was largely inspired by TV pundit Alan Hansen. The former Liverpool skipper had earlier predicted on Match of the Day that the tie was set up for a cup upset, with the little Second Division club supposedly going through at our expense. We had the satisfaction of forcing Hansen to eat humble pie after our comfortable 2-0 win, but there was no pay out from the bookies on first goalscorer this time.

The Cat occasionally collects a fiver from each player and puts it all on whoever the lads agree will be our first scorer. On this occasion, we gave the money to club photographer Steve Bacon to bet on Jeroen Boere . . . but Yosser limped off with an ankle injury in the second half, when headers by me, then Kenny Brown, sealed the tie. Whenever I hand over my fiver, I always ask Les to make sure the players don't back me for the first goal, because when they don't bet on me, that's usually my cue to score and it happened again at Wycombe. I'm not sure Harry was too pleased with Les and the lads, though, as he commented that they should have backed me at odds of 4/1 against!

You wouldn't have wanted to have bet too much on any Hammer scoring at QPR in the fourth round, where we were shocking and rightly deserved the tongue-lashing we received from Harry. At half-time he pointed the finger at a few players and demanded that we all raised our games for the second half. We put Rangers under a bit of pressure, but couldn't claw back Andy Impey's first half goal and it was a very disappointing way to go out of the Cup. After having a right go in the dressing room after the game at QPR, Harry held a players' meeting at training the following Monday, with everyone giving their views.

Harry made the point to the players that if we went down, we would have only ourselves to blame, because he had absolute belief that we were better than the other sides in trouble. To build us up, he'd say things like: "There's more talent in this dressing room than there is in most other Premier League dressing rooms." He gave rollickings when they were needed, yet still had the ability to pick the players up again after a defeat. He might have been tearing his hair out on the bench on a Saturday, but by Monday morning Harry was back to his usual bright and bubbly self and projecting a positive image that helped to keep the players' spirits up, too.

Our league form was also causing increasing concern, although we suffered a major injustice when my old 'friend', referee Paul Danson, cost us three points when he sent off Alvin just 10 minutes into the game at home to Sheffield Wednesday. He obviously didn't have the same perfect view of the incident that all the Sky TV viewers did, but it was obvious that Alvin brought down Mark Bright inside the Wednesday half and, even though Bright did appear to have a clear run on goal, Steve Potts would have easily come across to cover, so there was no call for the red card. The only thing I will say in Danson's defence is that at least he had the courage to later admit he got it wrong, so Alvin didn't suffer a suspension. Having previously lost the last home game, to Tottenham, we didn't need the nightmare of having two players sent off – Tim Breacker later joining 'Alv' down the tunnel for two bookable offences.

The new year began well for me, with eight goals in eight games, but there was a special significance about the one that set us on our way to a 2-1 victory at Leicester City on February 4. I knew that our next game would be against Everton at Upton Park and I didn't want to face my former team mates with the added pressure of wanting to break the magic 100 league goal milestone for West Ham.

Julian Dicks saw to it that I wouldn't have to wait long, though, as he surged to the bye-line in the 25th minute and cleverly pulled the ball back for me to side-foot it home from close range. Dicksy did brilliantly for me and I was pleased to 'assist' him before half-time when I was brought down for the penalty that Dicksy thumped into the net.

One of our best young prospects, Danny Williamson, made his first league appearance of the season at Filbert Street. One of the most technically gifted youngsters I've seen, Danny's only problem is that there are so many good midfield players at the club. He loves reminding me of the fact that, as a 10 year-old, he once came to the training ground and had his picture taken with me, which is his little way of rubbing it in about my age!

The Sky cameras were back at Upton Park for the visit of Everton, a game that turned into a personal triumph for me, even though it was disappointing to only draw 2-2 against a side who were only just above us in the table. My first goal was probably my best of the season and gave me an unbelievable feeling. I put the ball through David Unsworth's legs and, as it rolled about 10 yards ahead of me, I knew that Gary Ablett might get there before me . . . unless I slid in on the muddy pitch and toe-poked the ball low past Neville Southall, which turned out the right thing to do.

Paul Rideout scored their equaliser and, personally, I was really pleased to see that he'd come through all the speculation about who would be coming and going at Goodison to re-establish himself alongside Duncan Ferguson. Hutch set up my second when he won possession on the left – who says he doesn't win tackles – and put over a perfect outswinging cross for me to head home. Unfortunately, Anders Limpar equalised towards the end to push us into the bottom three.

Alvin Martin's problems continued at Coventry, where he went off at half-time with a pulled hamstring and didn't play any part in the remainder of the season. It was a big blow to lose our most experienced player, especially as he'd been outstanding and making a mockery of his 36 years. The Sky Blues' 'killer' second goal was scored by Mike Marsh, who was inspired for his new club shortly after leaving the Hammers. We were unfortunate to face Coventry in their first game since the appointment of Ron Atkinson as manager, although our performance was well below standard.

We were still languishing in 20th position after Chelsea came from behind to beat us 2-1 at Upton Park. I thought I'd squeezed the equaliser in the dying minutes but it was disallowed for a foul by Trevor Morley on 'keeper Kevin Hitchcock. I've always maintained that goalkeepers are over-protected and this was another such example. I came off at the end of the Chelsea game fearing that, if we weren't careful, we would be fighting a relegation battle by the end of the season.

Another London derby, at Highbury on the first Sunday in March, brought better fortune – and a rare goal from a set piece. On the previous day in training, we practiced some set pieces and Harry came up with the idea of John Moncur, laying the ball into me, holding off my marker and then laying it back to Moncy who had to cross to the far post, where Hutch was coming in. It's a real rarity to work on a specific free-kick like that and then see it actually come off during a game, but that's exactly what happened with our crucial winning goal.

Things definitely didn't go to plan, though, on our midweek trip to Newcastle where, one of the few times in the season, we were outclassed and could have no complaints with the 2-0 defeat. We chartered a plane to the north-east and were just about to taxi down the runway when Les Sealey alerted the stewardess to the fact that he'd notice a crack in the window next to him and Ludo. It meant a delay while the problem was sorted out, followed by a further hold up when our coach was a little late picking us up at the airport in Newcastle. It was just one of those days when nothing went right.

Another nightmare followed against Norwich City, who took a two-goal lead at Upton Park and prompted our disillusioned fans to chant: "We're going to Endsleigh." Many of them had already left the ground when, with just eight minutes to go, I managed to score twice to earn us a priceless point.

Yet it could have been so different had the substitute referee, Mr. Sims, sent off Spencer Prior, who had a good game as one of Norwich's three central defenders, instead of Johnson, when I was brought down by Prior just outside the area in the first half. I tried to spare the ref embarrassment by informing him that he'd shown the red card to the wrong player, but I think he had the impression that I was trying to claim a penalty and chose to ignore me. Days later, Prior was handed a one match suspension and the official received a rap on the knuckles from the Premier League for his cock-up. We were entitled to wonder what might have been if he'd sent off the right man in the first place, but my two goals ultimately cost the Canaries dearly.

It's funny sometimes how a team can embark on a long unbeaten run on the back of what was a disappointing result, but that's what we did after drawing with Norwich. Not that Harry was too pleased after we could only draw our next game, 1-1, at Southampton in midweek. He had apparently been shouting instructions to

Hutch from the far side, to track back with their full-back, but Hutch claimed he hadn't heard the manager.

It got very heated and after appearing to cool down a little bit, Hutch made another comment and after exchanging a few more words with Harry, the manager picked up a tray of sandwiches that were on the medical bench in the middle of the dressing room, and threw them over Hutch's head. I was sitting two away from Hutch and had to pick pieces of tomato off my shirt after the sandwiches had splattered against the wall.

No one said a word as Harry left the room to cool down, but he managed to quickly get over the incident by jokingly saying to Stevie Bacon, who had been in the dressing room at the time of the inquest: "Did you manage to catch any of those sandwiches!"

Fortunately the sandwiches remained on the tray after our very pleasing 2-0 victory at Aston Villa, thanks to a cracking 25-yarder from John Moncur and a tap-in from Hutch. Moncy and Ian Bishop disproved the common theory that playing two ball-players in the centre of midfield is a luxury no team can afford by producing a string of brilliant performances in the closing months of the season.

Moncy is a mad character, a typical East-ender from Bethnal Green who includes the equally zany Gazza among his best friends. Gazza would have been proud of John's antics at the training ground one morning, at the time the builders were in to refurbish the Chadwell Heath facilities. Always guaranteed to brighten up a drab day, Moncy borrowed a paint brush and emerged on to the field with his hair absolutely covered in white paint!

I also recall his exploits on a piano while we were staying at an hotel prior to an away game. Moncy sat down at the piano and discovered that, at the push of a button, it played a tune automatically. He was giving it all the arm actions, swaying from side to side like Dudley Moore, and really looking the part . . . so much so that a few couples, in the restaurant having their meal, actually started clapping his entertaining performance!

The only West Ham player affected by the March transfer deadline was Lee Chapman, who joined fellow strugglers Ipswich Town with that immortal quote: "I've never been relegated." One of the very few middle-to-upper class players I've come across, 'Chappie' was still a down-to-earth and likeable character, with his passion for obscure wines and the London social scene! As a player, Chappie had a difficult time in 1994/95, playing few games, but his contribution the previous season, when he scored the goals that did so much to ensure the Hammers stayed up, should not be forgotten. The deal that brought him, Burrows and Marsh to Upton Park, with Dicksy going to Liverpool, proved crucial.

I'll always remember Chappie for the funniest exercise routine he introduced to a warm up session at Chadwell Heath one morning. There were about 20 of us gathered round in a circle and each player in turn had to suggest a little exercise that everybody else had to do. About 18 players had gone through all the usual routines – calf, thigh and hamstring stretches, press-ups, the lot – when it came to Chappie's turn. His 'warm up' consisted simply of clenching the fist and stretching the fingers, which was a bit typical of a player who was hardly renowned as our best trainer!

After the victory at Villa, we had a ridiculous wait of three weeks until our visit to Nottingham Forest, due to an England friendly and the Coca-Cola Cup Final between Liverpool and Bolton. Dicksy thundered a tremendous free-kick past Crossley into the top corner at the City Ground and although we conceded a second half equaliser to Stan Collymore, it was still a good point away to the fourth-placed team.

Just prior to Easter, we climbed three places up the table to 17th with a convincing 3-0 home win over Wimbledon. Michael Hughes set up what was my 13th goal in the Premiership and with two more in the cups, I was confident, with six games to go, that I could reach my target of 20. At already-relegated Ipswich Town on Easter Monday, I helped to set up Yosser's very late equaliser in another game we really should have won easily. The 1-1 draw saw us slip down to 18th in the table and although I didn't know it at the time, I'd played my last game of the season at Portman Road.

We were already facing another frustrating two-week break from the action due to an England get-together, but I pulled my calf in training on the Wednesday after the Ipswich game and it got progressively worse. I rested the injury, believing I would comfortably be fit for the Blackburn game, but I failed a fitness test on the pitch prior to the match at home to Rovers.

Without me, the lads put in an absolutely tremendous performance to beat the eventual champions 2-0, with Bish outstanding in midfield. A creative player, Bish was one of the main reasons why I was so looking forward to rejoining West Ham and he proved his quality by playing so well, particularly in the closing weeks of the season, despite the handicap of a hernia that required an operation in the summer. Matthew Rush also deserved credit for winning the ball and making our second goal for Hutch, Marc Rieper having headed us in front earlier in the second half.

I was pleased, too, for Simon Webster who finally made his long-awaited first team debut that day, albeit as a late sub. 'Webbo' has shown so much courage and determination to fight back from his broken leg and we were all delighted that he got on in that epic win over Kenny Dalglish's men.

On the morning of the home game with QPR, John Green and I went to Hainault Forest to test my calf, with the intention of getting fit for the following Saturday's vital visit to Crystal Palace. But after doing some medium-paced running, I suddenly felt a sharp pain in my calf and Achilles area and I had to accept there and then that I wouldn't kick another ball in the season. At least it was better that my calf 'went' at Hainault, where we'd gone to take advantage of the softer ground, rather than in the opening five minutes against either Rovers or QPR, which would have been a big blow to everyone.

The only notable recollection of the tame, goalless draw with QPR was that the referee somehow managed to book 10 players and sent off Martin Allen, who had enough worries on his mind at that time as his dad, Dennis, was undergoing treatment for cancer.

Our eight-game unbeaten run came to an untimely end at Palace where, less than a week after our brilliant showing against Blackburn, we looked very jaded and didn't play at all well. The 1-0 defeat put us right back in the mire, just one point above the relegation zone, with only two matches to play.

Even so, Harry and the players believed all along that we had the ability and team spirit to get us through, although Leeds did us a big favour by beating Palace the night before we met Liverpool at Upton Park. Liverpool had already qualified for the UEFA Cup and seemed to be going through the motions by that stage of the season, but we still had to beat them.

Despite losing Dicksy with a chipped ankle bone after just 15 minutes, we dominated the game, with Mattie Holmes scoring his first of the season on the half-hour mark, followed by two strikes by Hutch in the space of a couple of minutes in the second half. The 3-0 victory put us on 49 points. moved us up to 13th place and, most importantly, ensured our survival. It meant that Palace, stranded on 45 points, couldn't catch us and were condemned to the Endsleigh League along with the bottom three of Norwich City, Leicester City and Ipswich Town . . . exactly as I'd predicted in the club's Hammers News Magazine a good eight weeks earlier!

With Premiership football assured for 1995/96, there was a carnival atmosphere at Upton Park for the finale against Manchester United on Sunday, May 14 – and the party went with a swing for all Hammers fans. If there was pressure on the clubs fighting against relegation, then there was just as much tension at the top, where Blackburn and Man. United were slugging it out for the championship. There was no doubt in my mind who I wanted to win the title – with United having dominated for the past two seasons, I wanted Rovers to break their monopoly of the main honours, for the good of the Premiership as a whole. I'm sure our fans felt the same way.

Rovers couldn't have done more to stop United winning their third consecutive league title if they'd been out there on the Upton Park pitch themselves that glorious day. West Ham went out, gave their all and took the lead through Michael Hughes. United equalised and Andy Cole had a few chances to have won the game and the league for his side, but he found Ludo in brilliant form and Upton Park rejoiced as the trophy went to Ewood Park. The way our fans celebrated at the end, you'd have thought we'd won the title.

It was funny to watch Match of the Day that Saturday night and hear the Blackburn players singing their heads off in the Anfield dressing room . . . to the tune of 'I'm Forever Blowing Bubbles!' No doubt Tony Gale instigated their choice of song and it was very appropriate.

Man. United never lost the title on that dramatic last day in East London, they threw it away on a cold winter's night at Crystal Palace in January, but that's another story.

Despite missing a number of games due to injury and suspension, and the fact that I arrived with the campaign four games old, I was quite pleased with my first season back at West Ham. A return of 15 goals was satisfying. I thought I worked hard for the team and it was nice to round off the season by being voted runner-up in the Hammer of the Year award.

First place deservedly went to 'Mr. Consistency', skipper Steve Potts, a quiet defender who gets on with his job without fuss. In the last three games of the season, Steve and Marc Rieper easily got the better of three of the deadliest strike partnerships in the country in Alan Shearer/Chris Sutton, Robbie Fowler/Ian Rush and Andy Cole/Mark Hughes (who came on somewhat belatedly as sub.).

Steve and I had to collect our awards on the pitch after the drama of the United game had ended. The fans observed the club's request to stay off the pitch – West

Ham had the threat of a suspended FA sentence hanging over them after a pitch invasion near the end of the last game of the previous season against Southampton – but what a great reception they always give the players. I've seen them run on to the pitch after the last game and chair-lift the players back to the dressing room, gathering in front of the directors' box waiting for their heroes to re-emerge for one last salute before the summer break. And that's at the end of a season in which we've nearly been relegated . . . just imagine their reaction if, at long last, we were able to give them the success their fantastic support truly deserves . . .

CHAPTER 54

Claret & Blues

BACK TO EARTH

HARRY Redknapp is the best manager I've ever worked under, so I was just as pleased for him as I was for myself and everyone else connected with West Ham when we survived in the Premiership last season.

The manager had been under tremendous strain, particularly in the last couple of months of 1994/95, but he came through it. You can only ever speak personally about a manager – and this is not meant to sound like I'm sucking up to Harry – but he is the best one I've had.

He has given me confidence in my ability, treats me how I want to be treated. I like his coaching and his attitude to the game and one of his main strengths is his ability in the transfer market. Julian Dicks, Don Hutchison, John Moncur, Marc Rieper, Michael Hughes on loan . . . Harry deserves all the credit for bringing those quality players to Upton Park. At the end of the season, Harry declared publicly that he was looking to strengthen the squad for the following season by signing a striker and someone wide on the right.

Above all, Harry wants West Ham to be successful, which is great.

Once again, my good/bad syndrome struck the day after we had ensured our survival against Liverpool when my dad phoned to tell me that nanny Griffiths, who'd been ill with Alzheimer's Disease for the past three years, had died at the nursing home where she lived, aged 83. With her funeral set for the following Thursday – three days after we were to fly out on our tour of Australia – I faced a difficult dilemma, but my family realised my commitment to the club and, knowing nan, she would have wanted me to have been on that plane to Aussie.

Although I knew before we left that it was doubtful whether my calf injury would allow me to play in any of our four friendlies against state and local teams, I was happy to go along with Peter Storrie's request that I went on the tour to make P.R. appearances in Perth, Melbourne, Sydney and Brisbane during the course of the 17 days. Dicksy, Rushie and Moncy were in the same boat and a lot of our spare time was spent meeting ex-patriots, who were there in force wearing their old Hammers shirts, and I also appeared on national TV.

It was a good experience to visit a country I'd always wanted to see and, naturally, we took in the usual tourist attractions like the Sydney Opera House. I also enjoyed a very enjoyable day at Canterbury racetrack with Pottsy, even though we didn't back a winner.

I was luckier, though, when we sat down at our hotel, at midnight, to watch the FA Cup Final between Everton and Manchester United. There was no hint of bitterness as I saw my good friend Paul Rideout head the match-winner that completed United's misery at missing out on their second successive double. Besides, I was £80 richer and looking forward to collecting my winnings from William Hill on my return to England!

Everton had had a difficult season and I was pleased for the players and everyone associated with the club that it had ended on such a big high.

But just to show that footballers don't always make loads of money, I received a phone call from Lorraine while I was in Australia to say that a couple were interested in buying our house in Birkdale, but we had to accept a £45,000 loss on the selling price! We were glad, though, to have finally found a buyer, so that we could pack up all our gear and well and truly re-establish our roots in Essex.

We returned to Southport for one last week, when we packed our gear into containers ready for storage, and I took the opportunity to meet up with Paul Rideout and Matt Jackson. It was the end of an era as we shook hands before Lorraine, Chloe and I opened a new chapter in our lives. In fact, we were expecting to move into our new home in Essex just when this book is due at the printers.

Our holidays were spent in America before flying on to the Cayman Islands, where we were awakened at 5.15am one morning by a tremendous rumbling sound. Our bed was shaking, and the blinds were moving. We thought at first that it might have been someone trying to break into our apartment . . . but it was actually an earthquake measuring 5.5 on the Richter Scale!

After a check confirmed that there was no break-in in progress, and we agreed that it was an earthquake, I turned to Lorraine and said: "Well, did the earth move for you or what?" When I spoke to one of the locals the following day, he confirmed that it was the first earthquake ever recorded on the Cayman Isles!

Soon after we returned to England, West Ham raised a few eyebrows with the signing of Dutch striker Marco Boogers from Sparta Rotterdam for a fee reported to be just under £1m. Several established Premiership names had been linked with us, including Mark Bright (Sheffield Wednesday) and Dean Holdsworth (Wimbledon), but the 33 year-old Bright could not be considered a long-term prospect, while Holdsworth's transfer fee, which would have been in the region of £4.5m, on top of his big wages, put them both out of the reckoning. Bristol Rovers striker Marcus Stewart was another mentioned as a possible signing, but he lacked senior league pedigree and signing him from a Second Division club would have been just as much a gamble as signing the unknown Boogers, who, ironically, visited Everton for talks before ending up in East London.

I was looking forward with interest to playing alongside my new strike partner, who could not have imagined quite what an impact he would make in the weeks ahead . . .

CHAPTER 55

Claret & Blues

ROVER AND OUT

IT won't be the most important goal I'll score this season, but I felt a huge weight lift from my shoulders when I completed the scoring in our 3-0 home win over Bristol Rovers in the Coca-Cola Cup second round.

The tie was already settled, having already taken a one-goal lead from the first leg, but to any striker your first goal of the season is always a significant moment and, hopefully, for me it was a turning point.

I felt I went into the game, our tenth of the season, with something more to prove after being dropped for the Premiership match at Southampton 48 hours earlier. Harry explained that he was leaving me out for "tactical reasons" but I was still very disappointed.

Yet the 1995/96 campaign began so brightly when Danny Williamson scored the first Premiership goal of the season against Leeds United after only five minutes. I had a couple of half-chances in the first half and, if anything, probably connected too well. But we were destroyed in the second half by Tony Yeboah, who scored twice to win Leeds the game, and then proved it was no one-off performance by scoring even more spectacular goals in subsequent matches against Liverpool and Wimbledon.

It was clear from the first game that we had to improve our overall performance throughout the 90 minutes and the following few games did nothing to dispel that theory. We played quite well to hold Manchester United goalless at half-time in midweek, but faded again in the second half and lost 2-1. Steve Bruce's own goal – with me standing right behind him waiting to tap the ball home from close range – meant that another season has gone past without me scoring at Old Trafford.

You could have heard a pin drop when we equalised, because one side of the ground had been closed for redevelopment and United hadn't allocated any tickets to West Ham fans. I felt that was wrong, because all Premiership clubs have had to cope with restricted capacities as they rebuilt their grounds in the wake of the all-seater recommendations and West Ham, like most other clubs, have always attempted to make at least a small allocation of tickets available to away fans. Surely Manchester United could have offered at least 500 seats for Hammers' fans, who ended up watching what the club later admitted was very poor closed circuit TV coverage of the game beamed back to Upton Park.

If they had difficulty seeing Marco Boogers clatter late into Gary Neville, then nobody else at Old Trafford did. I think Marco was unhappy that he hadn't started in either of the first two games and seemed out to make his mark. The Dutchman has obviously had his problems settling in at West Ham, gaining himself some unwanted bad publicity that did neither him nor the club any good, but I know from experience that it is never easy to settle in new surroundings. I only moved to another club in England, but Marco has had to adapt to a new language, new team mates, new tactics, a new manager and a totally new way of life. With his wife also experiencing problems in pregnancy, it was a difficult time for him.

I'm certainly not in any position to criticise his behaviour at Old Trafford that night! What is it about West Ham strikers who get themselves sent off on their debuts? . . . first there was Jeroen Boere, then myself, followed by Boogers in our first away game. I hope Marco sorts himself out and becomes an important addition to the squad, because we're not exactly overloaded with strikers following the departure, in the last year, of Steve Jones, Lee Chapman, Trevor Morley and 'Yosser' Boere. Danny Shipp and Chris Moors have shown potential at youth and reserve team level but it's a huge step up to Premiership class.

Almost as soon as they left the club, Trevor and 'Yosser' suffered the injury jinx that also struck two more who moved on soon after the season started, Matthew Rush and Martin Allen. I was particularly disappointed to see Rushie join Norwich City. He has everything: electrifying pace, skill and strength, although his crossing let him down at times. I'm convinced, though, that once he has recovered from the knee ligament injury he sustained in training, he will prove a very good bargain at only £350,000. I just hope we've inserted a sell-on clause in the deal.

It was Martin Allen who headed us into the lead at Nottingham Forest in our third game but, yet again, we let them back in it, although the penalty awarded against Hutch was highly debatable. I missed a very good one-on-one against their 'keeper, Mark Crossley, while our new Australian signing from Blackburn Rovers, Robbie Slater, also missed a clear chance to have made the game safe.

Robbie is a very busy player who can operate on either flank and he grew in confidence once he got a few games under his belt. He arrived as part of the shock deal that took Mattie Holmes to Ewood Park. I don't think Mattie would have wanted to leave Upton Park – he is a classy little player with excellent touch and ball control – but the chance to join the reigning champions and European Champions League contenders, where he has been playing alongside the likes of Alan Shearer, was too good to resist and I don't blame him for taking the opportunity.

Our home game against Tottenham was another case of points slipping from our grasp. Hutch gave us the lead with a cracking free-kick that flew into the top corner, but Ronny Rosenthal equalised in the second half. Everyone at the club realised that the fixture list had given us a very tough start to the season and our results reflected that.

After the Spurs game, 'Mad Dog' became the latest player to depart when he joined First Division Portsmouth, initially on loan but with a view to a permanent move. We all knew how upset Martin was by the death of his father, Dennis, during the summer. They were obviously very close, with Dennis and Martin's mum present at every match, and Martin admitted that with his dad no longer watching from the stands at Upton Park, it would never be the same again.

Neither were the players' socks after Martin paid a sneaky visit to our dressing room – while we were all out training – to clip the toes off all our socks before he left the training ground for the last time!

After the disappointment of the 1-1 draw with Spurs, we had to wait another 12 days until we were in action again – at home to Chelsea in Sky's Monday Night Live game. We put the Blues under quite a bit of pressure but, again, conceded two bad goals, although their 3-1 win didn't really do us full justice.

I missed a couple of half chances, one after I managed to 'turn' Ruud Gullit, who was outstanding on the night. He started the match playing as sweeper but showed what a world class player he is with his second half forays that caused us more problems at the back.

The Chelsea defeat was Iain Dowie's debut after his £500,000 arrival from Crystal Palace in the deal that took 'Yosser' to Selhurst Park. It was on the Friday morning before the game at Forest that Harry told me he was thinking about bringing Dowie back to the club. I couldn't really comment because I'd missed Iain by about three years in our previous spells at the club, but I knew that he'd given us a hard time in our last away game of the previous season and he is an international regular.

Both the Chelsea game and the following one, at Arsenal, were overshadowed by incidents involving Julian Dicks. But I'm sure I speak for all the players when I say that none of us realised an incident had even taken place when Julian's boot came down on John Spencer's head and forced the Chelsea striker off to have stitches before half-time.

Normally when there is a bit of friction between two players the other players sense it, but this was an innocuous looking challenge and none of the Chelsea players complained on the night or, indeed, after it had been replayed a hundred times on Sky. In fact, at the time, I didn't even realise Spencer had left the field. The referee couldn't have thought on the night that Julian was guilty of stamping on Spencer, because the card he showed him was yellow, not red.

In the dressing room afterwards, we made the usual sort of ribbing comments to Julian, but he insisted to us and Harry, who asked him outright if he meant to stamp on Spencer, that there was no intent.

Alas, Dicksy had a close look at both coloured cards in yet another derby game, at Arsenal a week later, when he was sent off for two bookable offences. They were simply two misstimed tackles but the media overreacted and we woke up on Sunday morning to hysterical headlines all about the sending off . . . even though it was the first time he'd been sent off since January 1993 – and I've been sent off more often than him in that time!

The morning after it appeared in the papers that one of Julian's young twin daughters had been harassed at school over her father's on-field problems, there were TV camera crews and a posse of press outside the training ground sniffing around for more stories, but I just felt as usual, the media went way over the top and I know Julian was surprised by all the fuss.

I really felt for our fans at Highbury, who sat out in the rain and saw such a dreadful performance on the day. We defended poorly, created nothing from midfield and never looked like scoring up front. My disappointment was compounded 15 minutes from time when Harry decided to take off me and Hutch. It was quite obvious that I wasn't suited to playing left midfield – as we attempted to reshuffle following Dicksy's departure – but within a minute or so of bringing on our new Australian signing, Stan Lazaridis, and Alvin Martin, to try and shore up the defence, we conceded the crucial penalty to Dennis Bergkamp, from which Ian Wright scored their winner.

Minutes later, we were down to nine men, as John Moncur was caught in the eye by Ray Parlour and had to leave the field minus one contact lens. To give Harry credit, it would have been easy for him to have simply played on with only nine men, but he had the guts to send on our substitute goalkeeper, Les Sealey, for his debut – up front!

Of course, he was well out of his depth, but at least he put himself about. I think he now has a better understanding of what we strikers have to put up with, though, having been a little upset to have received Tony Adams' forearm in the back of his neck! On the bus afterwards, I asked 'The Cat' if he had any decent tips for me on how to end my goal drought that was beginning to cause increasing concern.

We didn't create much in the midweek Coca-Cola Cup tie at Bristol Rovers either, but we did a professional job on what could have been a difficult night at Twerton Park. 'Moncy' scored a good goal from outside the box to win the game, although I was again disappointed to be taken off five minutes from the end, this time so that Marc Rieper could bolster our defence.

Not only was I growing more and more concerned that I hadn't scored yet this season, but the lack of chances was just as worrying. There would have been no better time to have ended my barren run than against Everton, the visitors to Upton Park on September 23, but it was another dismal day for me.

It began with a bit of a moan from a few of the Everton lads, who weren't too pleased with my comments in a couple of tabloids on the morning of the match. One set of quotes had been taken from an interview I gave six months earlier, while the other was based on quotes lifted from West Ham's Clubcall line, which was a bit naughty.

I smoothed it over with the Everton players but the afternoon ended on another bad note for me. To be substituted for the third game in succession, and against my former club, hurt me even more. Again, we created hardly any chances, so it was just as well that Julian came through a high profile test of character to ram two unstoppable penalties past Neville Southall who, although he went the right way, was simply beaten by the sheer ferocity of Julian's shots.

The day before the Everton game, Iain Dowie and I asked Frank Lampard if we could stay behind for shooting practice. I felt I needed to get back into the habit of getting in shots at goal, but my confidence dipped even further after I fired about 25 shots at 'The Cat' and not one found the net.

Being honest, I think that every now and again it doesn't do any player any harm to be reminded that he must always have to earn his place, so I had to look at myself after Harry dropped me at Southampton. Although he told me it was for tactical reasons and said to me there and then that I'd be back for the second leg at home to Bristol Rovers, I was still gutted to be left out. But it was never one of those situations where I was going to be knocking his door down, because I always believe that if you are going to argue about something you should do so from a position of strength. And the fact was, I'd gone eight games without scoring.

After Harry told me his decision, as we were inspecting the pitch at The Dell before the game, my mind flashed back to the last time I was dropped as a West Ham player. It was at Southampton, almost 10 years ago, that John Lyall replaced me with Greg Campbell. Even more coincidentally, I came on for the last 20 minutes, as I did in 1985, and, just like then, we drew the game.

More significantly, I scored in the next game after being dropped, as I did against Bristol Rovers on this occasion, scored in the next six matches and ended up with a personal best for the season of 26 goals.

When I told Harry that, he laughed and said: "Well, I won't be too unhappy if you can do that again!"

I could have let my head drop and start feeling sorry for myself, but I reacted positively and felt determined to prove myself again as a goalscorer. I care a lot about the club and about football, and things were beginning to get to me. As you get older, you are aware that there is more to life than football, but that still doesn't mean you don't care about the game or your own lack of form.

If I'd played eight games and missed 40 chances, then I would have been seriously questioning my ability as a forward, but I think I counted that I had only six shots in those first eight games, which proved how few chances we'd created as a team. But few people go into statistics in that detail and I had to accept that strikers will always be judged by their goal ratio.

When I scored against Bristol Rovers from Robbie Slater's pass, it was a wonderful feeling of relief and emotion to look up at the Chicken Run and see so many happy, smiling faces. I think those fans, who have been brilliant for me and very patient, were just as relieved as I was when I finally scored.

I know I'll never lose that special buzz that only scoring a goal brings. It's a feeling I've had 233 times in my professional career and hopefully I'll celebrate many more goals before I hang up my boots.

A nice, bright sunny day back on Merseyside, September 10, 1994 . . . until the red mist descended.

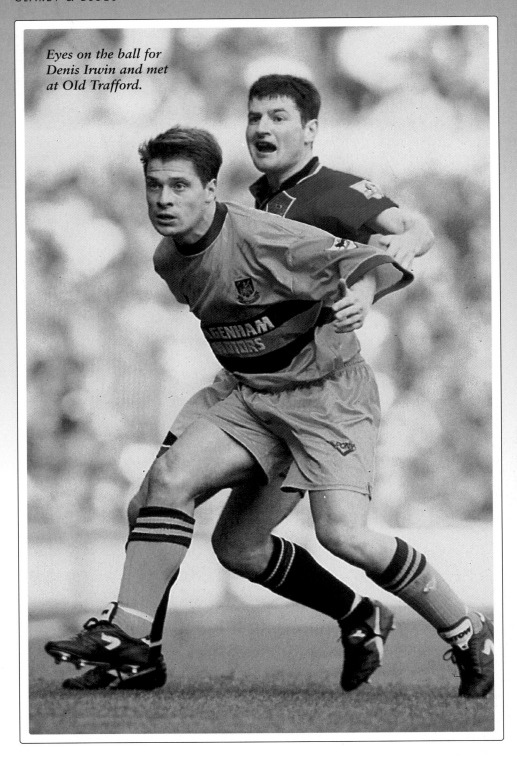

Eyes on the ball for Denis Irwin and met at Old Trafford.

Left: *A new ball-boy for Chadwell Heath.*
Below left: *I said I always claimed to be a 'Mod'.*
Below: *A pose up on Bondi Beach, Sydney.*

Below: Composure on the ball at Upton Park.
Below left: After scoring one of my late goals against Norwich, March 1995.
Below right: Stuart Pearce doesn't look too pleased about my goal against Forest on New Year's Eve, 1994.

On our way to a
crucial 2-0 victory at
Villa, March 1995.

Above: Me and my sponsored car.
Left: In action at Chadwell Heath on my first day back, September 1994.
Below: A back-stretch in Germany, July 1995. I hope I remembered to take my watch off for the game!

Above: Almost a tackle from me
on John Pemberton of Leeds.
Right: A race to be won.
Below: Let's all dance . . . with
Arsenal's Nigel Winterburn.

Above: Who said we're 'playing pony?' . . . my first goal of the season, at the 10th attempt, against Bristol Rovers in the Coca-Cola Cup, October 4, 1995.
Below: "Had to come" . . . my response to the Chicken Run after my goal sealed our 3-0 win over Rovers. The fans looked as relieved as me.

Claret & Blues

MIND GAMES

O NE of the worst feelings a player will ever experience is being dropped, or
left out of the team, because it can be a long and lonely road back to the first
team – and I should know!

I've already written about my own personal – sometimes selfish – feelings after
being dropped by three different managers at Everton. I don't care what players may
say to people around them at the time, if they have an ounce of pride in themselves,
then deep down they are feeling sick and desperate to get back in.

Occasionally, I've seen that desperation manifest itself on the training ground,
where the player who has been dropped vents his frustration on innocent team
mates. The tackles fly in and people can get hurt. At Everton, we had a situation
where one player – I won't name him – had to be 'pulled' by one or two others for
his over-zealous tackling of the man who'd been brought into replace him.

I've known one or two players who've been absolute poison when they're left out
of the team. They've tried to manipulate the press or the manager to put the other
man in a poor light, and you'd be amazed at some of the ducking and diving that
goes on behind the scenes in football.

As I've said before, the last thing in the world an out-of-favour player wants is his
replacement to do well. I know, because I experienced it with Mike Newell and Graeme
Sharp, and I'm certain that they would have felt the same way when I was keeping either
one of them out of the side. It's just human nature and you'll never change that.

The psychology of football is quite amazing, because there is no doubt that the
modern game is played as much in the mind as it is with the feet.

Most players adopt a pre-match routine that they stick to religiously, and I'm no
different in that respect. My preparation for a Saturday game begins at lunchtime the
day before at the training ground, where we usually enjoy Shirley's spaghetti bolog-
nese before either going home in the afternoon, if we're playing at Upton Park the
next day, or meeting up with the boys about to travel for an away game.

I take it easy on Friday afternoon – you'll never see me shopping in places like Romford or Lakeside! – and in the evening at about 6pm, whether I'm at home or in an hotel, I always prefer to eat avocado and prawn cocktail, followed by fillet steak, chips and beans or peas. The night before a game I relax by watching telly before going to bed between 11-11.30pm. I never make arrangements to go anywhere on a Friday night, or invite anyone, including family, to our house, because otherwise I'll never know how late I'll end up going to bed.

If we're playing at home, I always have a lie-in on Saturday, while Lorraine and Chloe get up early. Lorraine will bring up a cup of tea at 9.00am and I'll get up by 9.30am to enjoy freshly-squeezed orange juice which is always prepared and ready for me in the fridge. It may sound funny to some people, but this is a routine we follow prior to every home game, and I know that most other players follow similar pre-match habits that never change over the years.

My usual Saturday morning breakfast consists of scrambled eggs, two sausages, baked beans, two slices of toast and another cup of tea. I used to eat again at midday but I don't anymore and after breakfast I won't eat anything else until after the game.

After breakfast I'll sit down and watch the Italian football programme on TV at 11am, perhaps play with Chloe, then take a bath and get changed. I'll be back downstairs by 12.15 to watch Football Focus, have another cup of tea before leaving at home at 12.45pm. The journey from Hornchurch to Upton Park usually takes around half-an-hour.

Immediately before the game, I'll sometimes have a bar of chocolate and, as I've got older, I've got into the habit of drinking glass after glass of still mineral water – up to a litre – which prevents dehydration during the game and helps to keeps me going.

Players have their own individual way of preparing for the game once we've all arrived in the dressing room. For instance, Tony Gale always used to make himself sick, to ensure his stomach was as empty as possible before kick-off. My own way of coping with nerves is to go to the toilet about 10 times, sometimes even a minute apart, even if it's only a trickle!

Billy Bonds used to do the most strenuous exercises in the dressing room, jumping and running up and down, but then laid-back players like Julian Dicks and Gary Ablett simply sit around, drink a can of Coke and then go out and play football. Alan Devonshire used to fall asleep in the medical room for half-an-hour, wake up and still be the best player on the pitch.

There is no right or wrong way of preparing to play football, it's all down to individual preference, and the same applies to diet. At West Ham, we've been given advice by expert dieticians who tell us what we should and shouldn't eat and drink at certain times of the week. Gordon Strachan reckoned that eating porridge and bananas probably helped to extend his playing career by five years, but I think we can sometimes be too fussy about the food we eat and its effect.

When I was younger, I used to eat fillet steak and beans at midday before a first team game and still score a goal, but the experts would discourage me from eating that today and suggest something like pasta. I know of one top club who always used to take their players away to a hotel on a Thursday night, on the basis that they would all eat pasta, the benefit of which would become apparent 36 hours later, at

3pm Saturday! But, in between, the players were free to go and spend Friday night at their homes. So, whilst the pasta meal the players ate on Thursday might have done them a lot of good, who's to say that some of them didn't feast on eggs and chips and drink two pints of lager on Friday?

Everyone is different. I know a player who drinks a bottle of wine every night, including Fridays, and yet still plays well on Saturday. So how can anyone turn around and tell that player that he shouldn't drink wine. There are a lot of legendary players who have been self-confessed heavy drinkers, and yet have enjoyed enormous success.

I think players should be treated like adults, because by treating them like kids, they'll behave like kids. If a team is away on tour and the manager tells everyone to be back by 11pm, you can bet your life that some will either return at one in the morning or get back for eleven, and then go out again later. If I was a manager, I'd simply tell the lads to go out and have a good time, but keep out of trouble and make sure you're on the team bus at nine o'clock in the morning.

It's the same with food. I heard that when Lou Macari became manager at West Ham, he stopped the players eating chips before a game, which is silly. Apparently, Mark Ward was one who rebelled against Lou's chip-ban and it's hardly surprising since Wardie had probably been eating chips for the past 12 years! At Everton at one stage, the physio, Les Helm, actually banned us from eating cheese. For four years, every day we had a choice of cheese and tomato or cheese and ham on toast . . . until we were suddenly told it wasn't good for us!

It's all very well dieticians claiming the benefits of eating food like pasta, chicken, baked beans and scrambled eggs at certain times, but when the ball comes to your feet on a Saturday, you're not eating a banana or pasta . . . if you can't control a ball or strike it properly, it doesn't matter what you've been eating all week!

If I were a manager, I wouldn't worry too much what my players did during the week. The bottom line is what they do at three o'clock on Saturday.

Claret & Blues

FAME AND FORTUNE

IT is amazing how the valuation of players has changed since I joined Everton for the British record transfer fee of £2.05m in 1988. We're now talking £8.5m – the amount Liverpool paid Nottingham Forest for Stan Collymore.

It's almost frightening the way players' wages have increased since the start of the 1990s, with a number of Premiership stars now earning in excess of £10,000 a week – way above the figure I earned at Everton.

For a footballer to suddenly enjoy such wealth, it must be difficult for some of them to handle, especially if they are young with no wife or children to support. I found it difficult to handle myself, when I more than doubled my weekly wage following my transfer to Everton.

Quite honestly, I don't know why clubs need to pay players some of the huge wages that are banded around today. Surely a player should be able to survive very comfortably on three of four grand a week.

I don't want to take anything away from Stan Collymore, or any other player who can command big wages – I say good luck to them, because a player owes it to himself and his family to earn as much as he can while he can. Besides, it wasn't Stan Collymore who set his record-breaking fee at £8.5m, it was Forest.

But clubs should be careful that they don't pay out £10 million on one player - the equivalent of one season's gate income - with no guarantee of a trophy on display at the end of the season.

The problem is that it's not only leading strikers who fetch enormous fees. More and more average players are being bought and sold for silly money, with no international pedigree and very little experience of playing in the top flight.

What youngsters earning big money need most is someone who genuinely cares for their interests, who can advise them financially and point them in the right direction. I think Alex Ferguson deserves a lot of credit for the way he protected Lee Sharpe and Ryan Giggs from the glare of media and public spotlight when they first burst through onto the scene at Manchester United.

I was lucky to have my dad to advise me, from the age of 17, to invest my earnings in a pension fund, which should net me a nice, tidy sum when I'm 35 years-old. It's my advice to all young players to do the same, even those who may now be earning 10 grand a week. If they are fortunate to steer clear of serious injury and finish playing at 35, the big question is what will they do then? It's easy to simply say, go and get a job, but it's far from easy to do that. Imagine going for a job interview and saying: 'I've just finished playing football, and now I want a job. I'm 35, have no qualifications and what's more, no experience at all.' How many employers would give you the time of day, especially with unemployment running at just less than three million.

Of course, many players now employ agents to handle all their financial arrangements with clubs and it's obvious why. You need to be a very upfront type of person to sit down and talk turkey with much more experienced negotiators, like managers, chairman or chief executives who are representing the club.

It's very pleasing to see the Professional Footballers' Association become more and more involved in player transfers in recent years. They are a marvellous organisation who have only the player's best interests at heart, but there is still room for individual agents to get involved.

To try and eliminate illegal agents and protect the reputable ones, FIFA introduced a rule last year that all agents had to provide a hefty financial bond before they were licensed to work in football. As it happens, my agent, Jon Smith, was one of only three British agents who paid it straight away, so at least I know my representative is legitimate and acceptable to the game's authorities. Jon played a vital role in my move to Everton and did very well for me. We came to an arrangement where I agreed to pay Jon 'x' amount of pounds once the transfer was completed, but a lot of agents insist on 10% of the player's signing on fee, or even of their basic wage. Some players get themselves into an awful mess financially.

If an agent negotiates a big transfer deal, then I think he should be entitled to earn between £5,000 and £10,000, but I don't see how they can justify charging more than that, regardless of the fee. When you think of all the money agents have taken out of the game, just remember this: when Chris Sutton moved from Norwich City to Blackburn Rovers for £5m in the summer of '94, he used the PFA players' union to represent him . . . and paid them the standard fee of just £250! By doing that, Chris must have saved himself anything between £10,000 and £50,000. So to any young players who are lucky enough to be involved in a big-money move, my advice is use the PFA, because they will look after the player and not charge them the earth to do it.

Unfortunately, though, there have been too many agents over the last 15 years who have been bad news for football, people who have no care for anyone but themselves. We should get rid of the 'cowboys' and deal only with agents with a good reputation, like Jon Smith, Jerome Anderson and Jon Holmes. And although I've never dealt with him personally, Eric Hall comes across as a larger than-life character who is now a well-known figure in football. At Upton Park last season, my mum made him laugh when she remarked that he "had a big one" – a cigar, that is!

With some young players, you fear that they will press the self-destruct button, and I can see why managers tend to encourage their new, young stars to marry early and settle down. I fear for the future of some clubs, too, because if they maintain their spend, spend, spend policies for many more seasons to come, some could end up facing bankruptcy. No matter how big a club it is, there must come a cut off point where they have to balance the books. Blackburn Rovers won the Premiership title last season and, despite the invaluable input of owner Jack Walker's millions, the club still traded at a loss.

If British clubs are not careful, they will find themselves going down the same road as clubs on the continent, where there have been major financial problems, largely as a result of spiralling wages and transfer fees. Let's face it, it's only a matter of time before we, in England, are proclaiming the £10 million player.

I don't know how clubs can bring a halt to escalating transfer fees and ridiculously high wages but it's a problem they will need to address soon. If the Premiership or FA tried to cap players' transfer fees and wages, it wouldn't work. Every player would end up going for £5m, while there are always other ways of paying players – through sponsorship and endorsements, etc. Perhaps the Jean-Marc Bosman court case might just change the transfer system as we know it, but only time will tell what direction the game will travel in after the European ruling.

Looking back, I don't think I capitalised as much as I possibly could have on the fact that I was the British record transfer. Jon did well for me, arranging a boot contract with Patrick and a few other bits and pieces, but once I fell out of favour at Everton it obviously had a knock-on effect. In my first year at Goodison, I suppose my income from outside sponsorship and appearances, etc, came to £20,000. That is put into perspective when I read that David Platt has reportedly signed a £5m deal, over five years, with Mizuno!

I would have earned more had I been based in London, where there are more commercial opportunities than in other big cities like Liverpool or Manchester. Indeed, when I returned to West Ham I earned more from off-the-field sponsorship in just nine months than I had in my last three years at Everton.

But I'm not complaining about missed opportunities. I did as much as I wanted to and was never one to keep phoning my agent looking for work. Besides, if a player takes on too much, it can affect his game. There is no point in having loads of money coming in if you neglect the two most important things – your family and football.

Players have to be wary of hangers-on, people who just want to be around them simply because they are very well off financially and famous. Players should be cautious about the places they visit in their social life, because no matter how well behaved they are, there will always be someone looking for a punch up, a drunkard trying to make a name for himself. But that's the price of fame and it's obviously not only footballers who have problems dealing with difficult members of the public.

Players must not forget, though, that we owe the fans a lot for their support and the fact that the money they pay at the turnstiles pays our wages. I've rarely declined an autograph or photo request from a fan and on the rare occasions when I may have felt a little inconvenienced – usually when someone interrupts a quiet, family meal at a restaurant – my dad will swiftly remind me that, in 10 years time, I'll be complaining if I wasn't asked for my autograph.

If players are honest with themselves, they will admit that being recognised in public does give them a little buzz, so it's nothing to spend a few seconds signing a little kid's autograph book.

Being a well-known footballer may be great for the player himself, but it is not always easy for other members of his family. At times I feared for my brother, Paul, and sister, Joanne, as it crossed my mind that they might attract 'friends' who wanted to know them for the wrong reasons – like the attraction of being attached to a 'glamourous footballing family'. It's a situation that will be familiar to footballers all over the world. But Paul's girlfriend, Jane, comes from Wolverhampton and had no interest in football when they first met, while Joanne has married Andrew, who is a great fella and married her because he loves her dearly and not because he happens to be a West Ham season ticket-holder who is looking for inside info on his club!

Family members can be affected in various ways. Lorraine's mum and dad, June and Bill, who have always been brilliant with me, often get people knocking at their door asking them to get me to sign things or arrange tickets. When there was talk of me coming back to West Ham, Paul's mates in his Sunday football team kept on asking when, and if, it would happen. It must be annoying at times to be constantly asked questions about your brother, but it's just the knock-on effect of being related to someone who is relatively well-known.

Claret & Blues

NOW FOR THE BAD NEWS...

WHAT all major signings quickly realise, if they didn't already know, is that almost everything they do will become public property thanks to the media circus. It's a sad reflection on the society we live in that the tabloid press will happily devote more column inches to scandalous stories about what players get up to in their private lives than what they do on the field.

As Ian Botham pointed out in an interesting TV interview a few months ago, it seems to be a peculiar trait of the British press that they enjoy nothing more than creating new sporting heroes, only to knock them down again.

The press are a powerful force in modern football, but it can't be good for the game that they have effectively hired and fired the last three England managers. The tabloid newspaper campaign waged against both Bobby Robson and Graham Taylor was despicable, regardless of what you might think about their abilities as football managers. Terry Venables actively courts the press and does it very successfully. He was undoubtedly the media's choice to replace Taylor but I'd advise him not to turn his back for too long, particularly if England fail in Euro '96. If that happens, and I sincerely hope it doesn't, then make no mistake, the 'friends' Terry thought he had could very quickly turn their backs on him.

With England hosting its first major international tournament since the 1966 World Cup, I think there will be unprecedented hype surrounding the event here next summer. I just hope the English press don't pile unnecessary pressure on Venables and his players, putting them in a no-win situation where they are expected to win because we're playing at home. Wouldn't it be nice for the press to get right behind the England team and encourage and praise good play . . . or am I just being naive?

England tours can be interesting. The players are under the spotlight throughout the trip, not just for the 90 minutes of action on the field, and you can bet your life that any misdemeanor will make the front or back pages the next morning. Yet the behaviour of certain hypocritical journalists has been known to be much worse than the people they are there to report on.

Footballers are only human but it saddens me that any mistakes they make in their private lives automatically become the subject of intense media scrutiny. The trouble is, tabloid papers are no longer content to send a sports journalist to cover the major events, he is invariably accompanied on the plane to an England game by a news-hound, assigned specifically to dig the dirt on the England team. We don't want these characters inside football grounds or furtively hanging around hotel receptions.

It's a shame, but nevertheless a fact, that bad news and scandal usually sells more papers. If I picked up the phone and told a journalist on a national daily or Sunday paper that me and a group of West Ham players were going down to a pub or club to get pissed, the chances are a reporter and a photographer would turn up to get the pictures and quotes from eye-witnesses. But if I rang them up and said I was visiting sick young children in hospital for charity, they wouldn't want to know. And that's a sad state of affairs. Footballers do a lot of good things for charity and other good causes – last year I visited Newham schools to help campaign against racism – but apart from a bit of local coverage, the nationals won't touch it. It's good news, but it doesn't sell papers.

Since I came into professional football 12 years ago, the press and the media have become an increasingly powerful force in football. Top footballers are no longer mere sportsmen, but celebrities in the sense that pop stars and actors and actresses are. They are front page news, prime targets for the newsdesk never mind the sportsdesk, but the standard of sports writing has undoubtedly deteriorated, too.

You know full well that if you score a hat-trick, you will be portrayed as the hero and if you miss a sitter you're the villain. But I read some reports and wonder if the people who wrote them were even at the game in question. They praise players who have had a bad game, don't understand why certain things have happened and are tactically naive . . . and yet their sports editors still ask them to give the players marks out of 10! Sometimes I'll look at the Sunday papers and expect to see me given a mark of, say, eight, and only get 4. Or, alternatively, after a rubbish performance, when I've deserved four or five, they'll given me seven or eight.

I once heard a story that a reporter phoned through his report and marks out of 10 for each player, having been sat at home that afternoon. He hadn't even gone to the game! He was quite rightly sacked when he was found out, but I just wonder how many other times it happens!

The frustrating thing is that reporters, whose football playing experience is limited to their Sunday pub side, are informing millions of readers what a bad player so and so is.

I have been appaled by the treatment some people in the game have received at the hands of the press. How must Tony Adams, and his family, have felt when they picked up the paper and saw a picture of him with donkey's ears superimposed on his head? Imagine they'd done that to your son or another member of your family. I've already given credit to Tony for proving the press wrong, but instead of ridiculing him in the way I've mentioned, why didn't they criticise constructively, by saying what a player should or shouldn't have done?

It's very easy to generalise, though, and I'd like to say that the 'quality' papers do attempt to provide their readers with a considered account of the match by reporters who are quite knowledgeable. I'd like to see a few more ex-pro's writing about the game

– Johnny Giles and Alan Hansen contribute excellent columns for the *Daily Express* and *Today* newspapers respectively, which are the two I have delivered, while I also read the *Mail On Sunday* and *Sunday Express*., who give good accounts of the Saturday matches.

Giles and Hansen have an insight into the game and I respect their opinions. Unfortunately, I can't say I feel the same about the controversial column John Sadler writes for The Sun. He very rarely has a good word to say about any player, quite often slaughtering them, but he's never even played the game at a respectable level.

I've had my moments with the press when I've been slated, but I think I've always maintained a good relationship with them, At times, perhaps I've made myself too available for my own good but I've never shied away from reporters and will usually give an honest opinion, even though my views have landed me in trouble with my managers.

But I can count the journalists I trust on one hand. Rob Shepherd of *Today*, is one, John Keith, based at the *Daily Express'* northern office, and Tony McDonald, of *Hammers News Magazine*, are two others who have been good, trustworthy friends. Trevor Smith, of the local *Newham Recorder*, is another I have found very reliable. I actually confided some personal information to Rob about my transfer in 1988, but it never went any further than his ears and I respected him for that. Otherwise, I take the well-worn phrase "off the record" with a pinch of salt.

I recall a few disappointing personal encounters with the press. Harry Harris of the *Daily Mirror* phoned me for my reaction to Alan Shearer's £3.6m move from Southampton to Blackburn Rovers. I said that as a record signing, the fee could prove a big weight on his shoulders if he wasn't careful and the move didn't work out, but as it turned out Alan has done fantastically well for Rovers. I didn't receive a penny for the exclusive interview and was amazed, the next day, to see a sensational spread with the headline 'SHEARER CAN GO TO HELL!' plastered across the two inside back pages. It was an ambiguous headline that caused me a bit of embarrassment, although luckily Alan never made anything of it at the time.

I realise that the journalists who write the copy don't write the headlines – a potential problem that had surfaced years earlier with Jack Steggles and *The Mirror*, when my comments about my training ground fracas with Billy Bonds and Ray Stewart were blown out of context in the form of a big splash headline that bore no real resemblance to the point I'd tried to make in the interview I gave Jack.

I was disappointed with *The Independent's* Patrick Barclay, one of the most respected football writers, following a problem that arose soon after I joined Everton. Ironically, Patrick had been one of the first journalists to interview me in depth after my scoring debut for West Ham against Spurs five years earlier. He was writing a paperback book called *'From Schoolboy To Superstar'* and I was very pleased with how his chapter on me came out.

But on this occasion, Patrick decided to contact my agent instead of me to arrange our interview. I can perhaps understand to a degree why Jon, who thought he was acting in my best interests, asked Patrick if there would be any fee for the piece, but Patrick said 'no, there wouldn't be any money involved' and didn't pursue the conversation. I knew nothing of this until I picked up his paper and read a piece criticising me for how I changed from an innocent, fresh-faced kid, who he'd interviewed all those years earlier, to an arrogant so and so who would no longer give interviews without payment and employed an agent. If only Patrick had rung Everton in the first place – presuming that he didn't have my telephone number at the time – I would have gladly given him the interview for nothing. Instead, I was portrayed in a bad light when I didn't even know he was seeking an interview in the first place.

But how often are people who are misquoted or misrepresented given the right of reply? The papers, caught up in an intense circulation war with their rivals, can print more or less what they like knowing full well that footballers can't afford to bring a libel action against them. What good is a four-line apology, buried somewhere on a page 17, after a damaging piece that may have made the front page?

Many of today's football reporters are not only unknowledgeable about the game, but lazy too. It's a bit concerning to note the growing trend of journalists 'lifting' quotes from the Clubcall telephone line that virtually every Premiership and Endsleigh League club now operates. The players at West Ham freely give interviews to Chris Raistrick which obviously appear on the line either later that day or the next day. But the players have realised that it's not unusual to see the comments we make to Chris crop up again in a separate daily newspaper piece, which has been re-hashed and, in some cases, distorted out of all context. I've also known the national press lift other interviews I've given to our club magazine, Hammers News, not even bothering to call me for an update!

If you are doing a special exclusive interview, then it's fair enough to ask the nationals for payment, but in the main I never do. I always make myself readily available for comment because it is a two-way thing. I realise that whilst the papers undoubtedly need players, there are a lot of times when players need the press, and will try and manipulate them to their advantage.

Over the past six or seven years football has seen the growth of fanzines, written by supporters, which present an alternative view. Some of the articles and drawings they print can be quite cruel and, although I'm against people who slag off players simply for the sake of it, there is nothing wrong with constructive criticism and there's definitely a place in the game for fanzines. The fans' views have regularly been ignored over the years and the fanzines provide a platform for them to air those views. I would probably have bought them myself if they'd been around in my days as a fan.

During my time at Everton, I met four writers from *'When Skies Are Grey'* and gave an interview for their fanzine. I've done the same for Phil Daniels of the West Ham fanzine *'Over Land And Sea'* , visiting his house to give an interview last season, and I recently contributed the foreword for a book written by another regular *'OLAS'* writer, Robert Banks, called *'An Irrational Hatred Of Luton'*. The fanzine editors and contributors speak from the heart, and whilst I might not always agree with their opinions, they are supporters through and through and I respect that. Their views do get through to the players and I think it's important to keep in touch with what our fans are thinking.

If I get to the bit where someone is calling me a w--ker, I'll just turn the page!

Having said my piece about the deteriorating standard of football journalism, it's a career I would seriously consider pursuing after I've finished playing, if the opportunity presents itself. It must be great to be sent, all expenses paid, to watch a football match every Saturday, as well as the major international tournaments, particularly if you enjoy it and understand it like I do.

Claret & Blues

SEASON OF SLEAZE

WHAT a year that was! I'm referring, of course, to 1994/95 and the troubled campaign that was dubbed the 'Season Of Sleaze' by the media, who certainly didn't have too look hard for their front and back page stories.
It seemed that all the good work achieved by many to rebuild football's credibility in the wake of Hillsborough had been undone in one bizarre season tainted by allegations of match-fixing, bungs, drug and alcohol abuse and crowd violence.

Here's my view of events as they happened . . .

MATCH-FIXING

When I first heard the allegations against Southampton goalkeeper Bruce Grobbelaar in November 1994, my reaction was one of total surprise. Football is such a close-knit community that players nearly always know of something that had occurred before it gets into the press. If a player has a drink or drugs problem, even if he plays for another club, we invariably get to hear about it on the football grapevine before it makes the papers.

That's what really surprised me about the allegations that players had been deliberately throwing Premiership games for a Far East betting syndicate. In 15 years involvement in professional football, I'd never heard of anyone taking bribes or anything like that.

There was a lot of whispers that Everton's dramatic 3-2 victory over Wimbledon in the last game of the previous season had been rigged, but, as I said earlier, there was not even the slightest hint at Goodison that afternoon that anything untoward had been planned by anyone. Sure, we scored what was a very poor goal from 'keeper Hans Segers' point of view, but none of the Everton players were aware of any possibility that the result had been fixed . . . it looked to us like a bad blunder by Segers which allowed Graham Stuart to score our last-gasp winner that ensured our survival. The former Wimbledon striker John Fashanu also faces charges, along with Grobbelaar and Segers, and I can't believe that they are guilty.

If it is proven that any player is found guilty of these allegations, then they should be punished as severely as possible . . . a life ban from the game and, if it involves fraud, then the police will obviously press charges. There is no room in football for cheats.

On the other hand, if the players are eventually cleared of all allegations, as I sincerely hope they are, then they should sue the pants off whoever has levelled the allegations against them.

BUNGS

In December 1994, Arsenal manager George Graham was at the centre of bung allegations surrounding transfer deals involving Scandinavian players Pal Lydersen and John Jensen, arranged through Norwegian agent Rune Hauge.

When it was alleged that Graham had received an 'unsolicited gift' from Hauge – or 'bung', to coin the popular phrase – Arsenal reacted by conducting an internal inquiry and then sacking their manager, despite all the success he had brought them.

If Graham is, indeed, guilty of the allegations against him, then the one-year ban he received from the FA was probably appropriate – it could have been even more severe.

Having said that, I believe that George has been made a scapegoat . . . if he's guilty, he can't be the first football manager to have received a bung and, most likely, won't be the last.

The ban has cost Graham considerably in lost earnings but when he is eligible to return from the start of the 1996/97 season, I'm sure that there will be a queue of clubs lining up for the services of one of the game's most successful managers.

What the George Graham affair underlines is the need for the manager to look after only team affairs and a managing director to handle all the financial arrangements, player transfers and contract negotiations, etc, as is the case with Peter Storrie at West Ham and Cliff Finch at Everton.

BETTING, BOOZE, BIRDS AND DRUGS

Arsenal dominated the headlines again just prior to Christmas when Paul Merson 'came out' and revealed that he had a gambling and alcohol addiction, and had also dabbled in cocaine and women. A lot of players fall into one, two or maybe three of those traps, but the shocking thing is that 'Merse' succumbed to all four.

It's easy to see how he landed himself in trouble. Paul obviously earned a lot of money from a young age and at a very high profile club it's easy to get into bad habits. We all like a drink, just like most other people, and some of the most talented players in the game's history have had a reputation for boozing, so Paul certainly wasn't unique in that respect. There is nothing wrong with drinking in moderation.

It's easy to see how a top player can end up gambling heavily too. Football and racing seem almost to go hand in hand, and there is always someone at the training ground with a "good tip" to whet your appetite. With the saturation coverage racing receives nowadays, it's easy to go into a betting shop at, say, 1pm and sit there all afternoon watching the racing on the TV screens and fritter your money away until 6pm. Footballers are particularly vulnerable to betting because they tend to have lots of spare money and spare time.

I don't think players bet large amounts with the sole aim of winning even more cash, because many of them have enough already. They back heavily simply for the sheer thrill of it.

I enjoy a bet and have a credit card account with William Hill, but I gamble only in moderation – no more than £100 per month – and that will cover horse racing, greyhounds and football. For example, before the 1995/96 season started, I had a £10 accumulator bet on Newcastle United, Wolves, Carlisle United and Preston to win the four English divisions, which will net me about six grand if it comes in. It's a fun bet and my dad and my grandads have always enjoyed a little flutter, too. In fact, my dad used to own a dog, called Irish Joe, that ran at Romford for two years.

I've talked in this book about the card schools that exist at all football clubs, and we even stake a small wager on practice matches in training, where each member of the losing team has to pay £5 per head to their opponents.

It is hardly surprising that women or young girls – 'groupies,'as the lads call them – want to hang around famous footballers and are willing to do anything to be near them, and you have to be careful. Some of them can't wait to have a 'conquest' with a player and then run off to the papers with their 'kiss and tell' exclusive.

The most emotive subject surrounding Paul Merson was the drugs aspect. Drugs were not readily available when I was in my last years at school but in the last 10 years they have become a regular part of many young people's social lives – they take them like people in my youth would smoke cigarettes. So if more and more youngsters today are experimenting with drugs, is it really any surprise that young footballers do, too? Most players are working class lads who enjoy going down the pub like everyone else in their age group, so the same temptations will come their way. Footballers are more vulnerable to drug peddlars than most because, again, they earn relatively big wages.

A number of players have been found guilty by the FA for the use of illegal substances, but I have heard that there are two very well-known Premiership footballers (nothing to do with West Ham or Everton), who have not been caught, who are heavily involved in 'social drugs' and playing football. I would never name them but I know that it's an aspect of the game that the FA should clamp down on.

There is a difference however, between the use of social drugs, which only harms the player who uses them, and performance-enhancing drugs, which are far more worrying as far as football is concerned. The authorities should be wary of the possibility that players might take stronger drugs to make them fitter and faster for a limited amount of time, such as 90 minutes! I've got no time for cheats, like the Canadian athlete Ben Johnson, who took drugs to beat the opposition and, again, if any footballer is found guilty of doing so he should face a long ban, possibly for life.

What concerns me is that I believe it would be relatively easy for players to get away with it if they wanted to. In 12 years of playing football, I've been randomly tested for drugs only twice – at Leeds United and Manchester City, both after playing for Everton. It basically involves urinating into a bottle, which is an absolute nightmare because it usually entails having to drink gallons of water before you're able to produce the required sample for testing.

As I understand it, the Sports Council carry out their test at only one game every weekend, so the chances of a guilty player being caught are minimal.

After the Merson story broke last winter, the FA made a big fuss about how they proposed to clampdown on drug offenders and would be visiting clubs' training grounds to carry out tests. Well, I've never seen anyone at West Ham's training ground to carry out a drugs test on anyone – and I've been there since September 1994!

One of the former Everton youngsters, Billy Kenny, had a drugs problem which we all knew about, but it only came to the FA's attention because it was reported to them by club. There weren't only rumours about Billy circulating at Bellefield, but also one of the first team players, which were never proven. The rumours about him persisted even though he was tested and cleared following a drugs test after a Premiership game.

I would hate to be tested, because I'd view it as an insult to my intelligence, but if the threat of the FA's drug-busting team paying a surprise visit acted as a deterrent to every player at the club, particularly the YTS lads and young pros, then I'll willingly take it.

I don't know why youngsters take drugs anyway . . . why don't they simply go down the pub and drink 10 pints of lager to 'get happy?'

ERIC CANTONA

Like everyone who saw the incident at Selhurst Park in January 1995, I couldn't believe what Eric Cantona did to Crystal Palace 'fan' Matthew Simmons. I first knew of the trouble when I turned on Teletext later that evening and read the headline 'CANTONA ATTACKS FAN', but I went to bed that night thinking it was probably an over-exaggeration and that all the Manchester United star had done was grab a fan by the scruff of the neck after he'd run onto the pitch – as Cloughie did once at Forest.

I couldn't believe it when I picked up the morning papers and then saw the incident for myself on breakfast TV. The sight of Eric aiming a kung fu kick at the fan's chest was an unprecedented sight in British football.

Of course, he should never have retaliated in the way he did, but the extent of verbal and racial abuse and spitting some players have to suffer at football grounds all over the country, has reached unacceptable levels.

Cantona certainly paid a hefty price for his moment of madness – and so did United, especially where the Premiership title was concerned. They really missed him.

Cantona was initially charged in court with assault and given a two-week prison sentence, but it was quashed on appeal and instead he was ordered to do 120 hours of community service, coaching schoolkids. Common sense prevailed, although you couldn't help thinking what crowd problems would have ensued had the incident occurred at a more intimidating ground.

As a player, I think Cantona is great for English football and we need world class players like him here to entertain the public with his brilliant silky skills and creativity. He came back for the Liverpool game on October 1, 1995, as though he'd never been away. I just hope that he doesn't step out of line again, for we can't afford to lose players of his talent.

DUBLIN RIOT

Between 1990, when the European club ban was finally lifted, and 1995 the reputation of English football improved considerably.

So it was a bolt from the blue when, in February '95, we turned on our TV sets to see English 'fans' behaving disgracefully at the friendly international in Dublin, causing the game to be abandoned after 27 minutes with Ireland leading 1-0.

It was quite clear that these were not real football supporters, there to support Terry Venables' team. They were politically-motivated right and left-wing extremists who had travelled to Southern Ireland simply looking for a fight and to further their cause.

The trouble is that because there is no war or national service where young men can channel their energies in a disciplined way, there are too many young people around with pent up aggression, just waiting to explode. They have little or no interest in football, but the massive publicity major football matches attract provides them with an ideal platform for their activities. You see the nutters on telly, giving Hitler salutes. What has that got to do with football? The actual match is simply their excuse. The fact that the Irish have never known football hooliganism like it, only added to the outrage felt by so many back home.

There were questions asked of the local Garda and the Irish authorities, especially as it was later claimed that there had been advance warning of trouble at the match. Okay, so they may have been somewhat naive, but who could blame them? I have visited Ireland many times and can honestly say that the people, both north and south of the border, are among the friendliest you could ever wish to meet. They can't do enough for you. They were ready to welcome the English team and its supporters with open arms, especially in the wake of the peace protest in operation there at the time.

The genuine majority of English fans in Dublin that night must have been absolutely horrified and disgusted with what went on. No one in their right mind would defend the kind of moron who throws an iron bar down on to other people in the crowd. The picture of that little Irish boy, standing frightened and bewildered as the violence erupted around him, was used throughout most English tabloids the next day and I really felt for him and the many others who must have shared his sadness.

A lot of things went wrong at Lansdowne Road that night and lessons have got to be learned, particularly with the European Championships in England approaching rapidly. For instance, it defies belief that English supporters were issued tickets for the top tier of the stand, from where they launched their dangerous missiles on to the innocent men, women and children below.

As I've said, we should ban the people responsible. If that means banning English fans from travelling to future matches abroad, so be it. It will never be possible to stop every determined Englishman from entering a country, but with good police work at airports, ports, stations and along main road links, the vast majority of trouble makers would be apprehended and sent back home.

The people who brought shame on our game in Dublin are the products of a sad society in which too few offenders are sent to jail and there is little deterrent. The punishment rarely fits the crime and it makes me sick because these people are trying to destroy our game. In the last decade English football has made much progress in the fight against hooliganism, which has seen the return of an increasing number of youngsters and families to grounds up and down the country.

We can't allow the idiots to undo all that good work, but it's a problem we must quickly get to grips with.

Racism is another problem that has blighted the English game for far too long, and I know the football and government authorities have joined forces to try and eradicate it from our grounds. I got involved personally last season by visiting schools in the borough of Newham to stress to the kids that football is an international multi-cultural sport, and it doesn't matter whether they are black, brown, white, yellow or whatever, they are all welcome to enjoy football either as players or supporters.

Some of England's best players today are black, including big names like Les Ferdinand, Andy Cole, Stan Collymore, Paul Ince and Ian Wright.

I think a lot of clubs should have done more in previous years to wage war on the problem of hooliganism and racism, and both of the two clubs I've been at have had their problems in respect of the race issue. I've seen bananas thrown onto the pitch at Upton Park when Cyrille Regis has played there, John Barnes has also come in for a lot of racist abuse, while Everton signed their first black player for 21 years (since Cliff Marshall) when Daniel Amokachi went there last year.

We'll know we've turned the corner in the fight against racism when a player of Asian origin, an Indian, Pakistani or Chinese, breaks through into the Premiership ...

CHAPTER 60

Claret & Blues

MY TOP 10

AFTER studying the way other strikers play for all of my career in order to improve my own game, I am experienced enough to pick the top ten strikers I have played against. This isn't necessarily my top 10 goalscorers' list – although obviously goalscoring is a major part of any striker's game – but the forwards I've admired most over the years.

In no particular order, here is my top 10:

CLIVE ALLEN:
The highlight of Clive's career was no doubt the 1986/87 season when he smashed 49 goals for Tottenham Hotspur. It's amazing to think that one player could score that many goals in one season, even nowadays with the likes of Shearer, Cole and Ferdinand around. I've played in testimonials and England squads with Clive and his finishing is second to none. He is one player who gets in purely because of his goalscoring – it can't be ignored – and I find it very hard to believe that Clive had trouble finding a club earlier this season after being given a free by Millwall. Before he finally joined Second Division Carlisle United for a month, Clive spent a few weeks training back at West Ham and I saw, at first hand, that he still has that instinctive knack of finding the net. If I was manager of a lower division club, I'd be champing at the bit to sign him.

IAN RUSH:
One of the best modern day strikers around, Ian has been Liverpool's top marksman for the majority of his 13 seasons on Merseyside. He played in a great Liverpool side, with players like Dalglish, Beardsley and Barnes providing great service, but it still takes something special to put the ball in the net as many times and as consistently as he has. Rushie also holds the ball up well and sets up goals for other players – more recently young Robbie Fowler.

Rushie was scoring goals when I first started playing and is still scoring goals 12 years later!

IAN WRIGHT:

Came into the game late, signing for Crystal Palace at the age of 25. He forged a prolific partnership with Mark Bright before his big money move to Arsenal in 1991. A very gifted finisher in the sense that he can score with his right foot, left foot or head. This is the reason that he has scored so many goals for both Palace and Arsenal. Even though he is 32 years-old, he still runs around like a 19 year-old and looks very sharp. Very temperamental, but I think if you take that away from Wrighty, you take away the player.

ALAN SHEARER:

Made it into my Premier League dream team simply because he is one of the greatest strikers in the world at the moment. Has really shone since he joined Blackburn for £3.6 million in the summer of 1992. Many critics said that the fee was too much for a player of Shearer's inexperience, but he proved them all wrong by scoring plenty of goals and showing that he has more to his game as well. Holds the record for being the youngest ever player to score a hat-trick in the top division, when he scored three on his debut against Arsenal for Southampton in 1987 at the age of 17.

Was the best 'signing' of last summer when Dalglish and Harford persuaded him to sign a new contract to stay with Rovers.

LES FERDINAND:

Another who was in my Premier League Dream team, Les, like Ian Wright, came into the game late, and I think that may be a blessing in disguise for some players. They have the appetite and want to make up for all the years they have lost. Les has done just that and was a revelation for QPR before getting his dream £6m move to Newcastle last summer. I would call Les a target man although he does have more than that. He has pace, a good shot and amazing spring in his jump. Les will definitely do the business for Newcastle and it must be great to play with him.

GARY LINEKER:

Has to make the top 10 even though he is retired. Was the star of the mid and late 80s and probably reached his peak in the 1990 World Cup even though he had been outstanding in the same competition four years earlier. Without a doubt, the best English finisher since Bobby Charlton – certainly on the international front. 48 goals for your country is phenomenal and I think he learned a lot from his time with Barcelona. Not the most skillful of players but when it comes to scoring goals Gary was number one.

PETER BEARDSLEY:

I played with Peter at Everton and he is one of the most enthusiastic players I have ever met. He is an amazing trainer and runs around like a schoolboy. Obviously not a prolific goalscorer, most of Peter's goals are spectacular ones, normally finished from around the edge of the penalty area. Unlike most of the strikers I have mentioned, Peter doesn't rely on service to score his goals, he usually creates them himself and also creates chances for other strikers. Peter looks after himself – he doesn't smoke or drink – which is probably the reason he is still playing so well at the top level.

MARK HUGHES:

Another player who has been around the same number of years as me. Has consistently played well for Manchester United in his two spells at the club. A great target man, 'Sparky' is so strong and – this has been said before – is not a great goalscorer, but a scorer of great goals. He does score some spectacular ones and generally his all-round game is superb. Chelsea are extremely lucky to get a player of his talent for only £1.5 million.

KENNY DALGLISH:

Kenny stopped West Ham winning the league in 1985/86 when he led Liverpool to the double as manager and also star player – something I'll never forgive him for! However, there was no doubting his talent. Not unlike Beardsley in the way that he not only scored goals himself but also set them up for his fellow strikers. He must have been responsible for at least half of Ian Rush's goals when they played together and was always a joy to watch. A world class striker.

MATT LE TISSIER:

Although not an orthodox striker – his best position is the floating role where he has the freedom of the pitch – Matt does score a lot of goals, most of which are spectacular. He always chips in with a few contenders for Goal of the Season – and actually won it in 1994/95 with an absolutely amazing effort at Blackburn Rovers. His return from free-kicks and penalties is also astounding – I think he has missed something like one penalty out of 40 in his career. It is also interesting to note that Le Tissier is a very creditable third in the Premiership top scorers over the past five seasons (behind Shearer and Wright) – a fact he can be very proud of considering some of the world class names on that list.

It's a travesty that he has been ignored for so long by England – you should always find a place in your squad for someone as classy as Le Tissier.

Claret & Blues

PREMIERSHIP TEAM TO BEAT

PEOPLE are now placing our top division on a par with Serie A in Italy, so I have formulated my own Premier League team. It is a fairly cosmopolitan line-up with a variation of English players and foreign imports. I'll challenge anyone to come up with a better all round side to beat this one!

PETER SCHMEICHEL (Manchester United/Denmark):
By far and away the best goalkeeper in the league. When he first came over to England he was a good goalkeeper, but in the last few seasons he has improved tremendously. A very commanding 'keeper, he comes out for crosses and most of the time he wins the ball, although sometimes he takes the player with him! He is such a big lad and seems to fill the goal, which makes him very hard to beat. His distribution – either throwing or kicking – is second to none. An easy choice for the number one spot.

GARY KELLY (Leeds United/Republic of Ireland):
Gary is a very young player who has only come into the game in the last couple of years, but his performances for both Leeds and Ireland have shown maturity beyond his years, particularly in the 1994 World Cup when he earned himself a permanent place in the right back position for Ireland with some outstanding displays.

Although not a very tall player, what Gary lacks in inches he certainly makes up for in pace. Pace is of vital importance in today's game – every team needs at least a couple of players who can turn a game with a burst of acceleration and Kelly does just that. He can defend, tackle and looks comfortable on the ball. It's a shame he's not English! Seriously, though, Leeds will definitely benefit from his talent in the years to come.

GRAEME LE SAUX (Blackburn Rovers/England):
Some people may not agree with me on this choice, it seems as though fans either

love Graeme or hate him. Personally, I think he is a very good player. Like Gary Kelly, he is very quick and has been outstanding for his club in the last couple of seasons. He has a tremendous left foot and his distribution into the forwards is good. However, his strongest point would have to be his ability to overlap the midfielders and whip in dangerous crosses – that Alan Shearer is normally on the end of! Le Saux can also play in midfield and is very adaptable.

PAUL McGRATH (Aston Villa/Republic of Ireland):

I accept that Paul is probably coming to the end of his career but I've chosen him on his performances over the last 10 years – the era that I have played in. He was always my hardest opponent and is still making it hard for strikers in the Premiership today. His reading of the game is superb, he is a good tackler and can push forward and score important goals.

For Paul to have played this long with all the problems he has encountered – for example his 'dodgy' knees – then it underlines what a great player he is. He was a tremendous signing for Aston Villa and rightly earns a place at centre-half in my team.

TONY ADAMS (Arsenal/England):

An outstanding defender who has had his fair share of problems over the years, on and off the field, yet always manages to rise above them and silence his critics. Tony was a born leader and I don't think it will be too long before he is the regular skipper of England. He leads the Arsenal defence superbly, reads the game well and, more importantly, doesn't over-elaborate. He wins the ball, controls it and passes it simply, which is just what you want from your centre-half. Again, Tony scores some vital goals for Arsenal and is probably their most important player. Definitely my captain.

RUUD GULLIT (Chelsea/Holland):

I know that Gullit has been playing as a sweeper for Chelsea, but I still think he could play a holding role in midfield to great effect. He's not the greatest tackler, but the rest of his all-round game is marvellous and I have admired his talents for a long while, particularly in the 1988 European Championships when Gullit and Holland were a different class. He would make my team tick and add a touch of flair to the midfield.

GARY McALLISTER (Leeds United/Scotland)

To sum up how much I rate Gary McAllister, I once suggested to my old Everton manager Howard Kendall that we should buy the Scottish captain from Leeds, as we were in need of a creative midfielder. Sadly, he didn't take my advice and Gary has since gone on to become one of the most respected midfielders in the game.

He has everything a midfielder needs. He can tackle, pass well, bring other players into the game and although he isn't very fast, he beats opponents with close ball control, change of pace and sheer power. Above all, he has one of the fiercest shots in the game, with the ability to hit the target from all angles and distances. Gary would be the first name on my teamsheet.

ANDREI KANCHELSKIS (Everton/Russia):

One of the quickest players ever to be seen in the Premiership. Andrei has two great feet, crosses a ball superbly and can finish well too. He'll guarantee you over 10 goals a season, which is a great record for a winger.

He's had four great years at Manchester United and, once he is over his injury problems, should settle in well at my old club Everton. He sets up numerous chances for forwards and it's just a shame that the Toffees didn't buy him four years ago!

RYAN GIGGS (Manchester United/Wales):

Has had a lot of problems over the last year or so, what with injuries, loss of form and intense media pressure, but on his day, Giggsy is as good as any winger in Britain. Again, another pacy player who can beat defenders so easily. Ryan's crossing can sometimes let him down, but then I have seen him swing in some near perfect ones.

It's so exciting when he gets the ball and goes on one of those mazy runs, beating three or four players and then either crossing or shooting. I only hope he can get over his injury worries and return to the Ryan Giggs of two years ago.

LES FERDINAND (Newcastle United/England):

Has been exceptional for QPR in the last few years and fully deserved his transfer to Newcastle United last summer. With no disrespect to QPR, Les needed to be in a team that was capable of challenging for honours, and I am confident that Newcastle will do just that. Les will score lots of goals – who wouldn't with Beardsley and Ginola supporting them? Good on the floor, Les also has a tremendous ability to rise above defenders and head for goal. Should definitely be in the England set-up.

ALAN SHEARER (Blackburn Rovers/England):

There are a lot of excellent foreign forwards I could choose, but I've got to go with our own Alan Shearer. Probably the best striker in Europe at the moment, Alan's all-round game is unbelievable. Despite suffering what many people would term a career-threatening knee injury, Alan has still averaged over 30 goals a season and there seems to be no stopping him. He's strong, fast, mobile and takes great penalties! There's no one in England at the moment with his talent.

This team would definitely be one to fear. With Kelly and Kanchelskis on one wing and Le Saux and Giggs on the other, the pace would be frightening and not many teams would be able to deal with it. A solid back four that can all attack, behind a midfield full of skill as well as determination, would guarantee some exciting matches . . . and with two of the best goalscorers in the business up front, this team would entertain to the fullest. Add me as manager, and they'd be unstoppable!

Claret & Blues

DREAM TEAM

THE two clubs that I have had the honour to play for have both included an array of talented players in their line-ups at some stage during my career. This is the all-star team I would pick if asked to choose the best players I had played with during my 12 seasons at West Ham and Everton:

NEVILLE SOUTHALL (Everton):
Nev would have to be the best all-round goalkeeper that I have ever played with, particularly when I first joined Everton. He is a great shot-stopper, is agile and mobile and is still denying the best Premiership strikers at the grand old age of 37! Neville did face tough competition from Phil Parkes to get in my team – Parkesy was an excellent shot-stopper, but perhaps didn't have such a good all-round game as Neville, although injuries did hamper Phil's performances. I have only played with Ludek Miklosko for around a year, so I can't really include him. However, when I finish playing in a few years time, Ludo will hopefully be my No.1.

RAY STEWART (West Ham):
Ray would definitely be my penalty taker! His record from the spot was second to none. His nickname was 'Tonka' because of his ability to hit the ball so hard and he scored some very important spot-kicks during his time with West Ham, including the one that took Hammers to the FA Cup semi-final and the one that earned them a replay in the 1981 League Cup Final. Ray was also one of the most underrated defenders of his time – he was a good tackler, very committed and good going forward – yet never quite received the praise that his efforts deserved. An easy choice for the right-back position.

JULIAN DICKS (West Ham):
This wasn't such an easy choice. I've played with several very good left-backs, including Frank Lampard, Pat Van Den Hauwe and Andy Hinchcliffe, but Julian just gets the nod.

He works very hard in training, has a wonderful left foot that has scored some tremendous goals, and is probably one of the hardest players to beat in a one-on-one situation. It's a real shame that his reputation over the last few years has cost him an England place because he certainly has the talent to succeed at international level.

BILLY BONDS (West Ham):

Definitely my captain. Bonzo takes one of the centre-back positions. He was as brave as a lion and a tremendous athlete, but Bill could also play a bit as well. He had good touch and always weighed in with a few goals – he actually finished top scorer for the Hammers one season with 13 goals. 'Mr. West Ham' was one of my boyhood heroes and it was great to then play with him. He was still as fit as a fiddle after he retired at the age of 41 and has to go down as one of the greatest player's never to have won an England cap.

ALVIN MARTIN (West Ham):

This was another hard decision to make. Players such as Tony Gale, Dave Watson, Steve Potts, Kevin Ratcliffe were all worthy nominees for the other centre-back place, but in the end I had to go with Alvin alongside Bonzo. It really amazes me that Alvin is still playing. You have to be something special to carry on in the Premiership at the age of 37 and 'Stretch' comes in that category. His partnership with Bonzo in the early 80s was as good as there was anywhere in that era. Alvin is another one who can win the ball and then play with composure and skill, something that is very rare in today's central defenders. He is a credit to himself and the game.

ALAN DEVONSHIRE (West Ham):

Purely and simply the best player I have ever played with. Dev's link up play with the forwards was amazing to watch. He came back from an horrific knee injury to play some of the best football of his career in 1985/86, when we finished third in the league, and it just summed up how respected he was when Trevor Brooking declared that Dev's absence was one of the key reasons why he decided to retire early. Peter Beagrie and Kevin Sheedy were the nearest contenders for this spot but Dev was up there on his own.

MARK WARD (West Ham/Everton):

I was lucky to play alongside Wardie for both West Ham and Everton. Another very underrated player, he was 5ft 5ins of dynamite! Wardie could tackle, shoot and ran up and down the right wing all day, even though he always said he wasn't a winger! His greatest strength though was his crossing – probably one of the best crossers of the ball I have ever seen. Pat Nevin, Paul Allen and Trevor Steven were also in with a chance. Wardie is now doing a great job in the centre of midfield for Birmingham City.

PETER BEARDSLEY (Everton):

The most creative player I have ever played with. A wonderful servant for football and all the clubs he has played for, Peter is still wowing the crowds for Newcastle and England at the age of 34. His dedication to the game is second to none and I can see him playing until he is 40. It was an honour to play with him and he would definitely take one of the forward positions in my team.

FRANK McAVENNIE (West Ham):

No real surprises here. Obviously Frank's best season was 1985/86 – his first season at the club – when the team finished third in the league and Frank and I shared probably the best partnership I have ever experienced – in terms of goals, understanding and enjoyment. To give Frank the nod over players like Paul Goddard, Graeme Sharp and Paul Rideout just shows what a good player he was and how much I thought of him. He always worked tremendously hard for the team and was a great character to have in the dressing room.

TREVOR BROOKING (West Ham):

One of the all-time greats ever to play for West Ham and England. I only played one season with Trev but it was enough to prove to me that he was as good as I thought he was. There aren't many words that describe Trevor's influence on the players he played with and I was just glad to have had the chance to play one season with him. One contender for this position was Alan Dickens. I would have liked to have included Dicko because we had such a good relationship on and off the field, but his career fizzled out way too early and Trevor had to assume the role of ball-player in the centre of midfield.

STUART McCALL (Everton):

My ball winner in the centre of midfield. Peter Reid, in his prime, or Geoff Pike, another underrated player, were other contenders but Stuart gets the nod – not only because he's a good friend of mine but because he was also a tremendous player. I often felt that Stuart's role at Everton wasn't as defined as it should have been. He never really knew whether he was expected to be a ball-winner or a ball-player and sometimes fell between two stools. But he has a tremendous engine who won the ball well and created chances, too.

SUBS (As I'd fully expect my team to be competing in Europe, I've taken the liberty of naming five subs…):

PHIL PARKES:

A great shot-stopper and a real character, too, who was impossible to beat in shooting practice.

DAVE WATSON:

Another player, so inspirational, who is still playing well into his 30s and marking people out of the game. I was so pleased for him when he collected the FA Cup this year.

PAUL INCE:

I only had a year or so with Incey but I had to have him as a sub, as he's improved so much since he went to United, and now Inter, that he's a quality international.

ALAN DICKENS:

I had eight great years with Dicko and it was such a shame his career didn't reach the heights it should have. He did an awful lot for me and Frank McAvennie in our golden season.

PAUL RIDEOUT:

I only had one season with Graeme Sharp, whereas I had probably 18 months partnered with Paul and it was my most productive partnership since Frank. We had a good understanding and Paul is a target man who not only heads the ball well, but has good touch and knows where the goal is, as he proved last season.

CHAPTER 63

Claret & Blues

MANAGING TO SUCCEED

AFTER more than 12 years as a player I am already looking forward to the next part of what I hope will be a continuation of my football career – in management.

My long-term ambition to manage is not something that has just crept up on me. Even as a schoolboy I always had it in mind to become a manager one day, and said as much to my careers officer when she doubted whether I would ever fulfil my dream to play professionally.

Not that I'm thinking about hanging up my boots yet. Although I've turned 30 years-old, I feel a youngish 30 and still look after myself reasonably well. I'd like to think that I can play on for West Ham at the top level for another three, maybe four, years yet. I have played the whole of my career so far in either the old First Division or the Premier League and hopefully I'll see out my playing days in the top flight with the Hammers.

I would like to at least continue playing up until the age of 35, when I can draw my pension, but I'm not the type who will sit back and take it easy when that day comes. I won't want to completely turn my back on the game that has really been my life for 30 years.

I mentioned earlier in the book that I would enjoy writing about football, having contributed weekly columns for the local *Liverpool Echo and Recorder* newspaper, as well as my 'Down Under Diary' from Australia for *Hammers News Magazine* earlier this year. I would like to write a weekly conversation piece for a paper, but it's difficult while I'm still playing, and of course I've thoroughly enjoyed writing this book.

Another possible option is to get involved in my dad's insurance company, Chase Cross Insurance Brokers. I currently own 14 per cent of the business, as the third major share-holder, so I've got an interest there and who knows what is around the corner . . .

But football management appeals to me even more. I realise it is a high risk profession, with managers losing their jobs each season, but I still fancy a crack at it and, given the luck of being in the right place at the right time, believe I could do a good job in the so-called 'hot seat'.

As a player who has experienced the highs and lows of football, scoring a hattrick on my debut and then being banished to the reserves, even the 'A' team, I feel I'm well qualified to give an opinion on what I believe it takes to succeed in football management. I would go into the job and put into practice all the best aspects I've learned from the five club managers I've played under and dismiss their faults and weaknesses.

The main key to success is man-management and the way in which a manager handles his players will ultimately determine his and their fate. Whilst the boss obviously needs to clampdown on indiscipline among his players, and give a rollocking where and when it is due, it is important that he and his assistant or coaches, also give praise where it is deserved.

It's all very well managers saying that on the money players earn, they should all be self-motivated, which is true to an extent, but even the stars lose form and confidence at times and need encouragement to help them regain it. I've seen quite a few youngsters show promise, only to have the stuffing knocked out of them at an early stage of their careers and never recover psychologically. A good example is Mark Schivai, who played outside-left in my West Ham youth team days. He had lots of ability but lost confidence after coach Mick McGiven got on his back and never fulfiled that potential, finishing up playing at non-league level.

There is no sadder example of wasted talent than my old mate, Alan Dickens. His move to Chelsea turned into a nightmare, he fell out with the management and coaching staff and within four years of his big move to Stamford Bridge, 'Dicko' had also drifted into the lower divisions and then out of the pro game altogether. He is now learning the knowledge to become a London taxi driver and plays football in the Brentwood Sunday League. Yet I can't help feeling that with his ability, Dicko would still be playing in the Premiership today if only he'd been handled properly.

All players react differently when they are struggling for form. I know I always respond better to someone putting an arm around my shoulder – not giving me a rollicking – and I'd say the same applies to Don Hutchison. But then again, Julian Dicks and Martin Allen are the type who will probably respond better after stern words or a 'gee up' from their manager. We're all different and it's up to managers and coaches to identify the needs of all their players.

A good manager will always leave his door open for players to enter his office for advice – not only in football terms, but personal, too. It's no good to anyone if a player is fretting about his unhappy wife or sick child, so a reassuring word here and there, or perhaps the offer of a day off when it's needed, can work wonders for that concerned player's spirits.

Having dealt with the press regularly since the age of 17, I don't believe I would have any difficulty handling that aspect of the job. The media have a job to do and I would never shy away from them. It's a two-way relationship that can be as important to the manager as it is to the journalist. But you wouldn't see me slating any of my players in the papers, because that sort of thing should remain inside the dressing room after the game has finished. I see nothing wrong with a manager publicly criticising his team if he feels they deserve it, but it's not good to single out individuals for blame. As a player, there is nothing worse than picking up the paper and reading a piece in which you're own manager is slagging you off.

Players should be told they've played badly to their faces, and that's also the way I'd tell them they're dropped. Players may not agree with the manager's decision, but they will respect him for being told personally, rather than hearing it third hand from another source.

Injury problems often cause a manager to delay naming his side and when there are doubts surrounding the fitness of one or two players, there is obviously no point in one day telling a player he is in the side only to inform him the next day that he is not playing after all because so and so has made a rapid recovery overnight. But, wherever possible, I would want to name my team the day before the game. I would always try to send my players to bed on a Friday night settled in the knowledge that they are on the team sheet. I know from past experience how the uncertainty surrounding your place in the side the next day can lead (often unnecessarily) to anxiety and a restless night.

Perhaps some managers don't like to reveal their teams too soon for fear of alerting the opposition – Kenny Dalglish, when he was in charge at Blackburn, liked to leave it very late before announcing his team and I believe Newcastle boss Kevin Keegan does, too. But why worry about the opposition – let them worry about you, and by confidently announcing your team early it could be said that you are striking the first psychological blow.

Players like to keep to their preferred routine as much as possible, so preparation for a game is all important. At West Ham last season, the team travelled on the day of the game to Manchester City by coach and, after I rejoined, we did the same for a midweek visit to Everton. After four hours or more on the road, there was hardly time to eat our meal and relax at the hotel before we had to get back on the bus for the ride to Goodison and the match.

On another occasion, back in the mid 80s, our coach broke down soon after setting off from London for a game at Leicester, so we had to sit at the side of the motorway for half-an-hour waiting for a replacement coach to come and collect us before we could continue our frantic journey to the Midlands.

Thankfully, Harry Redknapp soon adopted the policy of travelling overnight to all away games that involve more than an hour-and-a-half's journey, which is only sensible. I don't agree, though, with what they used to do at Everton, where we'd stay overnight at an hotel even for local away games against Liverpool and the Manchester clubs!

One thing about managers that has always amazed me is that almost all of them watch matches from the dug-out . . . which nearly always provides the worst view in the ground! At Everton, until they changed it last year, the dug out used to be situated below pitch level. So if a player was dribbling with the ball on the opposite wing, he was only visible from the knees upwards. I know, because Colin Harvey and Howard Kendall regularly asked me to keep them company on the bench!

I thought George Graham had the right idea, when he used to sit up in the directors' box at Highbury, gaining a much clearer overall picture of the game. At pitch level it's so much more difficult to appreciate space and where people should and shouldn't be running, but from 'upstairs', George would often be captured on TV phoning instructions down to his assistant, Stewart Houston, on the bench.

I don't know why managers rant and rave on the touchline anyway. Half the time the players can't even hear what they're saying and the other half they don't want to hear!

It's interesting that football clubs do a lot of things out of tradition. Is there any reason, for instance, why we train every day in the week from 10.30am until mid-day, bearing in mind that all our games kick off at either 3pm or between 7.30pm and 8pm? It's just a thought.

Having expressed some of my own thoughts on the best way to manage a foot-ball team, I know full well that it's never as easy as it sounds. As a player, I only have to worry about myself initially, whilst obviously contributing to the team's cause. But a manager has to consider around 25 pro's and all the many other aspects that come under his control, including the running of the vitally important youth and reserve teams, the coaching and scouting network, training and the business that is carried out in the office, in conjunction with the managing director.

The only slight reservation I would have about becoming a manager is the enor-mous amount of time I would have to devote to the job, and the effect that could have on my family. Anyone who goes into the job must be 100 per cent committed to it – and if I did, I would only go into it on that basis.

If the chance came along and I did decide that management was right for me, I would perhaps be attracted first by a player/manager role at a club in the lower divi-sions, where I could learn the trade. I don't know how I would handle working with lesser quality players, having spent my whole career in the top flight, and playing as well as managing at the same time must be a big strain, although Glenn Hoddle, Bryan Robson and Ray Wilkins have proved it can be done successfully.

I've got to be honest, though, one day it would be a dream come true if I became the manager of West Ham and completed my eventful journey from the terraces to the dressing room and on to the manager's office. If not at Upton Park, then I'd love to be given a similar opportunity at Everton, a club who will always remain very close to my heart. Only time will tell but, so far, it's been a wonderful life playing for both the claret and blues . . .

TC goals trail

JUNIOR FOOTBALL

Year	For	Goals	Total
1973/74	Romford Royal	17	17
1974/75	Romford Royal	82	82
1975/76	Romford Royal	99	99
1976/77	Chase Cross United	53	
	Warren School	40	
	Barking district	3	96
1977/78	Chase Cross United	39	
	Warren School	23	
	Barking District	1	
	West Ham United U-14s	3	
	Arsenal U-14s	3	69
1978/79	Chase Cross United	66	
	Warren School	64	130
1979/90	Personal records (including Essex County) mislaid!		
		Total	493

YOUTH & RESERVES

No.	Date	Opponents	Comp	Venue	Goals

WEST HAM UNITED

1980/81

No.	Date	Opponents	Comp	Venue	Goals
1.	23/8/80	Crystal Palace	SEC 2	H	1 (V)
2.	6/9/80	Gillingham	SEC 1	A	1
3.	13/9/80	Ipswich Town	SEC 1	A	1
4,5.	4/10/80	Gillingham	SEC 1C	A	2
6.	8/11/80	Cambridge United	SEC 2	A	1
7,8,9.	22/11/80	Peterborough United	SEC 2	A	3
10,11.	29/11/80	Reading	SEC 2	H	2
12,13.	7/2/81	Brentford	SEC 2	A	2
14,15,16,17.	25/2/81	Bristol Rovers	SEC 2	H	4
18.	28/2/81	Cambridge United	SEC 2	H	1
19,20.	7/3/81	Luton Town	SEC 2	A	2
21.	21/3/81	Norwich City	SEC 1	H	1
22,23.	18/4/81	Peterborough United	SEC 2	H	2
24.	20/4/81	Portsmouth	SEC 1	A	1

1981/82

No.	Date	Opponents	Comp	Venue	Goals
25.	12/9/81	Leyton Orient	SEC 1	H	1
26.	19/9/81	Hereford	RES	H	1 (V)
27.	26/9/81	Tottenham Hotspur	SEC 1C	H	1
28.	5/10/81	Luton Town	SJFC 1	H	1
29,30.	10/10/81	Crystal Palace	SEC 1	A	2
31.	17/10/81	Queens Park Rangers	SEC 1	H	1
32,33,34.	24/10/81	Fulham	SEC 1	H	3
35.	31/10/81	Southend	SEC 1	A	1
36,37.	14/11/81	Fulham	SEC 1C	A	2
38,39,40.	17/11/81	Derby County	SJFC 2	H	3
41.	21/11/81	Tottenham Hotspur	SEC 1	A	1
42.	2/1/82	Norwich City	SEC 1	A	1
43,44.	20/1/82	Shrewsbury Town	SJFC 3	H	2
45.	23/1/82	Chelsea	SEC 1	A	1
46.	30/1/82	Portsmouth	SEC 1	H	1
47,48.	6/2/82	Crystal Palace	SEC 1	H	2
49.	9/2/82	Arsenal	SEC 1	A	1
50.	13/2/82	Queens Park Rangers	SEC 1	A	1
51,52.	20/2/82	Fulham	SEC 1	A	2
53.	27/2/82	Southend	SEC 1	H	1
54.	4/3/82	Tottenham Hotspur	SEC 1	H	1
55.	20/3/82	Ipswich Town	SEC 1	A	1
56,57,58.	27/3/82	Watford	SEC 1	H	3
59,60.	14/4/82	Charlton Athletic	SEC 1	H	2
61,62,63.	17/4/82	Arsenal	SEC 1	H	3
64.	22/4/82	Millwall	SEC 1CF	A	1
65	24/4/82	Leicester City	RES	A	1

No.	Date	Opponents	Comp	Venue	Goals
66.	28/4/82	Chelsea	SEC 2CF	A	1
67,68.	4/5/82	Millwall	SEC 1CF	H	2
69.	8/5/82	Luton Town	RES	A	1
70,71.	11/5/82	Chelsea	SEC 2CF	H	2

1982/83

No.	Date	Opponents	Comp	Venue	Goals
72,73,74.	28/8/82	Queens Park Rangers	SEC 1	H	3
75,76.	14/9/82	Birmingham City	RES	A	2
77,78.	18/9/82	Millwall	RES	H	2
79,80.	25/9/82	Fulham	SEC 1C	A	2
81.	27/9/82	Luton Town	RES	A	1
82,83.	11/10/82	Coventry City	SJFC 1	H	2
84.	16/10/82	Swansea City	RES	H	1
85,86.	19/10/82	Norwich City	RES	H	2
87.	30/10/82	Arsenal	SEC 1	A	1
88,89.	6/11/82	Fulham	RES	H	2
90.	13/11/82	Tottenham Hotspur	RES	A	1
91.	16/11/82	Luton Town	SJFC 2	H	1
92,93.	30/11/82	Folkestone Town	FAYC 2	A	2
94.	4/12/82	Chelsea	RES	H	1
95.	6/12/82	Luton Town	SJFC 2	A	1
96,97.	11/12/82	Charlton Athletic	SEC 1	H	2
98,99,100.	13/12/82	Crystal Palace	FAYC 3	H	3
101.	29/1/83	Tottenham Hotspur	SEC 1	A	1
102,103.	5/2/83	Birmingham City	RES	H	2
104,105.	15/3/83	Southampton	RES	H	2
106,107.	26/3/83	Tottenham Hotspur	RES	H	2
108.	21/3/83	Ipswich Town	SEC CSF	H	1
109.	27/4/83	Southend United	SEC CF	A	1
110.	30/4/83	Reading	RES	H	1
111.	4/5/83	Southend United	SEC CF	H	1
112.	12/5/83	Norwich City	RES	A	1
113,114.	19/5/83	Charlton Athletic	RES	A	2

1983/84

No.	Date	Opponents	Comp	Venue	Goals
115.	18/10/83	Leicester City	RES	A	1

EVERTON

1989/90

No.	Date	Opponents	Comp	Venue	Goals
1.	21/9/89	Manchester United	RES	A	1
2.	31/1/90	Leicester City	RES	H	1

FIRST TEAM

No.	Date	Opponents	Comp	Venue	Goals

WEST HAM UNITED

1982/83

No.	Date	Opponents	Comp	Venue	Goals
1.	1/1/83	Tottenham Hotspur	D1	H	1
2.	4/1/83	Luton Town	D1	H	1
3.	5/3/83	Brighton & Hove Albion	D1	H	1
4,5.	14/5/83	Coventry City	D1	A	2

1983/84

No.	Date	Opponents	Comp	Venue	Goals
6,7.	27/8/83	Birmingham City	D1	H	2
8	6/9/83	Leicester City	D1	H	1
9,10,11,12.	25/10/83	Bury	LC	H	4
13.	12/11/83	Wolverhampton Wanderers	D1	A	1
14.	27/12/83	Luton Town	D1	A	1
15.	31/12/83	Tottenham Hotspur	D1	H	1
16.	21/1/84	West Bromich Albion	D1	H	1
17.	4/2/84	Stoke City	D1	H	1
18.	7/2/84	Queens Park Rangers	D1	A	1
19	11/2/84	Coventry City	D1	A	1
20.	3/3/84	Ipswich Town	D1	A	1
21.	10/3/84	Wolverhampton Wanderers	D1	H	1
22.	31/3/84	Queens Park Rangers	D1	H	1
23,24.	17/4/84	Luton Town	D1	H	2

1984/85

No.	Date	Opponents	Comp	Venue	Goals
25.	4/9/84	Coventry City	D1	H	1
26.	25/9/84	Bristol City	LC	A	1
27.	6/10/84	Leicester City	D1	H	1
28,29.	9/10/84	Bristol City	LC	H	2
30.	20/10/84	Stoke City	D1	A	1
31.	27/10/84	Arsenal	D1	H	1
32.	17/11/84	Sunderland	D1	H	1
33,34.	22/12/84	Southampton	D1	H	2
35.	26/12/84	Tottenham Hotspur	D1	A	1
36,37.	29/12/84	Coventry City	D1	A	2
38.	2/3/85	Arsenal	D1	A	1
39.	4/3/85	Wimbledon	FAC	A	1
40,41,42.	6/3/85	Wimbledon	FAC	H	3
43.	30/3/85	Nottingham Forest	D1	A	1
44,45.	8/4/85	Queens Park Rangers	D1	A	2
46.	13/4/85	Chelsea	D1	H	1
47.	11/5/85	Sheffield Wednesday	D1	A	1
48.	17/5/85	Ipswich Town	D1	A	1

No.	Date	Opponents	Comp	Venue	Goals
1985/86					
49.	7/9/85	Sheffield Wednesday	D1	A	1
50.	14/9/85	Leicester City	D1	H	1
51.	21/9/85	Manchester City	D1	A	1
52.	24/9/85	Swansea City	LC	H	1
53.	28/9/85	Nottingham Forest	D1	H	1
54.	5/10/85	Newcastle United	D1	A	1
55.	8/10/85	Swansea City	LC	A	1
56,57.	19/10/85	Aston Villa	D1	H	2
58.	26/10/85	Ipswich Town	D1	A	1
59.	9/11/85	Oxford United	D1	A	1
60.	30/11/85	West Bromich Albion	D1	H	1
61.	5/1/86	Charlton Athletic	FAC	A	1
62.	2/2/86	Manchester United	D1	H	1
63.	4/2/86	Ipswich Town	FAC	A	1
64.	6/2/86	Ipswich Town	FAC	A	1
65.	12/3/86	Sheffield Wednesday	FAC	A	1
66,67.	29/3/86	Chelsea	D1	A	2
68.	31/3/86	Tottenham Hotspur	D1	H	1
69.	2/4/86	Nottingham Forest	D1	A	1
70.	15/4/86	Chelsea	D1	H	1
71.	19/4/86	Watford	D1	A	1
72.	26/4/86	Coventry City	D1	H	1
73.	3/5/86	West Bromich Albion	D1	A	1
74.	5/5/86	Everton	D1	A	1
1986/87					
75.	6/9/86	Liverpool	D1	H	1
76,77,78.	13/9/86	Queens Park Rangers	D1	A	3
79,80,81.	7/10/86	Preston North End	LC	H	3
82,83.	11/10/86	Chelsea	D1	H	2
84.	25/10/86	Charlton Athletic	D1	H	1
85.	15/11/86	Wimbledon	D1	A	1
86.	18/11/86	Oxford United	LC	H	1
87.	22/11/86	Aston Villa	D1	H	1
88.	25/11/86	Chelsea	SC	H	1
89.	6/12/86	Southampton	D1	H	1
90.	20/12/86	Queens Park Rangers	D1	H	1
91.	27/12/86	Wimbledon	D1	H	1
92, 93..	1/1/87	Leicester City	D1	H	2
94,95,96.	24/1/87	Coventry City	D1	A	3
97.	27/1/87	Tottenham Hotspur	LC	H	1
98.	31/1/87	Leyton Orient	FAC	H	1
99.	28/2/87	Luton Town	D1	A	1
100,101.	8/4/87	Arsenal	D1	H	2
102.	20/4/87	Tottenham Hotspur	D1	H	1
103.	9/5/87	Manchester City	D1	H	1

No.	Date	Opponents	Comp	Venue	Goals
1987/88					
104,105.	29/8/87	Norwich City	D1	H	2
106.	5/9/87	Liverpool	D1	H	1
107.	12/9/87	Wimbledon	D1	A	1
108.	17/10/87	Oxford United	D1	A	1
109.	31/10/87	Watford	D1	A	1
110,111.	21/11/87	Nottingham Forest	D1	H	2
112.	1/1/88	Norwich City	D1	A	1
113.	9/1/88	Charlton Athletic	FAC	H	1
114.	30/1/88	Queens Park Rangers	FAC	A	1
115.	13/2/88	Portsmouth	D1	H	1
116.	23/4/88	Coventry City	D1	H	1
117.	30/4/88	Southampton	D1	A	1
118.	2/5/88	Chelsea	D1	H	1

EVERTON

No.	Date	Opponents	Comp	Venue	Goals
1988/89					
119,120,121.	27/8/88	Newcastle United	D1	H	3
122.	3/9/88	Coventry City	D1	A	1
123,124.	8/10/88	Southampton	D1	H	2
125.	30/10/88	Manchester United	D1	H	1
126,127.	29/11/88	Oldham Athletic	LC	A	2
128.	3/12/88	Tottenham Hotspur	D1	H	1
129.	20/12/88	Millwall	SC	H	1
130.	26/12/88	Middlesbrough	D1	H	1
131.	14/2/89	Aston Villa	D1	H	1
132.	11/3/89	Sheffield Wednesday	D1	H	1
133.	27/3/89	Middlesbrough	D1	A	1
134.	1/4/89	Queens Park Rangers	D1	H	1
135,136.	30/4/89	Nottingham Forest	SC	Wembley	2
1989/90					
137.	28/10/89	Norwich City	D1	A	1
138.	5/11/89	Aston Villa	D1	A	1
139.	9/12/89	Tottenham Hotspur	D1	A	1
140.	10/2/90	Charlton Athletic	D1	H	1
141.	17/2/90	Oldham Athletic	FAC	A	1
142.	10/3/90	Oldham Athletic	FAC	A	1
143,144.	17/3/90	Crystal Palace	D1	H	2
145.	21/3/90	Millwall	D1	A	1
146,147.	24/3/90	Norwich City	D1	H	2
148,149.	4/4/90	Nottingham Forest	D1	H	2
150.	7/4/90	Queens Park Rangers	D1	H	1
151.	14/4/90	Luton Town	D1	A	1

No.	Date	Opponents	Comp	Venue	Goals
1990/91					
152,153,154.	25/9/90	Wrexham	LC	A	3
155,156.	29/9/90	Southampton	D1	H	2
157.	9/10/90	Wrexham	LC	H	1
158.	18/12/90	Blackburn Rovers	ZDS	A	1
159,160.					
161,162.	22/1/91	Sunderland	ZDS	H	4
163,164.	20/2/91	Liverpool	FAC	H	2
165.	23/2/91	Sheffield United	D1	H	1
166.	13/3/91	Barnsley	ZDS	A	1
167.	16/3/91	Southampton	D1	A	1
168,169.	21/3/91	Leeds United	ZDS	H	2
170.	10/4/91	Wimbledon	D1	H	1
171.	13/4/91	Chelsea	D1	H	1
172.	24/4/91	Tottenham Hotspur	D1	A	1
173.	4/5/91	Luton Town	D1	H	1
174,175.	8/5/91	Derby County	D1	A	2
1991/92					
176.	20/8/91	Arsenal	D1	H	1
177.	1/10/91	Oldham Athletic	ZDS	H	1
178,179,180.	5/10/91	Tottenham Hotspur	D1	H	3
181.	26/10/91	Queens Park Rangers	D1	A	1
182.	30/10/91	Wolverhampton Wanderers	LC	H	1
183.	16/11/91	Wimbledon	D1	H	1
184.	23/11/91	Notts County	D1	H	1
185.	7/12/91	West Ham United	D1	H	1
1992/93					
186,187.	15/9/92	Blackburn Rovers	PL	A	2
188.	7/10/92	Rotherham United	LC	H	1
189,190.	16/1/93	Leeds United	PL	H	2
191,192.	26/1/93	Wimbledon	PL	A	2
193.	6/2/93	Sheffield Wednesday	PL	A	1
194.	3/3/93	Blackburn Rovers	PL	H	1
195,196.	13/3/93	Nottingham Forest	PL	H	2
197.	24/3/93	Ipswich Town	PL	H	1
198.	12/4/93	Queens Park Rangers	PL	H	1

No.	Date	Opponents	Comp	Venue	Goals
1993/94					
199,200,201.	21/8/93	Sheffield United	PL	H	3
202.	11/9/93	Oldham Athletic	PL	A	1
203.	18/9/93	Liverpool	PL	H	1
204.	22/9/93	Lincoln City	LC	A	1
205.	3/10/93	Tottenham Hotspur	PL	A	1
206,207.	6/10/93	Lincoln City	LC	H	2
208.	23/11/93	Leeds United	PL	H	1
209.	4/12/93	Southampton	PL	H	1
210.	3/1/94	Chelsea	PL	A	1
211,212,213.	15/1/94	Swindon Town	PL	H	3
214.	19/2/94	Arsenal	PL	H	1
215.	2/4/94	Sheffield Wednesday	PL	A	1
216.	9/4/94	West Ham United	PL	A	1
217.	16/4/94	Queens Park Rangers	PL	A	1

WEST HAM UNITED
1994/95

No.	Date	Opponents	Comp	Venue	Goals
218.	17/9/94	Aston Villa	PL	H	1
219.	30/11/94	Bolton Wanderers	LC	H	1
220,221,222.	17/12/94	Manchester City	PL	H	3
223.	26/12/94	Ipswich Town	PL	H	1
224.	31/12/94	Nottingham Forest	PL	H	1
225.	2/1/95	Blackburn Rovers	PL	A	1
226.	7/1/95	Wycombe Wanderers	FAC	A	1
227.	4/2/95	Leicester City	PL	A	1
228,229.	13/2/95	Everton	PL	H	2
230,231.	11/3/95	Norwich City	PL	H	2
232.	13/4/95	Wimbledon	PL	H	
1995/96					
233.	4/10/95	Bristol Rovers	LC	H	

TC career record

WEST HAM UNITED

Season	League Apps	Gls	FA Cup Apps	Gls	League Cup Apps	Gls	Other Cups Apps	Gls	Totals Apps	Gls
1982/83	3/5	5	1	0	0	0	0	0	4/5	5
1983/84	37/2	15	4	0	4	4	0	0	45/2	19
1984/85	40/1	17	5	4	4	3	0	0	49/1	24
1985/86	41/1	20	7	4	3	2	0	0	51/1	26
1986/87	42	22	5	1	6	5	1	1	54	29
1987/88	40	13	2	2	2	0	0	0	44	15
1994/95	31	13	3	1	2	1	0	0	36	15
Totals	234/9	105	27	12	21	15	1	1	283/9	133

EVERTON

Season	League Apps	Gls	FA Cup Apps	Gls	League Cup Apps	Gls	Other Cups Apps	Gls	Totals Apps	Gls
1988/89	35/1	13	8	0	5	2	4	3	52/1	18
1989/90	25/2	13	3/2	2	1/2	0	0	0	29/6	15
1990/91	20/9	10	1/3	2	3	4	4/2	8	28/14	24
1991/92	17/7	8	1/1	0	3/1	1	2	1	23/9	10
1992/93	25/1	12	0	0	2/1	1	0	0	27/2	13
1993/94	36/3	16	2	0	5	3	0	0	43/3	19
1994/95	3	0	0	0	0	0	0	0	3	0
Totals	161/23	72	15/6	4	19/4	11	10/2	12	205/35	99

CAREER TOTAL

	League Apps	Gls	FA Cup Apps	Gls	League Cup Apps	Gls	Other Cups Apps	Gls	Totals Apps	Gls
	395/32	177	42/6	16	40/4	26	11/2	13	488/44	232

INDEX

Abbott, John, 18
Ablett, Gary, 247, 256, 280, 283, 284, 286, 295, 296, 297, 302, 324
Aberdeen FC, 124
Adams, Neil, 209, 221
Adams, Tony, 156, 193, 198, 263, 313, 331, 344
Airdrie FC, 72
Aldershot FC, 41
Aldridge, John, 184
Allen, Clive, 125, 199, 245, 340
Allen, Dennis, 305, 312
Allen, Martin, 305, 311, 312, 350
Allen, Paul, 42, 53, 67, 69, 83, 88, 89, 94, 116, 125, 190, 255, 347
Amokachi, Daniel, 286, 287, 288, 339
Ampofo, Chris, 52
Ampofo, Gerhard, 40, 42, 43, 52
Anderlecht FC (Belgium), 91
Anderson, Jerome, 327
Angell, Brett, 46, 275, 276, 277, 278, 279, 283, 284
An Irrational Hatred of Luton, 333
Arsenal FC, 11, 12, 16, 19, 28, 31, 32, 37, 38, 51, 53, 91, 106, 110, 113, 124, 134, 136, 137, 139, 140, 142, 143, 144, 145, 155, 156, 157, 158, 159, 160, 161, 162, 163, 165, 170, 171, 173, 176, 182, 186, 193, 216, 217, 224, 243, 245, 253, 262, 275, 277, 278, 286, 292, 296, 303, 312, 313, 335, 341, 344
Ascoli FC (Italy), 124
Ashby, Gerald, 114
Ardiles, Ossie, 125, 278, 286
Aston Villa FC, 31, 35, 42, 50, 52, 53,106, 110, 122, 172, 200, 217, 221, 239, 258, 262, 275, 279, 285, 304, 305, 344
Atherton, Mike, 33
Athletic Bilbao, 166, 263
Atkinson, Ron, 19, 258, 303
Atteveld, Ray, 209, 240, 243
Avis, Clive, 24

Bacon, Steve, 51, 301, 304
Baily, Eddie, 31, 41, 42
Bailey, Gary, 107, 118
Bamber, Dave, 75
Banks, Robert, 333
Banton, Dale, 53
Barcelona FC (Spain), 91, 117, 156, 191, 341
Barclay, Patrick, 332, 333
Barking & Dagenham Post, 51
Barking District athletics team, 33
Barking District football team, 22, 38
Barlow, Stuart, 263, 274
Barnes, Bobby, 42, 51, 89, 119
Barnes, John, 87, 122, 158, 185, 191, 196, 199, 237, 339, 340
Barnet FC, 85
Barnsley FC, 35, 134, 171, 239
Bassett, Dave, 171
Batson, Brendan, 215
Bayern Munich FC (Germany), 274, 286
Beagrie, Lynn, 249
Beagrie, Peter, 195, 217, 226, 235, 241, 242, 243, 245, 249, 253, 254, 261, 262, 278, 347
Beardsley, Peter, 113, 119, 133, 141, 157, 174, 191, 192, 196, 197, 236, 242, 243, 244, 245, 246, 249, 250, 252, 254, 255, 258, 259, 260, 290, 292, 340, 341, 342, 345, 347
Beasant, Dave, 168
Beauchamp, Joey, 85, 284, 285

Beck, John, 171
Beech, Ronnie, 19
Benfica FC (Portugal), 91
Bergkamp, Dennis, 286, 313
Besiktas (Turkey), 209
Bingham, Billy, 174
Birmingham City FC, 19, 51, 55, 67, 75, 114, 135, 138, 176, 256, 347
Bishop, Ian, 296, 304, 305
Blackburn Rovers FC, 85, 238, 244, 252, 256, 279, 280, 299, 300, 305, 306, 311, 327, 328, 341, 342, 343, 345, 351
Blackhall, Bill (Father-in-law), 168, 329
Blackhall, June(Mother-in-law), 66, 168, 329
Bland, Tony, 180
Blissett, Luther, 87
Boere, Jeroen, 299, 301, 305, 311, 312
Bolton Wanderers FC, 12, 274, 275, 298, 305
Boogers, Marco, 309, 311
Bonds, Billy, 31, 35, 46, 48, 49,55, 67, 84, 85, 87, 88, 117, 125, 128, 129, 131, 135, 140, 141, 199, 200, 238, 240, 284, 285, 324, 332, 347
Booton, Mr, (Warren deputy head) 25
Botham, Ian, 330
Bournemouth, AFC, 278
Bowles, Stan, 199
Boyce, Ronnie, 38, 41, 42, 45, 51, 87, 294, 300
Bracewell, Paul, 184, 209
Bradford City FC, 87, 88, 164, 169, 170, 176, 178
Brady, Liam, 124, 135
Breacker, Tim, 85, 295, 296, 302
Brennan, Mark, 111
Bright, Mark, 260, 302, 309, 341
Brighton & Hove Albion FC, 70
Bristol City FC, 190, 240, 297
Bristol Rovers FC, 42, 309, 310, 313, 314
Brøndby FC (Denmark), 299
Brooking, Trevor, 19, 32, 34, 35, 46, 51, 53, 54, 67, 68, 71, 72, 74, 75, 76, 84, 88, 116, 117, 160, 347, 348
Brown, Kenny, 301
Brown, Terry, 295, 299
Bull, Steve, 199
Burke, Stan, 294
Burnley FC, 35, 186
Burns, Mickie, 40
Burnside, Dave, 186, 187
Burrows, David, 287, 291, 294, 304
Burvill, Glenn, 41, 45
Bury FC, 73, 74
Butcher, Terry, 114
Butler, Peter, 296

Cantona, Eric, 337
Cambridge United FC, 30, 171
Campbell, Bobby, 52, 55
Campbell, Greg, 42, 52, 55, 105, 119, 314
Capps, Brian, 19
Carlisle United FC, 336, 340
Carr, Tony, 40, 41, 42, 52, 53, 294
Carter, Andy, (PE teacher) 24
Carter, Philip, 159, 161, 166, 216
Cartwright, John, 186
Castilla FC (Spain), 36, 92
Castle, Sid, 19
Castle, Steve, 19

Cearns, Len, 53, 145
Celtic FC, 85, 134
Chapman, Eddie, 128
Chapman, Lee, 87, 137, 181, 304, 311
Charlton, Alfie, 40
Charlton Athletic FC, 35, 106, 111, 122, 137, 140, 173, 175, 220, 221
Charlton, Bobby, 249, 341
Charlton, Jack, 53
Chase Cross United FC, 23, 27
Chelsea FC, 19, 28, 55, 92, 106, 112, 115, 116, 122, 130, 135, 140, 164, 170, 190, 191, 216, 217, 218, 221, 240, 245, 257, 260, 261, 264, 274, 277, 280, 286, 303, 312, 337, 338, 342, 344, 350
Christie, Linford, 96
Clapton FC, 13
Clark, Sandy, 56, 66, 67, 70, 72
Clarke, Allan, 165, 183
Clarke, Colin, 135
Clarke, Wayne, 156, 165, 170, 176, 200, 209
Claesen, Nico, 137
Clemence, Ray, 35, 50, 67
Clockhouse Infants School, 15, 24
Clough, Brian, 19, 180, 337
Clough, Nigel, 195, 199, 257
Coe, Mr (Commerce teacher), 25, 26
Cole, Andy, 306, 339, 340
Collymore, Stan, 256, 305, 326, 339
Cook, Mr (Junior school teacher), 15, 16
Cooper, Paul, 106
Coppell, Steve, 69, 171
Cornwell, John, 19, 23, 28, 30, 31, 32, 36, 40, 43, 50, 54, 71, 140, 143, 179, 200, 209, 245, 291
Cornwell, Sandra, 200
Cottee, Alan (Uncle), 11
Cottee, Carole (Mother), 12, 13, 15, 45, 71, 80, 155, 162, 192, 195, 289, 291
Cottee, Chloe (Daughter), 14, 66, 248, 249, 258, 277, 282, 289, 292, 309, 324
Cottee, Charles (Great-grandfather), 11
Cottee, Clive (Father), 11, 12, 13, 14, 17, 19, 20, 21, 23, 25, 26, 28, 29, 34, 36, 38, 45, 53, 66, 71, 75, 78, 80, 127, 129, 155, 158, 159, 160, 161, 162, 185, 192, 195, 200, 276, 283, 289, 291, 300, 308, 327, 349
Cottee, Janet (Aunt), 11
Cottee, Jane (Grandmother), 11, 32, 66, 198
Cottee, Joan (Aunt), 11
Cottee, Joanne (Sister), 15, 155, 329
Cottee, Lorraine (Wife), 27, 66, 68, 71, 78, 79, 108, 109, 117, 119, 127, 128, 131, 139, 160, 161, 163, 165, 167, 168, 172, 175, 176, 178, 179, 195, 198, 199, 200, 221, 223, 242, 248, 258, 259, 277, 278, 282, 283, 288, 289, 292, 295, 309, 324
Cottee, Paul (Brother), 12, 13, 14, 16, 17, 28, 30, 31, 32, 66, 143, 163, 185, 195, 209, 276, 289, 291, 329
Cottee, Roy (Uncle), 11, 66
Cottee, William (Grandfather), 11, 12, 68
Courtney, George, 75
Coventry City FC, 19, 35, 70, 71, 75, 85, 86, 114, 122, 124, 135, 140, 168, 211, 214, 215, 218, 224, 243, 253, 256, 263, 264, 279, 291, 298, 303
Cowans, Gordon, 136
Cowell, Ian, 40
Cowie, George, 51
Cowley, Carl, 17, 19, 21
Cox, Harry, 11, 12
Cox, Tony, 13
Crandon, Graham, 19
Cranson, Ian, 114
Croker, Ted, 75

Crosby, Gary, 239
Crook, Ian, 19, 176
Cross, David, 34, 35, 50
Crossley, Mark, 305, 311
Cruyff, Johan, 20
Crystal Palace FC, 53, 70, 85, 111, 221, 239, 243, 255, 263, 296, 298, 305, 306, 312, 337, 341
Curbishley, Alan, 55

Daily Express, 332
Daily Mirror, 128, 129, 332
Daines, Barry, 30
Dalglish, Kenny, 19, 75, 92, 115, 122, 174, 237, 238, 299, 305, 340, 341, 342, 351
Daniels, Phil, 333
Danson, Paul, 294, 295, 302
Darracott, Terry 'Tex', 165, 173, 184, 185, 214
Davenport, Peter, 135, 137
Dean, Dixie, 244, 293
Deane, Brian, 299
Derby County FC, 50, 72, 126, 172, 179, 240
Derry City FC (Rep. of Ireland), 255
Dettori, Frankie, 143
Devonshire, Alan, 34, 35, 53, 55, 67, 74, 76, 81, 84, 86, 95, 96, 112, 119, 122, 124, 133, 324, 347
Dickens, Alan, 15, 38, 41, 42, 53, 55, 56, 65, 66, 67, 69, 70, 72, 84, 86, 95, 96, 105, 112, 113, 114, 118, 119, 121, 124, 134, 141, 182, 186, 187, 188, 348, 350
Dicks, Julian, 138, 209, 246, 248, 289, 296, 298, 300, 302, 304, 305, 306, 308, 312, 313, 324, 346, 347, 350
Dibble, Andy, 106
Dixon, Kerry, 135, 190, 191
Djurgardens IF (Sweden), 209
Donald, Warren, 40, 42
Doncaster Rovers FC, 186
Dowie, Iain, 312, 313
Dreyer, John, 240,
Drinkell, Kevin, 135
Dublin, Dion, 274
Dundee FC, 250
Dundee United FC, 260

East, Trevor, 126
Eastbrook school, 33
Ebbrell, John, 239, 243, 252, 253, 262
Ekoku, Efan, 262
Ekstrom, Johnny, 122, 191
Elliot, Bill, 13
England, Youth, 55, 186, 187; U 21, 88, 190, 194, 195, 263, 295; Full, 185, 186, 190, 191, 199
Espanol FC (Spain), 209
European Championships 1988, 91, 144, 193, 194, 196, 197, 249, 344; 1992, 91; 1996, 330, 338
European Cup Final 1985, 90
European Cup Winners' Cup Final, 1965, 12, 299; 1976, 91
Evans, Roy, 289
Exeter City FC, 38

FA Cup Final 1964, 12; 1966, 22; 1975, 1980, 12, 32, 34; 1989, 165, 177, 180, 181, 183, 184, 185, 186, 199; 1995, 297, 298, 309
Fagan, Joe, 90, 92
Fashanu, John, 137, 160, 199, 280, 281, 334
FC Bruges (Belgium), 338
FC Haarlem (Holland), 209
FC Schalke 04 (Germany), 53
FC Twente (Holland), 53
Ferdinand, Les, 339, 340, 341, 345
Ferguson, Alex, 326

Ferguson, Duncan, 260, 302
Feuer, Ian, 298
Finch, Cliff, 335
Findlay, Jake, 69
Finn, Tom, 127, 248
Fiorentina FC (Italy), 126, 128, 136
Flowers, Tim, 194, 300
Fogg, Dave, 243
Fowler, Robbie, 306, 340
Friar, Ken, 158
Frith, Jimmy, 40
Fulham FC, 29, 38, 51, 53, 55, 74, 84, 137, 138

Gabriel, Jimmy, 220, 225, 226, 274, 276
Gale, Ronnie, 37, 38, 279, 294
Gale, Tony, 84, 85, 95, 112, 113, 118, 120, 122, 133, 137, 140, 239, 282, 306, 324, 347
Gallagher, Joe, 67
Galleon, Paul, 15
Galvin, Tony, 125
Gascoigne, Paul, 140, 158, 195, 197, 198, 199, 221, 222, 284, 304
Gibson, Lee, 26, 27
Giggs, Ryan, 327, 345
Giles, Johnny, 332
Gillam, Eddie, 294
Gillespie, Gary, 174
Gillingham FC, 40
Ginola, David, 345
Glasgow Rangers FC, 72, 128, 136, 138, 172, 200, 242, 244, 250, 260, 262, 273
Goddard, Paul, 31, 34, 35, 56, 66, 67, 70, 72, 73, 77, 78, 79, 85, 87, 88, 90, 94, 95, 113, 118, 119, 132, 134, 255, 348
Godden, Tony, 113
Gordon, Dale, 300
Gornik Zabrze FC (Poland), 239
Gothenburg FC (Sweden), 240
Graham, George, 143, 155, 156, 157, 158, 161, 277, 292, 335, 351
Gray, Andy, 106, 160
Greaves, Jimmy, 23, 125
Green, John, 40, 87, 291, 305
Greenwood, Jim, 156, 159, 161, 162, 220, 259, 289
Greenwood, Ron, 54, 285
Gregory, Ernie, 55, 131
Griffiths, Arthur (Grandfather), 11, 12, 31, 68
Grimstead, Eddy, 291
Grobbelaar, Bruce, 184, 237, 262, 280, 334
Gullit, Ruud, 286, 312, 344
Gunn, Bryan, 176

Hackett, Keith, 239
Hall, Eric, 327
Hammers News Magazine, 332, 333
Hammerton, Paul, 22
Hampden Park, 85, 186, 193, 199
Hansen, Alan, 92, 160, 185, 301, 332
Harford, Mick, 135, 197
Harford, Ray, 341
Harper, Alan, 226, 243, 252
Harris, Harry, 332
Harvey, Colin, 124, 143, 155, 156, 157, 158, 159, 161, 165, 166, 170, 172, 173, 175, 176, 184, 209, 210, 211, 214, 215, 216, 217, 218, 219, 220, 221, 223, 224, 225, 226, 236, 242, 254, 257, 273, 274, 281, 286, 351
Hateley, Mark, 119, 191, 192, 196, 197
Hateley, Tony, 197
Hatter, Steve, 38
Hauge, Rune, 335

Hawkes, Malcolm, 19
Haynes, Garry, 14
Haynes, Iris, 14
Hazdell, Mr, (Science teacher) 25
Heart of Midlothian FC, 263, 273
Heath, Adrian, 156, 209, 226
Hedworth, Chris, 113
Helm, Les, 248, 276
Hendry, Colin, 300
Hereford United FC, 50, 51
Heysel Stadium (Brussels), 90, 92, 93
Hickson, Dave, 244
Hill, Jimmy, 111
Hillsborough, 176, 178, 179, 180, 181, 334, 338
Hilton, Paul, 119, 134, 140, 294
Hinchcliffe, Andy, 224, 237, 241, 252, 254, 346
Hitchcock, Kevin, 245, 246, 303
Hockton, Michael, 143, 212
Hoddle, Glenn, 23, 67, 261, 352
Hodge, Martin, 105
Holdsworth, Dean, 280, 309
Holmes, Jon, 327
Holmes, Matt, 300, 306, 311
Hornchurch FC, 13
Horne, Barry, 250, 252, 253, 262, 280, 283
Houghton, Ray, 51, 113
Houston, Stewart, 351
Howard, Martin, 19
Howard, Roly, 243
Hudson, Alan, 199
Hughes, Charles, 19, 187
Hughes, Emlyn, 165
Hughes, Mark, 88, 116, 290, 306, 342
Hughes, Michael, 299, 305, 306, 308
Hurst, Geoff, 87, 117
Hutchison, Don, 297, 298, 302, 303, 304, 305, 306, 308, 311, 312, 350
Hysen, Glenn, 191, 237

Ilford FC, 19
Ilford Palais, 66, 71
Impey, Andrew, 301
Ince, Paul, 37, 123, 248, 339, 348
Independent, The, 332
Inter Milan, 123, 136, 348
Ipswich Town FC, 29, 85, 88, 106, 110, 111, 114, 115, 132, 197, 244, 254, 257, 263, 277, 279, 280, 282, 283, 288, 300, 304, 305, 306
Irvine, Ian, 184

Jackson, Matt, 244, 252, 297, 309
Jenkins, Rob, 12, 50, 87, 121, 125
Jennings, Pat, 116
Jensen, John, 335
Johnson, Andy, 303
Johnson, Ben, 336
Johnson, Peter, 274
Johnston, Maurice, 244, 245, 247, 253, 254, 260, 263, 273, 274
Jones, Rob, 294, 295
Jones, Steve, 311
Jones, Vinnie, 171
Joseph, Roger, 255
Juventus FC (Italy), 90

Kanchelskis, Andrei, 344, 345
Keegan, Kevin, 19, 243, 351
Keen, Kevin, 138
Keith, Adrian, 51, 53
Keith, John, 225, 332

Kelly, David, 182
Kelly, Gary, 343, 344, 345
Kendall, Howard, 41, 166, 209, 210, 219, 226, 235, 236, 237, 238, 239, 241, 242, 243, 244, 245, 246, 248, 250, 252, 253, 254, 255, 256, 257, 258, 259, 260, 262, 263, 264, 273, 274, 275, 281, 286, 289, 292, 300, 344, 351
Kennedy, Alan, 35
Kenny, Billy, 337
Kenwright, Bill, 274
Keown, Martin, 200, 224, 241, 242, 249, 255, 256, 259, 263
Kerslake, David, 187
Klinsmann, Jürgen, 285, 286, 297
Kray, Reggie, 85

Lampard, Frank, 46, 87, 88, 138, 290, 294, 313, 346
La Ronde, Everald, 51
Latchford, Bob, 117, 244, 293
Lawson, Nigel, 137
Lawton, Tommy, 293
Lazaridis, Stan, 313
Lazio FC (Italy), 284
League Cup Final 1981, 346
Lee, Sammy, 35
Leeds United FC, 31, 92, 116, 165, 224, 239, 245, 253, 255, 279, 299, 306, 310, 336, 337, 343, 344
Leicester City FC, 29, 51, 73, 106, 110, 123, 200, 298, 302, 306
Leonard, Jason, 38
Le Saux, Graeme, 343, 344, 345
Le Tissier, Matthew, 298, 342
Lewin, Gary, 16
Leyton Orient FC, 19, 31, 43, 50, 95, 123, 216, 217
Limpar, Anders, 278, 280, 302
Lincoln City FC, 124, 263
Lineker, Gary, 117, 119, 141, 156, 160, 191, 192, 193, 196, 197, 246, 249, 256, 293, 341
Liverpool Echo, 349
Liverpool FC, 35, 50, 53, 70, 73, 74, 75, 85, 88, 90, 91, 92, 96, 106, 110, 113, 114, 115, 116, 117, 122, 133, 135, 142, 143, 169, 170, 171, 176, 178, 179, 180, 181, 182, 184, 185, 189, 191, 199, 224, 236, 237, 238, 239, 242, 243, 247, 262, 273, 278, 279, 282, 289, 294, 296, 298, 301, 304, 306, 310, 326, 337
Lukic, John, 139
Luton Town FC, 29, 52, 69, 74, 75, 95, 96, 106, 135, 197, 217, 220, 240, 244, 248
Lyall, John, 32, 34, 41, 45, 46, 48, 49, 51, 53, 55, 66, 70, 72, 73, 75, 78, 79, 81, 82, 83, 84, 85, 86, 88, 94, 96, 105, 108, 109, 115, 118, 120, 121, 123, 126, 127, 128, 131, 135, 136, 137, 139, 140, 143, 144, 145, 155, 158, 164, 165, 182, 189, 200, 240, 282, 283, 285, 295, 314
Lyall, Murray, 94
Lyall, Yvonne, 94
Lydersen, Pal, 335
Lyons, Mick, 214

Mabbutt, Gary, 262
Macari, Lou, 238, 240, 285
MacDonald, Malcolm, 51
MacMillan Stadium, Newham, 33, 48
Maddix, Danny, 249
Mail On Sunday, 332
Manchester City FC, 50, 114, 123, 125, 135, 144, 169, 170, 224, 226, 243, 253, 261, 277, 278, 286, 300, 336, 351
Manchester United FC, 69, 85, 86, 91, 95, 96, 106, 107, 110, 111, 112, 113, 116, 117, 122, 123, 135, 143, 168, 209, 210, 215, 221, 243, 249, 252, 263, 264, 274, 277, 290, 296, 297, 299, 306, 308, 310, 311, 337, 342, 343, 345
Maradona, Diego, 119
Marsh, Mike, 294, 303, 304

Marsh, Rodney, 199
Marshall, Cliff, 339
Martin, Alvin, 35, 67, 74, 84, 85, 95, 110, 113, 118, 119, 120, 133, 137, 191, 192, 294, 297, 299, 302, 303, 313, 347
Martin, Jimmy, 260, 263
Matthews, Stanley, 112
McAllister, Gary, 253, 344
McAllister, Tom, 51, 55, 87, 131, 140
McAvennie, Frank, 82, 84, 94, 95, 96, 105, 106, 107, 109, 111, 112, 113, 115, 116, 117, 118, 119, 120, 121, 122, 123, 124, 125, 130, 131, 132, 133, 134, 141, 157, 158, 172, 190, 195, 255, 260, 282, 289, 348
McCall, Stuart, 164, 171, 173, 175, 184, 185, 210, 218, 226, 237, 242, 255, 259, 292, 348
McClair, Brian, 277
McClure, Dougie, 187
McCleary, Alan, 186, 187
McDonald, Neil, 164, 165, 166, 167, 168, 175, 195, 209, 219, 237, 243, 244
McDonald, Tony, 332
McDermott, Terry, 35
McGiven, Mick, 38, 41, 65, 82, 120, 136, 350
McGrath, Paul, 258, 344
McKnight, Allen, 169, 182
McMahon, Steve, 121, 174, 184
McManaman, Steve, 262
McMillan, Colin, 38
McNab, Bob, 37
McPherson, Keith, 51
McQueen, Tommy, 124, 125
Melia, Jimmy, 70
Merson, Paul, 156, 170, 335, 336, 337
Metgod, Johnny, 112
Middlesbrough FC, 53, 171, 173, 182, 196, 257
Miklosko, Ludek, 247, 297, 298, 306, 346
Millichip, Bert, 195
Milligan, Mike, 224, 242
Millwall FC, 17, 19, 52, 173, 217, 337, 340
Milton, Steve, 40, 51, 53
Molby, Jan, 237
Monaco FC (France), 138, 286
Moncur, John, 296, 303, 304, 308, 313
Moore, Bobby, 12, 13, 42, 84, 117, 277, 278, 279, 288
Moore, Brian, 67
Moore, Dudley, 304
Moors, Chris, 311
Morecambe FC, 243
Morgan, Nicky, 56, 65, 66, 73
Morley, Trevor, 288, 294, 303, 311
Morton, Greenock FC, 118
Moseley, Gary, 44
Moseley, Graham, 70
Muhren, Arnold, 69
Mutch, Andy, 275

Neal, Phil, 117
Neill, Terry, 37
Nervik, Egil, 194
Neville, Gary, 311
Nevin, Pat, 113, 164, 166, 175, 176, 178, 184, 217, 225, 237, 241, 250, 347
Newcastle United FC, 19, 30, 43, 51, 106, 113, 114, 123, 131, 133, 140, 158, 164, 165, 166, 167, 168, 172, 182, 195, 200, 258, 262, 290, 291, 303, 336, 337, 341, 345, 347, 351
Newell, Mike, 199, 200, 209, 211, 213, 214, 215, 216, 218, 220, 224, 226, 237, 239, 244, 323
Nicholas, Charlie, 134
Northwich Victoria FC, 94
Norwich City FC, 13, 19, 86, 91, 122, 133, 135, 160, 171,

175, 176, 217, 243, 262, 274, 275, 297, 303, 306, 327
Nottingham Forest FC, 28, 31, 32, 56, 87, 112, 122, 135, 170, 176, 178, 179, 180, 181, 182, 195, 199, 216, 218, 221, 239, 243, 254, 257, 286, 287, 300, 305, 311, 312, 326, 337
Notts County FC, 29, 55, 73, 244

Oldham Athletic FC, 94, 169, 209, 221, 224, 225, 242, 244, 245, 251, 262, 274, 275, 277, 279
O'Neill, John, 160
Orr, Neil, 75, 95, 113, 118, 121
Over Land and Sea, 333
Oxford United FC, 53, 113, 122, 133, 136, 284

Pallister, Gary, 196
Parkes, Phil, 31, 35, 55, 67, 81, 86, 87, 95, 117, 131, 137, 139, 140, 182, 346, 348
Parker, Paul, 249
Parkinson, Joe, 278
Parlour, Ray, 313
Parris, George, 22, 23, 38, 40, 42, 88, 105, 118, 121, 135, 141, 186, 282
Pearce, Stuart, 199
Pearson, Stuart, 31, 51, 53
Pegram, Bill, 40
Penn, Graham, 20, 22, 24, 33, 34, 37, 66
Perryman, Steve, 106, 278, 279
Peters, Martin, 117
Pickering, Fred, 244
Pike, Geoff, 31, 53, 67, 70, 111, 113, 119, 121, 348
Platini, Michel, 90
Platt, David, 217, 248, 328
Pleat, David, 125
Plymouth Argyle FC, 19, 171
Pointon, Neil, 163, 187, 218
Poole, Kevin, 172
Portsmouth FC, 73, 189, 216, 257, 311
Port Vale FC, 86
Potts, Steve, 37, 82, 85, 119, 247, 294, 302, 306, 309, 347
Powell, Jeff, 130, 134
Preston North End FC, 122, 169, 336
Prior, Spencer, 303

Queens Park Rangers FC, 29, 55, 76, 85, 87, 95, 107, 113, 122, 133, 135, 169, 173, 209, 225, 226, 235, 240, 244, 246, 249, 263, 279, 285, 298, 299, 305, 341, 345

Radosavijevic, Predrag (Preki), 250, 254, 257
Raistrick, Chris, 333
Rapid Vienna FC (Austria), 92
Ratcliffe, Kevin, 166, 171, 178, 184, 185, 209, 210, 219, 245, 250, 347
Reader, Wayne, 40, 53
Real Sociedad FC (Spain), 241
Redknapp, Jamie, 282
Redknapp, Harry, 82, 87, 284, 285, 288, 289, 290, 294, 295, 297, 298, 300, 301, 302, 303, 304, 305, 308, 310, 312, 313, 314, 351
Regis, Cyrille, 339
Rehn, Stefan, 209, 240
Reid, Peter, 121,165, 167, 168, 173, 209, 348
Rice, Brian, 112
Richardson, Alan, 22
Richardson, Kevin, 76
Rideout, Paul, 136, 186, 250, 254, 255, 261, 262, 263, 275, 277, 279, 280, 285, 287, 297, 302, 309, 348
Ridley, David, 19, 20, 21
Riedle, Karl-Heinz, 194
Rieper, Marc, 299, 305, 306, 308, 313

Rioch, Bruce, 275
Robson, Bobby, 69, 90, 119, 135, 141, 144, 190, 191, 192, 194, 195, 196, 197, 198, 221, 240, 274, 330
Robson, Bryan, 69, 110, 111, 189, 198, 199, 352
Robson, Bryan (Pop), 28, 35, 75
Robson, Stewart, 124, 138, 186
Rocastle, David, 156, 192, 277
Romford FC, 13
Romford Recorder, 18, 296, 349
Romford Royal FC, 18, 19, 22, 50
Room At The Top club, Ilford, 71
Rosenior, Leroy, 137, 138, 140
Rosenthal, Ronny, 279, 311
Rossi, Paolo, 54
Rotherham United FC, 253
Rowett, Gary, 278
Royle, Joe, 199, 221, 225, 244, 274, 275, 297
Rush, Ian, 75, 184, 185, 236, 306, 340, 342
Rush, Matthew, 297, 305, 308, 311
RWD Molenbeek (Belgium), 53

Sadler, John, 332
Samways, Vinny, 284, 295
Sansom, Kenny, 189, 198
Santos FC (Brazil), 89
Saunders, Dean, 240, 242,
Schivai, Mark, 51, 350
Schmeichel, Peter, 264, 343
Scunthorpe United FC, 187
Sealey, Alan, 299
Sealey, Les, 298, 299, 301, 303, 313
Seaman, David, 122, 188
Segers, Hans, 280, 281, 334
Sexton, Dave, 188, 195
Sharp, Graeme, 96, 156, 167, 168, 169, 170, 172, 173, 174, 176, 183, 184, 200, 209, 210, 211, 215, 218, 219, 220, 224, 235, 236, 242, 244, 293, 323, 348
Sharpe, Lee, 263, 326
Shearer, Alan, 252, 300, 306, 311, 332, 340, 341, 344, 345
Sheedy, Kevin, 167, 172, 174, 176, 184, 209, 210, 218, 219, 220, 224, 235, 236, 242, 243, 245, 347
Sheffield United FC, 171, 194, 225, 235, 238, 243, 249, 279, 280
Sheffield Wednesday FC, 87, 105, 112, 122, 125, 137, 171, 172, 178, 215, 243, 245, 250, 252, 256, 260, 261, 298, 302, 309
Shepherd, Rob, 332
Sheringham, Teddy, 285
Shipp, Danny, 311
Shilton, Peter, 123, 189, 198, 199
Shreeves, Peter, 89
Simmons, Matthew, 337
Slater, Robbie, 311, 314
Slater, Stuart, 37, 182, 238, 248
Small, Paul, 22
Smith, Alan (ex-Arsenal striker), 156, 157
Smith, Dave, 23
Smith, Janine, 161
Smith, Jon, 133, 136, 137, 140, 142, 145, 155, 156, 157, 158, 159, 160, 161, 162, 163, 200, 209, 211, 214, 215, 216, 217, 246, 257, 259, 278, 282, 287, 290, 291, 327, 328, 332
Smith, Mark, 44, 51
Smith, Martin, 40
Smith, Phil, 161, 282, 285, 287, 288, 290, 291
Smith, Trevor, 332
Snodin, Ian, 167, 174, 186, 198, 255, 262, 281
Socrates, 54
Souness, Graeme, 75
Southall, Neville, 167, 184, 209, 219, 224, 235, 256, 302, 313, 346
Southend United FC, 19, 38, 43, 245, 275, 276, 291

Southampton FC, 70, 73, 74, 83, 85, 89, 105, 112, 113, 123, 135, 140, 168, 188, 215, 224, 239, 249, 250, 261, 264, 273, 279, 280, 296, 298, 303, 307, 310, 313, 314, 332, 334, 341
Spackman, Nigel, 113
Sparta Rotterdam, 309
Spencer, John, 221, 312
Spink, Nigel, 106
Statham, Derek, 115
Steggles, Jack, 128, 332
Stein, Mark, 280
Stephens, Bill, 12
Sterland, Mel, 245
Steven, Trevor, 167, 169, 170, 172, 176, 184, 186, 188, 200, 209, 347
Stevens, Keith, 186
Stewart, Marcus, 309
Stewart, Paul, 136, 144, 246
Stewart, Ray, 34, 67, 74, 85, 87, 95, 110, 111, 113, 114, 115, 117, 118, 125, 126, 128, 129, 246, 332, 346
St. Mirren FC, 94
Stockport County FC, 283
Stoke City FC, 83, 88, 217
Storrie, Peter, 287, 288, 290, 294, 308, 335
Strasbourg FC (France), 299
Strachan, Gordon, 324
Strodder, Gary, 124, 141
Stuart, Graham, 260, 280, 285, 334
Sun, The, 332
Sunday Express, 332
Sunderland FC, 70, 75, 209, 224, 236
Sutton, Chris, 158, 306, 327
Sutton United FC, 19, 291
Swansea City FC, 26, 31, 65, 70, 107
Swindlehurst, Dave, 70, 72, 73, 76, 77, 78, 85, 94
Swindon Town FC, 19, 43, 186, 240, 263, 275, 279

Taylor, Alan, 29
Taylor, Gordon, 215
Taylor, Graham, 91, 171, 187, 188, 240, 249, 330
Taylor, Lord Justice, 179, 338
Thorn, Andy, 168
Thomas, Clive, 35
Thomas, Martin, 113
Thomas, Michael, 139, 156
Today, 332
Torino FC (Italy), 284
Tottenham Hotspur FC, 11, 23, 28, 30, 42, 50, 56, 66, 67, 69, 73, 74, 89, 91, 92, 113, 122, 125, 137, 143, 144, 158, 169, 170, 180, 190, 209, 214, 216, 218, 220, 236, 240, 244, 248, 257, 259, 262, 277, 278, 279, 284, 285, 286, 297, 302, 311, 312, 332, 340
Townsend, Andy, 158
Tranmere Rovers FC, 250
TSV Munich 1860, 12, 91
Tuck, Jimmy, 66
Tucker, Tommy, 12

Unsworth, David, 256, 302

Van Basten, Marco, 193
Van Den Hauwe, Pat, 184, 209, 346
Van Der Elst, Francois, 56, 67
Vaughan, John, 40
Veal, Ian, 19
Venables, Terry, 246, 278, 330
Vitesse Arnhem FC (Holland), 283

Waddle, Chris, 125, 188, 192, 198, 199
Walford, Steve, 95, 118, 120, 121, 221

Walker, Des, 112
Walker, Jack, 238, 328
Walker, Mike, 240, 256, 262, 274, 275, 276, 278, 279, 281, 283, 286, 288, 289, 296, 297
Wallace, Danny, 186
Wallace, Rod, 245
Walsall FC, 182, 240, 296
Walsh, Paul, 69, 110
Walters, Mark, 186
Ward, Mark, 82, 83, 94, 95, 96, 107, 110, 114, 118, 119, 120, 125, 135, 137, 140, 141, 195, 242, 243, 248, 252, 254, 256, 261, 262, 264, 325, 347
Warhurst, Paul, 221
Warren Comprehensive school, 20, 22, 24, 33, 38, 42, 43, 66
Warzycha, Robert, 239, 240, 243, 252
Watford FC, 29, 65, 70, 76, 85, 87, 105, 113, 122, 138, 171, 187
Watson, Dave, 131, 164, 167, 184, 192, 209, 217, 219, 256, 286, 297, 347, 348
Webb, Neil, 197
Webb, Stuart, 126, 127, 128, 133
Webster, Simon, 305
Wembley, 12, 31, 35, 49, 85, 91, 176, 177, 182, 183, 185, 192, 197, 274, 299
West Bromwich Albion FC, 31, 68, 107, 114, 115, 171, 253
Whelan, Ronnie, 184
When Skies Are Grey, 333
Whitbread, Adrian, 85
'White Horse' Cup Final 1923, 12
Whiteside, Norman, 69, 86, 110, 209, 210, 217, 219, 221
Wigan Athletic FC, 74
Wilkins, Ray, 189, 352
Wilkinson, Howard, 188, 189
Williams, Barrie, 19, 20, 37
Williams, Dave, 275, 276
Williams, Steve, 19
Williamson, Danny, 302, 310
Wilson, Ian, 184, 209
Wilson, Kevin, 114
Wimbledon FC, 38, 86, 122, 137, 142, 160, 168, 171, 199, 216, 218, 236, 240, 244, 255, 279, 280, 282, 300, 305, 309, 310, 334
Winterburn, Nigel, 186
Wise, Dennis, 245, 246
Wogan, Terry, 131
Woking FC, 236, 250
Wolverhampton Wanderers FC, 182, 244, 336
Woodgate, Terry, 12
Woods, Chris, 198, 256
Woolley, Dave, 40
World Cup Finals, 1966, 13, 117, 330; 1974, 20; 1982, 54; 1986, 119, 191; 1990, 91, 221, 341; 1994, 53, 91, 284, 286, 343
Worthington, Frank, 199
Wrexham FC, 29, 36, 224
Wright, Alfie, 42, 43,
Wright, Ian, 313, 339, 341
Wright, Mark, 186
Wright, Roy, 275
Wycombe Wanderers FC, 301

Yeboah, Tony, 310
Youds, Eddie, 243, 244
Young, Eric, 263

Zanter, Peter, 194